Behaviour in a Business Context

Business in Context Series

Editors

David Needle
Currently Head of the Department
of Business Studies
The Polytechnic of East London

Professor Eugene McKenna
Currently Head of General
Management Department of
Business Studies
The Polytechnic of East London

Accounting Information in a Business Context
Aidan Berry and Robin Jarvis

Behaviour in a Business Context
Richard Turton

Business in Context
David Needle

Economics in a Business Context
Alan Neale and Colin Haslam

Law in a Business Context
Bill Cole, Peter Shears and Jillinda Tiley

Quantitative Techniques in a Business Context
Roger Slater and Peter Ascroft

Behaviour in a
Business Context

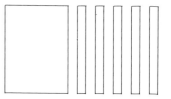

Richard Turton

CHAPMAN AND HALL
University and Professional Division
LONDON · NEW YORK · TOKYO · MELBOURNE · MADRAS

UK   Chapman and Hall, 11 New Fetter Lane, London EC4P 4EE

USA   Chapman and Hall, 29 West 35th Street, New York NY10001

JAPAN   Chapman and Hall Japan, Thomson Publishing Japan,
            Hirakawacho Nemoto Building, 7F, 1-7-11 Hirakawa-cho,
            Chiyoda-ku, Tokyo 102

AUSTRALIA   Chapman and Hall Australia, Thomas Nelson Australia,
            102 Dodds Street, South Melbourne, Victoria 3205

INDIA   Chapman and Hall India, R. Seshadri, 32 Second Main
            Road, CIT East, Madras 600 035

First edition 1991

© 1991 Richard Turton

Typeset in 10/11½ pt Times by Excel Typesetters Company

Printed in Great Britain by
Richard Clay Ltd, Bungay, Suffolk

ISBN 0 412 37530 3 (PB)

British Library Cataloguing in Publication Data
Turton, Richard
    Behaviour in a business context.
    1. Business firms. Personnel. Behaviour
    I. Title   II. Series
    658.314

    ISBN 0-412-37530-3

Library of Congress Cataloging-in-Publication Data
Turton, Richard.
    Behaviour in a business context/Richard Turton. – 1st ed.
        p.   cm. – (Business in context series)
    Includes bibliographical references and index.
    ISBN 0-412-37530-3
    1. Organizational behavior.   2. Industry and state – Great Britain –
    History – 20th century.   3. Industrial sociology – Great Britain.
    I. Title.   II. Series.
    HD58.7.T87   1990
    158.7 – dc20

                                                    90-42754
                                                    CIP

Dedication

In Memoriam
Diana Greenway

Series foreword

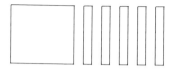

This book is part of the Business in Context series. The books in this series are written by lecturers all with several years experience of teaching on undergraduate business studies programmes. For a number of years we have been conscious that many of the books we were recommending to our students never catered specifically for business studies courses. Although there are some good books covering the different disciplines found in the business studies curriculum, very few of these texts are aimed specifically at the business studies student. Many of the best management texts assume a level of managerial experience and the worst take a simplistic and pre-scriptive view of business life. The interdisciplinary nature of business studies often means presenting students with a range of books dealing with various specialist topics, which can prove both daunting and expensive.

It is certainly not our intention to offer up our individual texts as a panacea. Indeed, our policy throughout this series is that books are well referenced and the student is guided to further reading on every topic area. However, we do feel that our books provide a focus for the student at-tempting to seek some meaning in the range of subjects currently offered on business studies programmes.

Business studies has attracted a growing band of students for a number of years and is currently one of the most popular undergraduate courses. Whilst many books have emerged to feed a hungry BTEC market, the undergraduate business studies student has been sadly neglected. One of the causes of that neglect has undoubtedly been the difficulty of many, academics and members of the business community alike, to define business studies, beyond a list of loosely connected subject headings. With this series we hope to make good some of those missing connections.

With the exception of the text, Business in Context, which takes the series title as its theme, all our texts take the approach of a particular discipline traditionally associated with business studies and taught across a wide range of business studies programmes. The first books in our series examine business from the pespectives of economics, behavioural science, law, mathematics and accounting. However, whereas in traditional texts it is the subject itself that is the focus, our texts make business the focus. All the texts are based upon the same specific model of business illustrated in the Figure overleaf. We have called our model Business in Context and the text of the same name is an expansion and explanation of that model.

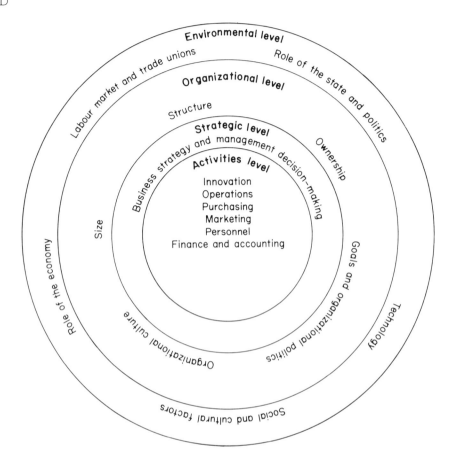

The model comprises four distinct levels. At the core are found the
activities which make up what we know as business and include innovation,
operations and production, purchasing, marketing, personnel and finance
and accounting. We see these activities operating irrespective of the type of
business involved, and are found in both the manufacturing and service
industry as well as in the public and private sectors. The second level of our
model is concerned with strategy and management decision-making. It is
here that decisions are made which influence the direction of the business
activities at our core. The third level of our model is concerned with organizational factors within which business activities and management decisions
take place. The organizational issues we examine are structure, size, goals
and organizational politics, patterns of ownership, and organizational culture. Clear links can be forged between this and other levels of our model,
especially between structure and strategy, goals and management decision-
making, and how all aspects both contribute to and are influenced by the
organizational culture. The fourth level concerns itself with the environment in which businesses operate. The issues here involve social and
cultural factors, the role of the state and politics, the role of the economy,
and issues relating to both technology and labour. An important feature of
this fourth level of our model is that such elements not only operate as

opportunities and constraints for business, but also that they are shaped by the three other levels of our model.

This brief description of the Business in Context model illustrates the key features of our series. We see business as dynamic. It is constantly being shaped by and in turn shaping those managerial, organizational and environmental contexts within which it operates. Influences go backwards and forwards across the various levels. Moreover, the aspects identified within each level are in constant interaction with one another. Thus the role of the economy cannot be understood without reference to the role of the state; size and structure are inextricably linked; innovation is inseparable from issues of operations, marketing and finance. The understanding of how this model works is what business studies is all about, and forms the basis for our series.

In proposing this model we are proposing a framework for analysis, and we hope that it will encourage readers to add to and refine the model and so broaden our understanding of business. Each writer in this series has been encouraged to present a personal interpretation of the model. In this way we hope to build up a more complete picture of business initially through the eyes of an economist, a behavioural scientist, a lawyer, a mathematician and an accountant.

Our series therefore aims for a more integrated and realistic approach to business than has hitherto been the case. The issues are complex but the authors' treatments are not. Each book in this series is built around the Business in Context model, and each displays a number of common features that mark out this series. Firstly we aim to present our ideas in a way that students will find easy to understand and we relate those ideas wherever possible to real business situations. Secondly we hope to stimulate further study both by referencing our material and pointing students towards further reading at the end of each chapter. Thirdly we use the notion of 'key concepts' to highlight the most significant aspects of the subject presented in each chapter. Fourthly we use case studies to illustrate our material and stimulate further discussion. Fifthly we present at the end of each chapter a series of questions, exercises, and discussion topics. To sum up, we feel it most important that each book will stimulate thought and further study, and assist the student in developing powers of analysis, a critical awareness and ultimately a point of view about business issues.

We have already indicated that the series has been devised with the undergraduate business studies student uppermost in our minds. We also maintain that these books are of value wherever there is a need to understand business issues and may therefore be used across a range of different courses covering BTEC Higher, and some professional and masters courses.

David Needle and Eugene McKenna
January 1989

Contents

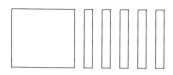

Acknowledgements

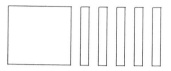

'Thought you'd finished that by now!' The more printable of a number of comments from those who have born the brunt of the efforts represented by this book and which has dominated a significant part of their lives, in one case 30%! I refer of course to my family, Pat, Joanna, Patrick and Caroline. In addition to taking more than her share of domestic responsibilities as a consequence of her partner's authorship ambitions, Pat's knowledge and understanding of the mysteries of word processing (and human nature) were crucial to the preparation of this volume.

Colleagues with whom I have taught at Hatfield, particularly the late Diana Greenway, and John Sykes and Ralph Stacey, contributed considerably to the refinement of ideas developed in this volume, as have students on business studies, computing and occupational psychology courses. Andrew Nicholas, Derek Dale and David Andrews have been sources of both encouragement and reassurance. I am also grateful to Paul Lyons and Diana Brown for their comments on drafts of Chapter 7.

The series editors, Eugene McKenna and David Needle are due a particular reference, David Needle because of the thorough and constructive way he read drafts of the manuscript.

Finally, my thanks are due to the perserverance of Stephen Wellings of Chapman and Hall. Stephen reponded to repeated, but only slowly improving, attempts to turn his advice into acceptable copy with remarkable equanimity. He moved on from Chapman and Hall to pursue his career in the same week as the manuscript went into production, assuring me that the two events were not related!

As always, the fault and inadequacies of this volume are to be laid at the author's door.

Preface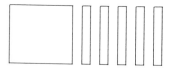

'If we are so clever, how come they are winning?'

The purpose of this book is threefold:

☐ To introduce the study of behavioural aspects of business organization to students on business and management courses, those taking business and management related courses on schemes such as computing and engineering, for example, and students following a variety of professional courses where the study of behaviour in business forms an important part of their studies. It is also intended that students on postgraduate courses who have no prior knowledge of the social science approach to organizational behaviour will find the book of benefit.

☐ To examine factors influencing behaviour in British business in the context of efforts to reverse the long-term relative decline of Britain as a manufacturing nation.

☐ To carry out the above in terms which examine behavioural aspects of contemporary approaches to the definition and solution of problems facing British business associated with such factors as the application of microelectronic technology, the Single Market, and the continued development of the 'Pacific-rim' economies.

The book considers (a) how individual and group behaviour at all levels of the business enterprise is influenced by strategies developed to cope with the process of industrialization, and (b) how policies designed to cope with differing experiences of industrialization can be seen to underlie efforts to define and solve contemporary problems in the UK and its competitors. These issues are explored by an examination of human behaviour at work which introduces students to the application of sociological and psychological research in a business setting. The approach adopted is equally applicable to those involved in private or public sector organizations.

The book attempts to explain the significance of behavioural factors in relative economic decline, and to suggest how, in the light of social scientific knowledge, behaviour in business organizations may be developed so as to halt and even reverse that decline.

Despite undoubted changes over the last decade, there still remain questions over the ability of British business to meet the challenges of the Single Market. One aspect of these questions concerns the attitudes and behaviour of British managers and workers, and their representatives.

Contemporary concern over the competitive ability of British industry, including the baleful influence of the establishment, educational theorists, and what the Chairman of the Institute of Directors refers to as the 'middle class salariat', echo concerns first expressed nearly one hundred and fifty years ago. Then, as now, attention focused on the apparent failure of British industry to compete effectively with the emerging economies of North America and Western Europe.

Later, in the decades spanning the end of the nineteenth and beginning of the twentieth centuries, business people, educationalists and politicians expressed worries over the apparent failure of British military and industrial institutions to maintain their place in the world. Apart from military weaknesses evidenced by the conduct of the Crimean and Boer Wars, particular concern was expressed over the economic and educational superiority of Germany and Japan.

The behavioural implications of UK policies which tend to emphasize free labour and capital markets, low wages and the reduction of the role and power of trade unions are explored. Major competitors in Europe have developed financial and employment systems geared to rather different sets of assumptions while still operating as effective capitalist economies.

The rights of workers to information and to participate in decision-making which are reflected in the Social Charter of the EC, and which operate in a number of EC and non-EC countries, provoke critical responses from those representing business industries in the UK. What has to be explained is why policies and strategies which are regarded as involving unacceptable interference in the market mechanism in the UK, and which have significant implications for behaviour at work, do not appear to have hindered to any significant extent the growth of other economies.

This book examines sociological and psychological explanations for this, explanations which suggest that lessons can be learnt, especially from the German or Japanese examples.

Introduction 1

The purpose of this chapter is to explain the context in which this book examines behaviour in business. The model of business around which this series is structured includes the socio-cultural and socio-political environment. At the centre of the model are the various activities which take place in any business enterprise whether it be run by a sole trader or a multinational corporation and whether or not the enterprise is a private or public limited company, a cooperative or even state-owned. Moving out from the centre of the model there are represented the strategic, organizational and environmental factors which make up the total context within which businesses function and which therefore influence human behaviour in business. This model of the 'business in context' is presented in Figure 1.1.

This book links the factors represented in the various strata of the model whilst establishing an understanding of the 'how and why' of human behaviour in work organizations. As regards the environmental sector of the model, the book starts from the well-established fact that since the last half of the nineteenth century Britain has experienced relative economic decline. The book examines some of the features of that decline in so far as they can be seen to be both a cause and a consequence of the behaviour in British business which appears, in comparison with major economic competitors, to have a detrimental impact on the competitive performance of the economy.

The historical element in the book is important because many of the ways in which the problems of the British economy are currently framed, and solutions identified and formulated, appear to concentrate on the idea that up to about 1945 everything was going well, that once upon a time, in some previous, happier period, British industry was supreme. The attitude can be summed up in the comment made by a manager, in his forties, on an MBA course when he got rather annoyed with a speaker who he thought went on at too great a length about the apparent superiority of German and Japanese management: 'How come you say they are so marvellous then? We damn well showed them a thing or to during the War!' He then went on to recite a litany of dates: '1918, 1945, 1966'. (The last, for the benefit of readers who are not ardent fans of association

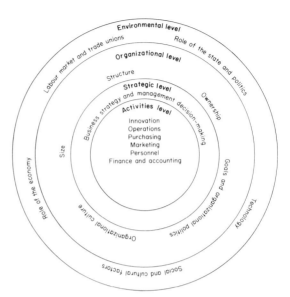

Figure 1.1 The Business in Context model.

football, refers to the English victory over Germany in the World Cup of that year!)

An important point is that the problems of the British economy today have been a cause of concern for nearly 130 years! For over one hundred years German economic performance has been a focus of attention, as has that of Japan for nearly ninety. Solutions to the factors underlying the relative decline of Britain as an industrial power must therefore require some fundamental reappraisal of assumptions that have been previously taken for granted. Not only must this reappraisal be at the level of public policy, but also at the level of the attitudes, assumptions and behaviour of managers and workers. As the book develops therefore we will touch upon all the components of the 'business in context' model.

The model itself can be viewed as an explanatory framework for this economic decline. Organizational behaviour can only be fully understood in the context of changing markets and economies, of the changing role of the state, changing technologies and labour markets and in the context of prevailing social and cultural influences. Such environmental contexts are dynamic and change over time. They help shape organizational structures and the behaviour of work groups; they play a part in influencing management goals and in shaping organizational cultures. It is such environmental and organizational contexts within which management strategy is developed and conducted and within which the behaviour of organization members takes place. It would, however, be wrong to view management strategy and the behaviour of organization members as simply products of the environmental and organizational contexts in which they operate. A key feature of the 'business in context' model is that influences operate both ways across the model. We shall see in Chapters 5, 6 and 7 of this book how behaviour goes some way to shaping the environment in which it operates. A more detailed view of the working of this model can be found in *Business in Context* (Needle, 1989).

The present situation

At the present time there is considerable talk about a British 'economic miracle'. The British economy appeared to be one of, if not the, fastest growing in Europe in 1988. This debate has obvious political implications, and discussion can therefore become not only heated but also confusing. This book is not about that debate itself, though it is very relevant to many of the factors which underlie it. The book is concerned with aspects of the behaviour of managers and workers as they go about their working lives under the influence of the dynamic factors represented in the two outer layers of the 'business in context' model. It is the attitudes and relationships of managers and those they manage which have a powerful influence on the effectiveness of enterprises in terms of productivity, profitability and competitive advantage. This is the case whether people are working in the public or private sectors of the economy and whether they are involved in manufacturing or the provision of services. Those students seeking an economic perspective on this debate are referred to the economics text in this series (Neale and Haslam, 1989).

Leaving aside the extent to which the present British economic miracle is a reality – and if it is, what factors are responsible for its occurrence – this book is about one set of factors that are crucial to the long-term consolidation of such a possible miracle, those factors which influence behaviour in business organizations. In order to maintain existing shares of world markets, and assuming that world trade continues to grow at the rate it did up to the early 1980s, British manufacturers will have to achieve the same rise in their share of the world market as Japan did during the 1970s – around 9%. Such a performance will have major implications for the organization and management of work in addition to the technological implications of product and process innovation. Rates of product and process innovation are crucially affected by the institutional and organizational structures and attitudes within which they must take place.

Ever since 1945, manufacturing output in the UK has grown at a slower rate than in major competitor economies. By 1979 British output of manufactured products was some 5% higher than ten years before. This compared with a 28% increase in the rest of the then EEC where France and Italy achieved over 30% growth in the same period. Between 1979 and 1981 manufacturing output in the UK fell by 15% at a time when Japan's increased by 10% and that of Italy by 4%. The fall in other major economies was much smaller with the USA experiencing a drop of 1½%, Germany 2½% and France 8%. The decline in manufactured goods in UK output in this short period was greater than that which occurred during the depression of the 1920s and 1930s. It was not until 1987/8 that output regained the level it had reached in 1974.

A point to note is that in the case of Britain, discussion focuses on 'relative' performance. It is not that the UK economy does not grow; it is simply that it grows at a slower – often significantly slower – rate than others. Some of the explanations that are offered for this concentrate on those aspects of business behaviour that are the focus of this book: the attitudes and qualifications of British managers and workers, for example, the power of trade unions, and the relatively low status of occupations centred on engineering and manufacturing in comparison with financial services, law and accountancy. (As an illustration of this last point only 9% of male students and 3% of female students were seriously considering a career in manufacturing according to a survey carried out amongst university and polytechnic students in 1989 (*The Financial Times*, 14 July 1989).) Such factors affect the orientations – and hence the behaviour – of managers and those they manage.

Whilst these are heated debates about the cause of the relatively intense decline of the British economy after 1979 and the role of government policy in that decline, there is evidence that the performance of British industry has for the last one hundred years at least lagged behind that of major economies which industrialized later. At no time in the century to 1980 did the British economy grow at an annual rate that exceeded 3%. Between 1870 and 1976 output per head in Britain grew four times, compared with an eightfold increase in fifteen other industrial economies.

A long-standing concern with national efficiency

At the turn of the century, there existed in Britain what amounted almost to a 'national efficiency' movement, involving politicians of all persuasions – the Fabians – and people such as Sidney and Beatrice Webb. Attention was focused upon the relatively poor performance of British industry, education, and political and social institutions. The countries with which unfavourable comparison was made then, as now, were America, Germany and Japan. Not only were these countries major economic and trading competitors, but they also had developed more ordered, systematic and efficient social institutions. Education and training were highly developed, their military organizations were efficient and effective, and their populations were not only better educated, but were also physically fitter.

The question of the fitness of the British population had come dramatically to the public attention following the often quoted example of the citizens of Manchester who, after volunteering for service in the Boer War, were rejected as physically unsuitable. Of the 11 000 volunteers only 1000 were considered suitable for military service, while a further 2000 were considered acceptable for the militia. The disastrous conduct of the war in South Africa had itself fuelled concern over the apparent decline of Britain as a world power.

In the comparison with Germany, attention in Britain focused on those factors which were considered to lie behind the efficiency of Bismark's state. These included a highly organized educational and training system and its influence on expanding science-based industries, the system of military service, and a social insurance scheme which was thought to prevent the German masses falling to the low physical condition typical of the British. Behind these three aspects of German superiority were the administrative systems of national and local government which made them possible. 'From 1885 onwards the newspapers were full of gloomy talk about Britain's stagnating exports, lost markets and technological obsolescence, contrasted with Germany's superiority in business methods, salesmanship and industrial research' (Searle, 1971).

As in the 1980s, the Administrative Reform Association of 1855, and a 'vigilance committee' that adopted the same name in 1900 when the mistakes of the Crimean campaign were apparently being repeated in South Africa, placed much of the blame for administrative, commercial and military failures upon the absence of a business approach in politics, the army and the administration of the country. At the turn of the century the role of education, business training and scientific research were all seen as central to reversing the decline of Britain as an industrial and political power. One of the objectives of those behind the establishment of the London School of Economics was to provide businessmen, politicians and administrators with a command of the economic and political sciences.

A study of technology, productivity and profits in the British and American whaling fleets between 1816 and 1842 identifies problems which characterize discussion of British industry today. In 1814, 200 British whalers operated in the North Atlantic against two American. Thirty years later the situation was reversed with 700 American ships and 27 British. A British whaling owner explained to a Parliamentary select committee that over a forty-year period British sailors who had been the best in the world in 1801 were no more than 'miserable wretches' by the 1840s. Among a number of factors in the decline of the British fleet was the quality of the crews in comparison with the Americans (Davis *et al.*, 1987).

British owners responded to the competition and superior profitability and productivity of the Americans by reducing costs, especially crew costs. This meant cheaper ships and less well-qualified crews. These strategies failed – as they have failed in business to the present day – to enhance the competitive capabilities of the British whaling fleet. Not only were the American ships superior, they were manned by larger crews who were technically better trained. They included among their numbers artisans such as carpenters, sailmakers, riggers, blacksmiths and coopers. The result was that the Americans could maintain their ships to higher standards without entering port. The British ships, with only a carpenter and his mate, would have to put into port to effect repairs which the Americans could undertake without interrupting the voyage.

Immediately after the Great Exhibition of 1850, British politicians, civil servants and businessmen were crossing the Atlantic to discover how American manufacturers were able to design and produce the sophisticated machinery they had exhibited and which laid the foundation for the development of large firms producing standardized machinery products thirty years later. Some of the features of the development of large firms in Britain and North America in the nineteenth and early twentieth centuries are set out in Case Study 1.1.

From the material covered so far it can be seen that the problems which face British industry today have a considerable history and their origins are to be found in the very fabric of early industrial society. Much of the concern over the peformance of the British economy in comparison with Japan and Germany in the late Victorian and early Edwardian period was subsequently muted by the defeat of Germany in 1918. However, assumptions about the inherent capability of British institutions as a result of being on the victorious side were as unfounded then as they have appeared to be since 1945.

CASE STUDY 1.1

GROWTH OF INDUSTRIAL FIRMS IN THE USA AND UK

Large firms displaying the organizational and managerial characteristics of modern companies first appeared in America in the 1880s. Growth was based upon a strategy of vertical integration. Businesses moved forward into wholesaling and even retailing (the Singer Sewing Machine Company pioneered direct canvassing of consumers) and backwards into the direct purchasing and control of raw materials and part-finished materials.

This process occurred in four types of industry. One was the production of low-priced, branded and packaged products such as cigarettes, flour, breakfast cereals, canned foods, proprietary medicines and paint. Companies involved included household names such as Quaker Oats, American Tobacco, Heinz, Libby, and Procter and Gamble.

A second group produced perishable products such as in the meat, brewing and fruit industries. Here the companies were meat packers such as Armour and Swift, brewers like Pabst, Miller and Anheuser-Busch, and United Fruit from the 1890s.

A third group consisted of companies engaged in manufacturing durable items such as sewing machines, typewriters and agricultural machinery from standardized interchangeables parts. Apart from Singer, companies involved included McCormick-Harvester, National Cash Register, Remington, Burroughs Adding Machines and the predecessor of IBM, Computer-Tabulator Recorder.

The fourth group manufactured standardized heavy machinery products and included among their number the forerunners of General Electric as well as Westinghouse Electric, Westinghouse Air Brake, Otis Elevators, and Babcock and Wilcox.

While there were variations in the speed and manner in which companies developed new management structures, they all displayed similar administrative structures. They had large central offices with salaried middle-managers supervising the lower levels via functionally defined departments. The operations and performance of the functional departments were in turn monitored by senior executives who defined the policies of the enterprise and allocated the scarce resources of capital and staff.

In Britain, while a similar process in similar industries started at about the same time, it developed more slowly and did not involve the formation of the large central offices managed by salaried managers which characterized the American experience. Until the 1930s mergers among British companies rarely resulted in economies of scale or the benefits of administrative coordination and control. British mergers tended to be arranged in order to maintain family control. In most cases the merged companies retained their autonomy and continued to be managed by descendants of the founding family. While consolidation may have permitted cooperation in the purchasing of raw materials, it stabilized the domestic market by avoiding price competition and increased advertising costs, and permitted the dividing up of overseas markets. These were the motives behind the mergers after the First World War and into the early 1920s that involved Cadbury and Fry,

Peek Freen and Huntley and Palmers, Crosse and Blackwell, Reckitt and Colman, and Tate and Lyle. Similar factors affected merger activity in brewing and tobacco.

Even this form of the process was less common in machinery production. Firms tended to produce relatively simple machines for older industries such as textiles and mining, many customers for which were in the relatively protected and low priced markets of the Empire. Until the expansion of the automobile industry in Britain in the 1920s, which itself was dependent largely upon American machine tools and the operation of the American Ford company, the major producers of standardized consumer durables for a mass market were American. In addition to Ford there were Singer Sewing Machine, International Harvester, General Electric and Westinghouse.

Although many British firms had developed sophisticated merchandising techniques for consumer goods, the need to develop new production and distribution methods meant that they were slow to move into mass production. This enabled American (as well as German) companies to take market share from Britain in the international as well as domestic market-place. The failure of British heavy machinery firms to develop marketing organizations meant that standardized producer goods of American origin were able to gain a foothold in the markets for harvesters, electrical equipment, elevators, printing presses and shoe-making machinery.

The way in which large British firms lagged in developing managerial hierarchies also meant a lag in the adoption of modern management techniques in mass production and distribution, including techniques of scheduling, inventory and quality control. Such methods were only adopted in British companies on any scale after the Second World War, and this was largely due to the presence of American consultants in the 1950s and 1960s.

Demand in America for trained production and marketing people in technologically advanced industries in the 1880s and 1890s resulted in state and private universities and technical schools, like the Massachusetts Institute of Technology, offering appropriate courses for such people. By 1890 the most prestigious universities and colleges in America were responding to the demand from consumer and producer goods industries for professional training in finance, production, marketing and policy-making.

In the British case, such demand was muted. Top managers came from the owning families, and the relatively few middle-managers were recruited from the travellers, buyers and supervisors. It is reasonable to conclude that the lack of technological and business training had less to do with an alleged bias against industry than of a lack of demand. As the historians of ICI and Unilever have pointed out, when such companies first required such people, they had no difficulty in getting those they wanted from the universities. Even today, the relative paucity of engineers and highly qualified people in industry is largely due to the perception that other areas of activity offer better rewards.

Source: Chandler, 1980.

It should be emphasized that reference to the lengthy time period over which concern with British economic performance in comparison with competitor economies has been expressed is not to be taken as an argument that British society should become more like that of either Germany or Japan. As will be discussed in some detail in Chapter 10, international comparisons are not as straightforward as they may at times appear. Additionally, the transplanting of policies and institutions from one country to another is as fraught with problems of 'rejection' as is a liver or kidney transplant. Nor is it the case that policies and institutions, which it may be agreed have played a large part in the success of economies like Germany, are necessarily those that will continue to keep it in the forefront of economic progress. The point is simply that, as far as one can see from the evidence which is currently available, there would appear to be some features of competitor economies that can possibly explain economic success, that are not inherently 'alien', and that these should be accorded some serious attention by policy-makers in Britain rather then being dismissed as aberrations.

The significance of the European Single Market

The context within which these long-standing problems must now be dealt with includes the Single European Market. The evidence that British firms lagged behind their American competitors in the late nineteenth and early twentieth centuries should not be taken to imply that American management methods and techniques necessarily provide the answers to current or future problems. It should be noted that the only economy to have performed similarly (relative to other major economies) to that of the UK since 1945 is the United States. The starting point of the relative American decline was of course much later, and from a higher level, than that of Britain, and it was not as abrupt. Even so, it is next to the UK in terms of relative performance when matched against major world economies. It has, in effect, been argued by some American authors that the management techniques which may have assisted in the growth of American industry up to the 1950s are a positive disadvantage in competing with major economies in the future.

In an article in the *Harvard Business Review* in 1980, which became one of the most influential published by that journal, Professors Robert Hayes and William Abernathy argued that American managers were concentrating on short-term gains. This they argued was in comparison with the features which were making Japanese management so effective: long-term competitive strategy, technological investment, customer service, quality and the importance of manufacturing as opposed to financial services.

Hayes and Abernathy suggest that the problem with American management derives from the fact that since the 1950s there has been a significant increase in the proportion of top managers whose primary interests are in the financial and legal areas rather than production. Not surprisingly, such people will tend to allocate time and effort to cash management and those activities for which their skills appear to fit them, for example, the process of acquisition and mergers. This approach tends to concentrate attention on issues associated with the return to be got from an investment in the short-term, rather than the longer-term issue of, say, growth in market share.

The result is a pervasive approach to manufacturing industry better suited to the management of stocks and shares portfolios. In comparison with their European and Japanese competitors, American managers appear to have a somewhat misplaced faith in the portfolio 'law of large numbers' as a means of reducing or spreading risk. Legally and financially trained managers concentrate on the acquisition of plants, products and technologies through acquisitions and mergers in the hope of relatively quick results and the avoidance of unforeseen setbacks.

While portfolio management techniques may be well suited to share portfolios where there is considerable evidence that setbacks are indeed random, in manufacturing this is rarely the case. Certainly there will be unforeseen and unforeseeable events which jeopardize a company's survival, but also there will be carefully orchestrated strategies by competitors to develop their own activities in particular markets. The basis of such a strategy may well be the readily identifiable extent to which new or existing consumer needs are not being met by the current suppliers (Hayes and Abernathy, 1980).

An overemphasis on financial management techniques and interests can also be seen to characterize British management. The constant search for short-term company results, from one quarter to the next, is associated with the role of financial advisors, merchant banks and the scale of take-over activity. Within companies, competition tends to be seen in terms of cost reduction to the exclusion of product and process innovation which will involve quite lengthy time periods and considerable investment. The latter may well have the effect of reducing the profit available for distribution to the shareholders. An indication of the scale of acquisition activity in a number of European countries is given in Table 1.1.

As in the case of the British whaling fleet in the 1820s and 1830s, British companies still concentrate on reducing costs, especially labour costs, to the apparent exclusion of other strategies. This ignores the fact that competition is not only, or even mainly, about **price**. It is about service, quality and delivery. The **cost** to a purchaser of a product is a function of the price paid in the context of its quality, reliability, delivery time and

Table 1.1 Acquisition activity across national borders (during year to June 1988, in $million)

	EC companies	Non-EC companies
UK	2 026	11 496
France	2 000	1 746
Netherlands	497	705
Italy	433	705
Spain	479	294
West Germany	352	32

Source: The Financial Times, 12 November 1988.

servicing costs. So higher priced products may well outperform lower priced ones. Quality products require considerable investment in process technology and skilled staff; these tend to be expensive in comparison with unskilled staff and older, simple products. A sound competitive strategy often requires a company to move out of the production of low priced items to concentrate on higher value-added products that require expensive resources and inevitably sell at higher prices. After all, most of the manufactured products that have penetrated British producer and consumer markets are not lower priced than domestically produced items (if there are any), but their cost to the purchaser is lower on account of high quality, quick delivery and lower servicing costs.

A British economic miracle?

Investment

A number of sources have questioned the extent to which recent improvements in the relative position of the UK can be taken to indicate a fundamental reversal of features of the economy and business which have been associated with relative decline since the 1880s. Much of the increase in productivity in the British economy in the 1980s can be seen not as a symptom of what is right with the economy, but of what was, and may well remain, wrong.

More than one third of the labour productivity growth between 1980 and 1986 was accounted for by capital replacing labour. This in turn was due to the reduction of underemployment which characterized the UK economy in the 1970s, and so leaves open the extent to which relatively modest levels of investment in technology and skilled labour will be reversed in the future. Also important in explaining recent improvements in the relative position of the UK, and which has important implications for estimates of the extent to which attitudes and strategies have changed, is that a significant part of the relative success of the UK has been due to the deterioration of the performance of other industrial countries rather than improvements in the performance of the UK. If a 2% a year margin over Germany could be sustained in labour productivity growth, it would still take the UK about ten years to catch up to where the Germans are now.

A constant feature of the relative decline of the UK has been the failure on the part of British businessmen to keep up with, let alone overtake, competitors in areas such as training, and product and process research and development. In these areas the evidence suggests that the problem is in large part due to 'market failure'. That is, competition for skilled staff has not resulted in either an increase in the amount spent on training, or training being perceived as an investment rather than a cost. What has happened is that rational actors in the market-place have resorted to poaching staff by higher pay and better conditions. The market has failed because, while it is in everyone's interest to have a highly trained labour force, it is in no one individual's short-term interest to invest in training when trained staff may be enticed away (Muellbauer, 1986; Spencer, 1987).

The problems that British managers will have to face in the areas of training and product and process innovation are illustrated by comparative figures for the installation of production and handling equipment in factories. A survey carried out in 1987 by an American market research company indicated that the expenditure in France on automated loading and handling equipment (which includes robots and automated guided vehicles) was nearly double that in the UK. The German figure was five times that of the UK. In fact UK expenditure on this type of equipment was below that of Sweden, a country of some eight million people but with very modern factories. A 26% increase in machine tool spending forecast for 1989 in a study for the Machine Tool Association would still leave expenditure in real terms some £195m below that for 1979. In 1987, West Germany installed machine tools worth £2,87bn compared with £669m in the UK (*The Financial Times*, 27 July, 4 October, 15 October 1988).

Training

In the case of training, serious problems have been identified in plans to establish a standardized system of vocational qualifications which will integrate with those in the EC. The problem in part derives from a long-standing approach by British managers to labour costs, including training. Historically, British companies have concentrated on reducing labour costs almost to the exclusion of other aspects of competitive advantage. This has meant that technology is introduced largely with the intention of cutting labour costs rather than increasing output or quality. Many of the benefits to be derived from electronic technology imply a more highly skilled and trained, hence expensive, workforce. A comparative study of the employment consequences of introducing new technology in Britain and Sweden suggested that despite dramatic improvements in labour productivity half the Swedish companies in the study raised employment levels between 1981 and 1986. Over the 13 companies studied, employment fell by 1.2%, while in comparable British companies the drop in employment was at least 8% with a maximum of 29% (Innovation Research Group, Brighton Polytechnic, 1987).

Plans by the National Council of Vocational Qualifications to establish a nationwide system of certification which would harmonize with that of the EC have been criticized by Professor Prais of the National Institute of Economic and Social Research in the Annual Review for 1989. The British system is planned to be one level below that in Europe. This is intended to make room for a lower starting qualification in Britain. The lowest grade of qualification, NCVQ Level 1, will cover only very narrow skills; for example, in the hotel work certificate 'bed-making' and 'answering the telephone' will be covered at this level. Such a level of skill certification has no equivalent in Europe. Moving up the scale, what European countries would include at NCVQ Level 2 will not be reached by British trainees until NCVQ Level 3. While European qualifications have an important content of general transferable skills, the British system will, as has always been the case, concentrate on the immediate needs of employers. The requirement that trainees pass written as well as practical tests, often supervised and assessed by outside bodies, ensures that the European system will require candidates to demonstrate a general understanding of principles which is the basis of flexibility and future learning. In contrast, the British system will involve only supervisors in the assessment of practical competence and will involve neither external examiners nor written tests.

What about services?

The discussion so far has proceeded on the basis that manufacturing is somehow the key to economic prosperity. What about the service sector? Does that have a part in future prosperity?

Indeed, services do have an important part to play in economic growth. The point is to what extent can they make up for the declining balance of trade in manufactured products? This is independent of the numbers employed in the various sectors of the economy. To argue that manufacturing industry has the major role to play in economic growth is not to argue that it ought to be the, or even a, major employer. While manufacturing is currently a major source of employment in advanced industrial economies, it would still be a key factor in economic growth even if the proportion employed fell to that of agriculture in the UK, around 3%.

While services are an important feature of all industrial economies, especially that of the UK with its emphasis on the financial aspects of business, a number of points need to be made about the role of financial services given the patterns of property ownership and the role of pension funds.

The growth of world trade in manufactured goods exceeds that in services, and for the advanced industrial societies trade in manufactures far outweighs that in services. There are two important factors involved here. First, much of the demand for services is derived from successful manufacturing enterprises. Increasing shares of markets, domestic or international, won by manufacturing industry will increase the demand for services. Likewise, declining shares in the markets for manufactured goods will reduce the demand for services. It is true that increased imports may stimulate distribution services, but many jobs in this sector are relatively low-skilled and do not stimulate or sustain strategies designed to reduce an imbalance in trade in manufactures. Indeed, distribution itself requires manufactured products which may well have to be imported – vehicles, computers, handling equipment and so on.

Second, as hinted in the previous paragraph, many services are not tradable internationally. By their very nature, many services are provided and consumed locally, certainly within one economy. While it is true that when hotel workers have foreign guests that amounts to an export, as it does when students come to study at British universities and polytechnics, there is only a limited extent to which such services can be taken to the consumer. Indeed, increasing recruitment of overseas students, even if it increases the income of a college, may reduce the capacity for home students.

A third factor which is important in terms of putting the services/manufacturing relationship into perspective is that the growth in services in terms of share of GDP has in recent years been due to the growth of expenditure on foreign holidays. Figures contained in the UK balance of payments (The Pink Book) for 1988 suggest that high exchange rates for the pound in the early 1980s had the same effect on services as they did on manufacturing output, that is they depressed exports and increased imports. While earnings from financial and other services have increased, there has been an equally rapid growth in the imports of, for example, shipping and aviation, and most important has been the growth in the expenditure of British tourists abroad.

As Eatwell (1984) and Hirst (1989) point out, there is a self-perpetuating dynamic centred around manufacturing since a failure of manufactured products to retain their share of domestic and international markets creates conditions which further hinder the growth of manufacturing. This happens because the deficit on manufactured goods, given the nature of services, leads those responsible for economic management of the economy to increase interest rates in order to attract overseas lenders, and to implement policies to maintain the value of the currency while curtailing inflation. The effect tends to be one which not only makes borrowing for industrial investment more expensive than in competitor economies, but also has the effect that firms will only undertake investment in order to retain market share in low risk areas, rather than take the risks involved in expanding.

On the other hand there can be established, in accordance with what Eatwell calls a 'principle of cumulative causation', a virtuous, upward, spiral as follows. First of all, the demand for manufactured products is almost infinite. Even growing service sectors of the economy require manufactured products. Travel agents depend on transport vehicles, planes, cars, trains, not to mention VDUs and all the electronic equipment. The dependence on electronic products is also a key feature of the financial services sector. Even the growth in office building in the City of London has increased imports of manufactured products such as steel frames, cladding, bricks, and even trees and plants from Holland for the landscaped courtyards!

Second, manufacturing provides almost unlimited scope for technological change and innovation, either in the products themselves or the processes by which they are produced. Related to this characteristic is the third one identified by Eatwell: the mutual reinforcement of production and demand. Technological changes promote new demands; these in turn encourage yet more product or process change which in turn affects demand, and so on.

Manufacturing, then, remains one of the key features of any economic growth pattern in an advanced industrial society. British businessmen and governments will ignore this fact at their – and our – peril. This then is the context in which this book discusses and examines behaviour in business in the framework of the 'business in context' model.

The modern world and behaviour in business

If British business is to maintain, let alone increase, its share of world markets in manufactured or service products then a number of characteristic features of UK enterprises which can be seen to date from the assumed apogee of British industrial strength have to be addressed. This book is concerned with those factors that relate directly to the behaviour displayed by people in work organizations, whether they be the managers or the managed. For this reason the book, while containing much of the material usually found in behavioural science books for business students, approaches the problems of behaviour in business from a slightly different perspective.

That perspective is one derived from a consideration of the issues and problems associated with the long-term decline of Britain as an industrial nation and the threats and opportunities presented by the establishment of the Single European Market. The behaviour observed in business and the factors which guide, motivate and modify it are dealt with in a manner which introduces students to the scientific factors involved and the associated research. This also places such behaviour in the context of what needs to be done at least to contain the long-term decline of Britain and to reverse it, involving some consideration not only of the origins of ideas about how work should be organized, but of how competitors handle similar issues. The assumption is that as human beings, British managers and workers are similar to their counterparts in, say, France, Germany, Sweden, Italy and Japan.

The orientation to the control of work displayed by managers in Britain, as indeed in any other country, is a consequence of their social origins, associated assumptions and expectations, and the institutional features of a society that have developed over a period of time and which will have been heavily influenced by the experience of industrialization itself.

Plan of the book

Following the view set out in the two previous paragraphs, Chapter 2 examines the origins of the modern work organization. Attention is focused especially upon the development of factories and the extent to which the so-called industrial revolution was mainly in fact a managerial one. What was significantly at stake was control over who did what work, where it was done, and how it was done. The process of gaining this type of control, and the resources that were mobilized, can still be seen to influence managerial and worker attitudes and behaviour today.

Chapter 3 looks at the responses to the factory system of work and the managerial control over work that were developed by workers and their organizations. Particularly important here are two concepts which are still of current interest although developed in the nineteenth century, and which can be seen as representative of the two ends of a political spectrum: 'alienation' developed by Karl Marx, and 'anomie' used by Emile Durkheim.

Chapter 4 examines the role and structures of modern organizations with particular attention paid to that form of organization which was, and remains, regarded as typical of industrial society – bureaucracy. The chapter considers the significance of organizational structures for human behaviour, especially when it is increasingly realized that the full commitment of highly trained employees is a major factor in competitive success.

Chapter 5 continues the study of organizations by considering the concept of strategic choice, and establishing the basis of power in organizations. The point is that much of what is regarded as inevitable in terms of organizational structure and policy becomes, on closer examination, very often a matter of the exercise of choice by powerful individuals or groups. The chapter considers what the basis of power in organizations may be.

Chapter 6 builds on the discussion so far by examining the nature of decision-making in organizations and what the informational requirements of such decision-making may be. Particular attention is paid to the impact of information technology on organizational decision-making and the impact on organizational structure as well as behaviour.

Chapter 7 changes the focus of attention so far by turning to individuals in organizations and the factors which affect their behaviour as individuals. Apart from an examination of theories of motivation, attention will also be directed at personality and ways in which it may be measured and categorized, and how this may be used in recruitment. Consideration will also be given to how individuals may adapt to organizational environments, and the significance of this adaptation for organizational performance.

The remaining three chapters focus very much upon the implications of what has been discussed so far, with particular reference to the issue highlighted in this introduction. Given the long-term decline of Britain as an economic power, what is to be done to meet the challenge of the Single European Market, as well as the increasingly competitive economies of the Pacific rim?

Chapter 8 looks at possible changes in organizational structures which will encourage increased commitment from highly skilled labour forces, and Chapter 9 examines the connection between notions of private property and the control of industrial organizations. The idea of the cooperative as an alternative form of organizing and controlling work will be examined here. Finally, Chapter 10 will examine the vexed question of the utility of international comparisons, both methodologically and in terms of what they can tell us about how British management and industry can – or should? – adapt to the challenges they face.

References

Chandler, A.D. (August 1980) The growth of the transnational industrial firm in the United States and the United Kingdom: A comparative analysis. *Economic History Revue*, Vol. 23, No. 3, pp. 396–410.

Davis, L., Gallman, R. and Hutchins, T. (1987) Technology, productivity and profits: British and American whaling competition in the North Atlantic 1816–1842. *Oxford Economic Papers*, No. 39, pp. 738–59.

Eatwell, J. (1984) *Whatever Happened to Britain?* BBC, London.

Hayes, R. and Abernathy, W. (July – August 1980) Managing our way to economic decline. *Harvard Business Revue*, 11–25.

Hirst, P. (1989) The politics of industrial policy. In Hirst, P. and Zeitlin, J. (eds) *Reversing Industrial Decline? Industrial Structure and Policy in Britain and her Competitors*. BERG, Oxford.

Muellbauer, J. (1986 Autumn) Competitiveness in British manufacturing. *Oxford Revue of Economic Policy*.

Neale, A. and Haslam, C. (1989) *Economics in a Business Context*. Chapman and Hall, London.

Needle, D. (1989) *Business in Context*. Chapman and Hall, London.

Searle, G.R. (1971) *The Quest for National Efficiency*. Blackwell, Oxford.

Spencer, P. (June 1987) *Britain's First Productivity Renaissance*. Credit Suisse First Boston.

The origins of the modern work organization 2

This chapter will examine the origins of contemporary ideas about how work should be organized and controlled. Such an examination is essential to our understanding of current issues in organizational behaviour and to our appreciation of its role within the business context model. In this chapter we will examine the related aspects of the Industrial Revolution: the development of the factory system, the division of labour, the development of management and the split between ownership and control, the control of labour and issues related to the work ethic. The chapter will close with an examination of the changing nature of work and control.

The purpose of this chapter is to show how the development and implementation of ideas concerning work and its organization rather than machines and technological developments formed the key attributes of the process known as the 'Industrial Revolution'. It was from these ideas that modern notions of the role of management, capital and labour – and the rights and obligations attaching to them – were developed. The origins of ideas about how work should be organized and the rights and obligations of management and workers will be examined in order to:

☐ Explain how those ideas came about and how they impact upon behaviour in modern organizations;
☐ Establish a framework for the examination in the following chapters of how contemporary ideas about work and its organization may have to adapt to changes in the nature of the competitive environment if British industry is to maintain, let alone increase, its share of world markets or defend its share of domestic markets.

In terms of the model informing the series of which this book is a part, attention in this chapter is focused upon the environmental context, not the immediate organizational environment, but the wider socio-political environment which gives credibility and legitimacy to the ideas used to organize business activities. Relevant ideas in this context are, for example, those concerning the role of markets and the state, the role and rights of the owners, management and workers in an enterprise, and their representatives. Underlying all these are the rights and obligations of private property which will be examined in more detail in Chapter 9.

The ideas mentioned in the previous paragraph influence the formulation and resolution of issues making up the inner rings of the model and influence, even if they do not determine, human behaviour in the workplace. Modern organizations are based upon ideas about where work should be done, by whom it should be done, under whose control and authority it should be done, and in pursuit of whose interest it should be carried out. These ideas were developed during the period known as the Industrial Revolution. Like all ideas, therefore, they relate to a particular social, political, cultural and historical time period.

These concepts were developed by a particular social group (merchants and entrepreneurs) who faced particular problems (controlling the quantity and quality of work) at a particular time in history, and who saw a particular solution (the 'manufactory' or factory-based work system) as being more readily available, or at least less inconvenient, than others in the context of a market-based economic system.

An industrial society is generally regarded as one primarily characterized by the presence of large-scale (in terms of numbers employed) organizations. This is the case whether those employed are making things (manufacturing), servicing those who are making things, or just providing services to the population as a whole – banks, supermarkets, insurance companies, hotels and holiday companies, for example. In terms of numbers employed 'large' may be defined by reference to a relatively small number, 200–250 employees. Organizations of this size employ far more people in the economy than organizations of the size of ICI or the Ford Motor Company for example. However, reflect for a moment upon the problem of organizing the work of ten people . . . or fifty . . . or eighty,

Table 2.1 Criteria for defining a 'small' business

	Annual turnover	No. of employees	Other
Companies Act 1981:			
Small	≤ £1.4 million	≤ 50 (weekly)	
Medium	≤ £5.75 million	≤250 (weekly)	
Department of Employment, Small Firms Division:			
Manufacturing example		200	
Construction example		25	
	£000's		
Retailing	315		
Wholesale	1260		
Motor trade	630		
'Miscellaneous services'	315		
Road transport			≤ 5 vehicles
Catering			**All** establishments except multiples and brewery-managed public houses

Source: Hill (1987).

let alone two hundred! How would you, how could you, know what each of those people were doing, how well they were doing it, what they ought to be doing next in order to achieve the organizations' goals, and what those goals ought to be in the future? Criteria that are currently used to characterize organizations by size are shown in Table 2.1.

An excursion into history is justified by the relevance such an exercise has for contemporary debate concerning the relative decline of Britain as an industrial power. This decline is commonly measured by a drastically reduced share of domestic and international markets for manufactured goods since the mid-nineteenth century. The debate over the causes and features of this decline focuses attention on the British experience of industrialization and the relevance of ideas developed up to 250 years ago for the solution to contemporary problems. Contemporary debate about the policies and strategies to be adopted in order to arrest and reverse the decline of Britain as an industrial nation are premised upon the view that either

☐ Ideas and principles which were effective in the past have been ignored; or, less frequently,
☐ such ideas anyway require at least some modification if they are to be appropriate for the last decades of the twentieth century and the pressures of the twenty-first.

The concepts and experiences which inform the debate about industrial decline and the ideologies of those who take part are all subject to the influence of the existing stock of ideas which derive from the experience of industrialization as it affected the interests of different social, economic and political groups in Britain. In this way historical factors have a continuing and powerful impact upon contemporary behaviour and attitudes.

Before we examine the Industrial Revolution it is necessary to dwell a little on the notion of **socialization**. This concept is important to our understanding of how individuals fit into our changing organizational world. Socialization is the process through which we acquire the roles we play in our daily lives. Current practice in the area of organizational structure and the roles of management and labour in work organizations is based upon ideas about the rights, duties and obligations of managers and workers which are very largely 'taken for granted'. Most people, whether managers or workers, find no reason to question them most of the time. In any kind of society, whether an industrial one or not, social life is possible because people have been socialized by family and school (or its equivalent) into behaving more or less 'properly', that is in ways found 'acceptable' or 'correct' by peers and superiors. In this way people learn what they are expected to do. They also learn what they can expect others to do. It is possible therefore to go into a shop, bank or post office, or catch a train or bus or hire a taxi, with a fair degree of confidence of what is likely to happen and with a minimal use of language.

Life in an office or factory also depends upon socialization for its effectiveness. The reason that a factory or office can operate at all is because the majority of people involved have expectations about their own behaviour and that of others that are sufficiently accurate to allow the interaction required by organizational life to proceed more or less smoothly. This taken-for-granted character of ideas about work and its organization is partly the reason for the fraught nature of organizational and industrial relations from time to time. When expectations about what is 'right and proper' or about what is 'normal' are not met, considerable frustration results. Frustrated people usually act without the forethought that complex situations demand which will further aggravate the issues underlying a disagreement. In order to understand social behaviour, whether characterized by cooperation or conflict, an observer (or even a participant) must attempt to make sense of the way those whose behaviour is being observed are making sense of the world in which they find themselves.

Socialization is discussed further in more detail in Chapter 7 on pp. 247–8.

An Industrial Revolution?

In order to understand the nature and significance of the changes which occurred in the eighteenth and nineteenth centuries and which are labelled as being the 'Industrial Revolution', it is necessary first of all to look at the notion of a 'revolution' as applied to the events which unfolded during that period. We need to do this because so much of current observation and analysis is based upon a model of what is thought to have occurred at that time in British history.

The notion of a revolution implies rapid change – as opposed to mere 'development' – occurring over a relatively short timespan. 'Change' is defined by what follows a particular event or point in time being both quantitatively and qualitatively different from what went before. It is precisely this 'revolutionary' character of events and processes in the eighteenth and nineteenth centuries which can be questioned in the context of industrialization in Britain.

There is considerable evidence in the case of England that many of the attributes of an industrial society were already in existence before either factories or machines came to play a dominating role in the popular perception of the modernization of society. For example, individual ownership of private property has been traced as far back as the thirteenth century in England, and by implication its origins lie even further back in history (Macfarlane, 1978).

We have identified six aspects of the Industrial Revolution: the notion of private property, the changes which took place in agriculture, the growth of towns, the importance of time, the concept of revolutionary change and the concept of industry. We will examine each of these in turn in order to understand more fully the basis of the 'Industrial Revolution'.

Private property

The notion of private property, the notion of a right in or to a material thing that can be sold or given away to others, will be discussed in more detail in Chapter 9, but for the moment it is sufficient to emphasize that such a notion is fundamental to a society in which the market is regarded as the major means of allocating scarce resources. A market economy presupposes the existence of private property. A key factor in the British experience of industrialization is the right of property owners to dispose of their property as they see fit, with minimal restrictions placed upon the enjoyment of such rights. This is reflected in attitudes to the relationship between captial and labour, the rights of management and trade unions, the duties of employees, and the role of the state.

As we will see later, contemporary British attitudes to the rights of workers and the obligations of the empolyment contract which distinguish British from, say, German or Scandinavian industrial relations systems derive from the perception that an effective means of disciplining a reluctant factory labour force was to be found, in part at least, by relying upon that part of the legal system that dealt with the rights of private property. This is one of the factors which underlies the British government's concern at the time of writing over the European Social Charter, and its characterization by the Prime Minister Margaret Thatcher as 'back-door Marxism'.

A second crucial aspect of modern industrial society which relates to private property and its exploitation was also present in Britain some considerable time before the advent of factories and the application of mechanical power. This was the organization of production around the **sale** of produce rather than its **consumption**, not just production for sale rather than for consumption, but production for sale which was organized in the interests of accumulating private wealth.

The agricultural revolution

Agriculture was well organized on a commercial basis, that is production for sale rather than for consumption by the growers, by the eighteenth century. Prior to the so called 'industrial' revolution had been the 'agricultural' revolution which incorporated innovations in husbandry resulting from discoveries of new crops in the New World, as well as land drainage techniques from Holland. The Norfolk Four Course Rotation system introduced by 'Turnip' Townshend (turnips being the key to the new crop rotation system), enabled landowners to make use of all their land each season rather than being required to leave a proportion fallow. These developments in agricultural and drainage techniques were accompanied by the extension of private ownership via the enclosure of common land which was itself motivated by a desire for the private accumulation of profit and which was well established by 1700.

'The British model of industrialization issued from an already well-developed market economy. The accumulation and concentration of capital as well as the creation of a wage labour force were already well advanced: agrarian relations had already been substantially transformed on capitalist lines . . .' (Kemp, 1983, p. 6).

At this point it is worth pausing to consider the concept of 'surplus' and its relationship to that of 'profit' as set out in Key Concept 2.1.

It should be realized that the pursuit of a surplus via the allocation of scarce resources that have alternative uses is not peculiar to just one type of society. **Any** society, if it is to survive, has to produce a surplus. There has to be a surplus over current consumption in order to ensure the continuation of production even if production is only for consumption. A proportion of this season's crop has to be available as seed for next season's planting; tools have to be replaced; items used in trade or barter for commodities not produced by members of society have to be available.

The necessity of creating a surplus is rarely if ever the point at issue in disputes over inequality in society. The point at issue is usually the size of the surplus to be attained in the light of to whom it accrues and how it is to be distributed. Important points to note about the development of the commercial production of agricultural commodities are the **ownership** of the surplus and the **motivation** for production – production for sale in the interest of wealth creation through market operations. These aspects of modern industrial society appeared first in agriculture and in the case of England have been shown to have a long history prior to the development and application of machine power in mills and factories.

It is important to appreciate the distinction between 'surplus' and 'profit'. A **surplus** is required to meet current obligations (pay the bills, wages, raw materials, etc.) and to invest in future activities – replace old-fashioned or worn-out equipment for example. **Profit** is that part of the surplus which accrues directly to the owners of capital. Chapter 9 explores the implications in greater detail. **Any** society or organization has to make a surplus to survive. Who owns that surplus, and who determines how it is to be divided (and by what criteria) between various uses, e.g. dividends, reinvestment or innovation, are factors which distinguish societies, e.g. 'capitalist' and 'non-capitalist', and organizational forms, e.g. cooperatives, partnerships and limited companies.

The growth of towns

To some extent dependent upon the surplus to be derived from the commercial production of agricultural commodities was the growth and development of towns. The existence of towns implies an adequate supply of food for sale. The urban population was augmented by those who left the countryside, partly as a result of the increased productivity of commercial agriculture which could support a growing urban population, and partly as a result of enclosures which forced landless peasants to seek employment in towns as wage labourers.

Medieval towns were the locale for the control not only of commerce but also manufacturing through a system of craft guilds. The organization of manufacturing and commercial trade was well established in towns long before the period generally regarded as the Industrial Revolution. Trade, including export trade, was well established in the woollen industry in medieval England, and the earliest craft guilds to be established in English towns were those of weavers, a factor of some significance when we come to consider the motivation behind the development of the factory system of production.

Evidence for the existence of a conflict of interest between town-based weavers and those based in the countryside – and which suggests the beginnings of a factory-based system of production – can be found in the Weavers Act of 1555. This Act limited the number of looms that a person could have in his house. To have been the subject of legislation the developing concentration of looms under one roof 'must have been a real economic threat to the independent weavers of the sixteenth century' (Marglin, 1974). That the town-based guilds were able to get this statute established, from which they of course were exempted, indicates not only their political strength but also the existence of a real threat from what may be recognized as the early stages of 'factory' organization as the number of looms physically located under the direct control of one person increased.

The importance of time and its measurement

Another important aspect of modern industrial life that also had its origins in medieval institutions is the concern with 'time' (Thompson, 1967) – time, that is, as it refers to a concern with schedules, with set times for working, with speed of work, time as money. The origins of this concern with time can be found in the development of the clock as a consequence of the discipline of the monastery. This required the day to be rigidly demarcated between various religious activities as well as between religious and secular ones. 'Not without reason can the Benedictines be identified among the ancestors of modern capitalism' writes Dickson (1974). The subordination of human activity to the dictates of the clock, as in 'time is money', was developed in the secular world by factory owners like Josiah Wedgwood and taken even further by the founder of the 'time and motion' study, F.W. Taylor, in his attempts to identify and rigorously impose minutely detailed work patterns on workers (set out later in the chapter in Key Concept 2.3).

Was the Industrial Revolution 'revolutionary'?

The factors considered so far suggest that the process of industrialization may not have been quite so rapid as the term 'revolution' implies. Some of the key attributes of modern industrial society – commercial production, wealth creation, the growth and importance of towns and private ownership, for example – all appear to have been well established in British society before machine tools and the application of water and steam power made their considerable contribution to the growth and development of modern society.

Having explored the allegedly revolutionary aspects of the Industrial Revolution, we continue in the following section to consider just how valid is the term 'industrial' in this context.

What was 'industrial' about the Industrial Revolution?

Even if we cannot regard many key aspects of industrialization as 'revolutionary' in terms of the timespan over which they appeared, surely there cannot be much doubt about the industrial nature of the changes that occurred? Even here matters are not quite as straightforward as might be expected. Yet again, taken-for-granted assumptions turn out to be more problematic than their widespread acceptance might indicate. Apart from the timespan involved, the changes which did occur – over however long a period – do not equate unambiguously with the concept 'industrial'.

Many writers have forced the facts of the case into an interpretation which stresses marked discontinuity (i.e. a 'revolution' that was 'industrial'), 'but the facts do not support this viewpoint' (Forres, 1981, p. 182). Despite the popularity and widespread acceptance of ideas about 'stages of growth', and the notion of 'take-off' into industrialization developed by Rostow (1960) to explain industrialization in both industrial and industrializing countries, the concept is a dramatic simplification in the British case, and does not stand up to the attempt to relate it to known facts (Deane, 1967).

There are at least four separate meanings of 'industry' (set out in Key Concept 2.2) which pervade debates about the process of industrialization in eighteenth and nineteenth century England, and which are implicit in contemporary discussions concerning the future development of industrial society. The relatively greater significance of change and development in the realm of social control and organization for the 'industrial revolution', as compared with innovation in technology, can be established by reference to statistical data concerning the growth of manufacturing industry.

The development of cotton manufacture has been at the centre of narratives concerning the English experience of industrialization (see definitions in Key Concept 2.2) between 1970 and 1840. However, even as late as 1841 only 14% of the employed British population were in textiles, and this sector included only 10% of the employed male population since 40% of the labour force were women and 30% of cotton workers were

KEY CONCEPT 2.2	The terms 'industry' and hence 'industrialization' have a number of possible meanings, each implying something rather different in the context of debates about the process of industrialization and the future development of industrial societies.
INDUSTRIALIZATION	

☐ **Industry** as in 'the motor industry' or the 'hotel and catering industry'.
☐ **Industry** as a reference to the manufacturing sector of any economy.
☐ **Industrialization** as the process by which factory methods come to dominate working life – even for those **not** employed in factories but in offices, shops and hotels, for example.
☐ **Industrialization** as the process by which modern, i.e. non-traditional, life develops.

Source: Forres (1981).

handloom weavers. Output of cotton never reached more than 5% of UK national income.

> 'Steam engines, like Manchester, Arkwright's invention, cotton manufacturing and factories, may have been taken as **symbolic** of the 1760–1840 changes, but they are hardly **typical** of the times.'
>
> *(Forres, 1981, emphasis added.)*

The events characterized as the 'Industrial Revolution' are more accurately applied to what happened in one industry, in one town, in one country: cotton, Manchester, England (Kumar, 1978). While the smoking chimneys of factories and mills may have been, and remain, **symbols** of modernity ascribed to industrialization, they were not typical of changes in the eoncomy or work experience of the majority of the population. However, the symbolic power of the 'dark satanic mills' has been a potent force in the articulation of the British experience of industrialization, and hence in the development and nature of the institutions which grew out of that experience, for example the public school and the 'professional' ethos. That reaction to the symbols of industrialization has had a powerful impact upon attempts to modernize British industry, institutions and policies in the twentieth century, as will be seen in Chapter 10 when some of the cultural factors argued to be behind the decline of British manufacturing industry are examined.

We now turn our attention to those aspects which are commonly associated with changes brought about by the Industrial Revolution, namely the factory system, the control of labour and the importance of the work ethic. We deal first with the factory system.

The factory system of organizing work

It is possible, however, to identify a significant change which, even if it occurred over a longer period than popular belief assumes, represented a significant departure from earlier times. This concerns the organization of work and the model presented by the development of factories. What was significant about factories was not the machines, but the fact that owners of capital came to exercise control over the location and organization of work. The changes in the location and organization of work which occurred during the period had implications for **all** forms of work, whether in factories, offices or on the farm. This involves an examination of Forres' first definition of 'industrialization' as set out in Key Concept 2.1.

The argument is that the development of the factory was motivated by the need to control work. In other words the factory was a managerial phenomenon. Acquisition of control over work subsequently facilitated and even motivated technological innovation, rather than technological innovation provoking the desire to control work, although this did and still does occur. Contemporary concerns over the organization of work and work groups as a consequence of the introduction of microelectronics into machine tools, and the competitive pressures involved in the introduction of new technology, are focused on the control over work exercised by workers and managers.

The development of the factory

Factory type work organization is associated with a number of features of modern society, for example the separation of home from work, the development of the notion of 'going to work', the opposition of work and leisure in human experience, as well as the development of modern ideas about the rights and duties of managers and workers. These aspects of social organization are crucial to an understanding of the development of industrial society and to the understanding of contemporary problems concerning behaviour in work organizations. They are also important for an understanding of popular ideas about how and why society may be changing. Many observers argue, for example, that changes in work organization, technology and leisure patterns are indicative of a future society which may be accurately and usefully described as 'post' industrial or even a 'leisure' society.

To understand the development of factory-based work as a managerial necessity it is useful to consider the changes which occurred in the textile industry. Wool had for centuries been the major commercial and manufacturing activity in England, and constituted a thriving export trade. Cotton in particular also has a central role in accounts of industrialization in England. This is illustrated in Case Study 2.1.

CASE STUDY 2.1 **TEXTILES AND INDUSTRIALIZATION**	Both spinning and weaving involved several intermediate processes: carding to straighten the fibres of raw wool or cotton, spinning the fibres into a long single thread or yarn, then dyeing and weaving. Each of these processes had their own craft guild, and it was in an attempt to avoid the restrictions imposed by town-based guilds that merchants first developed the 'putting out' system of textile manufacture. Work was 'put out' to rural workers on a cottage industry basis where the carding and spinning or weaving was carried out in addition to the other activities of a rural household. In many cases the work was organized around a division of labour within the family involving children as well as adults. 'Putting out' is still a feature of the clothing trade where it is often referred to as 'outworking' or 'home-working' and usually involves women working from their own home on part finished materials. While putting out enabled merchants to avoid the restrictions exercised by craft guilds, they were now at the mercy of the erratic life styles of their new, predominantly rural, labour force. Agricultural and other pursuits of rural life meant that the consistency of both quality and quantity demanded by an expanding trading network were difficult to control. The amount of spinning or weaving actually done in any one period of time would depend upon the other demands of daily life such as planting or harvesting, the care and feeding of cattle, and so on. These other pressures not only affected the quantity produced, but could also affect quality. There was also the problem that the quantity

available for the merchant could be reduced by embezzlement – cottagers might be tempted at times to sell some of the cloth or thread on their own account, or to use it to make needed clothes for themselves and their families. In addition of course, raw material and part finished material had to be distributed to each cottager and later collected for onward transmission to the next homestead in the production chain.

Merchants then had little effective control over weavers and others based in rural homesteads, and the dependence of the merchants upon the cottager for delivery, quantity and quality constrained the power of the former while enhancing that of the latter.

These to some extent long-standing problems were exacerbated by developments in spinning technology in the 1760s as a result of Hargreaves' work on the spinning-jenny which resulted in a substantial increase in the amount of yarn available. Exploitation of the cost advantages of this development was frustrated by the merchants' lack of control over the final stages of cloth production – especially weaving.

To cope with the problem of lack of control in a situation of expanding markets and trading opportunities, merchants developed the idea of establishing workshops where the punctuality, attendance, effort, sobriety and honesty of those employed could be kept under observation. The establishment of workshops in itself was not a new idea since town-based guild workshops occupied a section of the merchants' or financiers' own houses. The myth of the large and extended pre-industrial family is in part due to the existence of households which included not only servants but also apprentices and journeymen who were legally under the rule of a 'pater' or social father, the employer. As we saw earlier, the Weavers Act of 1555 can be seen to indicate awareness of the existence and effectiveness of workshops made up of a number of machines.

The control of work by merchants

The establishment of workshops was motivated by the need to exercise control over work. This had been the point of going to the country in the first place. These workshops were to be under the control and observation of the merchants and not the craft guilds. Evidence for an interim stage in the development of the factory system can be seen in places like Trowbridge in Wiltshire. Here the townscape of the old part of the town, where it exists today, is formed by large merchants' houses surrounded by weavers' cottages which had been built in the grounds of the merchants' houses to aid supervision.

The need to exercise control over labour was also felt in another industry, pottery. Josiah Wedgwood is quoted as claiming that he had turned 'worthless workmen' into a 'very good set of hands' by virtue of the enforcement of a discipline emphasizing punctuality, constant attendance, fixed hours, cleanliness, minimal waste and sobriety. The point is that the factory-based organization of work was not directly derived from the availability of new machines. Many of the machines assumed to be characteristic of industrialization were developed **after** the workers and their hand-looms had been collected together under the watchful eyes of merchants and their overseers. Once the fact – and more importantly for our case – the legitimacy of determining where work based on hand-tools was to be carried out had been established, investment in the development and application of mechanical power became an economically attractive proposition. The construction of 200 hp water-wheels and associated civil engineering works, let alone the installation of steam driven machinery, would not have been economic unless a large number of looms were to be operated.

The role of machines

The writings of contemporaries like Andrew Ure and Samuel Smiles all assert the role of machines in terms of their contribution to the enforcement of merchants' and owners' control over the organization of work in terms of who did it, when it was done, and where it was done.

Machines undoubtedly made possible vast increases in output, and eventually in quality. They also made possible an increase in the standard of living of the vast majority of the population. However, the prime motivation behind the development and application of technology in the eighteenth and nineteenth centuries was the managerial need of the merchants to control the work of cottage-based weavers and others. At least four reasons for the establishment of the factory method of production can be identified. 'Manufactories' enabled merchants to exercise:

☐ Control over the output of the weavers;
☐ Control over the hours and intensity of the weavers' work;
☐ Control over technical innovation; and also
☐ Served to emphasize the role of the 'capitalist' as one who actually owned the tools and equipment necessary for production, as well as supplying the raw material and disposing of the finished product (Dickson, 1974).

The major significance of the role of capital rested on the extent to which capitalists interposed themselves between the workers and customers. Under a craft form of production producers deal directly with the customer; there are no intermediaries because the product is consumed locally. A product, not labour, is being bought and sold. The factory division of labour is not just a division of tasks, important as that is, but also a division of **function**.

As a result of the factory system craftsmen become dependent upon the capitalist and financier not only for the organization of the supply and distribution of raw material and finished or partly finished goods, but also for the integration of the work of one craftsman with that of another until the end product reached the consumer. Labour was no longer independent but reliant upon the role, function and resources of capital and finance (Marglin, 1974).

The development and application of expensive and complex machinery implies the existence of work organized in accordance with what is recognized as the factory system. Today, for example, systems analysts and computer programmers can be supervised as closely as supermarket checkout operators since the very technology of which they are the apparent masters and mistresses can facilitate supervisory observation of even complex intellectual activities.

As the cost of computing technology falls dramatically and it becomes available on an individual basis, the possibility of people once again working from home arises. While work was removed from the home to the factory in order to facilitate control over it, the same motivation operates in the reverse direction. With Information Technology the time people put in at work, how fast they are working, and the quality of their work can be monitored at a distance. In addition, of course, it is the worker who carries the overheads of lighting and heating!

The Industrial Revolution, then, was primarily a social and managerial rather than a technical process. It was primarily, in terms of sequence and causes of events, a change in the way in which two social groups related to each other, a change in the way one social group came to control the activities of another. This change was important for the eventual development of a third group which came between capital and labour – that is mangement as a group of people rather than as an activity. As a group managers were not owners of the means of production, but they did not share the same social situation as other non-owners.

Technology and control

The material reviewed by Dickson (1974), Littler (1982) and Freeman (1974), for example, which examines the historical origins and development of modern methods of organizing work, provides considerable insights into the way technology is involved in the exercise of power in organizations, and into subsequent attempts by those affected to exercise countervailing power. We will return to this issue in greater detail when examining the factors behind contemporary attempts by management to introduce new technology and trade union responses. Modern as well as historical material suggests quite emphatically that while technology may certainly constrain human choices under certain conditions, it only rarely **determines** them. While technology may place limits on the range of options available to management, the introduction of technological innovations does not inevitably necessitate one particular course of action on the part of management in terms of the impact on the degree of skill and autonomy of those involved.

Recapitulation

As we said at the beginning, this chapter is concerned with establishing the origins of contemporary ideas about work, the way it should be organized, and the way in which control over the organization of work could be legitimated. Since much of the contemporary debate over the declining fortunes of British industry in comparison with major competitors is premised upon the validity and effectiveness of ideas taken for granted about the control over work which originated during the period known as the 'Industrial Revolution', the chapter so far has explored the natures of both the terms 'revolution' and 'industrial'. This has been done in order to show how ideas taken for granted (i.e. unquestioned) require examination if an understanding of why social groups behave the way they do is to be developed. Such an understanding must be based upon attempts to make sense of the way social groups attempt to make sense of the world in which they find themselves, since the perception of that world is powerfully influenced by ideas taken for granted.

The pressures which eventually resulted in the modern factory form of work organization have been explored in this context. The following sections of the chapter extend the investigation by considering the consequences of the division of labour in terms of the problems of coordination it created as enterprises increased in size, with the consequent emergence of a group of people known as 'managers'. Important in this discussion are ideas about the relative importance of managers in relation to ownership and the degree of control which ownership may entail. A third aspect to be explored is the nature and role of ideology, expressed in terms of the 'work ethic', for the contemporary debate about present and possible future developments in British industrial society.

The division of labour

In this section we will explore the significance of the division of labour for the relationships, and hence behaviour, of those in industrial organizations.

All societies display some division of labour. Particular tasks are allocated to particular social groups, either by systems such as the traditional caste system in India, or simply by age and sex. In all societies a **social** division of labour exists which allocates tasks to particular groups: the old, the young, men, women. Industrial societies maintain this principle even if there have been some recent, and slight, modifications. Some jobs are still seen as being primarily 'womens'' work while others are seen as unambiguously 'mens''.

Mechanization involved breaking a craft skill down into its constituent parts. The machines themselves were specialized, such as those for spinning and weaving in the early days, followed later by machine tools designed for turning, milling, boring, grinding and so on. These functions became the province not only of particular machines but also of their specialist operators. The final result is that no one individual actually makes a complete artefact any more, or even knows how to. Work has been reduced to a specialized activity which is determined by the nature of the machinery and the decisions taken by those who commissioned its designed and installation. There is a real sense in which the skill of the individual craftsman has been appropriated by the designers of new machinery, or by the creation of new tasks and task groups such as programmers for computer numerically controlled (CNC) machines. The process of mechanization produces a **technological**, as opposed to merely a social, division of labour.

This process does not mean that workers or jobs must necessarily be 'de-skilled'. The level of manipulative and cognitive dexterity required to control the new machine may exceed that required under the old methods, and in an expanding economy utilizing new production technologies and methods the demand for skilled workers may actually increase. However, if the economy, or a particular market, is static or in decline, then the productive potential of new methods may well lead to a reduction in demand for skilled workers or pressure to recruit cheaper (i.e. less highly trained) labour. One of the advantages of developments in textile machinery for factory owners in the eighteenth and nineteenth centuries was that at a time when skilled workers were protesting about the relocation of work into factories and mills, and the subsequent loss of control, the application and development of machines enabled owners to reduce the demand for skilled weavers. The new machines enabled a skilled worker, supervising a number of women and children, to produce the same or greater output than a number of skilled workers working individually on hand-looms. In this way machines enhanced the ability of owners to impose discipline upon recalcitrant skilled workers.

With the development of both private and public bureaucracies in, for example, central and local government, and financial and insurance industries, a similar technological division of labour has occurred in office work. Routine clerical work is the result of designing administrative processes such that the level of knowledge required is specific to those carrying out each particular process. In manual work the typical example of the technological division of labour is of course the mass production track, as epitomized in the car assembly line of the 1960s and 1970s. Much office work, however, can also be seen to follow just the same 'production line' flow pattern as standardized forms are processed according to standardized methods.

In both types of work, control rests firmly with a group whose existence is the result of the increased need to coordinate the multitude of tasks created by the technological division of labour. This group is known as 'management'. However, in particular circumstances a work group, or section of it, may be able to resist the exercise of that control and even impose their own will upon management due to the fact that they carry out a particularly crucial function which management does not fully comprehend, or for which they cannot recruit other forms of labour or technology. There were a number of instances during the 1989 wage round campaign of the local government union NALGO where some employers were considerably embarrassed by specialized groups (mainly concerned with various computer processes) withdrawing their labour.

The origins of management

An important aspect of the development of the factory system and the technological division of labour was the appearance of a group who, while not themselves owners, acted in the interests of the owners in the operation of the enterprise. 'Management' as a process of controlling and coordinating was a necessary part of the business of being an owner of the new type of enterprise appearing in the nineteenth century. Managing was intrinsic to the position of 'owner'. However, as organizations increased in size and complexity they outgrew the ability of the owner to manage directly on a person-to-person basis. This is a problem faced today by those who establish a successful business which then grows in terms of the numbers employed.

To cope with this situation supervisors were appointed and, as Pollard (1968) points out, these people were chosen for their reliability and ability to maintain discipline amongst the workforce. The predominant concern of the early factory owners was the recruitment for supervisory positions of people who could be relied upon to keep discipline. Technical knowledge, if any was required, would be acquired after appointment. This is reflected in the contemporary concern with the personality and schooling of recruits to many management training programmes, rather than concern with technical knowledge, as represented by a specific degree qualification for example.

Owners were advised by Adam Smith to take care over the selection of those appointed to supervise enterprises since in a world in which the individual pursuit of self-interest was positively praised, owners could not rely upon others to protect or act in sympathy with their own best interests. Consequently there was great concern over the personal qualities of those appointed. One way of ensuring the appointment of trustworthy staff was to appoint family members to management positions, including members of the family into which a son or daughter had married. That this may have raised other, equally difficult problems, is undoubtedly the case!

The development of a group known as managers and the articulation of a distinct activity of managing is significant because it provided an opening for the growth of a 'middle class'. This group were not owners of the means of production but as a result of representing and furthering the interests of the owners they occupied a very different situation in society from those who made up the remainder of the wage earning labour force. The experience of industrialization in England and the responses that experience provoked has had a profound effect upon the nature of British management and its technical competence in comparison with that of other industrial nations.

The work of people like Channon (1973), Chandler (1977) and that edited by Hannah (1976) all illustrate the very different character of British organizations as a result of differing responses to the problem of management. Modern management in terms of the development of techniques of accounting, reporting and monitoring the operations of departments and functions developed first in America in the late nineteenth century, as did the notion of mass production. The first 'modern' firms in Britain did not develop until the 1920s, for example when Mond put together what was to become Imperial Chemical Industries (ICI) from a loose cartel of firms still very much under the control of families and without a well developed tier of technical managers.

Familiarity with the historical origins of an institution can go some way at least to providing an account for why an institution is as it is, and so give some indication of what strategies may be available and appropriate for changing it. British managers are less technically qualified than many of their peers in other countries because technical qualification was never a major concern of those who were responsible for the appointment of managers and supervisors. British education for the élite did not stress technology for the same reason. Even natural science went under the euphemism of 'natural philosophy' in nineteenth-century public shools, if it was taught at all (see Chapter 10 for a fuller discussion). The 'old school tie' is a powerful totem precisely because it was an important proxy for the attributes sought by those making managerial appointments . . . and still is. Even the preponderance of accountants on the boards of British firms can be related to the desire to identify reliable managerial recruits. The early counting house was, according to Pollard (1968), a popular source of recruits to managerial positions since those employed in this area of the business had displayed honesty and were likely to have gained some commercial acumen.

The role of subcontractors

One other aspect of the supervision problem in the early factories centred on the role of subcontracting. This was an adaptation of earlier attempts to escape the rigid controls of town-based guilds, and involved the hiring of skilled workers who brought with them their own 'assistants'. In other words, a labour gang was hired and paid as a gang. The gang 'boss' distributed the money according to some agreed (or physically enforced!) formula. The position of such a gang leader was the basis of the 'hire and fire' foreman which characterized some industries right up to the Second World War. Such an individual is also part of the Japanese experience and was a focus of opposition to attempts to reorganize working practices during the development of modern Japanese industry. The role and power of subcontractors was important in the development and application of the principles of 'scientific management' by F.W. Taylor in America at the turn of the century as explained in Key Concept 2.3.

Ownership v. control

The role of modern management as a group exercising control over resources they do not own but who are accountable to shareholders is highlighted by the questions raised by insider dealing and some takeover bids. On occasion, contested takeover bids are marked by much advertising by the predators and their intended prey as to which of the two managements are best able to enhance shareholders' interests. The extent to which takeovers are funded by huge borrowings which can only be repaid by selling components of the newly acquired company ('unbundling' as Sir James Goldsmith called it in his bid for BAT in 1989), focuses attention on the extent to which modern management displays interests distinct from both labour and capital. The debate over the extent to which merger activity really does represent attempts to improve company performance rather than self-aggrandisement by managements is also part of this question, and relates to the debate over the creation of a European

KEY CONCEPT 2.3 ***SCIENTIFIC MANAGEMENT***	F.W. Taylor was an eminent American engineer of the late nineteenth century who developed a number of innovations which greatly increased the speeds at which metal-working tools could operate. Since the machines could now for the first time work faster than the people responsible for them, the resulting pressure upon human working methods caused him to develop a system of job design based upon the careful analysis and recording of how individual tasks in the workplace were, and in his view should be, carried out. The objective was to identify the 'one best way' of carrying out any task in terms of physical movement and the length and distribution of rest periods, and then ensure that workers only operated in that manner.

Taylor was concerned to overcome what he termed 'systematic soldiering' – 'skiving' as it would be termed today – and to wrest control over working practices from subcontractors in order to place it firmly in the hands of managers. Reward systems were to be designed to encourage compliance with the specified methods. Taylor considered this to be a 'scientific' method of organizing and designing tasks since it was allegedly based on careful observation. His method of task analysis which was the precursor of 'time and motion study', was known as 'scientific management'. While Taylor's work is correctly considered to be concerned with the way in which manual work was carried out, he intended later to turn his attention to clerical and managerial jobs.

An important part of his enterprise in his own mind was the need to establish a sound basis for legitimating managerial work not just in the eyes of the workers, but also in the eyes of the owners. Part of the point behind 'scientific' management was not simply increased output, but a scientific basis for the exercise of managerial activity in relation to owners and workers.

See Sofer (1972) and Littler (1982) for further accounts of Taylor's work.

capital market after 1992 since a much greater proportion of the equity capital of companies is held by shareholders in Britain than is the case in other EC members.

Interest in the extent to which ownership was separate from the exercise of control was sparked by the work of Berle and Means (1947) originally published as early as 1933 in America (see also Chapter 3 of Needle, 1989). Managers exercised **allocative** control in that they, rather than the shareholders, exercised the major influence over how the resources of the enterprise were to be distributed amongst themselves, the owners and employees, and in what direction the efforts of the enterprise should be guided.

The appearance of a large mass of shareholders, the vast majority holding a small proportion of the total equity and mainly interested in the size and regularity of the dividend rather than the exercise of ownership rights, is argued to have resulted in specialist managers exercising control in their own interests rather than in the interests of capital. It is worth reflecting that, for an organization fighting for survival or pre-eminence in the market, the payment of a higher dividend or a wage increase both have the effect of draining cash from the company which might have been invested in product or process innovation. While investment in new products and technology may ensure the survival of the firm and provide rewards for the managers and employees, returns to shareholders may be reduced in the short term.

A managerial revolution?

The separation of ownership and control, and what it implies about the development of modern industrial society, has been described as a 'managerial revolution' (Burnham, 1941). Burnham maintains that a technically competent, technocratic managerial stratum has emerged in society. Technical in this sense implies the mastery of the techniques of administration such as accounting, legal principles and so on. The expectation that such a management will act in the interests of technical efficiency is taken to imply that modern capitalism has lost the stigma attaching to the bad old days of *laissez-faire* capitalism. Consequently, institutions and ideologies associated with the development of capitalism – trade unions, socialism, 'them and us' – are irrelevant to the concerns of modern citizens whether as workers or as citizens.

Subsequent critiques of Burnham's position in this debate have involved an examination of the extent to which the social origins and interests of managers, particularly senior managers and boards of directors, were very similar to those groups and individuals who hold significant proportions of equity. See particularly Nichols (1969) and Scott (1985).

Control and the division of labour

The fact, and nature, of the division of labour in industrial society, including the role of management, is crucial to an understanding of what goes on in an organization. In terms of relations between management and workers, and between the various departments and functions in a business organization (organizational and departmental politics), the key issue is that of **control**. The control of scarce resources that have alternative uses implies control over who does what, when, where, how and to what end. It implies control over the distribution of surpluses or losses resulting from operations in the market-place.

This approach to the examination of behaviour at work has obvious political implications. However, the approach is not political in the sense of supporting one 'side' or the other, nor is it political in the 'party political' sense. The approach is political in the way Child (1972) has argued, that management is a political process since it is concerned with the exercise of strategic choice, that is the ability to determine the objectives which the organization will set out to achieve, how it will go about achieving them, and how the costs and benefits are to be distributed.

As previously mentioned, the human condition is such that any social group, using whatever tools and ideas are available, has to make a surplus if it is to survive. This requires the creation of rules governing how that surplus is to be created and distributed – in other words a 'political economy'. If rules are going to be followed with any regularity (a basic requirement of any **social** entity), then control must be exercised over the members of society.

Ideology and control

In all societies this kind of control requires a shared ideology, a shared ethos as to what is 'right', what is 'normal', to what the concepts 'good' and 'bad' are to be applied. Shared ideas of this type govern important aspects of social life in **any** society. They govern how production and the creation of a surplus is to be organized, who does what and who can order or require others to carry out certain instructions and activities. Such ideas also determine who should get what share of the surplus produced as a result of the social activity of production. The key features of an ideology are set out in Key Concept 2.4.

In industrial and non-industrial societies such shared ideas are internalized by the members of that society as a consequence of the process of socialization. The way we are brought up by our parents and teachers, as well as the way we are influenced by our peers, results in these ideas being taken for granted. They have the function of organizing the way we view the world – they **are** the way in which we view the world. At the very least socialization serves to reduce the desire and ability to do something about the way in which a surplus is produced and distributed since it inculcates an acceptance, however reluctant, of the inevitability of things being the way they are.

A complication arises in the case of societies whose size or structure is such that not all members have the same experience of the operation of the social system. In such societies there is the probability that some groups will perceive the system as not operating in their case in accordance with the norms they share with others in society. Discontent may be the result of a specific incident – like the motorway that destroys or damages a community. More significantly for social order, however, discontent may arise and be fuelled by the perception, accurate or not, that one

KEY CONCEPT 2.4	Ideology refers to a set of ideas that deal with important matters for a group. At some minimal level these ideas will form a coherent system. They explain and justify to others what the group is about, and they explain and justify to the group members themselves what they are doing and why. Membership of the group implies acceptance to some significant degree of what the ideas say about the group, its objectives and its activities. Given these characteristics of 'ideology', group members may find it difficult to ask serious questions about the ideas forming the ideology. They may be forced eventually to confront the incoherent or erroneous features of the ideas when something goes seriously wrong, but will initially look elsewhere for explanations of failure.
IDEOLOGY	

community or section of a community constantly appears to carry a disproportionate share of any costs in comparison to any benefits. This is particularly the case with forms of discrimination.

A situation can exist where, at a fairly high level of abstraction, there is general agreement that whilst the system itself is sound, or the best that could be hoped for in the circumstances, its operation may be flawed. Since the operation of the system is dependent to some extent upon human agency in that someone, somewhere, exercised choice or power, it is not difficult to understand how particular groups come to see themselves as having **different** if not necessarily opposing interests.

Even the application of sophisticated decision techniques like cost-benefit analysis to such projects as the siting of airports or the impact of the Channel Tunnel or a nuclear power station may leave unresolved and even unaddressed the question whether the benefits that all recognize and may even welcome are distributed in a manner which reflects the actual or perceived distribution of the costs. It is worth reflecting on this point in the context of any attempt to understand the behaviour and attitudes of management and workers in British industry. It is often the case that there is no disagreement about the need for a surplus to be created, that such a surplus may be necessary to ensure products and processes are available for the future. Disagreements are much more likely to arise over who, exactly, carries the costs involved in surplus creation, and how and to whom that surplus is distributed.

Managers, workers and shared values

With a few notable exceptions the British labour movement has not, historically, been concerned to do away with a market-orientated capitalist society based upon private property. Historically the British labour movement has been concerned to ensure what was perceived as a 'fair share' of any rewards. It has been the operation of the system, not the system itself, that has given rise to the main sources of complaint.

Dissatisfaction with the way the system has appeared to operate, as opposed to dissatisfaction with the system itself, has from time to time given rise to attempts to influence policy at national level. At other times – and more usually – dissatisfaction has manifested itself as a dispute with a particular employer or industrial group of employers over the way costs and benefits are distributed. It is worth reflecting that a nineteenth-century alternative to the private control and operation of capital – the cooperative – despite (or because of?) being a native product rather than an exotic import, has failed to take root in this country in the field of production. (Cooperatives will be discussed in more detail in Chapter 9.)

The relative lack of interest in the cooperative as an organizational form in the United Kingdom characterizes both management and unions. It serves to reinforce the view that trade unions are an intrinsic part of capitalism, like the stock exchange, rather than dedicated to its overthrow or serious modification (Anderson, 1967). Cooperatives are as much of a threat to the role and status of trade union officials as they are to traditional management. After all, unions exist to represent the interests of workers to management. If the worker/management distinction disappears, then so does the *raison d'être* of trade unions. This aspect will be discussed in more detail in the next chapter when we examine the way in which historical experiences have moulded present-day unions and the attitudes and behaviour of their leaders and members. However, one other feature of the process of industrialization that retains an important role in the continued legitimation of the role and authority of management, as well as in the operation of the welfare state, is the idea of the work ethic.

The work ethic

The drive to exercise control over work and the associated development of the technological division of labour was the setting for the development of the so-called 'Protestant' or 'work' ethic. The phrase 'Protestant ethic' is taken from the work of the German sociologist Max Weber, who examined the role of religion in the rise of capitalism. Weber's thesis was that the appearance of modern capitalism in North-Western Europe rather than in the more commercially and culturally developed southern region of the continent could be explained by the dominance in Northern Europe of Protestantism in general and a specific sect – Calvinism – in particular.

At the time he was writing in the early years of the twentieth century Weber recognized that the religious element had declined in importance. The Protestant ethic had been scularized and was perhaps more accurately to be termed simply the 'work ethic'. However, the values implicit in the work ethic are closely allied to basic tenets of Calvinism in terms of strictures against conspicuous consumption and in favour of hard work, duty and thrift, as outlined in Case Study 2.2.

The development of the work ethic has involved the establishment of what can be termed the 'social role of work'. It is necessary to regard work as having a number of social roles other than that of simply earning an income. These roles are crucial to an understanding of industrial society and to an appreciation of the multifaceted problem of unemployment. Failure to comprehend the social role of work has two major consequences: not only will important aspects of employment be ignored by policies designed to cope with unemployment, but the implications of asserting the inevitability or desirability of a 'leisure society' will not be recognized.

There is a certain irony in that the debate over unemployment in terms of how it should be counted, what causes it and how it is to be dealt with demonstrates that the issue is of major political importance. Yet the people at the centre of the debate, the unemployed, are experiencing the fruits of a society in which work, to some writers, no longer forms a, or certainly the central life interest.

Work, in terms of its social role and significance, is like so many other aspects of contemporary society – a consequence of the process and experience of industrialization. It is part of the 'social technology' developed by a particular group of people who had to deal with particular problems at a particular time. (The nature of a social technology is set out in Key Concept 2.5.) As has been indicated several times already in this chapter, the key to understanding the development of main features of an

In this study entitled *The Protestant Ethic and the Spirit of Capitalism*, Weber attempted to explain the origins and dominance of capitalism as a social system. What is significant in the rise of Europe and capitalism is that as a distinctive form of social and commercial organization capitalism in its modern form appears to have taken root in a part of the world that was less well developed commercially and culturally than others. Southern Europe, for example, was home to the Venetian traders and merchants who developed sophisticated commercial techniques as well as extensive trading activities. Many of the early efforts to exploit the products of the Orient involved explorers and navigators from the southern part of Europe, not the north.

Lombardy merchants and bankers, remembered in the street name 'Lombard Street' in the City of London, developed double-entry book-keeping in the sixteenth century; Lombardy bankers used to sit on benches (*banquiers* – hence the word 'bank' in English) to couduct business with clients. If a banker could not meet his obligations, irate customers would tip him off his bench and beat him with it, hence the expression 'bankrupt'. Countries like India also had highly sophisticated financial and commercial systems, but also failed to develop what is now recognized as modern capitalism.

Weber identified what he claimed to be a significant feature of North-Western Europe which could account for the origins of capitalism. That feature was the Protestant reformation in general and the development of Calvinism in particular.

Weber's reasoning was the while the southern portion of the continent had well established and highly developed technical and cultural features, a key feature of capitalism was missing. While all merchants and traders were anxious to make a surplus – and the bigger the better – in the case of southern Europe this was spent largely on what might be termed 'conspicuous consumption'. Fantastic palaces were built, for example, and these were furnished with the work of the most famous designers and artists. Churches were built and lavishly decorated. Musicians were hired to write and perform for church services as well as for secular events, and so on.

Calvinism as a Protestant sect had features which, in addition to redefining a person's relation to God, had an impact on commercial behaviour as a consequence of that redefinition. Unlike Catholicism which characterized Southern Europe, Calvin's doctrine taught that salvation was by no means assured. There was no way for an individual to know whether they were 'saved', whether they were indeed one of God's children. In addition, the role of a priesthood as intermediary between an individual and God was absent in Calvin's teaching. Here, each individual faced God as an individual in a direct, one-to-one relationship.

In this context, one of the few signs that a person was safe from eternal damnation was worldly success. Success could be seen as an indication that God looked favourably upon an individual. In the commercial world this had important consequences since it went along with strictures

CASE STUDY 2.2

THE PROTESTANT ETHIC, WORK AND IDEOLOGY

Continued over page

Continued from previous page about consumption and lifestyle. The Calvinists' emphasis upon what Weber called 'inner-worldly asceticism', as opposed to the non-worldly asceticism of religious orders, is illustrated in the Puritan tradition as experienced in Britain in the sixteenth century: simple, plain costumes, strict limits on what were acceptable expressions of enjoyment, strict religious observation and so on.

However, as mentioned earlier, the strict regulation of personal behaviour went along with an emphasis on commercial success. So surpluses were created, and larger ones desired, but they could not be consumed. Work was a religious duty. So, what was to be done with the surplus? Weber's answer is that it was re-invested in the business and so created even larger surpluses, and so the process went on.

This explanation by Weber is no longer seriously considered, but it is still consistent with contemporary concerns with hard work, thrift, self-help and personal attitudes. Contemporary concern about the attitude of young people towards work, and how they should be introduced to it, illustrates the relevance of ideas associated with a particular religious development. While Protestantism may not have had quite the role ascribed to it by Weber, it nevertheless did have and continues to have a major influence in terms of the legitimation of ideas about how people should behave. This is the case even if the ideas are now put forward in a secular context, and not advocated in terms of religious teaching but of economic 'efficiency'.

KEY CONCEPT 2.5

SOCIAL TECHNOLOGY

'Social technology' refers to sets of ideas that govern social relationships and processes, that is 'technology' as in 'technique'. The notion of bureaucratic or hierarchic structures is an example of a social technology, as is the military model and associated metaphors: 'captains of industry', 'aggressive' sales people, and 'business' strategy. The 'market' is a social technology.

The development of the 'work ethic' was (and remains) a piece of social technology. It not only served to explain how people ought to behave, but also legitimated the actions of those who insisted that this particular 'ought' was indeed a legitimate imposition upon all members of society.

---

industrial society is to be found by trying to understand what particular groups saw as solutions to problems which faced them at a particular moment in history. For the merchants and financiers of the eighteenth and nineteenth centuries the solution to their problems involved seeking control over the processes of production and distribution.

The context in which the 'work ethic' was developed included attempts by writers like Adam Smith to undermine the influence of the aristocratic classes in order to establish the status of the rising class of manufacturers

The original notion of 'liberalism' referred to the extent to which in a market society individuals would be freed from the demands placed upon them by the reciprocal obligations characteristic of a feudal society. A feudal system is characterized by relationships between social groups which are in the form of reciprocal, personal obligations. Relationships do not depend so much on the feelings or attributes of individuals as individuals, but on the obligation which an individual member of one social group or category owes or is owed by an individual belonging to another category simply by virtue of the fact that they both belong to the categories in question. So a feudal lord is not only owed obligations by his feudal subordinate, but also owes that subordinate certain obligations. This could be summed up as: the lords defend all, the clergy pray for all, and the serfs feed all.

Under the liberalism preached by Adam Smith, for example, individuals were to be liberated from such obligations in order to pursue their own self-interest as they saw fit. The new basis for integrating and coordinating the social process of production and distribution was to be provided by the 'hidden hand' of free markets, combined with the individual's responsibility to work. In fact work was to be the basis of property rights since every one was to be entitled to the fruits of their own labour, whether in the form of interest (as a return on capital) or wages. (Further discussion of the nature and development of property will be found in Chapter 9.)

'Free labour' as required for the operation of a market economy is 'free' in two important senses. First, it is 'free' in that the labourer is not bound by feudal ties or other extra-economic considerations; such a labourer is therefore free to enter into contracts. Secondly, it is 'free' in the sense of having been divested of the means of production. These are now owned by the 'capitalist' rather than the worker.

As a consequence, the technological division of labour produces a situation in which human relationships are characterized by:

☐ **Individualism:** a concentration on the individual as individual, rather than as a member of a social group or category.
☐ **Impersonality:** playing down commitment to a person and emphasizing contractual obligations only.
☐ **Contractualism:** the sale of goods and the employment contract, which focuses only on what has been agreed between the individuals who are parties to the contract, whoever and whatever they are.
☐ **Competition:** the basis of allocating scarce resources, including labour, and of determining their price via the market-place.
☐ **Egoism:** self-interest as the main, and legitimate, motivator of actions in the market-place and in dealings with others.

These characteristics are moulded into some coherence by means of rational calculation – profit maximization. Relationships in such a society then proceed from sheer self-interest, unencumbered by any but minimal considerations of emotional or traditional constraints.

CASE STUDY 2.3

FREE LABOUR AND THE 'LIBERATED' INDIVIDUAL

and merchants. Smith's book *The Wealth of Nations* is not only a treatise on the social and economic superiority of a market society, but also a conscious attempt to replace one social order by another. Central to this objective was the notion of 'free labour' which is a component of the social technology of a market-based society. The role and significance of 'free labour' are set out in Case Study 2.3.

It is in such a society as described in Case Study 2.3 that the social role of work becomes central to the way people relate to each other as individuals and as members of social groups. An examination of the role of work in modern industrial society illustrates the extent to which modern industrial society is committed to a particular method of solving some perennial problems of human society. This examination not only highlights issues raised by the suggestion of the development of a post-industrial or leisure society as a consequence of a 'second' industrial revolution, but will demonstrate that once again what will be 'revolutionary' will not be the machines or the technology but the changes in social institutions and relationships.

A consideration in more detail of the components of the social role of work reinforces the argument that, while technology may make radical change feasible or possible, it will not necessarily make such change probable. The key components of the social role of work are identified in Key Concept 2.6, and are elaborated in more detail in the following sections.

KEY CONCEPT 2.6 **THE SOCIAL ROLE OF WORK**	The social role of work can be broken down into at least five constituents: ☐ The distribution of the surplus resulting from the social activity of production; ☐ The legitimation of that distribution; ☐ The creation and maintenance of self-identity; ☐ The creation and maintenance of meaning and purpose; ☐ Social control.

Distribution of the surplus

As already argued, any society has to produce a surplus if it is to survive. In a capitalist industrial society that surplus is distributed by means of a wage or salary to employees, and via dividends to the nominal owners – the shareholders.

Legitimation of the distribution

This is perhaps the most significant of the five components of the social role of work in the context of the nature and development of industrial society. While unemployment may not necessarily leave a person with no means of support in a modern industrial society – thanks to some form of welfare state – the share of the surplus allotted to people unable to work for whatever reason is usually small in relation to what they can earn in work. Furthermore, the allocation of that relatively small share is hedged about with constraints derived from tests of availability for work of one kind or another. Such tests underline the fact that 'work' is assumed to be a duty, the only accepted method of acquiring a share of the surplus, thus emphasizing the continuing significance of the work ethic.

In the case of social groups who do not have to 'work for a living' in the sense of earning wage or salary, those with private means such as the inheritors of large fortunes for example, work-like obligations are nevertheless presumed to be operating. The inheritors of large fortunes are under some obligation to be seen to be 'earning a living' . . . including the Royal Family whose workload is measured by the tabloid press in terms of the number of public engagements fulfilled by individual members each year! Heeding Adam Smith's strictures about *noblesse oblige* – the obligation of the wealthy to assist the poor – modern members of the rich still contribute their time and efforts in the interest of charities, local councils and 'acceptable' pressure groups such as the Country Landowners Association, Save the Children, Oxfam and so on. Many of these activities are performed under a sense of obligation and in that sense resemble 'work'.

In the same vein, the maintenance of large country houses and estates is explained, and any income legitimated, in terms of stewardship. The landowner is seen to hold the property in trust for the rest of us (and for generations as yet unborn) and is therefore carrying out a duty which legitimates his or her share of the surplus. This legitimation is held to operate however great the variation in income and work conditions.

Differences in income between groups at less exalted social levels are also legitimated by reference to the differential demands assumed to be made upon those carrying out different jobs. Allegedly 'skilled' workers are paid more than less skilled workers; managers responsible for a wider range of activities than those they manage are deemed entitled to a differential. Teachers in polytechnics and universities earn more for less hours of teaching to smaller classes of allegedly more socialized human beings than secondary or primary school teachers. Doctors get paid more than dustmen, though as was seen in the 1970s, the threat to public health from a strike by dustmen is more immediate than if the doctors were to withdraw labour, and requires troops to be brought in to contain the threat to the public. On the other hand, many but by no means all of those in hospital are there due to what may be termed 'preventable' causes.

The widespread concern over the matter of differentials, whether at the level of the chairmen of private and public corporations or between different occupational groups lower down the organizational hierarchy – electricians, toolmakers, programmers, analysts and so on – serves to illustrate the way in which the job one does legitimates the share of the surplus one gets. The attributes of the job become attributes of the person doing that job.

The whole question of job grading structures and equal pay for work of equal value arouses such concern and attention precisely because, while all generally agree that differentials are in some sense 'fair' and may even be necessary, decisions about the magnitude are usually the result of some exercise of power. It is not always possible to identify a coherent logic underlying the operation of a payment structure. Even Adam Smith noted that the most pleasant jobs seemed to attract the better pay and conditions, whilst the least pleasant had the poorer rewards.

(Further discussion about pay structures and their impact on behaviour can be found in Chapter 7.)

Self-identity

The third aspect of work and its social role concerns the way in which a job provides the basis for a individual to establish and maintain a self-identity. Once one enters the adult world of work, relations with other people will at the very least be mediated by one's work. At parties people are less frequently asked 'Who are you?' than they are asked 'What do you do?' A person's job will form part of the host's or hostesses' introduction: 'Oh! John, I'd like you to meet Jennifer. She's in the City too . . .' Even if the introduction were in terms of 'She's fascinated by the early Beethoven Quartets,' it will not be long before John asks, or is informed, what Jennifer does for a living.

In an industrial society, work establishes an individual's relative significance and status. An individual's job indicates to others and to the individual whether or not they are amongst 'similar' people, whether among people who can be expected to share certain ideas and expectations in common.

The significance of work as a means of creating and establishing a self-identity can be judged also by considering the reply to the question 'What do you do?' often given by married women who do not 'work' in the market economy: 'Oh! I'm just a housewife!' Feminist writers have long been exploring the implications of excluding from the market economy the contribution made by 'house'-work to the welfare of the economy as a whole.

Those caring for invalid and aged relatives are also excluded from the market economy and not therefore perceived as having a 'real' job of work. Such work is not regarded as being in the market economy even though it dramatically reduces the demands that would be made upon the state, and it certainly is not rewarded with market rates of pay. Work in the market, or it's absence, is a crucial factor in an individual's self-perception as well as the perception of the individual by others. An individual's perceived worth to society in the eyes of the individual as well in the eyes of others is powerfully influenced by the kind of job they do. Unemployment therefore is not simply a problem of low income; it also represents a problem of self-identity and social esteem. To be unemployed is to lack status in society. This can have important social and psychological consequences.

Purpose and meaning

Closely related to the issue of self-identity is the contribution work makes towards creating a sense of purpose and meaning for the individual. Work may have a purpose in terms of the reputation it enables an individual to establish, or the material comforts it enables an individual to enjoy whether or not the work itself is intrinsically rewarding. At the very least work is a reason for getting up in the morning. In this way it does at least structure the day, week and year. Work provides a sense of purpose whether it influences the individual's whole life in terms of its encroachment into non-work time, as is often asserted in the case of 'professionals', or whether it is regarded as a purely instrumental activity which in and of itself provides no rewards other than money which can be spent. In this case work will not be a central life interest, but will be seen as more of a drudge to be endured for the sake of objectives quite separate from work and which are intended to compensate for the experience of work.

Social control

The analysis of writers like Dickson (1974) and Marglin (1974) provide illustrations of the way in which the control of work was central to the development of industrial society and may still be seen to be so in the modern world. The examination of the nature of the employment contract on p. 71 will illustrate this.

The thrust of the argument put forward by writers such as Dickson and Marglin is that, whilst machinery was not the prime motivation for the establishment of factories, once established, machines provided a further dimension to the exercise of control over recalcitrant labour. The threat of machine utilization and the implied displacement or replacement of labour as a result of decreased demand for labour or a reduction in the skill levels could be used to contain or overcome resistance to new methods of working.

Equally important, however, was the need to legitimize the new order at the level of society as a whole, not just the exercise of proprietorial power in the workplace. Market individualism had to be accepted, reluctantly or otherwise, if the ideology of the market mechanism was to become the organizing principle of the new order. Work was central to this enterprise since the control of work was based upon the control of property and the exercise of property rights. Even today, the interpretation of the provisions of the contract of employment is based upon the rights of private property except in so far as the exercise of those rights are constrained by statutes limiting their unfettered exercise.

Having opened the chapter with a discussion of the reasons behind the establishment of factories and the factory method of organizing and controlling work, we proceeded to examine the implications of the division of labour and the appearence of an activity and social group known as 'management'. The coordination and control of work exercised by management on behalf of owners has made use of the ideology of the work ethic. In the following sections we will go on to examine the extension of the control of work into non-working life, and the meaning of terms such as 'post-industrial' and 'leisure' society to reinforce the fact that industrialization was much more about managerial activities than it was about technology.

Control over non-work life

Through the mechanism of the control of work at the workplace, non-work aspects of life also became subject to the same kind of organization. The discipline demanded of workers at work placed an equal emphasis upon discipline outside work. Perhaps the best known, and more extreme, of owners' efforts to exercise a similar discipline over domestic life as they exercised over employees' working life was that of Henry Ford who paid a monetary bonus to his employees based in part on the right to supervise them in their own homes. Inspectors would call to ensure that Ford's orders conerning lifestyle – no alcohol for example – were being followed. The status of being a 'ten dollar a day man' at Ford's plant depended not just upon performance on the production line but also conformity to Ford's views concerning the private life of employees (see Littler, 1982).

Much earlier of course, Wedgwood's attempts to turn what he considered unreliable, ill-disciplined individuals into 'reliable sets of hands' involved setting and enforcing acceptable standards of behaviour outside the factory as well. The paternalism of employers in providing accommodation for workers was also in part at least a desire to ensure some supervision over non-work activities. The works bands of Lancashire and Yorkshire were funded by employers partly in the knowledge that evenings spent in practice and playing were evenings not spent in the pub. The rules of the Huddersfield Choral Society contained strictures concerning drinking, and forbidding the librarian 'knowingly' to lend copies of music to 'socialists'!

Similar concerns are expressed by employers today. The reliability of an employee is of considerable interest to those who are responsible for the smooth operation of complex production and administrative systems. A worker's private lifestyle may not only affect their reliability in terms of time-keeping for example, but hangovers, other forms of drug abuse and marital breakdown may well influence effort, accident rates, absenteeism and quality standards. Lifestyle, then, may be a relatively cheap screening device in that proxies for reliability – such as being married, having a mortgage, work experience and good references – are relatively easy to come by from the employer's point of view. In an attempt to qualify the economist's respect of risk-taking, Alfred Marshall argued that gambling was 'impure' because it was likely to 'engender a restless, feverish character, unsuited for **steady work** as well as for the higher and more solid pleasures of life' (*Principles of Economics*, Mathematical Appendix, 1890, emphasis added).

Personal attributes of workers

The significance for management of a worker's general behaviour and attitude pattern was illustrated in a research project which sought to examine the definitions of shortages of skilled labour used by managers, and the strategies they used to cope with such shortages (Oliver and Turton, 1982). The majority of managers in this study found it somewhat difficult to be very precise about the concept of skill when pushed to define objective criteria of cognitive and manual dexterity. When questioned about what they meant by a shortage of 'skilled workers', these managers fell back upon references to the personal attributes desired of potential employees. This approach was summed up by one manager who said: 'What we want is good blokes.' The 'good bloke syndrome' has long been a major concern of employers and has little to do with objective tests of an employee's ability or potential.

The concern with the personal attributes of workers was further demonstrated when it was found that the same attribute actually sent different signals to employers depending on their geographic location. As is often the case, being married was generally taken as a proxy for reliability in terms of the obligations it was assumed to imply. However, in the case of employers who recruited from among the population of a new town, being married was taken to indicate potential unreliability. This was because, like many new towns, the rate of marriage breakdown was above the average for the population as a whole. Instead of indicating reliability, being married indicated a risk that marital discord and break-up, with all the associated stress, might disrupt work performance. Thus in one geographical area amongst the factors indicating reliability was **not** being married!

Robertson (1974) illustrates how, in the marine engineering industry of North East England in the closing decades of the nineteenth century, technical education was regarded as beneficial not because it would raise levels of skill and knowledge to those characteristic of German and American workers, but because it 'discouraged vandalism, promoted moral strength and broadened a man's outlook as well as giving him a better grasp of the job'. Its importance derived not from '. . . a better knowledge of the principles of shipbuilding and engineering, but because it helped inculcate habits of good conduct'. Robertson reports that evening schools for apprentices in shipbuilding were regarded almost as correctional institutions and he quotes sources showing that more public money was actually spent on schools of correction than on technical colleges in Newcastle in the last decades of the nineteenth century. The key function of the Education Act of 1870 has been described as not about instruction, but '. . . to discipline a growing mass of disaffected proletarians . . . to civilize the barbarians' (Landes, 1969).

School-leavers are regarded with some scepticism by many employers. Not knowing much about specific jobs they try one, and then finding it less congenial than they expected, they leave to continue the process of exploring the labour market, albeit this time a little better informed. Thus a pattern of several jobs over a relatively short time is taken to indicate unreliability, rather than a serious search of the opportunities in the market! Indeed, changes (1989) in the legislation covering eligibility for unemployment pay have increased to six months the time over which an employee who voluntarily leaves employment must wait before receiving unemployment pay.

Current concern over discipline in schools as well as with the content of the curriculum are further examples of how the demands of employers are fed into life and institutions outside the factory or the office. The general view that the streets are not safe, that property is not safe, that schools, teachers and parents are somehow to blame for much of the lawlessness of modern youth, are all manifestations of the general concern over the creation and maintenance of a trained and disciplined workforce. A century before the 1870 Education Act it was argued that children as young as four years of age should be actively occupied, whether in earning a living or not, since this would ensure that '. . . the rising generation would be so habituated to constant employment that it would at length prove agreeable and entertaining to them' (quoted in Thompson, 1967). The work of Bowles and Gintis (1976) in America, Willis (1977) in this country and Bordieu (1977) in France offer fascinating insights into the role of the education system in industrial society.

Work, control and changing ideas

Work, then, in all its forms is much tied up with matters of social control. Absenteeism in the office or factory is of equal concern to those charged with administering social order as is truancy from the classroom. The fact that certain groups of workers are required to 'clock in' while others are not, that the same groups are expected to lose pay for short absences while others are not, all reflect the extent to which some social groups are deemed worthy of greater trust than others. The fact that an increasing number of employers are now doing away with such distinctions, harmonizing working conditions around those applying to 'staff' groups, reflects the extent to which employers are increasingly aware that what Alan Fox (1974) calls the 'high trust' syndrome is a more effective way of motivating employees than its corollary, the 'low trust' approach. However, the awareness that is being displayed by such employers is not awareness of scholarly endeavour, so much as a reaction to the media hype about Japanese management and industrial success.

The Japanese approach

In many cases this change in approach by British managers is motivated by an assumption that industrial success is at least partly a result of the employment practices thought to be characteristic of Japanese firms. It is worth noting that what are regarded as peculiarly Japanese approaches to employee relations are also responses to very similar problems of control over work and those doing it experienced by those responsible for the modernization of Japan in the late nineteenth century. Japanese workers were no happier about being forced into factories than workers anywhere else. While more troops were engaged in keeping that Luddites down in England than were commanded by Wellington in the Peninsular War, the example illustrated in Case Study 2.4 from turn of the century Japan shows what problems of labour control were experienced there.

A leisured or post-industrial society?

Having examined the five aspects of the social role of work as represented in the efforts of one social group to exercise control over others, the closing sections of this chapter will briefly explore implications for the debate

In his book *Japan's Managerial System*, Yoshino (1971) records the labour turnover of a textile mill in 1990:

Total labour force	4000
Total recruited during 1900	6085
Total leaving employment during 1900	7071
Of whom: Dismissed	989
Died	71
'Escaped'	5798
'other reasons'	210

That the Japanese managers of this mill resorted to the term 'escape' indicates the prevalent attitude towards labour control of managers and the managed!

The convent-like accommodation conditions under which many female textile and factory workers lived in Japan well into the twentieth century were in part motivated by a need to overcome reluctance on the part of rural populations during the early stages of industrialization to let their daughters go off to work in the mills. The problem was not so much a concern about the well-being of the daughter but about the disgrace if she could not make a respectable marriage due to suspicions about what she had been up to whilst away!

Providing supervised accommodation enabled employers to demonstrate to concerned parents that they would look after the girls as though they were their own daughters. However, while the degree of supervision ensured that the girls were not troubled by the escapades of irresponsible youths, it also meant that the girls could not easily 'escape' back to their villages before their contract had expired!

concerning the likely future development of industrial society. In this way, the secondary role of machines in the first, and postulated second, industrial revolutions will be underlined as will be the significance of ideas developd at one time, by one social group, concerning the social role of work for behaviour in industrial societies. It is these ideas, ideas which have a particular social and historical foundation, that still dominate approaches to contemporary issues.

Post-industrial society

The term 'post-industrial' society is taken from the work of an American sociologist Daniel Bell (1974) and is based upon the assumption that contemporary changes in the kind of work people do and the nature of the location in which they do it are significant indicators of the kind of society such people inhabit. The growth of office work, the increase in the proportion of the population with formal qualifications, and the general decline in the number of people employed in heavy manual work are all taken as indicators of the appearance of a qualitative change in the nature of society.

When such indices are linked with the development of the welfare state and a high minimum standard of living in comparison with earlier periods, post-industrial theorists are persuaded to argue that the old ideas and extremes of nineteenth-century capitalism are no longer operative. Hence, we now experience a 'post'-industrial society which is both quantitatively and qualitatively different from previous eras.

However, the 'post'-industrial approach ignores the fact that despite the obvious changes in work and work conditions over the last century, the basic character of its organization has not changed significantly at all. If information technology now allows executives to work from home, or indeed anyone else, this is because the technology permits those charged with responsibility for overseeing this work to monitor it just as easily when the workers are not in the office as when they are. As with all outworking, a major advantage for employers is that they no longer have the overheads of insurance, lighting and heating for office buildings. So while the location and even the nature of work may change, the motivation underlying its organization is still consistent with that which motivated the establishment of factories in the first place. That motivation centres on control. To this extent, then, the term 'post'-industrial is both inaccurate and in-appropriate.

The leisure society

The concept of the 'leisure society' builds upon that of a post-industrial one, but adds to it the notion that current changes in technology and its applications will not simply result in changes in the kind of work people do and the conditions under which it will be carried out. Current changes, it is argued, will radically alter the proportion of the population required to work, or the proportion of an individual's life occupied by work. Those who speculate about the leisure society forecast a dramatic reduction in the demand for labour as a result of technological change, a not wholly unreasonable scenario. This reduction in demand for labour will have to be accommodated either by shortening working hours, or working lives, or by creating an acceptance on the part of the population at large (social control again) that not only will leisure take up a larger part of their lives, but for some people it may become the dominant activity of their lives.

The Real revolution

If one now reflects upon the five aspects of the social role of work examined earlier, then the radical, not to say revolutionary, implications of the 'leisure society' theory or programme become evident.

Since work is the way in which the surplus created by economic activity is distributed (whether by salaries or dividends), since work is also the way that that distribution is legitimated, that self-identity and meaning are established and maintained, and that social control is currently maintained, then the 'leisure society' scenario is no more useful or accurate an account than the 'post-industrial' one.

Service sector growth has been a feature of all industrial societies since the early stages of the industrialization process. The characteristic feature of industrial societies in terms of employment shifts has been from agriculture to services, not from agriculture to manufacturing to services. What happened was that activities characteristic of the 'service' economy were transferred from the home, where they were unpaid and so unreported in economic terms, to the public and private sectors of the economy where they did involve monetary transactions. Cleaning, laundry, teaching, care of the sick, entertainment and so on are examples.

The logical and psychological dependency of 'leisure' on 'work'

The 'leisure society' argument is potentially more revolutionary than that for the post-industrial future. This is because the concept of 'leisure' derives its meaning and significance from its contrast with 'work'. In the absence of a set of activities which the individual is obligated to carry out there can be no sense of 'leisure', of non-obligated activity. Importantly, the arguments put forward to support the notion of a leisure society also fail to take account of the fact that leisure costs money! In the economic sense leisure has a cost in terms of the income which is forgone by taking time off work, and in addition leisure activities require expenditure over and above that required for food and shelter. To be a realistic proposition the 'leisure' society requires a radical, not to say revolutionary, change in the way the surplus is distributed, the way that distribution is legitimated, the way self-identity is maintained and in the way social control is exercised, since none of these processes can remain the sole province of 'work'.

Summary

In this chapter we have undertaken quite a wide-ranging examination of the features and processes of the so-called Industrial Revolution and how it moulded contemporary ideas about the organization of work.

We started by examining the extent to which the terms 'industrial' and 'revolution' could be accurately applied to a particular historical process. Perhaps the term 'revolution' is the least applicable of the two given the very considerable timescale over which the process occurred. This is particularly the case given the date at which key aspects of modern society such as private property and production for sale in the interests of private accumulation developed. The term 'industrial' may also be questioned in terms of the proportion of the population actually involved. It is often forgotten that an important part of the process of modernization, the development of railways, represents the growth of a service industry (namely providing transport), albeit making heavy demands upon the iron and steel and manufacturing industries.

The chapter identified as a major feature of the process of industrialization the efforts by owners and merchants to gain control over work by controlling where it was done, who did it, and how regularly and consistently it was done. The factory was a managerial neccessity rather than a technological one. The idea of the 'manufactory' derived from efforts to locate hand-tools and the necessary labour under one roof where they could more easily be supervised. Only when this effort was successful did it make sense on any large scale to introduce expensive machinery. Machines were then an aid to the controlling of labour, and their development was in turn encouraged by the control over labour sought by owners.

The process of controlling work involved the development of the 'work ethic' as a means of justifying the exercise of control. Such a development produced the social role of work. By this means work became the central organizing feature of industrial society. Any significant or dramatic changes in the nature of industrial society then requires equally dramatic and radical changes in the social role of work.

That they fail to recognize this implication is the basis of major criticisms of the post-industrial society and leisure society scenarios. The first is shown to be not particularly accurate, and hence not very useful when applied to modern conditions, and the second is either preaching revolution or fails to comprehend what it is dealing with.

Understanding the behaviour of others

An important point to keep in mind when reading this book, and one which will be explored more fully in Chapter 7, is that a person's **attitude** is in large measure determined by the behaviour patterns they and the organization are constrained to adopt in coping with the world as they and it see it. For example, it is widely asserted that 'people do not like change' – this is especially asserted in the context of technology. If you look around you, however, it becomes apparent that **some** people do like or even welcome change. The point is, **which** people welcome **which** changes and at **which** point in time? If you perceive a change as being in your interests, or at least compatible with your interests, then you will accept or even welcome it; if on the other hand you perceive change as incompatible with, or destructive of, your interests then you will resist it.

In order to understand social behaviour we have to develop some understanding of how others perceive the world, how they came to perceive it in that way, and how they attempt to cope with it. We have to try and make sense of the way others attempt to make sense of, and cope with, the world. In this chapter we looked at the problems as perceived by merchants and owners, in Chapter 3 we look at the responses of workers and will consider the nature of institutions like trade unions, and the kind of society that industrialization brought about. In this way we continue our examination of behaviour in a business context.

Study questions

At the end of each chapter in this book you will find a number of questions which are designed to consolidate your understanding of the material covered in the chapter. Before proceeding to the next chapter answer them on no more than one side of A4 (though there is never any harm in doing more!). You could, on the other hand, use these questions as the basis for a group quiz. However you decide to use them, they will help to ensure that you are clear about the material covered, and its implications, before moving on.

1. Why might both the terms 'industrial' and 'revolution' as in the Industrial Revolution be questioned?
2. Upon what basis may it be argued that the factory was a managerial and social phenomenon rather than simply the result of technological development?
3. What five factors constitute the social role of work? What are the implications for (a) the unemployed; (b) the very wealthy?
4. How useful or meaningful is the term 'post-industrial' society?
5. 'People don't like change.' Under what conditions might this statement be (a) true, (b) false?

Further reading

For more detail about the process and nature of industrialization generally, and the British case in particular, the following sources (also referred to in the text) are useful.

Marglin (1974) is a classic article setting out the basic characteristics of industrialization and considers the process from feudal times. Two further books which would repay reading are Dickson (1974) and Kumar (1978). Both of these are tightly argued, but each has a chapter that is particularly useful in the context of the issues discussed here. Dickson's book is now out of print after going to three impressions in three years, but Chapter 3 is particularly good on the factors behind the setting up of factories. It also contains a useful discussion about the impact on social and political institutions of current technological developments in Chapter 7. Kumar's book is a very full account of the social, intellectual, political and economic aspects of industrialization in Europe. Chapter 6 is particularly useful in terms of the debate over the development of industrial societies and the concept of a post-industrial society. It shows how the growth of the service sector of modern economies was part of the process of industrialization rather than a subsequent development. Lastly, Littler (1982) provides a useful and accessible account of the development and characteristics of 'modern' methods of organizing work in Britain, the USA and Japan. It is important for an understanding of the debate surrounding current developments in the organization of working methods. Willis (1977) is a readable but disturbing account of a small-scale investigation into the development of attitudes to school and employment amongst a group of adolescents who will leave school with no formal qualifications.

References

Anderson, P. (1967) The limits and possibilities of trade union activities. In Blackburn, R. and Cockburn, A. (eds) *The Incompatibles: Trade Union Militancy and the Consensus*. Penguin.

Bell, D. (1974) *The Coming of Post-Industrial Society*: *A Venture in Social Forecasting*. Macmillan.

Berle, A.A. and Means, G.C. (1947) *The Modern Corporation and Private Property*. Macmillan.

Bowles, S. and Gintis, H. (1976) *Schooling in Capitalist America*. Basic Books.

Bordieu, P. and Passeson J. (1977) Reproduction in Education Society and Culture, Russell Soge.

Burnham, J. (1941) *The Managerial Revolution*. Penguin.

Chandler, A.D. (1977) *The Visible Hand*: *The Managerial Revolution in America*. Harvard University Press.

Channon, D.F. (1973) *The Strategy and Structure of British Enterprise*. Macmillan.

Child, J. (1972) Organization structure, environment and performance: the role of strategic choice. *Sociology*, **6**, (1).

Deane, P. (1967) *The First Industrial Revolution*. Cambridge.

Dickson, D. (1974) *Alternative Technology and the Politics of Technical Change*. Fontana.

Forres, M. (1981) The myth of a British Industrial Revolution. *History*, **66**, 181–98.

Fox, A. (1974) *Beyond Contract*: *Work, Power and Trust Relations*. Faber.

Freeman, A. (1977) *Industry and Labour*. Macmillan.

Hannah, L. (ed.) (1976) *Management Strategy and Business Development*: *A Historical and Comparative Study*. Macmillan.

Hill, T. (1987) *Small Business Production/Operations Management*. Macmillan.

Kemp, T. (1983) *Industrialization in the Non-Industrial World*. Longman. (Contains a very useful chapter on the British experience even though the book is mainly concerned with industrializing countries.)

Kumar, K. (1978) *Prophecy and Progress*. Penguin.

Landes, D. (1969) *The Unbound Prometheus*: *Technological Change and Industrial Development in Western Europe from 1750 to the Present*. Cambridge University Press.

Littler, C. (1982) *The Development of the Labour Process in Capitalist Societies*. Heinemann.

Macfarlane, A. (1978) *The Origins of British Individualism*. Blackwell, Oxford.

Marglin, S. (1974) What do bosses do? *Review of Radical Political Economics*, **6**, (2).

Marshall, A. (1920), 8th edn. *The Principles of Economics*, Macmillan.

Nichols, T. (1969) *Ownership, Control and Ideology*. Allen & Unwin.

Oliver, J. and Turton, R. (1982) Is there a shortage of skilled labour? *British Journal of Industrial Relations*, **20**.

Pollard, S. (1968) *The Genesis* of *Modern Management*: *a study of the Industrial Revolution in Great Britain*, Penguin.

Robertson, P.L. (1974) Technical education in the British shipbuilding and marine engineering industries. *Economic History Review*, **27**, (2).

Rostow, W.W. (1960) *The Stages of Economic Growth*. Cambridge University Press.

Scott, J. (1985) *Corporations, Classes and Capitalism*, 2nd edn. Hutchinson.

Sofer, C. (1972) Organizations in Theory and Practice, HEB.

Thompson, E.P. (1967) Time, work discipline, and industrial capitalism. *Past and Present*, (38).

Weber, M. (1965) *The Protestant Ethic and the Spirit of Capitalism*, Allen & Unwin.

Willis, P. (1977) *Learning to Labor*. Saxon House.

Yoshino, M. (1971) *Japan's Managerial System*.

3 The factory system of work and behaviour

In this chapter we will examine factors which influence the response of working people to the factory system of organizing and controlling work. The purpose is to develop an understanding of the way in which contemporary notions concerning the rights, duties and obligations of both management and labour have been developed in practice as a consequence of the experience of industrialization. An understanding of behaviour in modern business organizations depends in part upon a consideration of the responses of workers to the industrial organization of work. This is because workplace behaviour is strongly influenced by ideas – management's right to manage for example – and institutions such as trade unions, which have been moulded by the experience of industrialization. Contemporary differences in the attitudes and behaviour of management and workers in Britain, Germany and France, for example, and the legislative frameworks within which they operate, are due at least in part to the different experiences of industrialization as well as subsequent history – as will be discussed in more detail in Chapter 10.

This chapter represents a move from the outer rim of the model of business underlying the series, and is particularly concerned with the organizational context of the labour and ownership components. The chapter is also concerned with the environmental component in so far as this represents the framework within which management–worker relations are enacted.

As we saw in Chapter 2, the development of the factory system of organizing work was the consequence of attempts to gain control over the organization, location and rate of work. In this chapter, which is concerned with responses to this change, we will examine the exercise of **countervailing** power by those required to work under the new conditions. That is, we will examine attempts to contain or to limit rather than eradicate completely the exercise of power and control by a dominant group of owners and managers.

The discussion will start with a consideration of the two concepts around which the analysis and description of the nature of human relationships and the future development of industrial society have focused to the present day. We will then move on to consider the collective nature of the response to factory organization as represented by trade unions, and consider how this response has influenced the behaviour of management and labour in the modern workplace. Further aspects of the management–labour relations issue can be found in Chapters 2 (labour) and 8 (personnel management) of the companion volume by Needle (1989).

Power, control and behaviour

Contemporary attitudes towards industrial relations on the part of trade unions and employer organizations is the result of a history of attempts on the one hand to assert, and on the other to limit, the exercise of managerial power. In order to understand the way in which members of either group behave in the work setting it is necessary to have some insight into the way in which their concepts, expectations and attitudes were formed – not individually but as members of collective entities or groups. The socialization of individuals at home, school and work involves the introduction to and assimilation of ideas concerning the legitimacy of the exercise of control and what limits may be placed upon it which are shared by others.

Closely related to the exercise of control, and attempts to contain it, are two concepts which have been influential in the development of theories of social change and theories of human behaviour at work: **alienation** and **anomie**. These concepts have been influential at the theoretical level in thinking about society and represent two competing theories of the development of industrial societies. The first, alienation, focuses on the approach originally developed by Karl Marx, and the second, anomie, represents the more evolutionary approach of which the post-industrial theory developed by writers such as Daniel Bell is an example.

At the empirical level they have been used to account for patterns of human behaviour in society at large and in work organizations. In this context alienation and anomie underlie attempts by management to limit the negative aspects of the technological division of labour as represented in an extreme form by the popular image of the mass production assembly line with its repetition of very short timespan tasks, minimum demands for skill, and lack of variety. This concern is continued in contemporary efforts to ensure the commitment of workers to the firm so that the full potential of new manufacturing technology may be realized.

In our discussion of alienation we will deal first with the concept as developed by Marx. This sees alienation as a product of the market system and capitalism in particular. We end the section on alienation with an examination of how the concept has been adapted by industrial sociologists to focus somewhat narrowly on the impact of technology on human behaviour.

Alienation

A definition of alienation as used by Karl Marx is set out in Key Concept 3.1.

We begin with an examination of alienation since not only is it prior alphabetically but also historically. Personnel managers and job designers have defined alienation as a problem, a problem created by certain types of

KEY CONCEPT 3.1	The separation of people as workers from their creativity, the product of their labour, and from fellow human beings, to whom they relate merely as units of a commodity. All this is the result of being positioned within a structure of organization and domination. At work, people become the means for the pursuit of the ends of others – profit. The alienation of the modern worker in capitalism stems from the commodity-like status of labour power, the ability to do work.
ALIENATION	

technology and work organization. A considerable body of literature exists covering attempts to make work experience more fulfilling for workers by allowing them to make use of the human attributes of judgement, skill and

KEY CONCEPT 3.2	☐ **Job enlargement:** the term used to describe an approach developed in the 1950s to reduce the negative impact of extreme specialization on workers' attitudes and hence declining productivity. It involved job rotation programmes in which workers would rotate between different tasks, and was intended to expand the number of tasks or operations performed by individual workers so as to relieve some of the boredom associated with repetitive work patterns.
JOB ENLARGEMENT, JOB ENRICHMENT AND AUTONOMOUS GROUP WORKING	☐ **Job enrichment:** the term used to describe a development of the job enlargement approach by enriching jobs so that they include opportunities for achievement, recognition, responsibility and advancement. Job enrichment attempts to design jobs which require higher levels of knowledge and skill so giving workers more autonomy and responsibility for planning and directing their own work. Whereas job enlargement enlarges a job horizontally, i.e. more tasks, job enrichment enlarges a job vertically, i.e. more responsibility and autonomy.
	☐ **Autonomous group working:** most modern production systems do not allow work activities to be considered on a purely individual basis. The individual is always part of a collection of people whose tasks are interrelated. In a modern office or factory one can only work more effectively if everyone else also improves their performance. For this reason, the idea of autonomous group working was developed. Here attention focused not on individuals but on a group of related activities for which a team approach was more appropriate. The vertical enlargement of jobs associated with job enrichment was applied to a team which was considered as self-governing to a considerable degree and had considerable responsibility for output and quality standards. The group could organize themselves to achieve their targets in a manner suited to their own requirements.

These approaches to the design of jobs, and the important issue of motivation, will be considered in more detail in Chapter 6.

responsibility. The ideas of **job enlargement**, **job enrichment** and **autonomous group working** (see Key Concept 3.2), to name but three, are all concerned with explicit or implicit attempts to overcome the negative impact of the technological division of labour in hierarchic organizations. The almost hypnotic attention paid by British managers to the human relations aspects of their Japanese peers results from a concern to motivate employees to identify wholeheartedly with the enterprise and its objectives. Such a commitment is seen to be a major factor in the success of Japanese manufacturing companies.

For a number of years the debate concerning the relatively disordered nature of British industrial relations in comparison with our major international competitors has been identified as a major factor in the poor performance of the British economy.

A number of aspects of contemporary society are susceptible to a Marxist interpretation, in terms of the basic contradictions created by the operation of capitalist market economies. Increasing use of technology to improve labour productivity must, inevitably, in a static or declining market produce a surplus of labour – unemployment. This makes it difficult to integrate into society those groups who bear the brunt of unemployment. The problems of the motor vehicle, shipbuilding, coal, and steel industries, for example, highlight the impact of over-production on a world-wide basis as described by Marx.

This suggests a second reason for starting this discussion with alienation: it has an important role in the debate over the nature and development of industrial society. The concern with the concept at the level of personnel management is not totally divorced from the significance of the concept in the debate over the future of capitalism. The debate between supporters of alternative theories of capitalist industrial society is not far beneath the surface of contemporary industrial relations. This is not to say that in the boardrooms and works canteens of British industry intense theoretical debates over the nature of capitalism and its future take place at regular intervals. It is to say, however, that, as any cursory reading of a quality newspaper will illustrate, a concern with the way in which our society is working and ought to work is not far beneath the surface. Observations concerning the balance of power between management and labour, the role of central government in implementing industrial policy, the extent to which market forces may be enabled to operate more freely, all are frequently articulated in the media and speeches of businessmen, trade unionists and politicians.

What in fact is going on in these debates and discussions is a phenomenon noted some time ago by observers of the social sciences. The study of economics, sociology and politics in the Western world has taken the form of an ongoing debate with the ghost of Karl Marx, a 'noted nineteenth century author' as the German sociologist Max Weber referred to him. Love him or hate him, Marx's ideas underlie contemporary discussions about the state of British society whether articulated by left-wing politicians and union officials, or members of the Adam Smith Institute and the Bow Group. The notion of 'alienation' encapsulates the reasons why the name of this particular nineteenth-century maverick should be so well known by so many people who have never read even a secondary account of his work.

Human nature and alienated labour

Marx was not the first student of modern capitalism to identify one of the most significant human consequences of the technological division of labour. Some sixty years before Marx wrote, Adam Smith had recognized the commodity-like nature of labour in the society he was advocating in *The Wealth of Nations*. Smith also commented upon the negative consequences for the quality of human life of extreme forms of specialization.

According to Smith the performance of repetitive, simple, tasks is likely to result in human beings who are

> . . . as stupid, and ignorant as it is possible for a human creature to become. The torpor of his mind renders him . . . incapable of . . . conceiving any generous, noble, or tender sentiment, and consequently of forming any just judgement concerning many even of the ordinary duties of private life . . . His dexterity at his own particular trade seems, in this manner, to be acquired at the expense of his intellectual, social, and martial virtues. But in every improved and civilized society this is the stage into which . . . the great body of the people must necessarily fall, unless government takes some pains to prevent it.

(Book 5 of *The Wealth of Nations*, quoted in Winch, 1987, p. 83)

The reference to 'martial virtues' illustrates Smith's concern over the consequences of the division of labour for national defence. 'A man, without the proper use of the intellectual faculties of a man, is, if possible, more contemptible than even a coward, and seems to be mutilated and deformed in . . . part of the character of human nature.'

Smith's observations were more or less an 'aside'. For Marx on the other hand, the consequences of the division of labour were central to his analysis. More than that, they were the basis for a moral outrage at the way the division of labour not only reduced the labourer's humanity, but also extended from the economic to every other sphere of social life. The technological division of labour not only limited the labourer at work but also when he was not at work. The commodity status of labour pervaded all of society, even the family. Everything was reduced to what Marx called 'the cash nexus'. Human beings related to each other in important aspects of life only via the medium of the market, hence via cash.

The context in which Marx applied the notion of alienation, and which gave it its moral quality, was set by Marx's own ontology, that is by his view of the essence of human nature. For Marx, to be fully human meant to be creative. Work was therefore the most important of human activities since it had the potential to fulfil or distort a person's nature and their relationships with other people. 'Work' here does not mean 'paid employment'. It means the expenditure of energy to achieve some objective, some end result. People are not naturally lazy. One only has to consider the activities that take up non-work time to realize that. Apart from hobby activities and membership of voluntary bodies, clubs and associations, think of the number of DIY activities that modern individuals engage in and take pleasure and pride in. These are the self-same people whom management, or colleagues at work, may regard as less than committed to doing a fair day's work for a fair day's pay! The conditions under which one has to carry out paid employment may result in behaviour which prima facie indicates laziness, but that is precisely the point behind attempts to involve workers in their work. 'If only employees could be motivated to work like they do in their own time, then labour productivity would rapidly increase' perhaps sums up management frustrations.

Alienation, for Marx, was a situation or condition in which the creations of human beings came to control them. Such a condition is not unique to capitalist societies. All human societies have created systems of rules, codes of religious, legal and military conduct which appear as forces acting upon human beings over which humans have no control. Yet those rules or codes were not only created by human beings but are enforced by them. Alienation exists where people are controlled in their daily lives by forces they themselves have created yet which are now perceived as having an independent existence. Alienation according to Marx reached its most developed form in capitalist society. In such a society human activity and fortunes are subject to the operation of market forces that none can control, the impersonal mechanism of supply and demand operating through what Adam Smith called 'the hidden hand of the market'.

In this situation human beings lost control over what they produced. Their labour was itself a commodity, and what was produced was owned by the capitalist. Furthermore, their work was no longer an end in itself but a means to an end, survival. Not only that, the labourers' work was a means to someone else's end, the creation of profit. Alienation therefore contains the notion of a contradiction between ends and means.

Alienation, then, arises out of relationships between people, what Marx termed the 'relations of production': the fact that one social group can control the work, and labour, of another social group.

In the case of a market-oriented society, alienation exists since the idea that impersonal market forces should determine the fate of human kind is itself a socially constructed and maintained idea. That is, people behave as if the market **should** be the determining factor rather than some other considerations. People have been taught to behave as though the market **ought** to determine the allocation of scarce resources. This is not to say that alternatives are necessarily better or worse, only that there are alternatives and that these are evaluated in terms of dominant system of values. A system of values which was created and is maintained by human action.

A number of points should be noted concerning the nature and extent of alienation in industrial society.

☐ First, alienation is not a question of how people **feel** about their work situation. Workers may **feel** contented with the position they have obtained and with their prospects for the future. This does not alter in Marx's sense the alienated nature of their situation. How people 'feel' about a situation is one thing – and very important – but how a person feels should be distinguished from the objective characteristics of the situation about which feelings are expressed.

☐ Second, workers are not the only people to experience alienated relationships in Marx's scheme. Capitalists are equally at the mercy of the accidents of market operation, though they may well be able to survive the vagaries of the market over a period of time without experiencing the privation suffered by wage labour when unable to find paid employment. However, capitalists are also competing in a market and so are driven by the 'impersonal' forces of the hidden hand. Competition between self-interested actors may still force unsuccessful capitalists down into the wage earning classes. Capitalists, like workers, are forced to behave in a particular manner by the operation of the market. They are not necessarily free to choose how to behave if they wish to survive, and survival may mean beating others in the competitive environment of the market place. Not all can succeed. Capitalists and workers, argued Marx, will be maimed and deformed in terms of their human nature as a result of submitting to the authority of the market.

☐ Third, these two points illustrate the way in which Marx's analysis can both explain the stability of capitalism **and** the self-defeating nature of developments which have occurred in modern societies. Workers' acceptance of their position and attempts to ensure that acceptance by a management concerned to ensure order and predictability are consistent with the behaviour which Marx argued characterized capitalists in their efforts to create profit. Marx in fact used the expression 'false consciousness' to describe a situation where people were unaware of, or had been blinded to, the true nature of their condition. Thus the idea of 'false consciousness', expressed as a belief in the status quo as the best that is possible, can explain the durability and stability of capitalism despite being associated with a theory of its eventual collapse.

☐ On the other hand, attempts by capitalists to survive in the market have produced developments which strike at the heart of market-oriented capitalism itself, hence the role of the Monopolies and Mergers Commission in this country, the anti-trust legislation in the United States and concern with insider dealing in both countries. The operation of market forces has resulted in what is termed 'monopoly capitalism'. This is a situation where large organizations have achieved a degree of power that enables them to manipulate the market to their own advantages. In both Britain and America the anti-competitive potential of mergers and the creation of monopolistic enterprises raises serious questions for those responsible for the administration of a market society. American legislation on monopolies known as 'anti-trust' legislation is in fact more severe than is the case in the UK, and recent debates over the regulation of the City of London after the Big Bang deregulation highlights these problems. In both Britain and America the last decade has seen elected administrations commited to reducing the power of large organizations whether private or public. Such activities on the part of the governments of economies like Britain and America point to the accuracy of Marx's forecasts concerning the inherent contradictions within the capitalist system. The influence of Marx's work as an 'ism' derives from this capacity to cope both with stability and change in capitalism.

Contemporary interpretations of alienation and the role of technology

Marx used the term 'alienation' in a specialized way for a particular purpose. It was a piece of jargon. Today the term has become simply an

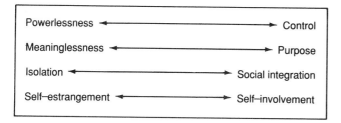

Figure 3.1 Blauner's concept of alienation.

expression of a persistant feeling of frustration, dissatisfaction and even aggression. It has become a term to describe the psychological state of mind of individuals with the implication that steps can be taken to deal with it which do not significantly alter the status quo. One of the most famous accounts of this approach is that of Blauner (1966) in his book *Alienation and Freedom*. In this work, and in the views of those who subscribe to the account offered there, alienation can be defined by reference to four dimensions as set out in Figure 3.1. Each dimension was considered as a continuum which could be identified and measured by means of questionnaires.

In Blauner's terms alienation existed when

> ... workers are unable to control their immediate work processes, to develop a sense of purpose and function which connects their jobs to the overall organization of production, to belong to integrated industrial communities and when they fail to become involved in the activity of work as a mode of self-expression. In modern industrial employment, control, purpose, social integration and self-involvement are all problematic.
>
> (p. 15)

Blauner went on to argue that technological developments would enable workers to move along the continuum illustrated in Figure 3.1 from left to right. Automated technology would enable workers to regain control over their work since the monitoring of expensive equipment and processes would to some extent force management to treat them as integral to the purpose of the organization rather than as an expendable commodity. Blauner assumed – with very little empirical justification it should be noted – that in continuous process industries labour tended to be regarded as a fixed, not variable, cost.

Blauner's view of the effect of technology on alienation can be represented diagramatically by an 'inverted U' curve as in Figure 3.2. In the craft situation workers' freedom is at its greatest; autonomy diminishes with the advent of machinery and is at a minimum in mass production assembly situations. With the development of continuous process technology utilizing feed-back and feed-forward (cybernetic) control processes, automation is assumed to increase workers' control over the work situation and so check further development of the technological division of labour.

The approach taken by Blauner fails to consider that it is not technology as such that causes alienation or leads to psychological states of frustration and dissatisfaction, but the way in which technology is used, installed and controlled. Alienation is due to the fact that labour is a commodity. Attempts by humanistic management to minimize the degree of frustration

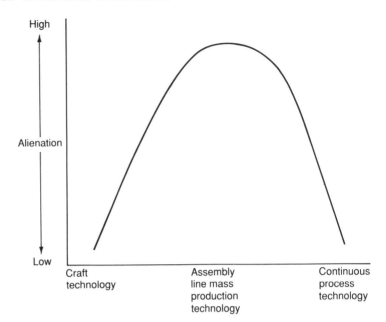

Figure 3.2 Blauner's inverted U representation of the relationship between technology and alienation.

experienced by the workforce do not alter the basic commodity status of free labour. The contradiction inherent in the very introduction of policies designed to reduce alienation **in the interests of achieving managerial goals** demonstrates this. Alienation is about the nature and quality of relationships, **not** about how people may from time to time feel about those relationships.

We have considered so far one of two concepts which have figured prominently in the examination of workers' responses to the factory system, and in debates over the nature and development of industrial society. The point is that, as we will see when we move on to consider the Human Relations movement later in the chapter, much managerial effort in modern enterprises is directed towards mitigating the effects of the factory system of work in so far as the effort and commitment of workers is concerned. One of the key concepts underlying such efforts is that of alienation. We will now move on to discuss what might be considered as an alternative to alienation in coming to terms with the negative aspects of the factory system: anomie.

Anomie: an alternative to alienation?

One of the most widely known and long-standing alternatives to alienation as an explanatory idea is that developed by a French sociologist Emile Durkheim. This is the concept of 'anomie', set out in Key Concept 3.3, which was further developed in its application to American society during the 1930s to 1950s.

Anomie is not simply a theoretical concept. It was the theoretical perspecitve taken by some influential academics who gave evidence to the Donovan Commission in its investigation of British industrial relations in

Anomie refers to the extent, or state, of moral regulation applying to work. The pathologies of modern work stem not from the economic context but from the disjunction between work activities, aspirations and their regulation by values and tradition. Work is anomic to the extent that it has lost its moral character and its cultural significance. Anomie describes a situation where shared values governing work, social life and the distribution of rewards have broken down.

The most succinct definition of anomie is that it is 'a state of normlessness'. A 'norm' is an ideal or standard of behaviour that can be seen to regulate behaviour even when actual behaviour does not conform to it. Thus a 'norm' is not standard or average in the sense of 'normal' or 'usual'. Norms represent values against which actual behaviour has to be justified, even when very few people act in accordance with them.

The very high salaries and 'golden hellos' paid to certain groups in the City of London after the 'Big Bang' reorganization caused considerable concern both to participants and commentators. This was because such a policy was seen to indicate a breakdown of established ideas about the relative worth of different activities and might have a disruptive impact on other groups in society.

KEY CONCEPT 3.3

ANOMIE

the mid-1960s. The Commission identified Britain's industrial relations problems as a breakdown of order which could be interpreted as anomic (Flanders and Fox, 1969). There had been a breakdown in the process of social regulation as far as the distribution of rewards in society was concerned. Consequently, it was everyone for themselves – since no one was apparently playing by the rules how could any one particular group afford to? It was not that there was no order, but that which did exist was based upon the exploitation of market opportunities and organizational strengths. This meant that some groups suffered while others benefited simply as a result of accidents of market fortune.

People or individuals who happened to work in particular jobs or industries, or who lived in particular regions, benefited or suffered independently of the extent to which they 'deserved' their fate. It did not matter how hard you worked or were prepared to work, if your industry or firm closed down you were out of a job. In some cases the way work is organized makes it impossible for individuals to improve output or quality by trying harder themselves. Other groups on the other hand, by virtue of being located in different industries or regions, could enjoy the same or higher benefits without any extra effort.

As Maitland (1983) has argued, the disordered aspect of British industrial relations is not because there is no consensus (or that one is unachievable) about the distribution of rewards, but a consensus which can actually be shown to exist concerning the relative worth of particular occupations cannot be effectively enforced or governed.

As with alienation, anomie offers not only an account of what is happening, but also a basis for a moral judgement. For Durkheim, the division of labour which characterized industrial society was a moral matter, not exclusively an economic one, since the very existence of individual freedom in his eyes was itself a product of the division of labour.

Markets, the division of labour and anomie

In the section we will examine the relationship between anomie, the division of labour and the workings of the market-place. We shall draw distinctions between anomie and alienation and examine the influence that the concept of anomie had upon human relations management, and its associated techniques.

While Durkheim regarded the division of labour as the basis of individual liberty he nevertheless regarded *laissez-faire* capitalism as a temporary stage in the process of the development of social order based on a harmonious division of labour. The basis of social order was to be found in the fact that, while the division of labour freed individuals to pursue their own interests and inclinations, this pursuit was constrained by the fact that the division of labour required all to cooperate for survival. The division of labour in its normal state was the basis for an **interdependence** between individuals, an interdependence based on difference rather than similarity. The division of labour was essentially a source of cohesion and should be welcomed rather than resisted according to Durkheim.

Unregulated markets, however, in which social order and regulation was assumed to emerge from the rational decision-making of self-serving actors, could not provide an adequate basis for social cohesion according to Durkheim. The closer a society approached such an individualistic model, the nearer it came to disorder. The consequences of a lack of market regulation would be periodic crises in which actions and expectations no longer result in anticipated consequences. Hard work to increase output can result in people being laid off when their increased output cannot be sold under existing market conditions. A work group who comply with management's requests and exhortations regarding working practices and pay may still find themselves redundant since the lack of a legislative framework serving to increase the cost of redundancy to the employer may actually make it cheaper to lay them off rather than more expensive workers in another European plant of the same company (Kraithman and Adams, 1983). Thus the operation of the market (involving minimal regulation over redundancy practice) results in unease, disillusionment and a sense of meaninglessness.

Durkheim was concerned (rather like Adam Smith) with the problem likely to arise if individuals followed no rule except that of self-interest in the occupation that took up nearly the whole of their time. How were such people to acquire a taste for disinterested or selfless behaviour? What would be the basis for socially responsible citizenship?

The regulation of exchange

Durkheim argued that the operation of the market should be governed by norms which would effectively regulate prices and wages. This of course implies some general agreement upon what constitutes a 'fair' day's work for a 'fair' day's pay as a basis for comparison between individuals and groups. It was the regulation of such matters by statutes going back to the reign of Elizabeth I that prompted merchants to move out of towns in order to escape the coverage of such regulatory provisions as we saw in Chapter 1. Unlike Marx, who saw the problems of industrial capitalism being swept away by the eventual downfall of the system, Durkheim saw the solution to the problem within the existing framework of industrial society. The dominance of self-interest should be replaced by ethical codes emphasizing the needs of society as a whole.

Durkheim argued that such a system of codes should be developed and administered by 'occupational associations'. Industries should be governed by freely elected administrative bodies upon which all occupations should be represented. These bodies would have the power to regulate relations between employer and employee, including the terms and conditions of employment as well as competitive relations. Such associations and regulations would eventually form the basis for rules to regulate all economic activity. This view of social order based upon functional interdependence and derived from Durkheim's optimistic (one might say Utopian!) view of professional associations emphasized codes of conduct and a sense of duty, responsibility and obligation to the community as a whole. The need was for a system of norms, the application of which would be regulated by such organizations.

Alienation v. anomie

The Anglo-American world generally holds a very negative view of the ideas and theories of Karl Marx. There are historical reasons for this which stem from the response in Britain to the horrors of the Terror during the French Revolution and the subsequent criticism of the ideas of people like Thomas Paine by Edmund Burke. The problems with the Luddites, and the turmoil occasioned by the Corn Laws in Britain after the Napoleonic Wars ensured that the revolutionary movements in continental Europe up to the middle of the nineteenth century were regarded with considerable apprehension in Britain. Since Marx and his writings were associated with the later stages of the political upheavals in nineteenth-century continental Europe, to the English speaking world Marxism represents a force for evil rather than a basis for a respectable method of the intellectual analysis of social phenomena, including the arts, as tends to be the case in continental European cultures.

For this reason, the ideas of Durkheim on the anomic form of the division of labour have offered an attractive alternative to Marxist accounts of the existence of conflict and tensions in industrial society since Durkheim was not apparently advocating revolution.

Anomie and the Human Relations Movement

One of the most influential, and still often quoted, pieces of research into work group behaviour and its effects on productivity was undertaken during the late 1920s and early 1930s by a team from the University of

Chicago under the general direction of Elton Mayo. These studies were intended to identify the underlying causes of disharmony in industrial relations, and the restrictions on output enforced by work groups. While they did produce many insights into work-group behaviour, they were considerably flawed by the assumption that managerial interests were somehow more valid than those of work groups. These studies are now known by the name of the plant of the General Electric Company where they were carried out – the Hawthorn studies. An account of the series of investigations making up these studies was published by the two people mainly responsible for carrying out the research, Roethlisberger and Dickson (1964).

Mayo was influenced to a considerable degree by what he took to be the applicability of the concept of anomie to the underlying causes of trade union militancy and industrial conflict. He believed that manifestations of conflict between management and labour were symptoms of the lack of a moral order which typified industrial civilization in the second and third decades of the twentieth century, rather than evidence of conflicting interests of management and workers.

The enterprise as a basis for social integration

Mayo argued that workers were non-rational in their effects to exercise countervailing power over management by regulating the productivity of their work groups. Consequently, the studies at the Hawthorn plant had two main objectives. One was the attempt to identify factors underlying and motivating efforts by work groups to restrict output. The second was to identify the processes by which such restrictions were imposed and maintained by work groups. The problem for Mayo and his colleagues derived from their view that such restrictions were not only against the interests of the employer but also the intersts of the employee.

The solution proposed by Mayo, and which formed the basis of the so-called Human Relations approach to the management of organizations, involved concentrating upon the role of the enterprise in re-establishing the role of community as a basis for social solidarity. In addition Mayo urged that managers should pay attention to their leadership qualities as a basis for improving relations in companies. It may be noted that even today attempts to emphasize the mutuality of workers' and managements' interests are still popular, while the issue of personal relationship skills still forms a very significant part of the work of consultants and the content of business and management courses. The emphasis upon the leadership skills of middle and junior management also continues, and has been taken up by those responsible for more senior managment for whom outward-bound courses are increasingly utilized.

As Lee and Newby (1983) point out, the prescription offered by Mayo and his disciples in the Human Relations movement was almost the reverse of what Durkheim had in mind since they advocated the kind of group commitment which contradicts the moral individualism he advocated. In a community, individuals are less 'free' almost by definition. They are not 'liberated' from mutual reciprocity, and pressure for conformity is considerable. Similarity, not difference, is the criterion for membership of a community; strangers are very nearly enemies.

Durkheim's notion of anomie has been examined in the work of a number of writers who have examined contemporary developments in modern British society. Colin Crouch (1978), for example, is one of a number of writers (Goldthorpe, 1978, is another) who contest the assumption that capitalist economies contain self-regulating mechanisms, that the market is a self-adjusting mechanism for allocating scarce resources. They argue as did Durkheim – and Marx from a different perspective – that the self-interested pursuit of gain in the market-place contains an inbuilt tendency towards failure and social disorder.

Social cohesion in a capitalist society

Crouch argues that modern capitalist society has undermined the very basis of social cohesion upon which it depends. The situation facing modern industrial society is not one brought about by overbearing trade unions, or 'unfair' competition from Far Eastern economies, but has been brought about by putting the whole emphasis of legitimation on the economy alone. This has occurred becasue of the separation, or uncoupling, of the sources from which societies derive their cohesion into separate areas of social thought. Political and social forms of control have become divorced from the economic sphere of life (the market-place) which is then made responsible for the total legitimation of the consequences of all that occurs in terms of life chances and the experience of plently or scarcity.

The result is that modern society ignores sources of cohesion which were the basis of modern capitalism in the first place: a social system in which religious, political and economic aspects of life were closely enmeshed, such that each was mutually supportive of the other in maintaining the status quo. Such an integrated system of activities and beliefs can be seen as an accurate account of society prior to industrialization. This system (feudalism) provided the basis upon which the exercise of power by a strong central state could be utilized in the establishment of a radically different social order. 'Capitalism depended on the survival of political institutions from an earlier (generally absolutist) period which made it possible to create the coercive legal framework it needed . . .' (Crouch, 1978, p. 220).

Evidence for the existence of such a separation of various aspects of modern life into apparently unrelated areas of thought (or 'universes of discourse') can be found in the debate over the pay and status of, for example, teachers and nurses in comparison with that of policemen, advertising executives, estate agents and financial dealers in the City of London. The debate between Mrs Thatcher's government and some bishops of the Church of England also illustrates the separation of moral, religious and market matters. The problems which are the focus of such debates derive from the fact that people are aware that allowing market forces alone to decide how much someone should be paid can result in morally and socially very important areas of work being apparently devalued. Opinion polls have consistently indicated a significant majority of the population are prepared for higher taxation in order to maintain the principles of a 'national' health service.

The market and the burden of legitimation

However, the radically different order that was capitalism uncoupled the religious, the political and the economic aspects of social order. The whole weight of the task of legitimating the distribution of wealth and opportunities was to be taken by the economy through the operation of the market. No other justification for good or bad fortune was to be accepted other than that available from market factors.

Widespread concern over the 'telephone number' salaries paid to certain groups in the immediate post-Big Bang City of London reflected a concern over the moral justification, or lack of one, of such a strategy by employers. The problem was quite explicitly one of 'normlessness': how to regulate the rewards of certain groups in a context which both emphasized self-interest but also social order. How can respect for order be maintained when there appears to be no rationale for what happens? How can people be expected to acquiesce in the distribution of income and wealth when the legitimation of the distribution makes no reference to any notion of moral justice or equity? Social order, and hence the self-interest of the élite, may well require some moderation in the exercise of sheer market forces.

This is a point taken up by Goldthorpe (1978) in his examination of the shortcomings of economic accounts of inflation and the policies adopted to deal with its consequences. Goldthorpe argued that since inflation is seen as a malfunction in what is in all other respects regarded as a sound and self-regulating system, then the problem is fundamentally one susceptible to purely technical solutions such as raising interest rates or manipulating the money supply. There is little respect for the idea that economic problems may derive from aspects of the social structure and market system. Goldthorpe asserts that '. . . in order to understand the relationships between economic quantities in terms of which the problem is defined, one must understand the underlying, generative relationships between social groupings – and that these will themselves present further "problems" of a kind which are not open to merely technical resolution in the light of economic science' (Goldthorpe, 1972, p. 212).

Summary

The discussion so far of the concepts of alienation and anomie provides an important framework for efforts to understand the nature of the employment relationship in industrialized market economies, and how behaviour in work organizations is thereby influenced. First of all, as already indicated, both alienation and anomie can be seen to underlie personnel or human relations policies developed by managers in business. The symptoms with which they are trying to deal – lack of motivation, apathy, various forms of conflict such as overtime bans, strikes, absenteeism for example – can be directly related to the insights expressed by Marx and Durkheim. These two observers of industrial society were, however, observing from two rather different political perspectives, one predicting and advocating the destruction of capitalism, the other seeing salvation in a more regulated form of capitalist society. The remainder of this chapter will consider the way in which institutionalized industrial relations has developed in Britain as the features of alienation and anomie have worked themselves out through the agency of human behaviour.

The employment relationship

In Chapter 2 we looked at industrialization from the point of view of the development of a 'social' rather than 'mechanical' technology. Attention focused not so much on the machines themselves as on the idea that machines could be used to facilitate the exercise of control over the work of others. The current chapter is concerned with the examination of factors affecting the behaviour of management and labour as they daily experience working life. In the first part of the chapter an examination in some detail was undertaken of the influential concepts of alienation and anomie in the context of behaviour in organizations. This section will examine the social technology that attempts to ensure the cooperation between relatively large numbers of people in modern organizations. What is important here are those aspects of the management of a businesss enterprise that are concerned with, for example, authority, hierarchy and delegation.

The quality and characteristics of management–labour relations are formed by efforts to exercise and contain power. It is important to appreciate that in a very real sense a work organization represents a 'community', not in the sense that every one agrees with everyone else and harmony pervades social experience (though in many workplaces that may be the case), but in the sense that a group of people have to live together and cope with that fact. They cannot, without considerable difficulty, just get up and leave! Managers may not wish to lose workers who are familiar with the enterprise way of doing things, and workers of course may not be able to find equally convenient employment elsewhere. Even if they could, the finanical and psychological costs may be sufficient to dissuade them.

When disagreements do occur under such conditions, the dispute is handled in accordance with customary standards of conduct. All know what the rules are, and are reasonably sure the other party will abide by them. Both parties to a dispute have some confidence that they know what rules will be applied in their case and that they will be applied 'reasonably' . . . or 'fairly' . . . or 'justly'. Just what exactly is considered 'reasonable', 'fair' or 'just' may itself be a matter of dispute rather than constituting simple so called 'facts of the case'. The interaction between the market system and the employment relationship is illustrated in Case Study 3.1.

Case Study 3.1 refers to the 'high' and 'low' trust patterns identified by Fox. These are set out in detail in Table 3.1, with examples of their likely consequences for behaviour.

We will now move on to examine the tension which exists between collective as opposed to individual responses to the factory system of work, and how both behaviour and the perception of behaviour by others may be influenced by the emphasis which a market system places upon individual responses while to some extent denying the legitimacy of collective

CASE STUDY 3.1

**THE MARKET SYSTEM
AND THE
EMPLOYMENT
RELATIONSHIP**

The transformation from pre-industrial to industrial society was a transformation from a situation in which relationships were 'diffuse' to a situation in which relationships became characterized by 'contractual specificity'. A diffuse relationship is one where the parties do not hold themselves or each other to a rigidly determined contract. Such a relationship is characterized by a non-specific pattern of mutual obligations, by mutual reciprocity. There is no strict calculation of cost and benefit as the basis of cooperation. The terms of the relationship, while well enough known, are not constantly referred to when considering whether or not to respond to a particular request, demand or order. There is considerable evidence even today that such diffuse relationships are widespread and are held to characterize small organizations.

Industrialization, however, resulted in an increasing scale of operations as well as the application of principles of contract to what were becoming impersonal relationships. The development and application of the theory or ideology of the impersonal market as the most efficient allocator of scarce resources, a market in which the pursuit of individual acquisitive self-interest (possessive individualism) was the dominant, required and admired behaviour, resulted in a narrow concentration on 'the contract' as the basis of employer/employee relations. No obligation other than that which was specified in the contract was held to be significant for the parties.

The idea of the market as an efficient allocator of scarce resources presupposes self-interested activity by individuals free to pursue their own self-interest in that market. This notion of freedom also requires the assumption that individuals are not only free but also equal. People in such a market must be unencumbered by non-economic restraints in order to be able to charge whatever the market will bear, however great the 'need' of any particular individual or group.

In such a situation calculation of the costs and benefits of actions and decisions is the basis of rational behaviour. Thus calculation becomes the basis of action taken in the pursuit of self-interest. There is no place for the operation of principles of mutual reciprocity unless established by the terms of the contract between the parties. Such pervasive 'calculative' behaviour, based upon individual pursuit of self-interest, implies a considerable degree of mutual distrust and suspicion.

A Question of Trust

It is this characteristic of relationships that is summed up by Fox (1974) in his use of the term 'low trust' to describe the employment relationship. Dore (1973) and Kahn-Freund (1972) are two other writers who have emphasized the extent to which the combination in Britain of a strong state, a well developed concept of individualism, and a belief in non-intervention (*laissez-faire*) played a key role in the formation of approaches to the employment relationship. These features continue to differentiate the British approach to labour relations from that in other European countries.

For example, in the British case employers welcomed the assurance offered by theorists of the market that they had only limited, responsibility for the well-being of their employees. The majority of British employers relied on the exercise of self-interest in the market-place as a mechanism for ensuring the well-being of free and equal human beings. In Germany and Japan on the other hand, authoritarian paternalism was exploited by employers for their own advantage.

As Dore illustrates, the concern of Japanese management with the well-being of (some of) their employees was a strategy developed to cope with the problems of a country industrializing in a world where there was already one other industrial country. Japanese management thus met the demand for skilled labour not through the operation of the labour market outside the company, but by the creation of a labour market internal to the enterprise. This involved considerable effort directed towards the training of employees. Having trained them, the next problem was to retain them. Pay and promotion scales based upon length of service were a response to this problem, and gave rise to the 'life-long' employment relationship which is widely regarded as characteristic of Japanese firms. It should be noted, however, that such policies only affect about one third of Japanese workers and even now are being put under the microscope by Japanese managements as they battle with the vagaries of inhospitable currency and product markets in a highly competitive world.

The Japanese approach contrasts with that adopted by British employers who resorted to the external market to supply the necessary quantity and quality of skilled labour. An adequate supply of skilled labour is a 'collective good' for firms competing in a free market since all firms benefit whether or not they actually undertake any training. In this situation firms behaving in accordance with market rationality will behave as 'free riders' and maximize their own utility by taking advantage of the training effort of others rather than doing any training themselves. They will attract already trained workers by poaching them from other companies by the offer of higher wages. Even where apprentice systems of training did exist in Britain they were, and remained, more concerned with time-serving than the attainment of specified standards at specified points during training. While this was in part the result of union attempts to maintain wages by controlling the supply of labour, it also suited employers. An over-long training period, especially when, as we have seen, employers placed relatively little emphasis on the technical component of training, could result in apprentices who were capable of adult performance while in receipt of junior rates of pay. Also in contrast to Japanese managements' paternalistic concern for the well-being of labour, British management, with one or two notable exceptions, concentrated on a narrow contractual approach which was accompanied by an emphasis upon the status of masters and servants.

This emphasis upon the highly individualistic relationship of master and servant, an emphasis which pervades the interpretation of contracts of employment to this day, resulted in contradictory, and self-defeating, Continued over page

Continued from previous page — assumptions by employers. On the one hand they held a 'low-trust' view of the employee associated with individualistic self-interest, while at the same time demanded the 'high-trust' response of willing compliance and loyalty. Thus it is possible to identify a contradiction at the heart of the approach taken by British employers to labour relations. The emphasis upon individualistic relations in a free market existed alongside the expectation that employee behaviour should be that associated with non-market-based obligation.

Free market principles have a natural appeal to employers in a world where unions do not exist, are weak or are prohibited by law. The problem for British employers was that by the time they sought alternative approaches, the existing market principles were firmly established and reinforced by the pattern of trade unionism itself. Trade unions were market maximizers on behalf of those who made up their membership. The British labour movement has never been concerned to eradicate the market principle – to modify it perhaps, but not to eradicate it.

Table 3.1 Discretion and status – two work-role patterns

1. The high discretion syndrome:
   (a) Occupant of the work-role perceived as committed to a 'calling', and/or to organizational goals and values;
   (b) Is an assumption, given (a), that close supervision and/or detailed supervision is inappropriate;
   (c) Where performance cannot (easily) be evaluated objectively subjective criteria are used by superiors, e.g. degree of loyalty;
   (d) Requirement for problem-solving relationships rather than for standardized, externally imposed coordination;
   (e) Conflict is handled on the assumption that at some level objectives are shared – given assumption (a) bargaining is not seen as appropriate since it is associated with the tactics of threats and gamesmanship.
2. The low discretion syndrome:
   (a) Role occupant's activities closely coordinated with activities of others;
   (b) Role occupant is subject to close supervision as a consequence of (a);
   (c) Failure or inadequate performance assumed to be result of indifference to rules and/or organizational goals – so resulting in punishment and even closer supervision;
   (d) Role occupant perceives superiors as not trusting him/her;
   (e) Conflict between role occupant(s) and superiors is handled on a group basis via bargaining.

Source: Fox (1974).

responses. The dichotomy between individual and collective interests and responses, and the extent to which these were consistent or not with the market system, shaped the nature of the British industrial relations system. Further aspects of these issues are covered in Chapter 2 and 8 of Needle's (1989) volume in this series.

Collective movements and legal constraints

The earliest unions were unions of craft workers who were particularly affected by the development of factory work and the imposition of machines, and who had a long history of organizing to protect their own occupational self-interest on the basis of the craft guild. British unions developed around craft-skill or **occupational** criteria, not industrial (i.e. all the occupations in one industry) criteria. Unions were a **collective** and a **calculating** (in the market sense) response to management strategies. While the response was collective, and thus counter to the prevailing ethos of market individualism, it was based on calculations concerning the exploitation of market opportunities and so was not a serious threat to the dominant ideology of the market as the means of allocating scarce resources.

Legal constraints

The collective nature of the response of organized labour has, however, been a source of some concern to employers and their representatives. As Kahn-Freund (1972) has forcefully argued, the idea that capital and labour meet as equals in the labour market has to be seen as a legal fiction required to maintain the essence of a contract. An agreement is not legally enforceable under English law, that is it is not a contract, unless **freely** entered into by both parties who intend to be legally bound by it. Any indication of coercion and a contract is void, that is it is not a contract at all in the eyes of the law. This fiction of equality between individuals in the labour market is necessary in order to '. . . exorcise the incubus of forced labour . . .' (Kahn-Freund, 1972).

British labour law has been characterized by the absence of positive legal rights. Where these have been established, they have been individualistic rather than collective. It is arguable that English law as a whole is weak in the area of collective compared with individual rights. It is not surprising that collective behaviour has been something of a problem for British employers since, unlike the individual exploitation of market opportunities, such behaviour represents a threat to the established order. An emphasis on the individual rights of individual union members has figured prominently in recent and proposed legislation in the field of industrial relations reform. This is seen as part of the process of redressing the imbalance of power which had developed between management and unions, and between the individual union member and the union hierarchy. This is one of the factors which can be seen to underlie the objections made to the articulation of the rights of workers in the European Social Charter.

Since the ethos of market exploitation was accepted by powerful groups on both sides of the labour market, historically neither management nor unions have been interested in seeing the law involved in labour market regulation when confidence in the ability to exploit market opportunities existed. This is illustrated by the emphasis placed on 'free collective bargaining' by both groups . . . when it suits them. Consequently, union recognition was achieved largely by industrial means in Britain rather than by political and legislative action. A belief in collective action is at the root of trade unionism in Britain where labour is seen as a commodity like any other in the market. The only criterion of the 'justice' of any claim is the ability to exploit market opportunities to enforce that claim.

In addition, the history of the role of the law in British industrial relations highlights the extent to which employee activity in contesting the exercise of managerial power and authority has created a climate of suspicion concerning the role of the law in the protection of collective interests. The history and experience of legal involvement in regulating relations between employers and labour suggest an emphasis upon the rights of employers as individual property owners rather than the collective rights of employees. In order to exercise countervailing power employees had to act collectively rather than individually. A legal framework emphasizing the rights of free individuals looked unfavourably upon attempts by groups to intervene in the exercise of that right. This characteristic of British employment law can be illustrated by comparison with the system in Germany where the legal rights of Works Councils and employee representation on Supervisory Boards entitle the workforce to take part in decision-making and to receive relevant information. In the British system, decisions concerning redundancy for example do not by law have to involve the labour force at all. At best unions are involved only after the decision has been made, and they have no right to information used by the company in arriving at its decision. It is in such a context that collective bargaining, to be discussed in the following section, has developed in Britain.

Collective bargaining

Along with the existence of trade unions goes the phenomenon of 'collective bargaining'. Collective bargaining is not the same as individual bargaining. When a collective agreement is made between an employer or employers' association and a trade union only the organizations on whose behalf it was signed are bound by it, and they are bound in honour only. Collective agreements in the UK are not binding in law since neither employers nor unions intend them to be legally binding. There is also a question over the extent to which, even if the actual signatories to the agreement (union and employer association officials for example) did intend to be bound by it, could they be considered to have bound their constituents (i.e. union or employer association members)?

All that is agreed in a collective agreement are the terms upon which individual workers may contract with individual employers. A floor has been put under the terms of the employment contract. There is nothing to stop any group of workers, or an employer, from exploiting their market situation by seeking or offering different terms from those in the collective agreement. There is nothing to stop an employer who is anxious to recruit labour from offering more than the terms of the agreement, nor anything to stop union members demanding better terms if they think they can get away with it. There is nothing to prevent lower benefits being offered if there are any takers, except perhaps collective action.

The behaviour of managment and labour in organizations is moulded by conceptions of the nature of collective bargaining. It is important to realize that the majority of union members and their officials are **not** interested in doing away with capitalism. Should the reader respond 'What about the likes of Arthur Scargill', consider just how much support that leader got from other unionists during the protracted miners' strike in 1985). His own union was split and many unionists considered Scargill's tactics were not appropriate for trade unionism in Britain. Evidence on voting behaviour has over many years suggested that at least one third of trade union members have consistently voted Conservative – in the 1987 election it was even more. It is dangerous to take the public utterances of either employers or union leaders (official or unofficial) at face value when they are giving accounts of their exchanges with each other over the negotiating table. Both groups may be 'playing to the gallery' in an attempt to satisfy their constituents that they are tough negotiators exploiting market opportunities.

The following sections of the chapter examine the nature of collective bargaining in order to establish an understanding of how behaviour in organizations may be influenced by the process. A model of collective bargaining as suggested by Fox (1974) is set out in Table 3.2. Each component of this model will be examined in turn so as to illustrate the nature of the response to the technological division of labour by organized labour and of the institutions formed to put that response into operation.

Table 3.2 A model of collective bargaining

---

1. The explicit or implicit acceptance by both parties of the pluralistic conception of the organization.
2. The notion of 'mutual survival' – both parties agree on definitions of the frontiers of control and influence; they agree the range of negotiable issues.
3. Both parties emphasize the ultimate goal of a negotiated compromise, in preference to arbitration where a third party imposes a solution.
4. The employee collective accommodates to the existing hierarchy, division of labour and authority relations.
5. The employee collective aims to improves its members' position marginally along a number of dimensions encapsualted in 4.

Source: Fox (1974).

Acceptance of the pluralistic concept of the organization

The notion of 'pluralism' is set out in Key Concept 3.4.

In the context of collective bargaining the acceptance (implicit or explicit) of the pluralist perspective implies that bargaining between representatives of the parties is likely to be an ongoing process. Acceptance of a decision does not place out of court an attempt to overturn or modify that decision at some more advantageous time in the future. A central aspect of pluralism is the notion of competing social forces where competition between equals operates as a check on the tendency towards absolutism, the unfettered exercise of power by just one group.

Miliband (1969) highlights a problem with pluralism:

KEY CONCEPT 3.4	Pluralism refers to a situation where the parties to a relationship accept that they each have differing interests and that those interests may be mutually exclusive. If one gains, the other loses. The heart of the pluralist idea is that conflicting interests may both be **legitimate**. A pluralist conception of democracy avoids problems that follow from the unitary idea that once the 'vote' has been taken then all should be equally committed to the achievement of the popular choice. The problem with the unitary view is that after a 'majority' has emerged, the pursuit of differing interests is seen in some sense as illegitimate. This leaves unanswered the criticism that the imposition of a majority view may represent the 'tryanny of the majority'. What, exactly, is to count as a 'majority' anyway? 51%? 66%? 75%? What is the evidence that the majority view is necessarily superior in any way to that of the minority? What is the evidence that the majority have been right more often than the minority?
PLURALISM	

Pluralism accepts that a decision, however taken, does not necessarily end the matter and that the interests of those who 'lost' must still be protected as far as possible. This means that the process of decision-making and implementation becomes an ongoing process rather than a point event in time. The hallmark of 'democracy' becomes the extent to which decision-making processes are senstitive to differing interests rather than merely the adoption of a procedural formality such as majority voting.

This is the basis of the case made by those advocating proportional representation in place of the 'first-past-the-post' system in British elections where 42% of the popular vote can produce a hundred-plus majority in the House of Commons.

> What is wrong ... is not its [pluralism's] insistence on the factor of competition but its claim (very often its implicit assumption) that the major organised interests in these societies, and notably capital and labour, compete on more or less equal terms, and none of them is therefore able to achieve a decisive and permanent advantage in the process of competition.

This problem was also forcefully identified by Kahn-Freund (1972).

In the case of relationships between management and labour the influence of shared assumptions about the pluralistic nature of the business organization is illustrated by the concern even in management circles over the abrasive, macho-managment style of people like Michael Edwardes at British Leyland or Ian MacGregor at British Steel and the Coal Board during the 1980s.

The notion of 'mutual survival'

Following from the pluralist perspective but having distinct implications for bargaining is the fact that the parties agree where the frontiers of control and influence lie. The significant boundary is that which defines the rights of property. While in a market economy it is not legitimate to question the existence of property rights, it is legitimate to exact, via the operation of market forces, a price for continued acquiesence in the exercise of those rights. The British labour movement, as a movement, has never been concerned to question the existence of property rights, only the way in which those rights are exercised in so far as they affect the interests of labour. This agreement over what is negotiable extends to the generally shared view that so-called 'political' strikes are illegitimate; industrial disputes should only be concerned with issures arising directly out of the employment relationship.

There is a real sense in which both employers and employees have a vested interest in the continuation of a relationship even if from time to time the quality of that relationship leaves much to be desired. This factor of mutual survival can account for the continued existence of institutions or practices which on first sight may be regarded as counter-productive, either for the parties themselves or the economy generally, as illustrated in Case Study 3.2.

The closed shop

A 'closed shop' can be one of two types. A 'pre-entry' closed shop exists where a worker must have a union card before they are taken on. A 'post-entry' closed shop exists where the worker has to join an appropriate union after being taken on by an employer. The closed shop in both its forms – both of which require a measure of cooperation from the employer – has been a bone of contention for those wishing to reform British industrial relations since the 1971 Industrial Relations Act. The closed shop has been seen as the prime example of the overbearing power of the union in relation to both the employer and the individual worker. Perhaps the most notorious example was in Fleet Street printing.

Attempts to legislate against the closed shop have run up against the caution of employers who actually see some advantages in the institution. A closed shop offers some protection against maverick employees who by their individualistic behaviour may disrupt stable relationships and expectations. A closed shop enables a union to exercise some control over recalcitrant members who might other-wise be persuaded to take matters into their own hands and ignore union advice and agreed procedures. Of course, where union officials are determined to take action against an employer then the converse is also true.

Attempts since 1979 to reduce the power of union officials and return the union to its members have a certain irony as far as the closed shop is concerned. The reduction of the power of union officials (never in fact very great anyway) has reduced further the ability of officials to take action against groups of members who take

CASE STUDY 3.2

**MUTUAL SURVIVAL:
THE CLOSED SHOP
AND THE
APPRENTICESHIP
SYSTEM**

Continued over page

Continued from previous page matters into their own hands and force a union executive to hold a strike ballot and then call a strike despite strong advice against such action by senior officials. This was to some extent the situation in the 1989 strike against the abolition of the Dock Labour Scheme, and the series of one-day strikes in the same year on British Rail.

The final 'nail in the coffin' of the closed shop now appears to be provided by the European Social Charter since the continued existence of the closed shop is inconsistent with the provisions of the Charter. Another little irony!

The apprentice system

Mutual benefit also accounts for the longevity of the apprenticeship system and its development into one of time-serving rather than the achievement of nationally recognized and externally assessed standards. It could take longer to train a bricklayer than a jet bomber pilot! Such a system had advantages for both employers and unions. Apprenticeship was a means of controlling entry to a trade by regulating the number of learners to each qualified person and by stipulating a minimum time period for certification. It has already been indicated that reliability rather than specific skill levels was, and remains, a prime concern of employers (Oliver and Turton, 1982), and if, as suggested by Blackburn and Mann (1979), skill levels were never very advanced anyway, then an emphasis upon time-serving meant that an employer would get a woman's or man's work for learners' rates of pay. Similarly, the requirement that a new entrant to a trade had a relation in that trade meant that again entry was controlled and that the employer could get a personal recommendation either from one of his own employees or that of another employer.

An emphasis upon negotiation and compromise

Given an emphasis upon market mechanisms it is not surprising that effectiveness in bargaining became a measure of an individual's ability to copy with the world. The ability to negotiate an agreement reflected upon the standing of those doing the negotiating since such skills were seen as worthy of respect. This aspect of collective bargaining is implicitly highlighted when both employers and union representatives describe arbitration an indicative of 'failure' and 'immaturity'. An emphasis upon the macho image of the negotiator has resulted in the rhetoric of 'free collective bargaining' used by employers and unions.

The employee collective's accommodation to existing hierarchy and authority relations

Unions tend to focus upon the way the system operates and the means of achieving some influence over the operation of the system rather than upon its abolition. The function of a trade union is quite simply to protect the interests of those it happens to organize. Not only does this mean they have relatively little concern for non-members, whether they are members of another union or not at all, it also implies that involvement in the management of the enterprise will require them to take account of interests they are not established to represent. A worker director may have to face two ways at once. Is he or she a director, or are they only to concern themselves with representing members' interests and get the best possible deal for them? Such problematic issues have resulted in a cautious approach to initiatives in the area of participation displayed by governments, employers and unions in the UK.

Trade unions have their origins in the distinction between capital and labour. They have developed to operate in the context of such a distinction. If the distinction is weakened then so will be the *raison d'être* of unions. As one shop steward from the aerospace industry put it: 'We don't want to run the . . . show, we just want gaffers who know their jobs!' The issue of industrial democracy and participation raises almost as many awkward questions for unions as it does for employers.

Aim to improve members position in relation to hierarchy and authority

It should now be apparent that what unions are concerned about – certainly what their members are concerned about – is in effect a marginal improvement in their position concerning the division of labour and the exercise of authority. The most obvious way in which this is done is by an emphasis on the commodity nature of labour, reinforced by employers' emphasis on the market, by bargaining over changes in working practices in terms of price. This aspect of the role of trade unions is highlighted by the sometimes acrimonious debates between and within unions over redundancy. It is argued that the present generation of job holders do not have the right to bargain away jobs since this has serious consequences for the next generation of workers. On the other hand, attempts by union negotiators to use arguments of a wider social responsibility often fail due to the eagerness of their members to take the redundancy money and run!

Summary

This chapter examined the nature of the relationship between employers and employees which developed in response to the imperatives of a market-orientated industrial society. The discussion started by considering the two main theoretical concepts, alienation and anomie, which underlie the analysis and description of both the nature of human relationships and the future development of industrial society itself. Alienation and anomie were examined as contrasting attempts to understand what goes on in relationships between management and labour in particular and society in general. The examination was in terms of their contribution to the development of strategies and tactics by both interest groups to cope with problems arising from the management of labour.

The chapter then went on to consider the way in which workers responded to the changes brought about by the development of factories. This response was in the form of collective organizations, trade unions, which in fact represented an adaptation to the demands of the new market-orientated society. Trade unions represent a feature of contemporary capitalist society which in their own way are as central to its functioning, as, say, the stock exchange or merchant banks. Even where firms or whole industries have highly developed policies designed to exclude or render trade unions unnecessary, these policies are themselves derived from the very existence of trade unions and their objective of protecting the interests of members.

These policies can be seen to emerge from the efforts of firms to come to terms with the factors represented in the business in context model which informs the series of which this volume is a part. Both union and employer bargaining power can be affected by changes in the environment, whether those changes relate to the market, the economy or to social and political attitudes. High levels of unemployment significantly weaken the ability of unions and work groups to contest management's exercise of power. The need of management for a highly motivated and skilled workforce may lead some employers to move away from traditional forms of collective bargaining towards those approaching Fox's 'high trust' model. Such employers calculate that they can do a better job than the unions and without the necessity of being seen to make concessions – often taken as a sign of weakness.

The much publicized 'new style' single union collective agreements incorporating pendulum arbitration, where the arbitrator has to make a choice between the case put by the employer or that put by the union – no 'splitting the difference' – and so-called 'no-strike' clauses are no exception. They also include provisions for training, consultation, information disclosure, and the abolition of status differentials which are all seen as central to the resolution of the problem of an alienating and anomic quality of working life.

In the next chapter we will go on to look specifically at the nature of modern work organizations with particular reference to the way their structure, size and technology influence the behaviour of their members.

Study questions

1. Define 'alienation' and 'anomie', and say why modern business people should understand the nature and role of these two concepts.
2. What insights, if any, do attempts to regulate market operations in free-enterprise economies such as those of North America and Europe provide into the debate between Marx and Durkheim concerning the nature of market economies?
3. What are the main features of Fox's model of collective bargaining? Are they relevant in the context of so-called 'new-style' agreements?
4. Upon what basis may it be argued that Blauner's approach to alienation is less than satisfactory?
5. 'The market mechanism for allocating scarce resources presupposes

equality and freedom; it cannot ensure equality and freedom.' Do you agree? Why?

Further reading

Since alienation and anomie are two seminal ideas in the debate over the nature and future of capitalist societies, the literature on them is vast! However, a few suggestions would be as follows.

Lee and Newby (1983) provide very accessible introductions to both the work of Durkheim and Marx set in the context of their relevance to modern society. Hill (1981) looks at the effect of technology and competion between interests on relations in the workplace. The book also considers the evolution of new forms of managerial organization. The essays by Bottomore on Marx and Tiryakian on Durkheim in Bottomore and Nisbet (1979) are also useful. Fenton (1984) both provides an account of Durkheim's work and relates it to contemporary concerns with conflict, work, race, education, religion and crime.

The literature on Karl Marx (who was led to proclaim on one occasion 'J'ne suis pas un marxiste') and Marxism is immense. This, coupled with the notoriety attaching to it, means that many people never read secondary sources let alone Marx's own work. To get some idea of the basic analysis developed by Marx it would be worth reading the very short *Manifesto of the Communist Party* of 1848. The first English edition came out in 1888, five years after Marx's death, and was edited by Frederick Engels who ran the Manchester branch of the family's cotton spinning business and contributed financial help to Marx during the period the latter was resident in London.

A readable account of the development of the trade unions in Britain can be found in Burgess (1975). Finally an acessible and useful critique of Blauner's approach to alienation is contained in Eldridge (1973).

References

Bassett, P. (1986) *Strike Free: New Industrial Relations in Britain.* Macmillan.

Blackburn, R.M. and Mann, M. (1979) *The Working Class in the Labour Market.* Macmillan.

Blauner, R. (1964) *Alienation and Freedom.* University of Chicago.

Bottomore, T. and Nisbett, R. (eds) *A History of Sociological Analysis.* Heinemann.

Burgess, K. (1975) *The Origins of British Industrial Relations.* Croom Helm.

Crouch, C. (1978) Inflation and the political organisation. In Hirsch, F. and Goldthorpe, J. (eds) *The Political Economy of Inflation.* Martin Robertson.

Donovan, Lord (1968) *Report of the Royal Commission on Trade Unions and Employers Associations* (chaired by Lord Donovan). Cmnd 3623, HMSO.

Dore, R. (1973) *British Factory, Japanese Factory*. Allen & Unwin.

Eldridge, J.E.T. (1973) *Sociology and Industrial Life*. Nelson.

Fenton, S. (1974) *Durkheim and Modern Sociology*. Cambridge University Press.

Flanders, A. and Fox, A. (1969) Collective bargaining – from Donovan to Durkheim. In Flanders, A., *Management and Unions*. Faber & Faber.

Fox, A. (1974) *Beyond Contract: Work, Power and Trust Relations*. Faber & Faber.

Fox, A. (1985) *Man Mismanagement*. Hutchinson.

Goldthorpe, J. (1978) The current inflation – towards a sociological account. In Hirsch, F. and Goldthorpe, J. (eds) *The Political Economy of Inflation*. Martin Robertson.

Hill, S. (1981) *Competition and Control at Work*. Heinemann.

Kahn-Freund, O. (1972) *Labour and the Law*, the 24th Hamlyn Lecture. Stevens.

Kraithman, D. and Adams, J. (1983) *The Impact of a Multinational on a Local Labour Market*. Paper to the annual conference of the APTE, Trent Polytechnic.

Landsberger, H.A. (1985) *Hawthrone Revisited: management and the worker – its critics and developments in human relations in industry*. Cornell University Press.

Lee, D. and Newby, H. (1983) *The Problem of Sociology*. Hutchinson.

Lewis, R. (1983) Collective labour law. In Bain, G.S. (ed.) *Industrial Relations in Britain*. Blackwell, Oxford.

Maitland, I. (1983) *The Causes of Industrial Disorder: A Comparison of a British and a German Factory*. Routledge and Kegan Paul.

Miliband, R. (1969) *The State in Capitalist Society: The Analysis of the Western System of Power*. Weidenfeld & Nicholson.

Needle, D. (1989) *Business in Context*. Van Nostrand Reinhold.

Oliver, J. and Turton, R. (1982) Is there a shortage of skilled labour? *British Journal of Industrial Relations*, **20**, (2), 195–200.

Roethlisberger, F.J. and Dickson, W.J. (1939) *Management and the Worker*. Harvard University Press. (A subsequent review and evaluation of the Hawthorne experiments came out in 1958 – see Landsberger (1958).)

Winch, D. (1978) *Adam Smith's Politics: An Essay in Historiographic Revision*. Cambridge University Press.

The role and structure of organizations 4 ||||||

In this chapter we move one step closer to the centre of the model of business used in this series. We will consider some of the issues raised by the predominance of organizations in industrial society before going on to consider organizational structure and the factors which affect it. These include size, technology and environmental variables such as the nature of the markets within which the organization has to operate. We start by considering the role of organizations because of the negative feeling that is generated by bureacracy, the organizational form which is typical of industrial societies both in terms of business organizations and the administration of the state.

This chapter will examine several aspects of organizations. First, we look at the influence of organizations on all our lives. Secondly, because of the power wielded by many organizations we must analyse how organizations are controlled by reopening the ownership and control debate from Chapter 2. Thirdly, our study of organizations focuses upon the concept of bureaucracy and we analyse the classic studies in this area as well as those professing alternative perspectives. Fourthly, we examine the influence of group behaviour on organizational life and introduce the concept of the informal organization. We end the chapter by taking a contingency view of organizations and those variables which influence the structure and functioning of organizations.

The extent and power of organizations

As many observers of modern society have noted, contemporary life is almost entirely based in or around organizations; people are born in hospitals, go to school and spend up to 50 years of their lives either in work organizations or their substitutes. For this reason if no other, modern society can be regarded as 'organizational society'. 'Pre-school children and non working housewives are the only large groups of persons whose behaviour is not substantially organizational' (March and Simon, 1958).

However, in addition to the significance of the time people spend in organizations, there is also the power which modern organizations and those who manage them can exercise over the societies in which they operate. For example, there are important issues raised by the role of multinational corporations in the economies of industrial and industrializing countries. These corporations have budgets which are sometimes several times greater than those of western nation states and their activities can have considerable impact upon foreign exchange markets which in turn may have serious implications for domestic economic policies. For example, in the spring of 1989 at a time of rising oil prices, a number of major oil companies threatened to stop supplying the Republic of Ireland, which had one of the highest price levels for petrol in Europe (I£2.72), because of a government price freeze policy designed to contain inflation.

Concern is also expressed by, for example, environmental, health and safety and consumer pressure groups over the social responsibilities of businesses. This concern focuses on the protection of the varying interests of those who have a stake in business activities and decisions, such as shareholders, employees, customers and the wider public. Issues of empolyee rights, health and safety, product liability, the environment, sponsorship and advertising can all be considered as part of the social responsibility of business and are associated with the power that large and wealthy organizations can exercise.

A key issue in the context of the debate about the power and influence of modern organizations and those who either own or manage them concerns the extent to which modern democratic society was developed to protect individual rights from encroachment by other **individuals**, rather than from infringement by organizations. As we saw in the two previous chapters, an important aspect of the development of a market economy was 'free labour'. People should be free to pursue their own interests. However, in contemporary society where economically powerful organizations are themselves regarded in law as individual entities, the problem of democracy may perhaps more accurately be seen as the problem of protecting individual rights from encroachment by those who **control** organizations.

For example, the problems faced by those who sought damages from the manufacturer of the anti-arthritic drug Opren arose largely from their economic and financial weakness. Quite simply, they could not afford the considerable legal fees they would have to meet had they not won their case. The manufacturers on the other hand, **could** afford such expenditure.

Similarly, the question has been asked whether or not the government should assist pressure groups at public enquiries into, for example, nuclear power station projects. Many of these groups, including locally based ones, do not have the funds to match those of the Central Electricity Generating Board in so far as the ability to call upon expert witnesses is concerned. Not only do the CEGB have their own experts whom they employ, they can also afford to fly in (and pay) others from around the world.

The problem is that individuals and groups may exercise power in society simply by virtue of their control over organizational resources such as finance, or the knowledge of experts that they employ or can hire. Similar concerns may arise in connection not only with commercial organizations, but also with the administrative apparatus of the state and other public bodies.

Ownership and control

The question of who actually controls modern commercial organizations was first raised in the 1930s by two American authors Berle and Means (1932) as mentioned in Chapter 2. Berle and Means suggested that the ownership of modern corporations had become separated from control over them. Modern shareholders were unable to exercise ownership rights since there was often a very large number of relatively small holdings. This made collective action by shareholders both difficult and (more to the point perhaps) expensive. The situation is illustrated in Case Study 4.1.

CASE STUDY 4.1

SHAREHOLDING AND CONTROL

Consider the breakdown of the shareholdings of two modern companies given in Table 4.1. The significance of holdings of more than 25000 shares is immediately apparent. Consider the financial implications in terms of stationery and postage alone of the organization of an action group amongst small shareholders. Whilst these costs are significant hurdles for such a group to overcome, the senior managers of the corporation have resources at their disposal, resources which significantly reduce the burden of such costs.

This issue is frequently raised at the time of major takeover battles when, in the context of expensive advertising campaigns by the bid participants, questions are asked concerning the true interests of shareholders (particularly private holders with only small holdings) and how they might be identified and publicized. An example was provided by the proposal in November 1988 from the management of R.J.R. Nabisco, the American food and tobacco group, to buy out the public shareholders in a $20bn deal financed largely by debt.

The problem was that the potential returns for the few members of top management involved were huge, running into tens of millions, if not billions, of dollars. The question was, at whose expense would this value be created? 'A conflict of interest is created whenever differences between the market value of company and its break-up value can be exploited by the managers for their own interests' (*The Financial Times, 21 November 1988*). A former merchant banker had argued earlier in 1988 that: 'Bids are often initiated and pursued primarily in the interests of management' (Stanley Wright, *The Victims of Bid Bias, The Financial Times*, 10 October 1988).

The debate over the extent or degree to which the separation of **ownership** from **control** has taken place as a result of the fragmentation of shareholdings involves the consideration of the interests and motives of three groups: shareholders, managers and financiers. The last group may become shareholders or simply loan funds to an enterprise. An important issue in the debate concerns the extent to which shareholders are really 'rentiers'. That is, they benefit from the use of capital (by buying shares on the stock exchange) but do not share in the exercise of control over it. While the legal framework provides protection for the

Continued over page

Continued from previous page   **Table 4.1** Two examples of the distribution of shareholdings in companies

Size of holding	No. of holdings	% of total holdings	% of stock held
A clearing bank			
1–100	13 759	11.0	0.2
101–250	19 293	16.0	1.0
251–500	25 731	21.0	2.8
501–1 000	27 618	23.0	5.8
1 001–5 000	28 968	24.0	16.5
5 001–10 000	2 024	1.7	4.0
10 001–25 000	757	0.6	3.3
25 001–50 000	274	0.2	2.8
50 000	576	0.5	63.6
	119 036	*100.0%	*100.0%
A manufacturing company			
1–100	1 762	7.8	
101–250	2 516	11.1	
251–500	3 483	15.3	
501–1 000	4 628	20.4	Not available
1 001–5 000	8 768	38.6	
5 001–10 000	943	4.2	
10 001–25 000	421	1.9	
25 001–50 000	188	0.8	
50 000			
	22 709	*100.0%	

* Not exact total due to rounding.

rights of ownership, this has become quite distinct from the exercise of control over the allocation of the resources of the organization.

Managers of an organization play a major role in the exercise of 'allocative' or strategic control. That is, the managers are in the position of being able (because it is within their remit) to make decisions over the allocation of resources to a number of (alternative) activities upon which the organization may be engaged. In addition, of course, they have at their disposal the knowledge and expertise of employees of the organization and who depend upon their superiors for career advancement. The result is that within varying limits managers can make decisions which other 'stakeholders', e.g. customers, employees or even shareholders, may neither approve of nor understand.

The issues raised by the debate over the relationship between ownership and control, and the various groups involved, are discussed in Chapter 3 of Needle's *Business in Context*, a companion volume in this series, and dealt with in considerable detail by Scott (1985). The point to bear in mind for our purposes in this volume is that, as suggested by the breakdown of shareholdings illustrated in Case Study 4.1, control, if exercised at all by 'owners' (shareholders), is likely to be minority control exercised through a 'constellation of interests'. A constellation of interests may be made up, for example, of minority holdings held by financial institutions (banks, insurance companies, pension funds), and the holdings of representatives of the founding family or families who may or may not be senior executives of the enterprise. Even these combined holdings will still represent a minority of shares. However, combining to protect shared interests will be easier than for the mass of individual shareholders, but still not necessarily 'easy'. On the other hand, management may be able to exercise what is termed 'allocative control' over the resources of an organization if the dividends satisfy the shareholders. The concept of allocative control is explained in Key Concept 4.1.

Allocative or strategic control refers to the ability to make decisions about how the resources (financial and human) of the organization are to be utilized, and the rate of return to be obtained. Managers as such do not 'own' the resources, but merely act in what they determine to be the interests of the various stakeholders with particular attention given to those of that constellation of interests which are able to influence the availability of finance in particular.	*KEY CONCEPT 4.1* ***ALLOCATIVE CONTROL***

The emergence of pressure groups as a force in modern society can be seen as evidence supporting the contention that society is basically 'organized', and indeed as being organized in the interests of those who exercise allocative or strategic control over large-scale commercial and governmental organizations. The existence and development of pressure groups is evidence of the forces acting upon those who wish to contest the decisions or operations of organized interests. To question such decisions and operations it is also necessary to 'organize', hence the crucial role of organization in modern society.

The modern organization: an overview

Concern with organizations and their influence upon society has grown with the experience of industrialization throughout Europe and also pre- and post-revolutionary Russia. This concern has focused on the nature and consequences of that form of organization most closely associated with the modern world – bureaucracy. The defining features of bureaucratic organization are set out in Key Concept 4.2. The term 'bureaucrat', if not a term of abuse, at least implies a highly critical evaluation of an individual's behaviour and/or the rules of the organization for which they work!

There are at least three reasons why an examination of the impact of organization structure on behaviour can usefully start with an examination of bureaucracy.

KEY CONCEPT 4.2

BUREAUCRACY

Bureaucracy is a form of organization consisting of a series of office holders whose 'offices' or posts are arranged in a hierarchy, and who are bound by strict rules governing their activities and responsibilities. The term is French in origin from 'bureau' meaning 'office', hence 'rule by office', in the same way that 'oligarchy' means 'rule by the few', autocracy means 'rule by one (absolute) ruler' and democracy means 'government by the people'.

The term first made its appearance in the aftermath of the French Revolution when what may be regarded as a modern, rational, administrative system was being developed for the administration of the new Republic. In this context the forms of government familiar to classical Greece (monarchy, aristocracy, oligarchy, democracy) were extended to include bureaucracy. The term was applied to a new group of rulers and system of government in which 'officials' were the key actors and the application of rules the basis of operation.

'Bureaucracy' passed into other European languages and political discussion largely as a result of the literary examination of nineteeth-century society, and through the work of political writers such as John Stewart Mill who wrote in 1859 'Where everything is done through the bureaucracy, nothing to which the bureaucracy is really averse can be done at all' (in *On Liberty*). This sentiment is expressed today by those who feel that the weight of administrative procedures and requirements of state intervention have stifled individual initiative and enterprise and should be drastically reduced if Western economies are to retain their prosperity in the modern world.

The defining characteristics of bureaucracy may be stated as follows:

☐ Members/employees of an organization are 'free' and owe allegiance only to the impersonal duties of the office they occupy (see earlier observations about free labour in Chapter 3). 'Impersonal' here means that the duties and obligations apply to an office or post and not to the individual who may occupy that office or post at any point in time.
☐ A clear hierarchy of offices or positions.
☐ Clear specification of the functions of each of these offices or positions.
☐ Individuals are appointed to an office on the basis of a contract.
☐ Selection and promotion operates upon the basis of formal qualifications attained.
☐ Officials are paid a salary which is graded according to their level in the hierarchy.
☐ There is a career structure, in which promotion is achievable by merit and/or seniority.
☐ The position held is that individual's sole or main occupation.
☐ Neither the post nor the resources associated with it may in any way be appropriated for personal use by the official who occupies that post for the time being.
☐ Officials are subject to disciplinary and control procedures whose rules are applied in a judicial manner.

☐ First, as indicated in the previous paragraph, there has been a long standing concern with the stifling impact of bureaucracy on individual freedom and behaviour.

☐ Second, those organizations which play an important part in everyday life are in fact organized according to bureaucratic principles.

☐ Third (and importantly) there is a basic tension between democracy as currently conceived in the West and bureaucracy.

CASE STUDY 4.2

HOW DEMOCRACY MAY IMPLY BUREAUCRACY

A democratic society based upon some conception of equality – of both treatment and opportunity – requires a form of administration which is based upon the application of relevant criteria. Justice not only needs to be done, but should be seen to be done. Administrative decisions have to be both predictable and defensible; they need to be based upon rules and the knowledge of rules by officials.

As the numbers of the elderly in the population of the UK increase over the next decade or two, and those with severe mental and physical disabilities survive longer due to advances in medical and nursing techniques, the problems of caring for these people will increase.

During the 1960s the traditional large Victorian psychiatric hospital was increasingly perceived as counter-productive. The rigid procedures of such organizations actually increased rather than decreased the dependency they were supposed to be dealing with. Patients became institutionalized, increasingly incapable of ever being able to cope in the outside world.

Those involved in the care of mentally and physically disabled people in such hospitals concluded that patterns of care should be modelled more closely on that provided by friends and family in the community. People should be treated in small groups in the community and helped to lead independent lives as far as possible. The closure of institutions was accepted by the government as a means of reducing costs, but the alternative form of care was not adequately funded. Community care was not a cheap option, at least in the short term, because of the need to establish the necessary facilities which were unlikely to be as cheap as the dormitory accommodation of the original institutions. A further problem was that responsibility for community care was split between a number of organizations: the social service and housing departments of local authorities (operating under increasingly constrained budgets anyway), voluntary bodies, community health services and private hostels and nursing homes.

The government's special health advisor, Sir Roy Griffiths, recommended that the social services departments of local authorities should be given the responsibility and funded accordingly. As a leader in *The Financial Times* pointed out: 'There are no easy solutions in community care. This is not an area where the market can play a big role: those in the greatest need of care are often those with the least cash and least able to make rational choices. **Responsibility has to be vested in a bureaucracy of some description and it has to be properly financed**' (12 April 1989, emphasis added.)

Let us deal with this third point first by considering Case Study 4.2.

One can argue therefore that democracy implies bureaucracy. However, the problem is, as many writers have testified, that bureaucracy does not imply democracy (see, for example, Lee and Newby, 1983). As mentioned earlier, organizations and those who control them have at their disposal resources of both knowledge and finance that make it very difficult for outsiders, and even others within the organization, to exercise any control. 'Who says organisation says oligarchy' was the aphorism of Robert Michels based upon his nineteenth-century observations of the behaviour of the paid officials of political parties in Germany. For them, organization ceased being a means for achieving the ends of those represented by the party and came instead to be a means for the ends of the officials themselves. The same charge is often levelled today at both company directors and trade union officials.

In the case of business organizations bureaucracy has been seen as problematic since it is generally regarded as being inflexible and slow to respond to change. In the current information technology revolution this characteristic of bureaucracy is seen as a hindrance, preventing businesses quickly and effectively developing the competitive advantages offered by the new technology.

A number of classic studies – Blau (1963), Gouldner (1964), Merton (1957), Burns and Stalker (1961) – have been carried out into the effect of bureaucracy on behaviour and efficiency in organization. Since these are directly concerned with the issue of the adaptability of organizations and their officials they form an important component of any examination of behaviour in organizations today and will be considered in some detail later in this chapter.

It should be remembered that modern industrial societies rely upon bureaucratic administrative systems and organizations, both in the public and private spheres. Many of the benefits of industrialization and Western-style democracy derive from the efficient administration and provision of the infrastructure – the legal system, transport, education, health – as well as the operation of large, privately owned organizations which provide products and services. Most of what we take for granted in the modern world as being the desired outcome of industrialism based upon a market economy is ultimately closely associated with the much criticized bureaucratic form of administration.

The examination of the nature of bureaucratic organization and their impact upon the development of industrial society represented by the four studies mentioned above has taken the form of a debate with one particular writer, the German sociologist Max Weber who died in 1920. As a result of his examination of the process of industrialization in Germany, Weber noted the very close association between the process of modernization and the extent of bureaucratic organization.

Max Weber and the problem of bureaucracy

In examining Weber's approach to bureaucracy, the key features of which have been set out in Key Concept 4.2, we need to spend a short time considering the distinction he made between action and behaviour, and three concepts that were central to Weber's approach. These are **rationality**, **authority** and **legitimacy**. It is necessary to do this because Weber's views on the role and nature of the bureaucratic form of organization derived from his ideas about the related concepts of social action, rationality, authority and legitimacy.

The basis of the distinction between social action and behaviour is set out in Key Concept 4.3. The three central concepts of rationality, authority and legitimacy are discussed now in turn. They are important because of their role in modern organizational life as justifications for the exercise of control by one social group over others.

Weber's starting point was a distinction between 'behaviour' and 'action'. Behaviour involves simple reflexes – blinking or flinching for example. 'Action', as opposed to simple 'behaviour', occurs when behaviour is influenced by the individual's dealings with others: when the intentions and actions of others are taken into account by the acting individual. If the actor is to take account of the intentions of others, then some interpretation has to be applied to the action or behaviour of those others as well as to that of the individual himself. In other words, when you respond to a gesture or comment from a friend, colleague or superior, your response implies some interpretation of what the other meant by saying or doing what they did and of what they will make of your response. In this way action, in contrast to mere behaviour, is 'social'. Even when 'others' are not physically present, for example when you are alone in the privacy of your room, your behaviour may still be influenced by your awareness of how others might react if they knew what you were doing.

KEY CONCEPT 4.3

SOCIAL ACTION

Rationality

Weber argued that it was possible to measure human action against some objective standard without necessarily resorting to value judgements. The value judgements Weber was trying to avoid were those associated, for example, with 'reason', 'efficiency', 'morality' or 'progress'. The problem with these four terms is that they are usually used as though there was no possibility of ambiguity over their meaning. Matters unfortunately are not so simple. Take 'reason' for example.

'Be reasonable!' is an injunction to adopt the same set of parameters as the speaker. Someone who accepts the same premise for an assertion as we do may nevertheless arrive at an alternative, and possibly equally legitimate, conclusion. This **may** be the result of faulty reasoning (i.e. getting the right answer for the wrong reasons), but equally it could be the result of using different values or criteria in the reasoning process. Both those who support and those who reject current policies on official secrets argue that they support 'free speech' and 'open government'.

Even 'efficiency' is not immune from such problems of ambiguity.

Efficiency may be attained by **either** maximizing output for given inputs, **or** minimizing inputs for a given output. Either course of action will be 'efficient', though they will have very different outcomes. During the 1984 miners' strike, for example, which focused on the issue of the closure of uneconomic pits, academic and professional accountants were engaged in public debates over how exactly an 'uneconomic' pit was to be defined. There is also the vexed question, in a democracy, of how to balance efficiency with equity. What is efficient may not be equitable, and what is regarded as equitable may not be efficient.

During the early 1960s British Rail produced many examples of similar problems. Closing branch lines which failed to 'earn their keep' when looked at in isolation resulted in considerable amounts of traffic being lost to road transport. Apparently 'uneconomic' branch lines were responsible for feeding a considerable volume of traffic (albeit in small amounts) to what were then seen as 'profitable' lines. Once the feeders were taken away, the 'profitable' became 'unprofitable'.

Factory closure decisions and subsequent unemployment may seem 'economic' or 'efficient' when looked at from the point of view of management or shareholders, but when seen from a wider perspective the loss of income tax revenue, and the decline in profits of local retailers who depend on a fully employed workforce (with a consequent decline in VAT revenue for example), plus the state's obligation to pay unemployment and social security benefits, may suggest a different evaluation. These other costs are distinct from the sociological and psychological costs to individuals and their families of course.

Similar problems arise with 'morality' and 'progress'. There are many 'moral' systems. How is it to be decided which should take precedence? Similarly with the concept of 'progress'. When an innovation produces something we consider beneficial, we don't have too much difficulty about defining it as 'progress'. To others though, it may be very different. Thus holidaymakers and conservationists may have a rather different attitude to industrial development in areas of natural beauty in comparison with those who actually live there and require work.

These were the type of problems Weber was trying to avoid by identifying some standard against which human action could be measured. The standard Weber eventually identified was that of human 'rationality'. There were two forms this could take: formal and substantive.

Formal rationality refers to the extent to which it is possible to calculate the relationship between ends and means. This could relate to quantitative methods, such as those used in accounting to prepare a profit and loss or trading account for example, or to less quantifiable contexts where nonetheless basing one's action on the regularity of the behaviour of others will not be considered 'irrational' or 'non-rational' even if on occasions people behave unexpectedly. One can always be on the look out for the unexpected, but this is not the same as predicting when it will happen. If one could, of course, it would not be 'unexpected'!

Substantive rationality refers to perhaps the majority of human action where action is influenced by the existence or operation of criteria relating to ultimate values, such as the enhancement of individual freedom or the idea of a health service which is free at the point of consumption, or a place in higher education for all who could benefit from it. In this sense action is 'rational' since there is a consideration of the relationship between ultimate values and means.

It is important to note that the operation of formal rationality does not necessarily imply substantive rationality. The existence and operation of an accounting system in a business enterprise does not imply that the business will make the desired profit, or indeed any at all! However, the system will tell you by how much the target was missed and it may even be possible to identify a trend and take remedial action before the worst happens. Not making a profit does not necessarily imply a lack of 'rationality'.

Formal rationality, therefore, does **not** imply 'efficiency'. All it does imply is the possibility of identifying relative inefficiency and hence the identification of steps to reduce it. But that in itself raises the question of whether a reduction in inefficiency is necessarily rational in the formal or substantive sense. For example, minimizing labour costs by hiring relatively cheap and untrained labour may well mean that adaptation to technological or product change is slowed down or prevented altogether.

The costs of reducing certain forms of waste may be greater than the amount that can be saved. In some cases this can be formally identified. Companies whose wage costs are a very small proportion of their total costs will spend less time worrying about a given pay increase than will companies whose wage costs are a very much greater proportion of total costs. In some cases such formal identification may not be possible, as when one is concerned about the impact of action on the 'goodwill' that surrounds a relationship. For example, the benefits which accrue from having a motivated and loyal workforce may outweigh the disadvantages of some theoretically avoidable cost or inefficiency.

The discussion of rationality, as defined by Weber, is important because it lies at the heart of the criticism by writers such as Blau, Gouldner and Merton that Weber assumed that formal rationality as represented by bureaucracy was efficient. The problem is that neither his translators nor his critics have kept the notions of formal rationality and efficiency sufficiently distinct. Weber argued that bureaucracy was the most **formally** rational system of administration because of the degree of calculation and logical analysis that went into it. He did not argue that bureaucracy was **synonymous** with efficiency. He was particularly concerned about the social and political implications for a society dominated by the power of large-scale bureaucracy. That this form of administration is typical of 'modern' industrial societies is not seriously doubted, however.

Authority and legitimacy

These two concepts are of considerable importance in the context of behaviour in organizations since they are implicit in the relationship between superiors and subordinates.

The arguments about bureaucracy and rationality are closely related to Weber's identification of at least three types of authority, in the sense of the legitimate exercise of power or domination by one group or individual over others. Each of these types of authority – traditional, charismatic, and legal-rational – can be seen as distinct bases for the domination of one group or individual over others.

'Traditional' authority

This is a form of authority based upon a belief in the sanctity of what has gone before. 'That's not how things are done around here!' is one of the common respones to those who suggest changes in many work organizations. What is done now, the way it is done and the reasons it is done are all based upon, and justified by reference to, the fact that that is the way it has always been done. That is what 'tradition' is about. There may well be other reasons for doing what is done, but the point is that they are not the ones used to support the action at this point in time. Such behaviour is not 'formally' rational although it may be 'substantively' rational. That is, the desired outcome may be achieved, but that will not be because there was a formally calculated relationship between the means and the ends.

'Charismatic' authority

This is a form of authority based upon a belief in the unique personal qualities of a particular individual which overrides both tradition and even the law. Things are done the way they are done because that is the way 'the leader' says they will be done. Means and ends do not relate in a calculated way, but via the personal qualities of an individual.

One of the problems with charismatic authority is that there comes a point in time when the authority and legitimacy derived from the charisma of an individual has to be passed on to a successor, upon the death of the founder of a business for example. This is the process known as the 'routinization of charisma', and within it there is a contradiction. Authority and legitimacy derived from the personal characteristics of one individual have to be passed to another, who may or may not be 'charismatic'.

It is possible to do this by establishing a process or routine for selecting and installing a successor. This should be done during the incumbancy of the charismatic leader so that the process is seen as legitimate be virtue of their charisma. One consequence of establishing such a routine for succession is that it is the 'office', rather than the office holder for the time being, which acquires the charisma and hence authority and legitimacy. 'The King is dead! Long live the King!' encapsulates this phenomenon. Since failure to establish a procedure for succession can result in dissent and schism, any organization if it is to survive has to establish a framework for the handing on of the authority of the leader. Since such a framework tends to imbue the 'office', rather than the current incumbent, with authority, and since adherence to the selection process legitimates the successor's exercise of the authority of the office, there then appears the beginnings of Weber's third form of authority.

'Legal-rational' authority

This is the form of authority Weber associated with the bureaucratic form of administration. It is characterized by a system of rules which are applied in accordance with ascertainable principles valid for all. In this sense the rules are 'legal', since they are applied in a judicial manner, and they are 'rational' since they are derived from the calculation of a relationship between ends and means.

Take as an example the examination regulations covering your course. (These, by the way, you are well advised to study since they will contain information about appeals procedures and how to protect your interests if, for example, ill-health undermines your performance on exam day.) Such regulations do not mean that mistakes will not be made, that justice will always be done and be seen to be done. After all, examiners are human too (really!) and therefore fallible. But the existence of such regulations does mean that it is possible to identify how well the system operates and how errors may be rectified or prevented in the future.

Weber was not equating rationality and bureaucracy with efficiency. He was asserting that:

☐ Rationality implied a conscious calculation (as opposed to mere unthinking or emotionional acceptance) of the relationship between ends and means. This is in contrast to tradition and charisma.
☐ That such conscious calculation was most highly developed in bureaucratic organisations.
☐ That organisations based on these principles were the dominant ones in industrial societies.

Other approaches to bureaucracy

The debate about bureaucracy concerns the extent to which the ten attributes given in Key Concept 4.2 can be claimed to enhance the rational and efficient operation of organizations. It was in the attempt to test this alleged assertion of Weber's about the efficiency and rationality of bureaucracy that a number of key studies were carried out. Perhaps the best known are those of Peter Blau, Alvin Gouldner, Robert Merton, and Tom Burns and G.M. Stalker, the latter being two British authors whose key book was entitled *The Management of Innovation*.

Each of these studies, although undertaken several years ago, speak to us directly today as managers and their organizations wrestle with the problems of adapting to changed, and still changing, economic and technological environments. For this reason we will spend a short time considering these classic investigations, starting with that of Gouldner.

Gouldner's model

Gouldner's study, set out in Case Study 4.3, although of limited generality, highlighted the significance of environmental factors for organizational structure as the business in context model suggests. It provided an example of a situation which supported the conclusion that general statements concerning the efficiency of bureaucracy were lacking in validity. However, it also suggested an insight that was to become an important aspect of

CASE STUDY 4.3

GOULDNER'S STUDY

Alvin Gouldner studied a gypsum plant in the United States which was taken over by a 'big city' firm which installed a new manager to run the plant in a more business-like manner than had the previous family owners. The new manager attempted to impose conventional business criteria for calculating efficiency and tighten up on what might be termed 'loose practices' by both the old management and their workers. He attempted to impose a more bureaucratic structure upon the company with clear sets of rules and responsibilities such that everyone would know what they were supposed to do and how they were supposed to do it and when they were supposed to do it. The new manager was particularly concerned to tighten up on the 'sloppy' procedures which characterized the business before he took over.

The plant that the new manager had taken over consisted of two separate operations. The first involved the mining of gypsum which was then used in the manufacture of gypsum building boards in a factory on the same site. While both these operations took place on the same site, they nevertheless displayed two very different sets of working conditions and practices.

The factory was organized for the routine production of a product that changed very little and was standardized. The situation in the mine on the other hand did not display such regularities. Working conditions could change quite rapidly due to geological factors confronting the miners as they worked the gypsum deposits, and this meant that output levels were not easily predictable. Additionally there were the dangers inherent in working underground which resulted in the men developing reliance upon their workmates in order to cope with the physical and psychological stress of mining. These related factors resulted in the miners having a very different attitude to, and organization of, work in comparison with employees in the factory.

Table 4.2 Three patterns of bureaucracy

1. 'Mock' bureaucracy:
   (a) Rules not enforced
   (b) Little conflict
   (c) Violation/evasion of the rules facilitated by informal sentiments of both management and workers.

2. 'Representative' bureaucracy:
   (a) Management enforce and workers obey the rules
   (b) Little overt conflict
   (c) Mutual support/respect for the rules.

3. 'Punishment-centred' bureaucracy:
   (a) Rules enforced by one group and evaded by the other
   (b) Tension and conflict in the relationship
   (c) Use of coercive sanctions.

Source: Gouldner (1954)

Under the previous management there had been what Gouldner called an 'indulgency' pattern or 'mock bureaucracy'. Under this form of bureaucracy the rules are not enforced by management. There is little conflict between management and workers, and it is the shared sentiments of the two groups that permit cooperation. Two other patterns were identified by Gouldner and their characteristics are set out in Table 4.2.

The indulgency pattern may be acceptable where the market environment does not put the enterprise under any pressure. If the product is unique, customers will either have to wait or pay whatever price is necessary to provide the required return on the investment made by the company. Even if the product is not unique, but the market for it is expanding, then a relatively 'inefficient' enterprise will be able to make adequate returns.

However, if the environment is not so benign, then the need to exercise tight control over the manufacturing process in terms of quality, quantity and costs will become irresistible. In such an environment bureaucratic control has certain attractions. Consider the following attributes of bureaucratic control (from Child, 1984) and reflect upon their attraction for managers coping with competition.

☐ Tasks are broken down into definable elements – specialization;
☐ Specified methods, rules and procedures are applied to these task elements;
☐ Standard budgetary and cost variation controls are applied;
☐ Technology is utilized to limit variations in pace, quality and methods;
☐ Routine decision-making is delegated within prescribed limits (this is the function of rules);
☐ Reward and punishment systems reinforce conformity to procedures and the rules.

In the factory, a control strategy based upon these six aspects could be implemented even if the workers responded with less than unqualified enthusiasm. Such a strategy could be implemented because the work situation was sufficiently stable – hence predictable – for rules to be formulated with some precision and with some confidence that they would be applicable over a period of time. Deviations from such rules could then be identified and variations from standard could be monitored within quite fine tolerances. Such a strategy has some advantages for the workforce. Compliance with clearly formulated rules – 'keeping your nose clean' – can carry rewards in terms of promotion and merit rankings. The very predictability of the rules may provide an opportunity for their manipulation, having the unintended consequence of creating some 'space' for the workers. At the very least, workers who are regarded as reliable by their supervisors are likely to experience less close supervision while supervisors concentrate on more problematic individuals or incidents. Workers may tolerate or even welcome bureaucratization in some circumstances.

However, in the case of the mine-workers circumstances were very Continued over page

Continued from previous page

different. Because of the unpredictability and danger of working conditions underground, the miners had developed their own procedures for dealing with their work. These procedures and their significance for the miners arose out of the need to rely upon fellow workers when coping with unexpected variations in the process of gypsum extraction as well as with life-threatening incidents associated with mining in general. In such situations each individual had to trust and rely upon the competence, and group and individual loyalty, of fellow workers.

When the new manager tried to impose his rules (based upon predictability and managerial control) in the mine he was resisted. The resistance of the miners was based on three factors:

☐ the irrelevance of specific rules in unpredictable circumstances;
☐ the interdependence among members of the work group; and
☐ the miners' commitment to their own working practices as a form of security in dangerous and variable conditions.

The interrelation of these factors enabled the miners to resist management attempts to impose rules upon them. A consequence of this conflict was the first strike the firm had experienced, discussed in Gouldner's later book *Wildcat Strike* (1965).

the relationship between organizational structure, performance and behaviour: that bureaucracy may be functional in predictable situations, but cannot easily cope with changeable environments. This insight, reinforced by subsequent studies such as that of Burns and Stalker, became the basis of a new approach to management and organizations, the so-called 'contingency approach', which will be discussed later in this chapter.

Gouldner developed a model of bureaucracy as illustrated in Figure 4.1. In this model, demand for control by management resulted in the use of general and impersonal rules. These were intended to reduce the visibility of power relationships by emphasizing the impersonal 'rationality' of the rules. That is, no reasonable person could object to rules designed to reduce waste and those who had to enforce the rules could deny personal commitment to them but simply insist that they were 'only doing their job'. The intended result of decreasing the visibility of power relations was to decrease the level of conflict or interpersonal tension. There was then an assumption of a 'virtuous circle' operating.

However, there is a problem with 'unintended consequences'. The problem is that rules give people employed in organizations an indication of the minimum acceptable level of performance: attendance between specified hours, for a specified number of days, with specified levels of output, and so on. This is likely to lead to a mismatch between actual performance and management's expectations. This in turn will lead to closer supervision in an attempt to reduce the discrepancy, which in turn will have the effect of increasing the visibility of power relations, which

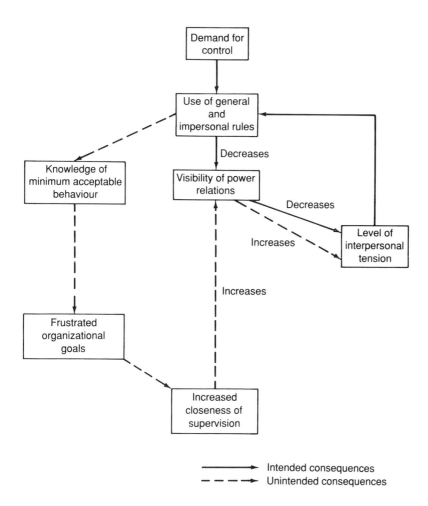

Figure 4.1 Gouldner's model of bureaucracy (from Katz and Kahn, 1966)

then increases the level of tension. In an attempt to reduce the tension, more specific rules are applied so that finally a 'vicious' circle develops.

Merton's model

While Gouldner's work is closely associated with the criticism that bureaucracy is not necessarily 'efficient' or 'rational', another equally influential critique of the Weberian view of bureaucracy is that of Robert Merton in *Bureaucratic Structure and Personality* (1952). This examination of bureaucracy provided evidence which suggested that such organizations had unfortunate implications for the personalities, and hence behaviour, of those employed in them.

Means and ends

Merton argued that constant compliance with rules resulted in individuals eventually losing the capacity to make decisions for themselves. In fact,

KEY CONCEPT 4.4

TRAINED INCAPACITY

'Trained incapacity' was the phrase Merton used to describe the effect on human beings of life in a bureaucracy. The effect was that people would lose the ability to think for themselves and fail to recognize contradictions between ends and means. Employers who emphasize adherence to procedures on the part of their employees will tend to recruit people who display evidence that such behaviour comes easily to them. Likewise, people who themselves prefer situations which are predictable and offer the security of clear-cut procedures and a minimum of ambiguity will tend to seek out employment which rewards such conformist tendencies.

constant reliance upon rules as guides for action resulted in the rules themselves becoming the be-all and end-all of working life. The stultifying consequence of rule-bound employment was that the rules became **ends** in themselves rather than the **means** to an end.

As a result of being forced to comply with rules that they did not originate, bureaucratic employees lose the capacity for independent thought. In Merton's terms the experience of bureaucratic life resulted in what he termed 'trained incapacity' (see Key Concept 4.4). The result was the stereotypical bureaucrat: an unimaginative, inflexible official applying a rule when it is obvious to all (but the bureaucrat) that the situation calls for its relaxation. Such a situation undoubtedly causes great irritation to the clients of the organization who then express considerable annoyance; such annoyance upon the part of the client forces the bureaucrat to re-emphasize the rule in order to deflect client anger and frustration. Another vicious circle results, fuelling the common sense view about red

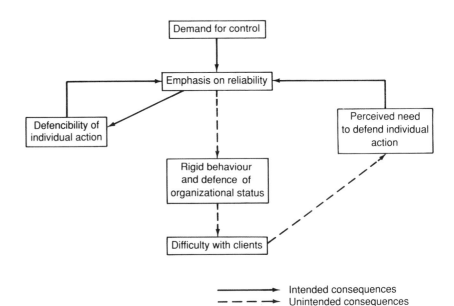

Figure 4.2 Merton's model of bureaucracy and 'trained incapacity (from Katz and Kahn, 1966)

tape, bureaucrats and the threat such organizations pose to ordinary people!

Merton's model (depicted in Figure 4.2) starts, like Gouldner's, with the demand for control. This demand is an attempt to foster reliable behaviour and performance. This in turn leads those employed to defend their behaviour to both organizational superiors and clients. The unintended consequence of such a 'virtuous' circle is rigid behaviour patterns which have the effect of frustrating clients. The irritation of clients leads the employees to feel the need to defend their actions. This they do by reference to the organizational emphasis on reliability and the existence of rules. Thus yet another 'vicious' circle develops.

The causal mechanism in Merton's model

What is the mechanism by which life in a bureaucratic organization produces the results Merton suggests? An individual's capacity to tolerate uncertainty is a function of their sense of security. Individuals who are secure in their status, whose status and expertise is constantly reinforced by the regard and opinion of others (whether at work or in some activity outside the work situation), will be more prepared to take a chance than someone whose status and skill is not so well regarded.

Within work organizations those who are in junior positions are, to some extent at least, dependent upon seniors for favourable evaluations for promotion, increased pay levels and even job security. Subordinates are therefore, by definition, in relatively insecure situations and will in consequence hesitate to exercise initiative where they are unsure what the relevant guidelines are. Equally, they will hesitate to display initiative when they are under some pressure to demonstrate their knowledge of the rules applicable to their level of the organization.

This dependency of subordinates is sufficient to produce the behaviour which Merton claims is characteristic of bureaucracies. A key characteristic of junior employees in organizations relevant to this discussion is that they are the ones who are likely to have most contact with the clients of the organization – telephonists, receptionists, clerks, counter staff, and so on. Even in schools and colleges it is the more junior members of academic and administrative staff who have the most contact with the 'customers'! It is a common experience in dealing with bureaucracies that when procedures require either modification or interpretation, difficulty is experienced in contacting the person who can make a decision, who has the authority to vary the application or interpretation of the rule in question.

Contacting this person is 'difficult' precisely because subordinates have to demonstrate that they can be relied upon not only to know the rules but also to apply them. From the client's point of view of course the subordinate's behaviour in insisting upon strict interpretation of the rules is just what you expect from a bureaucrat bound by red tape! From the superior's point of view, the subordinate is demonstrating reliability – a prized quality of all subordinates in all types of organizations, not just bureaucratic ones. An example is provided in Case Study 4.4.

In Merton's case, as in Gouldner's, a vicious circle is likely to develop. Subordinates attempt to conform to their superiors' expectations which

CASE STUDY 4.4

**BUREAUCRATIC
INTERPRETATION OF
A COMPANY'S RULES**

Smith & Jones plc, manufacturers of luxury fitted kitchens, have a rule that when a representative of their Design and Planning department travels to visit a customer, the representative must claim from their work location, not from their home address. John, who has just joined the company and does not yet have a car, submitted a travel claim on the basis of a train journey from Waterloo Station in London to a potential customer in Guildford, Surrey. He submitted the claim on the grounds that he lived in North London and had a season ticket to his usual place of work which he would not use that day. He saw no point in travelling to work only to retrace his steps to London in order to get to Guildford. He claimed £7.50 return rail fare which was rejected on the grounds that he could only claim from his place of work. Despite his explanations to the staff responsible for administering travel claims, they insisted on the application of the rules. Somewhat annoyed he rang the nearest railway station to his office and found that the return fare from there to Guildford was £8.20, so he made 70p! Subsequent journies netted him similar or even greater 'profits'.

The situation changed after John's colleague, Susan, who lived in Brighton and commuted to work by car, had occasion to visit a customer just a few miles west along the coast in Shoreham. Having overheard John's experience with his travel claim she made a claim from the office in South East London to Shoreham although she had travelled there from Brighton. This went on for some time before Susan's supervisor who countersigned travel claims realized that Susan actually lived only ten miles from the customer she was working with in Shoreham. Subsequently, several weeks later, the company issued a modified set of rules for the payment of travel expenses. In future, travel claims would be paid on the basis of 'from home or work, whichever is the cheapest'. It was not long before this rule produced its own problems of course!

provokes annoyance on the part of clients which in turn results in subordinates seeking justification for their behaviour by reference to organizational rules. It is this situation that Merton characterizes as 'trained incapacity'.

It should be emphasized that Merton's account may not be a particularly accurate or useful one since it ignores the control issues that impact on behaviour in any organization. All superiors need to be able to rely upon subordinates. Indeed, 'reliability' is perhaps the key quality desired by employers and one for which many indicators or proxies (to use the economist's jargon) are perceived to be available: for example, age, employment history or experience, educational qualifications, sex, race, marital status.

Reflections on bureaucratic control

The six aspects of bureaucracy as a control strategy identified by Child (1984) and listed in Case Study 4.3 (see p. 98) represent what might be regarded as perfectly normal methods of running a business or indeed any complex enterprise.

Businessmen continually discuss the problems of control, of the need to control variance, and of ensuring reliable estimates of costs, quantity and quality. Many successful businesses make use of all or at least some of the factors mentioned by Child; indeed, unsuccessful businesses can be shown to have ignored many of them. So, there appears to be some tension at least between the requirements for the running of a successful enterprise and the negative connotations of the concept 'bureaucracy'. Why?

Gouldner's study suggested that the six features of bureaucracy as a control mechanism were perhaps particularly suited to a stable situation. Under stable and therefore predictable conditions, such procedures were indeed capable of producing the desired results. In other words, in stable conditions set procedures are an effective means of attaining desired ends – they are 'rational'. Therefore in many business situations routine procedures and their enforcement will be a major factor in success even if such procedures and their observance are not the only reason for such success. They will be necessary even if not sufficient for success. Indeed, **any** business or enterprise will require routine procedures to ensure that such mundane activities as paying taxes and VAT, checking creditworthiness, chasing slow payers, paying suppliers, recording cash flow variations and demands and so on are carried out.

Any organization will have **some** requirements for routines, and therefore some requirement for bureaucratic processes. However, the survival of an enterprise also requires adaptation to changes in the environment. Markets do change, new products are developed, new processes for the production of conventional products are adopted by competitors. Pressure on subordinates to conform to routines may well hinder the exercise of discretion, judgement or intuition by those same subordinates which is crucial when environments are changing and established rules are no longer delivering the desired results. At this point one should ask whether the structure or procedure needs to be changed in order to allow subordinates greater flexibility or autonomy. **Means** to an end should not be raised to the status of **ends** in themselves. Case Study 4.5, researched by Peter Blau, illustrates this point. Blau studied a branch of a federal enforcement agency in the United States concerned with ensuring that firms observed laws regulating employment standards.

This case provides support for the view that bureaucratic structures are not particularly suitable in complex situations, but goes further in suggesting that informal (i.e. 'illegal' in the employer's terms) work practices developed by employees may actually enhance the performance of employees and of the organization as a whole. Informal processes in any organization may enable employees to function more effectively in the organization's terms as well as providing morale-enhancing experiences of autonomy for employees and self-respect based upon self-reliance. An important distinction has to be made therefore between the 'formal' organization as defined by rules and procedures formulated by management, and the 'informal' organization which results from the efforts of employees to cope with the world as it affects them in their daily work. We will now move on to examine this distinction, bearing in mind what we have so far considered about bureaucracy.

CASE STUDY 4.5

BLAU'S STUDY

The agents in the organization studied by Blau visited firms, interviewing employers and employees and auditing company records. About half their time was spent in the office processing cases which arose out of their investigations in the 'field'. An important rule governing the work of the agents required them to take any difficulties they encountered in applying the very detailed laws direct to their superiors. The requirement that work was not discussed with fellow agents was designed to protect the confidentiality of the information obtained by the agents from the firms they visited.

From what has already been said about the relationships between subordinates and superiors, you can probably predict how the agents might respond to the requirement that any difficulties should be discussed directly with superiors. Frequent requests for consulation might well lead the superior to doubt the ability of the agent whose promotion prospects were largely dependent upon the superior's appraisal of the agent's work. Consequently agents ignored the rule and discussed their difficulties with colleagues.

In this way agents not only protected their career prospects but also, argues Blau, improved the functioning of the agency in its enforcement activities. This improvement resulted from the fact that knowledge concerning the application of detailed and complex legal regulations was shared widely amongst the agents as a result of their discussions with each other and hence problem-solving was improved. In the case of this particular organization, not only were decision times reduced, but when cases were brought against employers they were successful, and cases which might not be successful were not brought. The reputation of the agency was therefore maintained.

KEY CONCEPT 4.5

FORMAL ORGANIZATION

The formal organization (as depicted in Figure 4.3) concentrates on how an organization **ought** to work, on how the work of the organization **ought** to get done. The most common representation takes the form of an organization chart which displays many of the characteristics of the bureaucratic form of organization. This form of chart is widely used to represent the structure of an organization by management and by writers on organizations. This widespread use to some extent demonstrates the nature of bureaucracy taken for granted as a means to organizational efficiency.

'Formal' and 'informal' organizations

The idea of the 'formal organization' is set out in Key Concept 4.5 and represented diagramatically in Figure 4.3. Note how the lines of communication and authority join positions in the hierarchy with those below them and above them. There is no attempt to represent what might

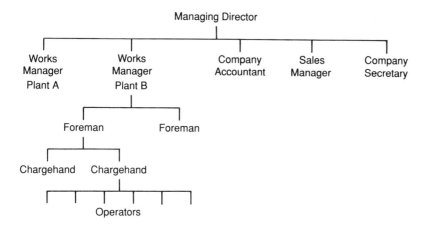

Figure 4.3 The formal organization.

be termed 'lateral' communication below a certain level. It is a representation of the type of situation described by Blau where employees were instructed **not** to discuss work with colleagues but only with superiors.

You will also note that this representation of relationships is consistent with the individualistic ethos of the employment relationship and contract of employment discussed in Chapter 2. In the light of this chapter so far then, it should be clear why such an individualistic representation of an organization may well lack both accuracy and utility in terms of any attempt to understand actual human behaviour.

The insecurity for the individual implied by the formal chart, along with the assumption that the only communication is with superiors, will produce efforts on the part of subordinates to minimize it. Such efforts will involve social activity amongst those who share similar experiences and expectations and who are likely to be able to communicate to each other their shared view of the world – shared experiences being a *sine qua non* of communication. It is highly probable, to say the least, that those who occupy similar positions in an organization will develop relationships and rules or conventions – customs if you wish – which will reduce their sense of insecurity and even perhaps enable them to exercise some countervailing influence upon their situation. This may simply be, as in Blau's case, collaborating with each other in contravention of the rules so as to screen their problems from superiors. Or they may collaborate in some other way to ensure that superiors do not know what, exactly, goes on in the process of getting the work done.

The most frequent, perhaps, example of this type of situation occurs in piece-rate payment systems where work-study engineers fix a price for a job on the basis of how long a worker should take to complete it, taking into account what bonuses will be applied. However, in a piece-rate system the workers' pay may be adversely affected by factors outside their control. The supply of components to their work station may be disrupted, substandard components or raw material may be involved, machines may break down, and so on. The effect will be to make earnings variable. Variability of income is a major source of uncertainty for anyone, especially where a regular income is a feature of a society such as ours where mortgages and other forms of credit are a significant aspect of material well-being and access to them depends on the regularity and level of income.

In such a situation, a work group will hesitate to pass on any innovations which they may develop to improve the speed at which work is done. They will use the knowledge to ensure that earnings remain stable even if work flow is disrupted. They will also fear that if such knowledge becomes known to management then the rates will be reduced and bonus targets reassessed.

A similar situation can occur in teaching organizations. In one business studies department, a junior member of staff consulted his senior colleague about rearranging the time spent in class by some accountancy students. The senior colleague advised the young lecturer to go ahead with the new programme but not to tell the head of department, '. . . because there will only be a great enquiry. You go ahead, I will take the can if anything goes wrong.'

Nothing did go wrong, all the students passed with flying colours, and the young lecturer was promoted to other work. Sometime later his replacement was found by the same senior colleague in some distress in the staff room. On enquiry, it transpired that she had had the same idea about how the teaching for the accountancy students should be organized and had gone to see the head of department to ask permission to try her idea. The head's reply? 'Nonsense, look at the results we got last year!'

What happens is that collections of individuals who share a similar situation or experience eventually form themselves into groups. A **group** is something more than just a number of individuals who happen to be in the same place at the same time, a 'collectivity' such as, for example, the passengers on a No. 14 bus or the 15:30 train from Paddington to Bristol. A 'group' compared to a collectivity has the real potential to impose its views or interests on the situation in which members find themselves. A definition of a group is set out in Key Concept 4.6.

KEY CONCEPT 4.6	A group is defined, according to Sherif (1966), as a social unit made up of a number of individuals who:
THE GROUP	☐ have role and status relationships with each other which are stabilized in some degree, and
	☐ have a set of norms or values which regulate the behaviour of individual members in matters of consequence for them.

Thus a group is distinct from a 'collectivity', people who just happen to be in the same location for the time being, e.g. on the 07:56 from Bristol to Paddington.

The characteristics of a group will develop whenever people share experiences with others who have similar expectations as themselves. This can happen, for example, amongst students in colleges as well as in work situations. When you first arrived at college your course was just a collection of individuals with no real sense of group identity. You had assumptions about what to expect, perhaps, and individual ideas about why you were there and what you expected to get out of the course, but otherwise you were just a collection of relatively isolated individuals.

There were, however, at least two factors which would facilitate the formation of a group identity among first-year students. First, the admissions tutor would have had some idea of the kind of student for which he or she was looking, so in some senses your colleagues would tend to come from similar backgrounds and have similar characteristics in terms of expressed preferences. Secondly, the team of tutors and lecturers would be anxious to create a sense of belonging amongst the new recruits, of belonging to a particular institution, of having joined a particular and identifiable group with some status in the world deriving from, for example, the importance to Britain of business and hence of students of business given their future role as managers and entrepreneurs.

The result of the operation of these two factors will be the creation of a group or at least of a number of groups within the course. Course members will find others whose expectations and approach to life are similar to their own, who have the same or similar ideas about how to cope with their new life, and who share similar problems about the work. Individuals who appear able to cope particularly well with difficult courses may become the centre of a network of communication as people seek help with course work. Such people will establish reputations for reliable advice and expertise. Thus they may become influential in determining how their group functions: they may acquire a certain kind of power and become leaders.

Individuals will acquire status positions in relation to others: Joanna will always know how to cope with the course work in Accounts; Patrick can always be relied upon for a cheerful word when one is feeling particularly depressed about something; Caroline is very articulate in representing the students' interests on the scheme committee and is likely to succeed in getting the burden of course work deadlines reduced if anybody can! In this way group identities and ethos are established.

An important consequence of the process of group formation is that, no longer being just a collection of individuals who lack a coherent framework for action, a group can actually start exercising – if it wishes – countervailing power. A group as opposed to a collection of random individuals can organize, can establish an agreed definition of the situation and identify a solution. The security, comfort and enjoyment of belonging to an effective group means that such agreed solutions or strategies can be enforced upon doubting members. The ultimate sanction of exclusion can make the cost of not supporting the group very high: it is likely that the thought of going against the wishes of the majority would never enter the heads of group members.

In this way, a social group can become a major influence upon events

KEY CONCEPT 4.7

THE INFORMAL ORGANIZATION

This is how the work **actually** gets done, how the organization **actually** works. It may well bear little resemblance to the situation imagined by the MD as he contemplates his organization chart. Figure 4.4 is a representation of the informal organization which actually operated in the case of the company illustrated in Figure 4.3. (This particular example comes from Rosemary Stewart's book *The Reality of Management* (1983) but applies to any organization.) The Company Accountant

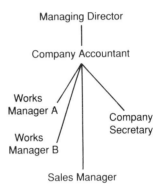

Figure 4.4 The informal organization.

was an old school friend of the Managing Director's; Works Manager B was younger and had been with the company a shorter time than Works Manager A and so, despite a position of formal equality, he actually behaved as a junior or subordinate to the older and more experienced man. The Sales Manager was actually an office boy amongst whose duties was filing sales office correspondence! The Company Secretary carried out the usual legal and administrative responsibilities of such a position. So, what the Managing Director knew about what went on was what was filtered through the Company Accountant.

since not only will knowledge and expertise be pooled, as in Blau's example, but the ability to control the actions of members produces what may be termed a 'disciplined force'. It is the operation of such processes that produces the 'informal' organization defined in Key Concept 4.7.

Mechanistic and organic forms of organization

We have now a link between the situations examined by Gouldner, Merton and Blau, and the next piece of research on organization structure and behaviour to be discussed, that carried out and reported by Burns and Stalker. Remember that one of the major criticisms of bureaucracy was that it was not able to handle complex or changing situations easily, although it was perhaps suitable for relatively stable situations. The concept of an informal organization enables us to observe a way in which organizations established according to bureaucratic criteria may yet be able

Burns and Stalker (1961) studied twenty firms, mainly in the electronics industry, in order to establish what the relationship was between technological innovation, rates of change, management procedures and organizational structure.

While they lacked any systematic measuring instruments and relied on in-depth interviews with managers and supervisors, Burns and Stalker were able to identify two distinct types of managerial system and organizational structure which they termed the 'mechanistic' and the 'organic'.

Under the mechanistic structure, seen by Burns and Stalker as characterized by stable environments, activities were broken down into specialist tasks performed by individuals almost independently of the activity of the organization as a whole. The feeling was that someone else, 'at the top', was responsible for integrating individual tasks into some meaningful purpose. The duties, power, authority and activity attaching to each role were clearly defined and working methods and operations were covered by instructions flowing down the hierarchy from superiors.

On the other hand, where technological and market factors were changing rapidly, it was not possible to give a precise breakdown of task activities – what may have been appropriate yesterday was not seen as applicable today. Individual tasks in such conditions have to be performed in the knowledge of the requirements of the enterprise, or at least the department, as a whole. Thus formal definitions of tasks and jobs break down. Interaction is not just vertical but also horizontal as tasks are redefined in exchanges with others directly affected by one particular activity. Consultation rather than command appears the main characteristic of interaction between superiors and subordinates.

CASE STUDY 4.6

THE WORK OF BURNS AND STALKER

The **mechanistic organization** displays the characteristics associated with the Weberian model of bureaucracy: vertical communication with instructions flowing downward and reports going upward, a specialized division of labour and coordination by a management hierarchy.

In contrast, an **organic organization** displays a less starkly defined range of responsibilities. While a hierarchy exists it is less important in terms of information flows. Rather than instructions and decisions flowing from top to bottom of the hierarchy, there is consultation and advice. This implies that management do not have a monopoly over decision-making or of the knowledge necessary for decision-making. In such organizations there is less emphasis upon status differentiation and the various ways of indicating differing status.

The organic organization is able to improve decision-making by virtue of the amount of information that can be handled in an informal context, thus avoiding overloading any one person or position. This kind of environment is also an important motivator since individuals are allowed

KEY CONCEPT 4.8

MECHANISTIC AND ORGANIC FORMS OF ORGANIZATION

Continued over page

Continued from previous page

considerable autonomy to suggest and try out new ideas which if successful will provide rewards of a material as well as psychological nature. However, as Burns and Stalker themselves stress: '. . . nothing in our experience justifies the assumption that mechanistic systems should be superseded by organic systems in conditions of stability' (1961, p. 125).

The key characteristics of a mechanistic system are:

☐ Work is broken down into specialized tasks;
☐ Such tasks tend to become ends in themselves for those carrying them out;
☐ Tasks are coordinated by superiors;
☐ Control, authority and communication is hierarchical (instructions flow down, and information flows up);
☐ Knowledge about overall purpose of the tasks is located towards the top of the hierarchy;
☐ The duties of, and methods to be used by, each task-holder are precisely defined;

The key characteristics of an organic system are:

☐ Individual tasks arise out of the problem situation;
☐ Knowledge and control may be located in a number of possible locations in the organization;
☐ While there may be a 'formal' structure, this is relatively unimportant in comparison with the 'informal' structure;
☐ Problem-solving will involve vertical **and** horizontal communication patterns in any pattern determined by the particular problem and perceived availability of skills/knowledge;
☐ Participation rather than 'instructions' characterizes communication and decision-making.

to cope with change and display innovative behaviour. In attempting to exercise some control over their work experiences, employees may, as in Blau's study, actually enhance the performance of the organization. The problem is that management will often assume that the excellent results are due to **their** rules, so demonstrating yet again the ease with which one can get the right answers for the wrong reasons.

Burns and Stalker's research is reported briefly in Case Study 4.6, and the nature of the two forms of organization they identified are set out in Key Concept 4.8.

Other approaches to organization structure and behaviour

We started our study of organizations in this chapter with an examination of bureaucracy since that is the form adopted by most public and private enterprises and the one associated in the minds of many people with negative evaluations of the behaviour of, and in, such enterprises. In contemporary thought 'bureaucracy' undoubtedly has pejorative connotations.

While bureaucracies may be, for good or ill, the typical form of organization in industrial society, there are at least two other related approaches to the study of organizational behaviour and structure that have been influential over recent years and which can be seen to develop from the insight that different structures and management styles may be appropriate to different environments. These are the 'systems' and 'contingency' approaches, which we will now consider.

The systems approach

The application of a systems approach to the study of organizational structure and behaviour became popular as a consequence of two factors: first, the successful application of operational research techniques and the development of cybernetics (the study of control systems in electronics and animal and human contexts) during World War Two; second, the influence in sociology of the 'functionalist' approach to the study of social life and institutions. The functionalist approach utilizes the analogy between biological structures seen as composed of circulatory, digestive and nervous systems for example, which interact to produce a functioning whole, and social systems dependent upon transport, communication, raw materials and socialization/education. (For a discussion of the systems approach to production systems see Chapter 6 of Needle's companion volume *Business in Context*.) The characteristics of the systems approach is set out in Key Concept 4.9.

The term 'systems theory' first appeared as a specific idea in a paper presented by Ludwig von Bertalanffy to a branch of the American Philosophical Association at its annual meeting in December 1950. This was published in the journal *Human Biology* in December 1951 as 'General systems theory: a new approach to the unity of science'. The idea that organisms should be regarded as 'open systems' had first been advanced by von Bertalanffy in 1932 and was based upon the realization that while physics and physical chemistry had been concerned exclusively with processes in closed reaction systems, developments in biology had resulted in the need to view cells and organisms as being 'open' to their environment and therefore not, in a technical sense, in a state of equilibrium but in a 'steady' state. That is, a state where a system remains constant though there is a continuous flow of component materials through it and its subsystems.

A critical feature of organizations is their ability, or lack of it, to adapt to changes in their environment. For example, changes in the product market characteristics brought about by competition will have an effect on outputs, and the availability of the correct quantity and quality of raw materials and labour will affect inputs.

The systems approach is extremely important in the design and implementation of information systems (discussed in more detail in Chapter 5), where 'system' is used both in its idiomatic sense – educational system, electricity supply system, computer system, transport system – and

KEY CONCEPT 4.9

THE SYSTEMS APPROACH

The basic model of a system can be represented as follows:

Input(s) → Process(es) → Output(s)

As Emery and Trist (1960) put it:

> Enterprises appear to posess ... these characteristics of 'open systems'. They grow by a process of internal elaboration and manage to achieve a steady state while doing work, i.e. achieve a quasi-stationary equilibrium in which the enterprise as a whole remains constant, with a continuous *throughput*, despite a considerable range of external changes.
>
> *(p.282)*

The systems approach to both organizations and management is very basic. It simply means that everything is interrelated and interdependent, just like the various layers in the business studies model used as a basis for this book and all others in the series. The important point is that changing one component of the system will have an impact upon other components and, following an 'open' systems approach, changes in the environment will have an impact upon the relations between components or subsystems of an organization. The organization must have contact with the environment since that is where inputs come from and to where outputs are delivered.

It is possible to identify a number of organizational subsystems contained within the organization viewed as a system, e.g. purchasing, personnel, marketing, production, finance. Subsystem outputs will be the inputs for other subsystems. For example, in a manufacturing company raw materials or components will be received from outside the firm, the environment. This will be handled by the purchasing or procurement subsystem which will have its own procedures for arranging the ordering, and meeting price and quality criteria. On receipt, the orders will be taken into the stores and checked, while the invoices will be sent to the finance department for payment.

Production will then be working on these materials or components which it draws from the stores as inputs to produce the finished product which is the output. This process will be linked with the sales function who deal with the world made up of customers outside the boundary of the firm. The sales department processes will link with the ordering systems of procurement and production as well as with finance to ensure payment is received.

in its technical sense in which the model shown in Key Concept 4.9 is used to represent the flows and processing of information. Indeed, modern organizations employ systems analysts to design not only information processing systems using computers, but also other control and work processes. This common use of the systems approach is important for our later discussions concerning the design of organizational structures. This is because the key factor which puts an organization as a system under stress is increased demands for information processing made on management and others. Such increased demands can result from changes in the environment which disrupt the routine processing activities of organizational subsystems.

As we saw from our earlier discussion of bureaucracy, rules can be effective when the situation for which they were designed remains stable. When that situation moves towards instability then the structure of the organization as well as those employed in it may not be able to cope with the extra demands for information processing necessary to adapt the rules to the changes. Or, as we saw in Blau's case, the extra demands are met by ignoring the rules. A computer system reacts to such overload by 'crashing' . . . as some of you may have found out already!

However, it is all very well asserting the usefulness of viewing organizations as systems but we must link this with the behaviour of those employed in organizations before we can appreciate its relevance. The **contingency approach** to management and organizational design attempts to do just this.

Before moving on to discuss the contingency approach to organizational structure and behaviour it should be noted that while organizations and systems are often spoken of as having 'goals' or 'objectives' or even 'needs', it is important to note that organizations (or systems) as such do not have these attributes. People do. Organizations and systems are constructed and maintained by people who see them as means of achieving goals or objectives, or of satisfying needs. Failure to remember this results in what is known as 'reification', explained in Key Concept 4.10.

'Reification' – literally 'thingification' – is the conferring of human attributes on non-human entities. That is, the attributing of thought and action to what is a social construct, e.g. Hatfield Polytechnic Higher Education Corporation, British Petroleum or the Ford Motor Company. To talk of the 'needs' of an organization is to attribute human qualities to an entity that is not human but simply the means utilized by social groups to obtain their objectives.	*KEY CONCEPT 4.10* *__REIFICATION__*

The contingency approach

This approach, the elements of which are set out in Key Concept 4.11, grew out of Joan Woodward's work, originating with *Industrial Organisation: Theory and Practice* in 1965. Woodward developed her ideas as a result of studying a hundred firms in South East Essex. She found that the ranking of these organizations in terms of relative success or failure did not in any way reflect the extent to which what at that time were the key principles taught on management course were applied by their respective managements.

A further application of the contingency approach is in the area of management accounting and information systems. Here it is assumed that there is no universally relevant accounting system applicable in all

KEY CONCEPT 4.11

***THE CONTINGENCY
APPROACH***

The contingency approach incorporates the environment using the open systems approach, but attempts to bridge the 'theory–practice' gap by assuming an 'if–then' relationship. 'The "if" represents environmental variables and the "then" represents management variables' (Luthans, 1981). So, **if** an organization is operating in a complex and changing environment **then** management should adopt an open and participative style which assumes that others than top management have the necessary skills to cope. However, **if** the organization operates in a stable market with a relatively simple product **then** management may appropriately adopt a rigid and authoritarian style and employ relatively unskilled workers.

It is possible to regard the environmental variables as **independent** variables, while the management variables are **dependent variables** – this is how the contingency approach usually views them. However, as we will see in Chapter 5, management may exercise some choice over the environment in which they operate.

organizations in all situations. Consequently accounting systems have to be designed to match the contingencies which may face a particular organization and its management at a particular time in a particular situation.

In the remaining sections of this chapter we will explore the issue of organizational structure and behaviour by looking at the three categories of contingency most frequently referred to in organizational and managerial literature, and which are represented in the two outer rings of the business in context model:

☐ environment (especially market related factors),
☐ size, and
☐ technology.

Before proceeding, however, it is necessary to clarify some issues related to the concept of control.

Control

You will recall that in Chapter 2 we discussed the Industrial Revolution in terms of its predominantly managerial nature since it reflected attempts to gain control over the location, nature and rate of work. 'Organization' too is about control. People 'organize' when there is too much information for them to handle on their own, because the collecting or processing – or both – imposes demands they cannot meet on their own.

Organizations are about the control of environments and the control of people. The organizations in which people are employed are structures of control and power, as we saw when discussing the employment relationship. The term control has a certain ambiguity: it is possible to observe the exercise of 'counter control', and it is possible to interpret control as 'domination' as well as regulation. In the latter sense, which is that of a control system, the concept may appear neutral and lacking any connotation of power since it is a requirement of any cooperative activity.

In the context of organizations, control operates on two levels. There is control at the level of capital and its provision, and (in the case of some organizations at least) control at the level of labour markets. Given the relative mobility potential of capital in comparison with labour, control over a labour market may be very real. A further level of control may be identified in the case of control over a production process and how employees perform their work.

The context in which control is exercised will display a combination of significant characteristics, namely complexity, unpredictability, uncertainty and risk. Two of the most important factors are perhaps complexity and unpredictability. The point is that whilst these terms are not necessarily synonymous they do have similar implications for those in organizations. A complex environment (in which there are many variables to handle) or an unpredictable environment (one which is changing in a way that is not readily foreseeable) increases the information processing demands upon organizational personnel and structures. Therefore either may produce uncertainty and actual or perceived loss of control. The relationship between uncertainty and risk is set out in Key Concept 4.12.

The point is that control is problematic; it depends upon the ability to identify and respond to factors which may undermine it. Effective control in organizations requires that attention be given to at least three contingent factors, namely the size, the technology and the environment within which the organization operates. The implications of these for organizational structure, and hence behaviour, are considered in the following sections.

Uncertainty (to be examined in more detail in Chapter 5) may be defined as the inability to assign probabilities to an outcome. This is important in distinguishing uncertainty from risk: risk arises when it **is** possible to assign probabilities to an outcome. One can assign a probability value beyond which one will not proceed with a course of action – one takes a risk, not a chance hopefully.

KEY CONCEPT 4.12

RISK AND UNCERTAINTY

Size and organizational structure

The argument that size is a major factor influencing organizational structure has a considerable history. Max Weber in his classic work on bureaucracy did not believe that small organizations would exhibit bureaucratic characteristics. You will remember that the term bureaucracy first came into common usage in European languages in the context of state administrative systems. Subsequently, studies by Pugh *et al.* (1969) and Blau (1970) have produced data indicating that increased size in terms of numbers employed produces structural differentiation within organizations, that is increasing resort to specialization and the consequent creation of departments. A useful account of the rise of large-scale organizations and administrative and managerial implications is contained in Presthus (1979). There are two strands involved in the argument concerning size and organizational structure according to Child (1972), that of size and specialization, and secondly that of impersonality.

☐ **Size and specialization**. This strand argues that increasing the size of an organization provides an opportunity to reap the benefits of specialization. Since increasing specialization is likely to result in increased differentiation as specialist departments arise, this will in turn increase the demand upon the information processing capacity of management as they attempt to coordinate the activities of the specialist departments. Impersonal control procedures are then likely to be designed and implemented.

☐ **Impersonality**. The second strand arrives at much the same conclusion by arguing that increasing the numbers employed makes it increasingly difficult to maintain personalized methods of managerial oversight and coordination. There appears to be some agreement that at some point between two and three hundred employees it becomes increasingly difficult for managers to maintain a personal contact basis for collecting, assimilating and transmitting information. In other words, at this point the personalized information system is in danger of becoming overloaded and if the organization is to survive then the information handling process has to be adapted to the new situation. It is in this kind of situation that a bureaucratic control strategy may appear inevitable, even if not actually attractive, to harassed managers.

One common response to information overload as organizations increase in size is to group together all those engaged in similar tasks. This of course is consistent with the idea of Adam Smith that specialization improves performance skills. Thus differentiation develops as departments are formed and responsibility for certain tasks are delegated to those departments and even sections within departments. This process may produce the form of organization where specialization is by function, e.g. finance, marketing, production, personnel.

By this process owners or entrepreneurs can reduce the information handling demands they experience. They can offload tasks which they like least or are least effective at, thus freeing themselves to concentrate upon key issues of strategy or those activities for which they have a particular aptitude.

Such a strategy on the part of management allows them to delegate without an inevitable loss of control over the activities of subordinates. Routine decisions can be delegated to junior members of the organization as a result of formalizing decision rules, setting them out on paper and requiring reports from subordinates. Thus the discretion of juniors is defined and actions outside the discretion limits are brought to the attention of superiors by regular reporting. What occurs is an apparent diminution in both centralization and personal supervision by superiors.

However, there are also motivational advantages to be gained from delegation. These will be dealt with in more detail in Chapter 6, but it is useful to consider them briefly at this point. The idea of individual freedom and initiative which can be said to characterize Western societies and

Western notions of democracy are likely to result in people giving more to their jobs when they feel able to exercise discretion and control over their work. While a worker's autonomy may be more apparent than real, the important point is that behaviour is affected by **perceived** autonomy and discretion. Even if senior management are still defining the parameters within which discretion is exercised, the fact that supervision is at a distance is crucial in enabling a worker to feel responsible, and so behave 'responsibly'. Bureaucracy as a control strategy may have advantages since employees may be able to use their initiative: they have the security of knowing what the decision rules are, and the security provided by the application of rules which minimize arbitrary treatment by superiors.

While the delegation, specialization and formality of a bureaucracy may have its positive side, it also has, as we have already seen, a negative side which becomes apparent when information overload again occurs. This may be because the organization continues to grow (fuelled by the employment of administrators required by the formalization associated with bureaucratization) or because of commercial success, or because the environment changes with the result that formalized processes are no longer effective and decisions are increasingly passed upwards to senior levels of management. At this point another form of structure may be available to management, that known as 'divisionalization'.

Divisionalization

A divisional organization structure is shown in Figure 4.5. In this case the firm is organized into product divisions, but it is also possible to have divisions based on geographical areas or even major clients or groups of clients.

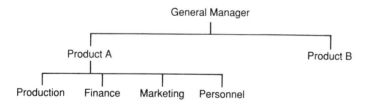

Figure 4.5 A divisional structure based upon products, but with each division organized into functional departments.

There are a number of advantages that the divisional form may have over a functional structure. First, important decisions can be taken nearer the centre of the action. Secondly, divisions can be assigned responsibility for profit and return on investment, thus enhancing motivation and training opportunities for general managers. Thirdly, shopfloor personnel may also be motivated if their monetary rewards are tied to their division's performance rather than being lost in the generality of corporate results where good performances in one area can be more than wiped out by poor performance elsewhere in the enterprise. Finally, the ability to evaluate the financial performance of the main activities of the enterprise separately makes it easier to formulate decisions concerning the allocation of investment funds.

Divisionalization may also have the potential to overcome what has been seen as a peculiarly British problem, the fragmentation of management due to a cultural emphasis upon professionalization. Functional specialists oriented towards the precepts and interests of professional bodies such as the Institute of Chartered Accountants or the Institute of Personnel Management and others, will tend to focus upon the intricacies of their specialism rather than the problems of the organization as a whole. Thus they are likely to identify with fellow specialists outside the organization rather than with colleagues in other functional areas. This is one of the aspects of contemporary British society deriving from the experience of industrialization, and social responses to it, that are blamed for the relatively low status of manufacturing industry in comparison with services like banking, law, finance and insurance (Child and Fores *et al.*, 1983).

A comparative study of manufacturing plants organized around functional and product structures found that the plant structured around products was characterized by functional experts who seemed aware of and acted in the interests of the plant as a whole (Walker and Lorsch, 1968). This suggests that while the problem of functional specialists is not confined to Britain, it is perhaps exacerbated in the British case by the cultural significance of professionalization as a means or raising an occupation's status in a society with a well-defined class system.

While the 'functional' plant in the Walker and Lorsch study was actually the most efficient, it adapted to change more slowly than the product organized plant. When variables are relatively few or stable there is time for adaptation and coordination of functional activities. When complexity or uncertainty are present a product division type of organization may be more appropriate since it will encourage communication and shared objectives amongst functional specialists.

However, a divisionalized structure assumes that organizational activities can be coherently grouped into self-contained divisions. In some cases the activities may not lend themselves unambiguously to such a grouping. What are the criteria by which such self-contained areas of activity are to be identified?

Assuming that coherent divisions with a minimum of interdependence can be identified, a further source of problems is that divisionalization may be a source of potential conflict. Conflict between divisions may occur over the funding of new investment or over the allocation of the costs of centrally provided services. The long-term interests of the enterprise as perceived by corporate managers at head office may not be consistent with the long- or short-term interests of general managers in the divisions, or those of their subordinates.

We have been discussing changes in organizational structure which may be brought about by increasing size though, as we have seen, environmental contingencies may also influence the selection of these structures as a response to information overload. It is worth noting before passing on to explore environmental factors in more detail that the divisionalized form is that followed by the majority of larger companies, especially those whose activities cross international boundaries. However, the precise basis of divisionalization may well be at the discretion of senior management.

Environmental influences on structure and control strategies

The systems approach is very much in evidence in this context since the basic assumption is that organizations depend upon exchanges with other organizations and with groups not involved in the organization itself. The management of an organization cannot define and attempt to achieve goals without taking account of the need to interact with others outside the organization. These others may control resources required by the organization and hence may be able to set the terms upon which they are acquired by the organization. Changing fashion, innovations and the action of competitors will all require that in the interests of survival management take account of the environment.

Three environmental conditions are commonly regarded as important for organizational structure and performance (Child, 1972):

☐ environmental variability;
☐ environmental complexity;
☐ the extent to which the environment is perceived as threatening.

Variability and complexity

Duncan (1972) provides a simple though persuasive representation of the variability/complexity aspect of environment as set out in Figure 4.6.

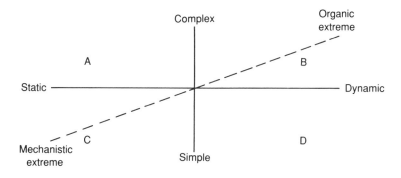

Figure 4.6 Dimensions of the environment.

Duncan's static/dynamic dimension relates to Child's use of the term variability. What is significant here is the degree of change occurring in the environment. The frequency, extent and rate of change are grouped under this heading. There is also a correspondence between Child and Duncan in terms of the definition of complexity. This refers to the number of variables which may change and which make up the environment. The idea is that change is problematic either because of the rate at which relatively few variables change, or because of relatively numerous variables that have to be coped with even if they are not changing rapidly or extensively. The most demanding environment will be one that contains relatively numerous variables (complex) that are changing rapidly and extensively (dynamic). Success in manufacturing for mass markets, for example, may well require tapping resources at the organic end of the continuum, and then moving towards the mechanistic to achieve market share. To move directly to the C quadrant may be unrealistic, but to move from B to A or D may be possible. The oft quoted apologia that the British are good at innovating but poor at implementation may be associated with this move from B. For example, Sir Clive Sinclair may be seen as an individual who operated very effectively at B, but was either uninterested or unable to make the transition from that quadrant. His association with Timex provided a link to an organization already established in one of the other quadrants.

A key point concerning complexity is that the greater the range and heterogeneity of environmental variables the greater will be the demands upon the information processing capacity of the organization. If the organization has slack in its system, then any given degree of complexity will not necessarily prove problematic. On the other hand, an organization that is already stretched in terms of information processing may find that a relatively small degree, or slow rate, of change is too much for its information processing capacities. The same thing goes for human beings. Those that are already stretched will find relatively minor events very demanding. Someone who is working within their capacity, and is not facing demands from outside work, will be able to cope with quite complex or dynamic situations.

Change can therefore represent a threat or an opportunity. If an organization or an individual has adequate resources and a relatively secure supply, then managers may well regard change as a challenge rather than a threat. As already mentioned individuals vary in their ability to tolerate uncertainty and this ability is a function of security, either the security that derives from having coped successfully in the past, or that which comes from the knowledge that adequate resources are or can be made available.

Whether perceived as threat or challenge, changes in the environment may well require that an organization responds in some way if it is to remain effective in terms of goal achievement – whatever and whosoever those goals may be. Thus there will be interaction between goals and the environment as the business in context model implies. If environmental changes make it less likely that, say, financial objectives will be attained then, rather than expend effort trying to maintain the expected rate of return in the existing field of business, an entrepreneur may decided to move into another area where the required returns may be more readily obtained.

The debate concerning the negative impact the City allegedly has on commercial innovation provides an example of a threat that managers may perceive in their environment. One consequence of the interest taken by the Stock Exchange in quarterly accounts is that firms are discouraged from making even essential investments if the immediate effect of that investment will be to reduce management's ability to maintain or increase the value of their dividends in the short term. The resulting possible drop in share price may make the company an attractive takeover proposition. While this may well be in the short-term interests of some shareholders, it can also be a considerable threat to the employees whose career and job prospects may be seriously threatened – directors included! While this particular environmental contingency is seen as a major problem for British businessmen (Plessey considered ceasing to publish quarterly results in 1987 – see *The Financial Times*, 21 August 1987), most authors who examine the impact of environmental factors on organizational structures and strategies concern themselves with more mundane, though not less significant, matters. For example, the product market in which an organization has to operate is seen as particularly significant.

The product market was a feature that the study by Burns and Stalker considered (see Case Study 4.6 earlier). Firms operating in stable markets, with few or very clear segments, will perceive the environment as lacking in (relative) complexity. Markets which are subject to variations in, say, fashion or rates of innovation may be perceived as complex and subject to rapid change. One response of course is to identify very clearly just what market segments or niches exist and concentrate on satisfying those for which the organization is particularly well equipped. This may reduce variability and complexity to levels which can be handled by current structures, but the identification of such niches may itself impose information processing demands which necessitate changes in the communication processes and hence changes in organizational structure.

The labour market

The labour market is another important source of variability and environmental uncertainty which may influence organizational structures. While the character of such a market may change relatively slowly, or at least with considerable warning, there are important implications for management. For example, the number of school-leavers in the population can be accurately estimated from birth rate figures sixteen years before the labour market is affected with possibly serious implications for employers who traditionally rely upon school-leavers for their labour force. The impact of changes in the birth rate on the numbers going on to higher education will also affect those who recruit graduates as well as the colleges, polytechnics and universities who produce them.

The state of the labour market also has implications for the training policies of firms. Depending upon the state of the labour market and decisions concerning the allocation of resources, a firm may cut back on training and poach skilled workers from other firms, or it may continue using outmoded technology since labour with the necessary skills is cheap and plentiful. Firms, both individually and as part of an industry, may find themselves having to respond to a labour market which is the result of actions they themselves have taken in the past. It is generally accepted that a major cause of the shortage of skilled workers in the engineering industry in the 1980s, for example, is due to the drastic cutback in the recruitment of apprentices in the 1960s and 1970s as firms struggled to adapt to a depression. Twenty years later, there is a shortage of 'prime age skilled workers', that is skilled workers between the ages of 25 and 45. Currently, of course, the more far-sighted employers are rigorously reassessing attitudes to training, recruitment and the retention of labour, especially women with children, as they come to terms with a dramatic decline in the numbers of school-leavers up to the mid-1990s.

Industrial relations

The state of the labour market may also be a major influence on the industrial relations policies pursued by firms. A tight labour market will tend to make firms 'price-takers' in terms of wage levels, and force them to accept working practices they might otherwise not. On the other hand, a plentiful supply of the necessary labour will mean that firms are 'price-setters', and will be able to get agreement on the working practices they want. Union recognition, and the facilities afforded union officials, may be susceptible to the perceived state of the labour market which, in a particular region or for particular skills, may also be a consequence of the state of the product market.

Union organization

It is worth noting that the same factors will influence the way unions themselves are organized and operate. Under the very tight labour markets of the late 1950s and early 1960s national union officials and managers alike were at the mercy of the power which shop stewards could exercise. Changes in the structure of employment as a result of the growth of part-time employment and of the proportion of women in the labour market has forced unions to reconsider both the service they offer and their methods of recruitment. Current debate over the need for trade unions to reassess their functions, structures and services reinforces the point that organizations other than commercial ones are affected by changes in the environment in which they operate.

Technology and organizational structure

There has been considerable interest in the way technology affects organizational structure and functioning since the pioneering work of Joan Woodward in the 1960s. Not only did her work throw doubt upon the practical relevance of much that had been written by the so called 'classical school' of management writers but it was also consistent with work on job design associated with the Tavistock Institute of Human Relations which developed the **socio-technical systems approach** to the relationship of technology and work experience described in Key Concept 4.13.

What is meant by 'technology'? 'Technology' itself is not a straightforward concept. Different writers have taken differing views as to what is implied by the term. Woodward, for example, defined technology in terms of the physical hardware, machines, tools, **and** what she termed the 'recipes' available at a given time for the execution of the production task. This approach tends to produce an emphasis upon the smoothness or otherwise of the workflow as illustrated by her typology of production technology set out in Table 4.3.

The problems associated with Woodward's definition of technology can be appreciated if one considers a company producing individual items to a customer's specification. Such a company would thereby fit in at the less sophisticated end of Woodward's continuum, with process production at

Utilising the notion of open systems the socio-technical systems approach argues that account has to be taken of both the social and technological variables when either designing a production process or attempting to understand the behaviour displayed by those working with it. 'Study of a productive system . . . requires detailed attention to both the technological and the social components' (Emery and Trist, 1960).

The concept of the 'socio-technical' system grew out of the study of early attempts to install mechanized systems of coal recovery in British mines after 1945 which were reported by Trist and Bamforth (1951). Prior to the installation of machinery the miners worked as almost self-recruiting and self-supervising groups. They were paid as a group for their output, and each group contained the necessary skills for the process of mining coal. After the installation of machines for cutting the coal, management reorganized working methods to get maximum machine utilization. This involved breaking up the relatively autonomous work groups and dividing them into specialized shifts. One shift would cut the coal, the second shift would prepare and load it for transport to the surface, they would be followed by the third shift who moved the machines forward and propped the roof ready for the first shift to return to do the cutting, and so on. This apparently rational response to the demands of mechanization by management disrupted production and morale to such an extent that the Tavistock Institute of Human Relations was retained to investigate.

They found that, rather like the situation in Gouldner's study, the miners depended upon the self-contained work group underground as a means of exercising some control over their work situation and earnings, and as a defence against the dangers of mining. Group loyalty and identity was important on both counts. In addition, a miner's status and his standing with his fellows underground was reflected in his status in the community on the surface. The reorganization instituted by the Coal Board not only destroyed the harmony which facilitated cooperation at work, but also reduced the range of tasks undertaken by the group and disrupted the system of social status in the wider community. Miners were confined to one specialized set of tasks and were dependent both for output and safety on people who were no longer part of their group and because of specialization might have different interests.

The Tavistock researchers suggested a 'composite' method of working the new machinery which took account of the social and psychological features of the old system of working.

the sophisticated end. However, such a company could make use of very sophisticated electronically controlled machine tools of the type associated with flexible manufacturing systems (FMS) or computer integrated manufacture (CIM). Such a factory would be regarded as automated and the use of such machinery would undoubtedly affect the way in which work was organized and controlled. On the other hand, as suggested by Table

Table 4.3 Woodward's typology of production technologies

Unit and small batch. Production to customer specification – prototypes or one-off large items of equipment such as power station generating sets.

Large batch and mass production. The 'typical' production line process of producing large quantities – motor manufacturing, for example.

Process production. Typified by the continuous-flow production of the petrochemical industry . . . and many processed food manufacturing techniques it should be noted!

4.3, petrochemicals and processed foods both appear at the more sophisticated end of the continuum. In the same way as one can envisage a unit production system using very sophisticated technology, it is also possible to envisage a situation where relatively unsophisticated tools are associated with a highly regulated production process with minutely prescribed tasks that produces a production flow similar to that obtained with far more complex machinery.

As Woodward (1970) and her colleagues pointed out 'The relationship between technology and behaviour . . . can be studied at two levels, by examining the *constraints* placed upon the behaviour of those individuals who come into direct contact with the technology of the organization; and by looking at those *salient* (i.e. important) features of the technology which limit the structure of the total organization to a greater or lesser degree.' However, while this is undoubtedly the case, there still remains to be investigated the social processes of decision-making which produce an observable outcome in terms of organizational structure.

A more useful conception of technology is provided by Perrow's (1970) idea of 'materials technology'. The argument is that the materials used,

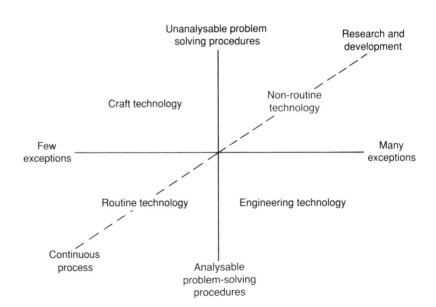

Figure 4.7 The Perrow model of technology.

and the extent to which problem-solving processes are analysable, will determine the extent to which work roles are highly structured or not, and hence influence the organizational structure. A representation of Perrow's approach is given in Figure 4.7. The vertical dimension indicates the extent to which the problem-solving methods available are programmable. However complex a decision process, if that process is analysable, via systems analysis techniques for example, then an algorithm can be prepared. The process can then be automated or less skilled workers can be trained to use the algorithm. The horizontal dimension reflects the variability an individual or group may face, the extent to which action is required in response to familiar events or unfamiliar ones. Familiar events tend towards the 'few exceptions' end of this continuum, while novel and unfamiliar events are at the 'many exceptions' end. In terms of structures and control mechanisms, the dotted line maps directly onto that in Figure 4.6 of Duncan's model. In continuous process technology many decisions concerning control and how it will be exercised are incorporated into the design of the plant and its equipment.

The similarity of Perrow's approach to that of Burns and Stalker is readily apparent. The easier it is to describe problem-solving or search procedures – and hence to program in the computer software sense – and the less variable the materials and processes are, then the more highly structured or mechanistic an organization will tend to be. The more difficult the problem-solving activities are to describe, and so to program, and the more variable the materials and process are, then the less structured and more organic the organization will be.

Implications for organizational structure

It is at the level of the implications for organizational structure that the idea of technology as an independent factor in organizational design is weakest. This is because it turns attention away from the choices which management can make concerning the implementation of specific technologies and the way they impact upon behaviour. The point is that the process of selecting and designing an installation of any given technology leaves room for a range of possible work and job design options. The key issue then becomes the choices that are made and by whom when decisions are taken about how an organization is to be operated and the type of market situation in which it is to operate. This issue will be further discussed in Chapter 5.

The preceding sections of the chapter have examined, very briefly, some of the major influences on the structure of organizations and on behaviour within them. One of the problems in understanding organizational structures and their operation is the uncertainty over the actual causal mechanism by which a particular environmental variable produces an observed effect. Such a matter is either of little interest to business people, or ignored altogether. For a particular environmental feature to have the impact of an independent variable, those operating in that environment much perceive its significance and consider it sufficiently important to be worthy of attention. Both this perception and the reaction to it, to do something **or** nothing, will be determined by the world view of those who are able to exercise control over the organization.

As we saw in Chapter 2, the factory itself was a social technology which facilitated the development and application of machinery **and** which also significantly determined the way in which that machinery should be used, that is the conditions under which work would be controlled. While those who were responsible for the industrialization process were undoubtedly responding to their environment, their response was itself dependent upon prevailing ideology and the formulation of objectives as a result of that ideology. In Woodward's terms, certain **recipes** were seen as being available and appropriate while others were not. As we will see when we look at international comparisons in Chapter 10, cultural and ideological factors influencing the availability of recipes are crucial in identifying what lessons if any can be learnt from the management strategies of other nations.

It is possible that any association between, say, size, technology and environment on the one hand and organizational structure on the other may well be the result of decisions and choices made by those who control organizations. It is to this question of strategic choice, and the ability to implement such a choice, that we turn in Chapter 5.

Summary

This chapter has considered organizations in modern society and the major factors which may influence the way in which they are structured. Attention was also given to the way in which organizational structures can influence the behaviour of members of the organization. Table 4.4 summarizes the major studies considered throughout the chapter.

The chapter started by examining the significance of organizations in modern society and some of the questions which this raises about the nature of modern democracy. It was noted that there is an important paradox at the centre of the debate over the nature and relevance of bureaucracy. This concerns the idea that in a democratic society citizens will be dealt with, and will deal with each other, according to criteria which are considered relevant and that are not applied arbitrarily. Such a society, which presumes the application of rules in a consistent manner, presupposes and indeed implies the existence of bureaucracy. The paradox is that the existence of bureaucracy does **not** imply democracy! This is due to the fact that those who control large organizations are able to exercise control over the resources of the organization and avoid close supervision by those nominally 'owning' them.

Discussion then moved on to consider the ideas of Max Weber on the nature of bureaucracy and the criteria by which it may be judged 'rational'. We further examined case studies undertaken by researchers who were basically sceptical of Weberian assertions concerning bureaucracy. This examination suggested that the differing perceptions of bureaucracy were due, in part at least, to the perceived compatibility of differing organizational structures with environments of varying stability and predictability.

The chapter went on to suggest that much of the negative evaluation of

Table 4.4 Major studies considered in Chapter 4

Writer	Main ideas and approach	Critique
Weber	The identification of an organizational form closely associated with industrialization. This represented a form of authority or domination referred to by Weber as 'legal-rational'. Bureaucracy was rational because it involved a consideration of the relationship between means and ends fundamental to the rule-making process. This form of authority distinguished industrial from non-industrial societies and was dominant in industrial society.	Weber failed to recognize the extent to which individuals or groups would use the positions they occupied to pursue their own ends. This renders bureaucracy less than 'rational' and not necessarily 'efficient'. Weber did not in fact argue that bureaucracy was 'efficient', only that it was rational in a way that other forms of authority such as traditional and charisma were not.
Gouldner	Bureaucracy was not 'rational', nor was it 'efficient'. This was demonstrated by a study in which the imposition of rules in a work situation characterized by informal accommodation between management and workers resulted in disruptions to output and eventually a strike, the first for many years. The disruption was due to the application of rules which assumed regularity in a work situation (a gypsum mine) in fact characterized by unpredictable changes in working conditions due to geological factors, and strong group cohesion amongst miners to combat dangers inherent in mining. In the factory which used the gypsum, which was characterized by a certain regularity or predictability, bureaucratic rules may be 'efficient'.	As stated above, the 'efficiency' of bureaucracy was not argued by Weber. Bureaucracy was 'rational' since it involved a means–ends calculation missing from other forms of authority associated with pre-industrial society. All organizations have some need for bureaucratic features to ensure survival.
Merton	The existence of rules which characterized bureaucracies resulted in the 'trained incapacity' of workers. The stultifying effect of rule-following meant that people lost the ability to use their own initiative and discretion. Instead of being the rational means of achieving a rational end or objective, the rules became ends in themselves, to be applied irrespective of their relevance to particular circumstances. It was this feature of bureaucracy that resulted in the pejorative connotations of 'red tape'.	Fails apparently to consider that it is the more junior members of an organization that will have most contact with the clients of the organization. These junior members are dependent upon superiors for favourable assessments. This source of insecurity puts juniors under pressure to demonstrate both their knowledge of the rules and their ability to apply them. Their dependent position within the organization makes it unlikely they will take it upon themselves to innovate.
Blau	Informal behaviour on the part of work groups ignoring or breaking organizational rules may actually enhance organizational performance and work group morale. Later editions of the study explicitly recognize the role of rules in providing a stable environment within which individuals may be able to calculate the risks of innovative actions or decisions.	Realistic overall assessment of bureaucracy as a control strategy. Recognizes that security derived from the existence of rules enables individuals and groups to engage in innovative behaviour which may enhance organizational performance. It is dependence or insecurity, rather than rules *per se*, which encourages rigid conformity.

Table 4.4 (continued)

Writer	Main ideas and approach	Critique
Burns and Stalker	The elaboration of the thesis that stable environments are consistent with, and may even require, routine formality – a 'mechanistic' style of management. Relatively unstable environments, those characterized by change, will require 'organic' structures and behaviour with little emphasis on formal hierarchy. This is in the interests of gaining maximum cooperation to complete tasks that no one group or individual could handle alone.	A classic study providing a foundation for the so-called 'contingency approach'. Within an organization different departments, functions or divisions may have different structural and behavioural requirements. Different structures and behaviour may be appropriate in different environments.
Woodward	The application of 'principles of management' could not be correlated with success, nor could failure to apply the principles be correlated with failure. The data gathered from 100 firms in Essex did, however, appear to show that a match was required between structure and technology. Technology could be defined in terms of the type of production process and the techniques available to the organization. It was possible to identify structural features which were compatible with production systems characterized by: 'one-off', small batch, large batch, and mass or continuous production processes.	A key study which had considerable impact on the understanding of organizational structures and behaviour. Originally criticized for an overly deterministic approach to technology, and a crude or simplistic notion of what constituted 'technology'. In the early studies, technology appeared to be equated with the smoothness of the production flow. Both these issues were addressed in later work by Woodward and, after her untimely death, by colleagues at Imperial College.
Perrow	The appropriateness of organizational structures to the demands of the product market environment, and hence their form, depended upon the extent to which problem-solving processes were analysable (i.e. programmable), and the frequency with which exceptions would confront decision-makers.	Overcomes some of the definitional problems of technology. Avoids an emphasis on the smoothness of production flow characterizing Woodward's earlier work. Recognizes that many routine production systems may use advanced technology, while advanced technology in terms of the machines may be used to produce 'one-off' items.
Crozier	A study of how a very formally structured system, that of the French cigarette manufacturing monopoly, may put quite disruptive power into the hands of a group whose role centred around the least, apparently, predictable events – machine breakdown.	Addresses the issue of power in a way many of the other studies do not, including Weber. The ability to cope with unpredictabe matters was what gave the maintenance crews in the cigarette factories their power to exercise control. In addition, none of the methods and procedures they used were written down, hence there was little danger that others would be able to understand what they did. This again illustrates how the existence of written rules and procedures characteristic of bureaucracy may actually facilitate rather than hinder adaptability. Planned preventative maintenance is not a widely used bureaucratic response to the type of situation described by Crozier.

bureaucracies and their employees was due to the fact that employees, especially junior ones, were required to demonstrate both knowledge of the procedures and reliable operation of them. This could provoke irritation from clients and so reinforce the negative stereotype.

It was also suggested that the existence of consistently applied rules enables organizations to adapt to changing environments. This is because knowledge of the rules provides a framework within which groups of workers can innovate, either by way of the 'informal' organization, or by calculating the likely consequences of any infringement both for themselves and the organization.

The systems and contingency approaches represent attempts to link theory and practice and lead on to a consideration of a number of factors which might affect the structure of an organization, such as size, technology and the market environment, be it bureaucratic or not.

A major problem arising from change is the extent to which managers and their organization structures may be overloaded with information. Thus, functional and divisional structures can be viewed as attempts to reduce the burden of information gathering and processing to manageable proportions.

Finally, it was suggested that any relationship between the factors discussed and organizational structures may be the result of the exercise of choice by management. In Chapter 5 we will examine the basis of power in organizations since this is crucial to the ability to exercise real choice. Chapter 5 will extend the discussion to a consideration of developments in information technology since these are likely to be as significant for future organizations and their management as mechanization was 150 years ago.

Study questions

1. Upon what basis may it be argued that bureaucracy is rational?
2. What is meant by 'trained incapacity' and how could managers avoid it in their subordinates?
3. Describe the forms of authority identified by Weber, and identify in your organization/college who might be grouped under each.
4. What are the basic assumptions underlying (a) the systems and (b) contingency approaches to organizations?
5. How might bureaucratic features of an organization actually facilitate rather than hinder change?
6. In the context of the administration of your course, or of the department within which it it located, or of your employing organization, construct a chart showing (a) the formal, and (b) the informal organization.

Further reading

The literature on organizations is immense – the major problem is identifying that which is most useful/relevant for one's purpose. A particularly useful guide to the main issues is contained in Burrell and

Morgan (1979). While this work is unashamedly sociological and theoretical, it is important to recognize that underlying the vast majority of writing on organizations are concepts drawn more or less explicitly from sociological analysis and theory.

Other useful texts include the following:

☐ Presthus (1979) offers an examination of the implications of modern organizations for the nature of contemporary society.
☐ A key article examining factors influencing organizational structure is that by Child (1972).
☐ An account of the development of the study of organizations and their impact upon those working in them is contained in Rose (1988).

References

Berle, A.A. and Means, G.C. (1947) *The Modern Corporation and Private Property*. Macmillan.

Blau, P. (1963) *The Dynamics of Bureaucracy*. Chicago University Press.

Blau, P. (1970) A formal theory of differentiation in organizations. *American Sociological Review*, **35**, 201–18.

Burns, T. and Stalker, G.M. (1961) *The Management of Innovation*. Tavistock.

Burrell, G. and Morgan, G. (1979) *Sociological Paradigms and Organisational Analysis*. Heinemann.

Child, J. (1972) Organizational structure, environment and performance: the role of strategic choice. *Sociology*, **6**, (1), 1–22.

Child, J. (1984) *Organisation: A Guide to Problems and Practice*, 2nd edn. Harper & Row.

Child, J., Fores, M., Gtover, I. and Lawrence, P. (1983) A price to pay? Professionalism and work organization in Britain and West Germany. *Sociology*, **17**, (1), 63–78.

Crozier, M. (1964) *The Bureaucratic Phenomenon*, Tavistock.

Duncan, M. (1972) Characteristics of organizational environments and perceived uncertainty. *Administrative Science Quarterly Review*, **17**, 313–27.

Emery, F.E. and Trist, F.L. (1960) Socio-technical systems. In Emery, F.E. (ed.) *Systems Thinking*. Penguin.

Gouldner, A. (1964) *Patterns of Industrial Bureaucracy*. Free Press, New York.

Gouldner, A. (1965) *Wildcat Strike*.

Katz D. and Kahn R.L. (1966) *The Social Psychology of Organizations*, Wiley.

Lee, D. and Newby, H. (1983) *The Problem of Sociology*. Hutchinson.

Luthans, F. (1981) *Organisational Behaviour*, 3rd edn. McGraw Hill.

March, J.G. and Simon, H.A. (1958) *Organisations*. Wiley.

Merton, R.K. (1957) Bureaucratic structure and personality. In *Social Theory and Social Structure*. Free Press, New York.

Perrow, C. (1970) *Organisational Analysis: A Sociological View*. Tavistock.

Presthus, R. (1979) *The Organisational Society* (rev. edn). Macmillan.

Pugh, D., Hickson, D., Hinings, C. and Turner, C. (1969) The context of organization structures. *Administrative Science Quarterly*, **4**, (1), 91–114.

Rose, M. (1988) *Industrial Behaviour*, 2nd edn. Penguin.

Scott, J. (1985) *Corporations, Classes and Capitalism*, 2nd edn. Hutchinson University Library.

Sherif, (1967) *Group Conflict and Cooperation: their social psychology*, Routledge.

Stewart, R. (1983) *The Reality of Management*, 2nd edn. Heinemann.

Trist, E.L. and Bamforth, K.W. (1958) Some Social and Psychological consequences of the Long Wall method of Coal Getting. *Human Relations*, **4** (1), 3–38.

Walker, A. and Lorsch, J. (1968) Organizational choice: product vs function. *Harvard Business Review*.

Wiener, M.J. (1981) *English Culture and the Decline of the Industrial Spirit 1850–1980*. Cambridge University Press.

Woodward, J. (1965) *Industrial Organisation*. Oxford University Press.

Woodward, J. (1970) *Industrial Organisation: Behaviour and Control*. Oxford University Press.

Strategic choice and the basis of power in organizations

In this and the following chapter we approach the central area of the business in context model around which this series is based. This area denoted as 'strategies' and 'information' surrounds the list of business activities at the core of the model. Information and decision-making are dealt with in Chapter 6, while this chapter will consider the issues of strategy and power.

The definition of 'strategy' which will be used in this chapter is given in Key Concept 5.1. Defined in this way, a strategy will have implications for both the structure of an enterprise and the relations between those activities listed in the centre of the model and which are usually (but not necessarily always) associated with specialized departments, as discussed in Chapter 4.

One of the major problems in manufacturing enterprises in the UK at the present time, and one which is argued to have hindered the competitive capability of British business generally, is that the organizational structure in terms of functional activities at the centre of the model of business not only separates the activities of key groups, but subsequently measures their performance by reference to different criteria. This is illustrated in Figure 5.1. Some of the problems likely to arise in this context, and which have important implications for strategy formulation and implementation, are demonstrated in Case Study 5.1.

Whatever the size of the company involved, there is the probability that

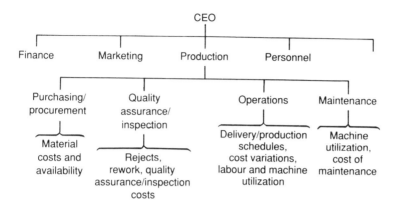

Figure 5.1 Departments and varying performance measures. Adapted from Hayes and Jaikumar (1988).

Martin Andrews is Managing Director of a medium-sized manufacturing business providing components to the automobile industry. The company has a good reputation and has been able to maintain a range of customers which enable it to avoid dramatic fluctuations in output.

Current changes taking place in the automobile industry as a result of increasing competition from Japan, especially the arrival of Nissan in the UK and efforts by other Japanese car manufacturers to establish themselves before 1992, were forcing Martin to improve the quality of his products and service while avoiding any price increase. His largest customer had indicated that in the medium term price reductions would be looked for.

Having studied production engineering and worked in Germany and the USA (where he had spent a semester at the Harvard Business School) before joining the firm ten years ago, Martin was aware of what steps he needed to take. The problem was going to be implementing them. For example, improving the quality of his products while remaining within the current price bands, was going to put pressure on the procurement, production and quality control functions. Waste and re-working would have to be reduced, 'right first time' must become the watch word, and some of the more aged machines would have to be replaced by up-to-date equipment. So the finance and training functions would also be affected.

Marketing would also be affected as they would be under pressure to develop marketing plans that reflected the new strategy. Sales reps may have to develop different skills and accept a different emphasis in their work. They may have to be more technically competent in order to liaise more closely with production and to help customers get the most from the higher quality products as well as to counter the efforts of rival sales staff.

A friend of Martin's who was employed by a major engineering company had a number of warnings for him. Efforts to reduce inventories, especially if associated with just-in-time systems and frequent deliveries of relatively small quantities, would create a number

CASE STUDY 5.1

FUNCTIONS, PERFORMANCE CRITERIA AND INNOVATION

Continued over page

Continued from previous page

of problems. For example, frequent deliveries of small quantities, perhaps a number of times a day, suggests the need to deal with relatively few suppliers who because of their flexibility and/or location could cope with the new demands. However, such suppliers may be unable to match the unit prices offered by those supplying large quantities. This would have the effect of making the procurement function look less effective under existing systems, while those responsible for materials handling would look more effective.

A reduction in work in progress would reduce, if not eliminate, buffer stocks, so increasing the chances of those responsible for production falling behind on their schedules, which in turn would put them under increased pressure. In addition, the effect of reducing scrap, re-working and the number of rejects would reflect favourably upon the quality control staff, but the effect may be to put the production workers under more pressure since they could appear less productive.

There would also be the question of the financial and accounting procedures. Not only could there be a problem about meeting conventional investment criteria if Martin was to invest in electronically based production technology, but once that investment was made, the cost accounting system would have to be adapted because it would be likely that direct labour costs would become a very much smaller proportion of total costs with implications for the design and operation of the costing system. A costing system designed when direct labour was a significant proportion of total costs would, if unchanged under the new conditions, result in the company spending up to 80% of its effort monitoring 15–20% of total costs.

Finally, if Martin was thinking of investing in new, microelectronic based equipment such as CNC (computer numerically controlled) machines he would need to be aware that maximum benefit would only be obtained if internal restructuring took place. For example, design staff might have to cooperate much more closely with production in order to realize the opportunities for flexibility in the new technology. On the other hand, rather than cooperation with production, designer staff could be organized to work more closely with sales and marketing staff in order to react more quickly to customer demands.

All of these issues would be extremely time consuming to sort out, but were crucial if the company was to survive let alone flourish under the new environment. A key question that Martin would have to consider is the extent to which his existing staff in various key positions would be able to cope, temperamentally as well as technically.

for any one strategic decision, there may well have been an alternative. For example, given the changes taking place in the motor industry, should the company in Case Study 5.1 decide to stick with that industry or look elsewhere for its markets? Instead of staying with mass producers in the industry, could it reduce some of the pressure by concentrating on other sectors of the industry, say speciality or quality vehicles where the demands on quality would be mitigated to some extent by the reduction in volume? Instead of maintaining a range of products for both the motor industry and other manufacturers should it concentrate on a narrower product range? For both types of customer? Or for only one? Should the company seek some form of association with a company that has a complementary product range and faces similar problems?

The point is that at the level of strategy and strategy implementation a choice amongst alternatives will be made by somebody (an individual or a group) with the power to do so. A particular interpretation of the threats and opportunities facing the enterprise will be established, as will the selection of one of a number of alternative strategies to deal with those threats and opportunities. It is possible of course that everyone involved shares precisely the same views about problems and solutions – possible, but by no means probable!

This chapter will examine the role and basis of power in organizations, and the implications for strategy formulation and implementation. In this way we will extend the discussion in the last chapter about organizational structure and the factors which determine it.

The implications of information systems for decision-making in organizations will be discussed in Chapter 6. The present chapter will start by examining the key role of theory in determining practical solutions, and will then move on to discuss the implications of considering management as a political process which involves the exercise of power over the process of selecting, defining and implementing strategic alternatives in business.

Why bother with theory?

The result of many years research into the factors affecting the structure of organizations and managerial strategies has been described as a 'theory jungle' (Luthans, 1973). This was not without some justification and reinforced the view of practising managers that academic research has little to offer those who must cope with 'real' life in the 'real' world. The so-called theory jungle was the result of research and writings in which, among other things, the definition of technology itself was confused and confusing, and which failed to distinguish between simplistic empirical relationships and causal explanations.

The major factor contributing to the growth of a 'jungle' was the almost total disregard for any effort to establish a theoretical basis for the research that was carried out, or for what was asserted on the basis of that research. In the debate over the role of technology and its influence on organizational structure this is exemplified by the confusion over what was meant by 'technology' in the first place. The actual process by which a given set of hardware ('technology' in the sense of the actual machines) resulted in the observed structure of an organization was virtually ignored. Little, if any, attention was paid to the social and political processes within organizations that moulded human behaviour so that a particular organizational structure resulted.

A feature of the study of human behaviour in work organizations up to the mid-1970s was a lack of interest on the part of managers and social scientists in questioning the assumptions underlying the very kind of questions they were asking and attempting to answer. In part at least this was due to the fact that social scientists, in order to be allowed to conduct research in organizations, were constrained to work on problems that management themselves had defined. Access by researchers to companies and employees was (and still is) on condition that research focused on what management thought the problem was, not what employees or social scientists for example thought the problem might be (Baritz, 1975). The result was that study followed study, data was heaped upon data, statistical association followed statistical association among taken-for-granted definitions of what were assumed to be relevant variables. Very few attempts were made to develop an underlying theory that might have made sense of the accumulating data, and which might therefore have prevented a jungle-like profusion of research findings.

In this chapter it will be argued that a way out of the jungle is available by means of the idea that while management decisions may be constrained by environmental and technological factors, they are not determined by them. There is some room for choice, even if it is a somewhat limited choice on occasions. The idea that management has a choice focuses attention on the processes within organizations by which options are identified and implemented, and this in turn directs attention to the question of who in the organization has the power to implement choices. This is wholly in keeping with the business in context model and its central theme that behaviour in organizations is not only influenced by its organizational and environmental context but also that some behaviour goes some way to shaping those contexts.

It will be argued that the idea of managerial choice in the context of strategy offers a better understanding of the impact of factors such as size, environment or technology on organizational structures and functioning than any number of statistically identified associations between these factors and organizational characteristics. In other words, the idea of strategic choice offers a theoretical framework lacking in much of the research work up to the 1970s, and consequently reduces the jungle-like confusion of accumulated evidence identified by Luthans.

The role and nature of theory

In the following paragraphs, the importance of a theoretical understanding for those dealing with the practical problems of running and managing a business will be explored. Subsequent sections of the chapter will build upon this discussion and focus upon the exercise of power in the process of strategy formulation and implementation.

Business people are by definition practical people; they are concerned to deal with the world as it appears to them, now. They do not have much patience with people who are considered to place too much emphasis on **analysing** problems rather than developing **practical** solutions. The practical person, the man or woman of action, is the entrepreneurial folk hero. If, as a result of such emphasis on practice rather than theory, the business flourishes, then positive reinforcement is given to the idea that the 'practical' is not just different from but superior to the 'theoretical'.

The notion that this distinction between theory and practice is at best naive was succinctly put by the economist John Maynard Keynes when he suggested that the so-called 'practical' person was usually the slave of some defunct theorist! The point is that practice is always based upon some theory – indeed, there is nothing quite so practical as a good theory.

The following paragraphs explore, briefly, the importance of theory for practical people. A definition of 'theory' is offered in Key Concept 5.2.

A 'theory' is a statement concerning a set of assumptions about the relationship that exists between observable (or even as yet unobservable) phenomena which is intended to provide an explanation of past or current events, and a prediction concerning future events.

The test of a theory, the reason for preferring one theory over another, is not 'truth' but 'utility', the economy with which it is able to produce reliable predictions. If what is predicted actually occurs and there is no *ad hoc* introduction of statements to account for what is observed on separate occasions, then the theory can be said to be **useful**. It cannot be said to be **true**. It is possible to get the right answer for the wrong reasons!

Arabian astronomers of the twelfth century were able to make very accurate observations concerning the movement of planets and stars and yet fitted all these into an erroneous (and complex) model of the solar system, with the earth at the centre. Copernicus hit upon the principle of the Sun centred system as a result of the application of what is known as 'Occam's razor'. Using the same basic observations as the earlier astronomers, but aware of the increasing number of irregularities and anomolies, Copernicus asserted that the system must be simpler than that represented by the Ptolomean celestial chart with its mass of circular orbits arranged as epicycles and deferents on epicycles. 'It must be more simple than that' is the basic principle of Occam's razor for selecting between competing theories. Copernicus found the required simplicity by substituting the Sun for the Earth at the centre of the system.

Copernicus was not totally without error himself, because he retained the idea of spherical orbits in his system, and it was not until Keppler showed that eliptical orbits removed even more long-standing anomolies that the modern view of the solar system was established.

Celestial navigation, however, using measurements by sextant of the angle of the Sun, Moon and stars is still widely used, is accurate, and yet is based on an Earth-centred solar system. Thus the Ptolomean system is still 'useful' in a limited way.

Einstein had the same effect on Newtonian physics as Copernicus had on astronomy. It was not that all Newton's ideas were demonstrably wrong, though some were. His ideas were replaced by Einstein's because Einstein could explain everything Newton explained **plus** phenomena that Newton had no knowledge of at all!

KEY CONCEPT 5.2

THEORY

The crucial role of theory in practical activity can be illustrated by undertaking the following simple, exercise.

Exercise
1. Stop reading and get a sheet of paper and pen/pencil.
2. Now follow the instruction in 3 below.
3. Observe, and then write down clearly what you observe.

You would have soon realized that without some indication as to what, exactly, you were supposed to be observing, the instruction was meaningless! This is precisely why any practical activity depends upon some theory, however limited in range. Without some idea of what you are supposed to be looking for, you have no idea what you are expected to see. Observations of the real world, and hence theories about how it works, are crucially dependent upon expectations and preconceptions. For example, the idea that people are motivated mainly by money, especially at work, derives from observations which are made about the operation of a system in which that idea is itself a key presumption. It is hardly surprising that people react towards monetary rewards in a particular way when that is the way in which work is structured.

The point is not that the statement 'people are motivated by money' is untrue, but that the extent to which it holds true is limited. The statement and theory of human motivation it presumes is of limited utility and only holds under limited conditions. One of those conditions of course is the domination of the idea that the individual pursuit of self-interest (or profit) is the most effective means of increasing the benefits received by all. (The question of motivation at work will be examined further in Chapter 7).

The point about practical people is that they actually pride themselves on **not** asking questions about their favourite theories. In this way 'theory' is defined as something separate and distinct from 'practice'. This approach can be summed up as 'Do not adjust your mind, reality is at fault.' An atheoretical attitude may not be a problem when the world is relatively simple and unchanging. In such a world, what worked today will work tomorrow because tomorrow's problems will be the same as today's, and **they** are similar to yesterday's problems. In other words, there is no change.

Where things do not change, or if they do then only very slowly, the prime requirement for success is experience. The longer a person's experience (i.e. the older they are) then the more they will know about what is going on since they will have seen it all several times before. This is the reason why in societies where change is slow, the old are accorded a special place and age is the prime criterion for advancing in status. In a society that is changing rapidly age, by definition, can easily preclude an individual from being perceived as having much of any use to say at all.

The relative utility of experience and theory

There are at least two problems with relying upon experience in a changing world. First, experience is like a rear-view mirror in that it tells you where you've **been**, rather than where you are going. Secondly – and importantly in terms of organizational careers – what exactly is meant by, say, 'ten years' experience'? Is it indeed ten years' experience, or is it one year's experience ten times over?

Does the same problem ever occur twice? Even acting on the assumption that today's problems are similar to yesterday's poses a theoretical problem. When it is argued that things or events are 'similar', they are always similar in certain respects. 'Similarity' presupposes a point of view – a theory – about what the key features are by reference to which two objects or situations may be said to be 'similar'. Even if the problem today is **identical** in all respects, as opposed to being only identical in major respects, the context of the problem will not be the same. Today's context in which the identical problem occurs is a function of how you were able to deal with it yesterday. If you dealt with it successfully, then today it is a problem you know how to handle. If you were unable to cope yesterday,

---

□ In about 1910 the International Commercial Truck Company of the USA issued an advertisement which included the following management consultancy advice:

CASE STUDY 5.2

INNOVATION VS EXPERIENCE

While the motor truck is an excellent substitute for the horse, the business which uses the truck simply as a substitute for the horse will be ignoring the new opportunities the truck makes possible. Not being a machine the horse can manage about five to six hours work a day and can cover up to twenty-five miles. The truck on the other hand can work for twenty-four hours a day and will cover the last twenty miles at the same rate as it covered the first twenty. To get the most from the new vehicle it will be necessary to change the pattern of routes and schedules. Hold-ups which may have been necessary to rest, feed and water a horse are time 'lost' for the motor vehicle. The point is to keep a truck busy for the entire day with as few hold-ups as possible.

(From Hayes and Jaikumar, 1988).

□ Isambard Kingdom Brunel wrote a letter to the Captain of the SS Great Britain pointing out that the new ship was not to be organized, managed or navigated as though it were a different type of sailing vessel. Being largely independent of the wind direction different attitudes and procedures were required if the full benefits of the new design and machinery were to be achieved.

□ A major problem in many plants and offices where microelectronic machines are introduced is that often these highly flexible machines are used as though they were no more than faster or more accurate versions of the ones they replaced. Thus word processors are used as though they were just the latest model of typewriter and machine tools capable of turning out a considerable number of different components are used to produce no more than a fraction of their potential range of items, albeit machined to finer tolerances than previously.

then today the identical problem is one that you have already failed to handle. So the same problem can be either one that you can handle **or** one that you cannot. In a very real sense it is **not** the **same** problem.

It is the very fact that the modern world is one characterized by change that makes concern with theory of practical importance. Since all practice is based upon **some** idea of how the world actually works, then there is nothing quite so practical as a theory that can account (without self-contradiction or *ad hoc* modifications) for a greater range of observable phenomena than other theories. Such a theory will allow a greater number of reliable predictions to be made: it is more 'useful'. Examples of the dangers inherent in relying on experience in a changing world are given in Case Study 5.2.

Theory and criteria of success

A further issue confronting the managers of organizations can be illustrated when we talk of dealing with a problem 'successfully'. We are implicitly talking about the selection of criteria by reference to which 'success' is to be defined. Such a selection also presupposes a point of view. In the case of business organizations this can be illustrated by the debate concerning what it is that business is supposed to be about. 'Profit maximization' is the most common justification, rationalization and explanation that is used – it is also the most naive! As we argued in Chapter 3, any enterprise has to create a surplus of outputs over inputs if the enterprise is to survive, but that is a very different proposition from one which asserts that a business person actually **maximizes** profits, or wishes to or even tries to.

One problem with profit maximization as description, explanation or justification is that no reference is included to a timescale. The selection of a timescale relevant to profit maximization has to be made. It is quite possible that steps taken to maximize profits this year, for example by cutting down on investment in training or new machines, may reduce profitability in the future. Increasing sales in the present year or six months by rewarding salesmen for persuading clients to take inappropriate or faulty products may well undermine the company's reputation to such an extent that future possible achievements are impaired.

Opportunities are also available to exercise choice in the selection of the criteria by which success is to be measured. The concept of the 'market share' or the rate of return on capital employed provide measurements, by which the performance of a company or its managers may be gauged. Share option schemes for senior management operate on the basis of the market price of the company's shares at some point in the future – yet another measure or criterion of performance. Ways in which differing interests may influence the selection of criteria are illustrated in Case Study 5.3.

The point is that some selection from a wide range of available criteria **has** to be made by someone. The question then is: by whom, for what purpose and upon what set of ideas about how the world actually works (i.e. by what theory) is that selection made?

Even if, say, the return on investment ratio is accepted as a useful means of measuring business effectiveness, questions still remain (Donaldson and Lorsch, 1983). There are at least three primary constituencies that corporate strategy has to satisfy:

☐ The external capital market;
☐ The product market; and
☐ The expectations of those within the organization.

All of these constituencies may have competing goals. For example, the capital market's requirement for returns may conflict with the demand for investment from the product market. Within the corporation different groupings may well ally their interests with the satisfaction of either (or neither) of the two other constituencies.

The return on investment ratio is a useful but nonetheless simplistic device for coping with such potentially varied demands. For example:

☐ The capital market, especially that portion made up of shareholders, may favour maximum return for minimum investment;
☐ The product market, especially customers, may prefer maximum investment with minimum return; while
☐ The organizational constituency, especially those whose career is in management, may opt for maximizing both returns and investment.

It may well be that one or another of the approaches to the return on investment ratio illustrated above will produce the desired results over some as yet undetermined time period. The problem is: how could you know which approach, and which timescale?

Selecting one of the approaches and a particular timescale presupposes a theoretical viewpoint since the decision to judge performance by reference to rate of return (or market share, or whatever), for example, implies some idea of how the world actually works. That is, the decision to use one or another criterion assumes a set of relationships between features of the real world that make market share, or return on investment, or whatever, a 'good' or 'useful' choice.

CASE STUDY 5.3

INFLUENCES ON THE SELECTION OF CRITERIA TO MEASURE SUCCESS

Theory and the role of statistical relationships

'Facts', established statistically, do not 'speak for themselves'. Facts are 'theory impregnated' – they derive from particular assumptions about the world and what is important for those for whom they are collected. Facts have meaning only in the light of such assumptions – on their own they are meaningless. Anyone could reel off any number of facts – age, address, place of work, favourite radio programme, for example – but in the absence of some means of setting them in context, of distinguishing the relevant from the irrelevant, of relating one to another, how would you – how could you – begin to identify what they 'mean'?

Theories tell us **what** facts are relevant, and **how** they are relevant. They tell us what **supposedly** relevant facts may **mean**. ('Us' refers here to those

CASE STUDY 5.4

MONETARISM AND THE PRACTICAL IMPLICATIONS OF THEORY

This issue is more fully discussed in Neale and Haslam's (1989) text in this series but it is relevant in the context of this chapter.

Milton Friedman's ideas on the role of money in inflation had been propounded some time before they became popular with economists and politicians. What gave them a boost was the apparent failure of the economic policies that had characterized the industrial world for three decades from the late 1930s. These policies had been based, more or less, upon the ideas of John Maynard Keynes, set out in *The General Theory of Employment, Interest and Money* published in 1936. These ideas concerned the role of demand in maintaining employment, and the role of government in maintaining demand.

'Keynesian' policies are those which are based on the assumption of the government's role in demand management via, for example, government spending and taxation. Since industrial societies experienced unprecedented economic growth for up to twenty years after the Second World War, and since governments had adopted policies based on Keynesian ideas, it was assumed that the one caused the other.

However, by the late 1960s things appeared to be going wrong. While inflation had been thought of as a lesser evil than unemployment, some economies, especially the UK, were experienceing rising unemployment and rising inflation without economic growth, a situation known as 'stagflation'.

Keynesian orthodoxy apparently no longer worked. Into the breach came the ideas of Friedman based on the assumption that increasing the supply of money (i.e. government expenditure) has only a temporary impact on unemployment but a permanent impact on inflation.

The point for our discussion here is that both the ideas of Keynes and Friedman are theoretical, based upon theories as to how the world works. But they can have considerable practical impact, and they have that practical impact because they are thought to be 'useful' by practical people.

In the case of Friedman, there is much evidence that the correlations that he quotes to support his thesis concerning the link between inflation and money supply are spurious (Hendry and Ericsson, 1983). As Hendry pointed out, Friedman **may** be right, we just can't tell from his evidence. An economist member of the House of Lords is reputed to have pointed out that it is rather like asserting that the increase in the money supply from November onwards is what causes Christmas!

When Sir Geoffrey Howe became Chancellor of the Exchequer, the staff at the Treasury had to re-write the model of the economy used by them because it was constructed to Keynesian criteria, not Friedmanite ones.

This example of the Keynesian v. Friedman debate, which has been conducted in a context where the same observable facts could be fitted into different theoretical frameworks, illustrates how and why there is nothing quite so practical as a good theory.

who share the same theoretical set of assumptions about the world and how it, and the parts in which we are interested, actually work.)

To rely upon statistically identified associations or correlations as a result of n number of case studies (where n is a large number) leaves the underlying causal process to be inferred. As in the natural sciences, any one collection of facts may be amenable to at least two explanations – the 'steady state' and 'big bang' theories about the origins of the universe for example. An example of more direct relevance to modern economies is discussed in Case Study 5.4.

Returning to the study of organizational behaviour, by studying a number of organizations we may be able to demonstrate an association between environmental characteristics and organizational structure. It may be possible to demonstrate, for example, that the majority of companies in a particular industry and operating in a particular product market all have structural features in common. This does not tell us about the causal mechanisms, however. Such associations say nothing about the **process** by which the observed relationship came about. We do not know what the people involved (management and employees) made of their situation. We do not know how they responded to it in terms of selecting from what they saw to be available and appropriate strategies or tactics. Until we can explain that process we are not able to claim knowledge or understanding.

Much research on organizations has proceeded upon the assumption that organizational structure is at least partly responsible for success or failure – Peters and Waterman (1982) is an example. However, could the relationship not be reversed? Successful organizations may instead adopt certain structures, so that structure could be the **consequence** of success, not the **cause**. That is, structure could be a dependent, not independent, variable. In order to understand causal relationships in the context of business behaviour it is necessary, having now some understanding of the role and nature of theory, to pay attention to the related issues of managerial choice and the exercise of power in organizations in the context of strategy.

It is the potential variety of meanings which an event or fact may have for different groups that is significant for the debate concerning the objectives which groups in an organization may have, and how these may influence their observed behaviour. Debate is confused to the extent that participants themselves confuse ends or objectives with the means to achieving those ends. Are profits an end in and of themselves, or are they the means by which those controlling the organization can obtain their objectives? Indeed, are profits the **only** means that could be used? What ends are those in control actually pursuing?

It is this complexity that underlies the plethora of research findings on behaviour in organizations. Such complexity, and lack of concern with theory, has resulted in relatively simple models and research methods. Any model, like the one used to link the books in this series, whether it is used in the natural or social sciences, represents a simplification of reality. The whole point of a 'model' is to provide a simplified representation of complex reality. If it were not simplified, then the model would be as complex as reality; it would **be** reality, and so just as impossible to deal

KEY CONCEPT 5.3

THEORETICAL
MODELS

Models are abstractions from reality that retain what are considered to be the key elements of the reality it is desired to comprehend. Being abstractions, models represent a **selection** from the real world, a selection made by a particular group with a particular problem attempting to identify an acceptable solution. Significant questions concerning the construction of a model are:

☐ Who made the selection (constructed the model)?
☐ Upon what criteria were elements selected and others ignored?
☐ For what purpose was the model constructed?

In some cases scientific and social-scientific research is limited by the technical qualities of the tools that are available: measuring instruments are sensitive only within limits; some questions cannot be answered because of the lack of suitable technology; some questions are not asked because anomolies are not recognized; anomolies are not recognized because assumptions are made about the relevance and completeness of what is already known. Some questions are considered worth asking, other are not. Research funds are available for some activities but not others. Those who control research funds determine the kinds of question which are acceptable and hence the acceptable answers. This goes for natural as well as social sciences (as anyone who has tried to get funding for a research project will confirm).

with. The significant features of a theoretical model are outlined in Key Concept 5.3.

At least two important points should be noted. First, the kind of questions you ask will very largely determine the kind of answers you get. This is well known to those who carry out opinion polls and market research surveys, for example. As Perrow (1972) noted, problems occurred in the literature concerning the impact of technology on organization structure over the definition of technology, and hence its measurement. What is the key distinguishing characteristic of different technologies: the kinds of machines used? how they are grouped? what they produce? or is it whether production is in terms of single items for specific customers or of standard products for a mass consumption market? What then are the implications for organizational structure and strategy of flexible manufacturing systems utilizing microelectronic technology that enable customized products to be produced on what was previously thought of as a mass production scale?

This problem of the question determining the kind of answer obtained has also been well known to natural scientists since the development of atomic physiscs in the early decades of this century, when it was discovered that it was not possible to locate a particle **and** find out how it was moving. Finding a particle's location disrupted its movement, and establishing the direction of movement disturbed its location. So the question you asked determined the answer you got. It was also established that the subatomic world did not behave with the law-like regularity of the macro-atomic world, but was probabilistic. That is, sense could only be made of it by resort to statistical probability theory. The utility of statistical probability in the study of atomic particles rests in part on the fact that (as far as we know) atomic particles are not **social** in the sense described in Key Concept 4.3! That is, they do not modify their behaviour, or their explanations for their behaviour, in the light of their perception of what the observer is up to. Human beings, unfortunately, do just that!

If there are a number of questions that could be asked, and if it is not possible because of the resources required or because of limited knowledge to attempt to answer all of them, then somebody (either an individual or a committee) will have to choose which questions are to be attempted. This of course is a basic characteristic of the human condition: resources are scarce and have alternative uses, choices have to be made.

Even in the case of research activity in the natural sciences, this choice cannot, of necessity, be a 'scientific' one. Prejudice, interests and assumptions will be involved, as illustrated in Case Study 5.5.

The experience of Louis Pasteur in gaining acceptance for his ideas on fermentation illustrate the problems associated with the exercise of strategic control and the impact on innovation. The idea that fermentation at least involved the activity of living organisms had been formulated in 1835, but when Pasteur came to study fermentation twenty years later, his preconception that fermentation was not simply a chemical process was at variance with the currently accepted view and was rejected without serious consideration. The controversy over fermentation was heated and acrimonious, with many protagonists refusing to accept Pasteur's conclusions even when they become widely accepted after several years. As Max Planck, one of the founding fathers of atomic physics, wrote in his *Scientific Autobiography*: 'A new scientific truth does not triumph by convincing its opponents and making them see the light, but rather because its opponents eventually die, and a new generation grows up that is familiar with it.'

Radio astronomers had an equally difficult time establishing their credibility after the Second World War against the prejudices of optical astronomers who naturally controlled access to research funds and refereed scientific journals. (For a very accessible account of the social processes involved in scientific innovation see Mulkay (1972).)

A study of the introduction of computer-aided design (CAD) by the Henley Management College illustrates this phenomena in the area of manufacturing. The study involved 20 British engineering firms and produced yet more evidence of narrow quantitative approaches to investment in new technology on the part of senior management, due at least in part to the dominance of the accounting perspective. However, it was found that in some cases those actually involved with the implementation of the technology tended to concentrate on qualitative criteria such as the improved quality of drawings and the production of design drawings that were previously impossible. In

CASE STUDY 5.5

SOCIAL FACTORS IN INNOVATION

Continued over page

Continued from previous page

addition they identified the advantages of improved lead time (time taken from the conception of a product through all the stages to delivery to the customer) in terms of non-price competiton. Senior management, it was found, particularly in the largest firms, tended to emphasize drawing-office productivity (often involving a reduction in numbers employed) and lead times in the narrow sense related to direct productivity. Thus both groups employed very different criteria (theories) for dealing with the world. The CAD engineers developed their response to senior management by couching their reports in the same quantitative language used by their superiors while maintaining their more qualitative approach. This produced a smokescreen which further reduced senior management's understanding of the technology. The Henley researchers suggest that in addition to senior management being dominated by quantitative accountancy rubrics, their insistence on quantitative measures was associated with their desire to maintain a quantitative control system since they understood such matters far better than they did the new technology. (See Campbell, Currie and Warner (1989).)

We have now established the basic components for the construction of a pathway out of what Luthans described as a 'jungle of theory'. The basic components are, (a) an understanding of the nature and role of theory, and (b) the notion of strategic choice exercised by whichever group in the organization has the power to frame such a choice and impose it upon the organization. Such an approach can provide **useful** accounts of how various environmental features such as technology and product markets come to influence the structure and functioning of an organization by concentrating attention on the strategies, behaviour and motives of human beings. The nature of strategic choice is illustrated in Key Concept 5.4.

KEY CONCEPT 5.4

STRATEGIC CHOICE

Strategic choice refers to the process of selecting one strategy from a number that are available. The role of strategic choice:

... extends to the context within which the organization is operating, to the standards of performance against which the pressure of economic performance has to be evaluated, and to the design of the organization's structure itself. Incorporation of the process whereby strategic decisions are made directs attention onto the degree of choice which can be exercised in respect of organizational design, whereas many available models direct attention exclusively onto the constraints involved. They imply in this way that organizational behaviour can be understood by reference to functional imperatives rather than political action.

(Child, 1972, p.2)

Later in the same article quoted in Key Concept 5.4, Child writes: 'In short, when incorporating strategic choice in a theory of organization, one is recognizing the operation of an essentially political process in which constraints and opportunities are functions of the power exercised by decision-makers in the light of ideological values.' The decisions which management make about the structure and organization of work are not determined by the technology. Technology, defined as simply the machines themselves, may facilitate the pursuit of particular goals in particular ways, but it determines neither the goals nor the means by which they are achieved. Different levels of management will perceive the same technology as helping them to achieve different, and possibly contradictory, goals, as illustrated in Table 5.1. It will be necessary to ensure that there is consistency among the strategic, operating and control objectives listed in the table.

Table 5.1 Perception of technology at different levels of management

Level of management	Objective	Concern
Senior management	Strategic	Costs Return on investment Competition
Middle management	Operating	Control of the workflow Reduce labour costs
Supervisors	Control	Reduce workflow disruptions Reduce human frustrations

Source: Buchanan and Boddy (1983).

'Ends and means are ultimately determined by by the decisions of those in positions to direct the use of the technology, and design jobs and organization structures around it' (Buchanan and Boddy, 1983, p. 255). The following sections of the chapter examine in some detail the notion of management as a political process, the significance of power and its basis within organizations.

Management as a political process

The human condition is such that it is not possible to have all relevant information when deciding between alternatives. If it were possible, if all relevant information were available and the relationships between what were considered 'facts' were clearly understood, then there would be no decision to take. The outcome would be given: the decision would have been made by rational calculation based upon complete information. The possibility of collecting complete information is unreal if for no other reason than that searching for, collecting and processing information itself has a cost (see Chapter 6 for further discussion of this issue). This is particularly the case when attempting to estimate the state of the world (or market) in five or ten years' time. At some point a halt has to be called – resources are never limitless and those available have alternative uses.

The cost of search limits not only what information can be acquired, but who can acquire it. This puts power in some hands rather than others. More resources may mean more accurate and up-to-date information, though not necessarily 'better' decisions. That searching amongst alternatives has a cost is a factor in the maintenance of the status quo. We can be more certain of costs if we stick with what we know, rather than trying something new which adds to the uncertainty. In this respect 'conservatism' (with a small 'c' please note!) is inherently self-justifying. Those proposing change are the ones who have to justify their proposals when by definition they cannot produce 'hard facts' as unambiguous evidence (since the same facts could support two interpretations, those of the 'conservatives' as well as those of the 'radicals'). The conservative, one who argues for the status quo, tends to rely on (historical) 'facts' that are held to 'speak for themselves', that is the facts have not (it is alleged) been selected for presentation by somebody with an interest in the outcome.

Since human decision-making cannot rely upon complete knowledge, the utility of the notion of 'maximizing' behaviour has to be called into question. In the absence of complete information, we cannot be certain that any particular action will result in the maximum return. We cannot try out alternatives, so have to do the best we can with the information available. A decision-maker in such a situation is said to display 'satisficing' behaviour. That is a decision is made to settle for some 'satisfactory' level of return, and this level will be satisfactory in the light of particular circumstances. For example, a company may pursue a rate of return on capital invested that is 'average' for the industry in which it operates; or that puts it in the 'top ten' in the industry; or that enables it to earn a surplus (and maintain a cash flow) sufficient to attain its aim of gaining any given market share in percentage terms. Again choice is being exercised and that choice, rather than some other, will be put into effect in so far as power is exercised by the chooser(s). Having a choice, a real choice, implies the power to implement it.

Given these points it is important to regard the selection of questions that are thought worth asking and the allocation of appropriate resources as political processes. This is so because they involve the exercise of power by one of a number of social groupings or individuals. In so far as social groups are able to mobilize resources more effectively than isolated individuals, it is possible to extend the political analogy and refer to such groups as 'coalitions'. Individuals or groups will join with others to pursue interests which may be shared, or at least are compatible. There can be no certainty over the stability of a coalition, however; as greater opportunities are perceived elsewhere allegiances may shift. The nature of political activity is defined in Key Concept 5.5.

The idea that management is a political process which can be understood in terms of relationships between coalitions will be explored in the following sections of this chapter. The idea has developed in an attempt to bring some sense to the vary large body of empirical data concerning behaviour in, and by, organizations and their managements.

The nature and operation of power in organizations will be examined

Political activity is activity to resolve questions about who gets what and when; it is about the exercise of power, the ability to influence the distribution of scarce resources in accordance with a particular set of interests. Such activity is political because it is undertaken in order to overcome opposition; if there is no contesting how resources are to be distributed, then there is no political activity – there is no need for it.

In order to legitimate the exercise of power in a political context, recourse will be had to claims concerning the rational and objective nature of the decision-making process. Some alternative courses of action will have been defined as inappropriate, as not **real** alternatives; facts will be put forward as 'speaking for themselves'; emphasis will be placed upon shared values at some higher level of reasoning. Every effort will be made to give the impression that the decision was taken according to rational and bureaucratic administrative processes based upon rules and the best available evidence. The key to the successful exercise of political power, necessary and sufficient for the legitimation of that power, is to persuade others that there was no alternative – this goes for party politics on the national and international stage every bit as much as it does within organizations.

KEY CONCEPT 5.5

POLITICAL ACTIVITY

along with the idea of a 'dominant coalition' and the role of such groupings in organizations. The role of power, and sources of power within organizations, will be the justification for suggesting that the processes of management and decision-making should be regarded as political if they are to be adequately understood.

The nature of power

'Power and domination remain real even when resistance and open challenge are not strong' (Rueschmeyer, 1986, p. 102).

Power is one of those words the precise definition of which causes some difficulty. One important reason for this is that it may be in the interests of the powerful to deny that they infact have any . . . or very much. In a democratic society demonstrable inequality in power can be the basis of a significant challenge to the legitimacy of the process of decision-making. The process of ensuring acquiescence from a group of people may lie in the group believing that they are choosing amongst alternatives. Or, people may be persuaded to do something they would rather not do simply because they are persuaded that there really is no alternative.

Any definition of 'power' must distinguish it from 'authority'. This is not necessarily straightforward since the exercise of power may well rely upon the perceived legitimacy of that power, i.e. 'authority'. Authority must itself be distinguished from the context in which it refers to specialized knowledge. Even 'knowledge' may in some sense be 'power'. What matters is the uses to which knowledge is put and the interests it may be serving.

Social order is maintained most securely when people can be left to conform to the dominant ideas and mores of their society or organization. If one has to station a policeman, soldier or supervisor at every street corner or office door to ensure order, then order has broken down. If people take for granted the 'normality' of everyday life then they will not regard what they do or the way they do it as worthy of investigation. They will react 'instinctively' towards those who transgress against the values and practices that are taken for granted. Within a system of order, the roles of particular individuals or groups will be accepted by the vast majority without question. Thus the policeman who can move people on because he 'has reason to believe' that a breach of the peace may occur does not have to provide justification for his belief before people move. Those who do demand such a justification will generally be regarded as deserving of what they get as a result. Here we are confronting the exercise of 'authority', i.e. legitimate 'power'.

The fact that power struggles and conflict are not obvious characteristics of relationships between managers and their subordinates (although they may be of some such relationships) suggests the acceptance, in general, of managerial decisions. If order is to prevail, with a minimum visible display of force or coercion, managerial actions must be seen as in some sense 'legitimate', they must be within the authority of management.

After considering a definition of power, we will move on to consider important distinctions between: (a) a definition of power, (b) the identification of the basis or source of power, and (c) the identification of the forms that the exercise of power may take. All three will be discussed in the following pages.

A definition of power and how it may be distinguished from authority is set out in Key Concept 5.6. It is important to recognize that while a superior may undoubtedly have the authority to give instructions, within the terms of delegation, that does not necessarily mean he or she can gain

---

KEY CONCEPT 5.6	What is POWER?
POWER AND AUTHORITY	Perhaps the most useful answer to this question is that provided by Max Weber: 'In general, we understand by "power" the chance of a man [sic] or a number of men to realize their own will in a communal action even against the resistance of others who are participating in the action' (in Gerth and Mills (eds), p.180).

Bachrach and Baratz (1962) offer an elaboration of the concept of power as a set of '... predominant values, beliefs, rituals, and institutional procedures ("rules of the game") that operate systematically and consistently to the benefit of certain persons and groups at the expense of others.' This formulation directs attention to the extent to which power may be exercised through the ability of a group to set the agenda for discussion, that is the ability to get others to accept that certain questions are illegitimate, that some alternatives are just not acceptable.

What is AUTHORITY?

Authority has at least two meanings: in the sense which it is used in the present discussion it can be taken to mean the exercise of 'legitimate' power. That is, A is able to get B to do what A wants, even if B objects, because B accepts that A has the right to order the former to carry out certain tasks. The order, and any sanctions applied as a result of B failing to comply with it, are seen as 'right and proper', or 'legitimate'. There may well be debate about the extent of any particular person's authority, and there may well be debate about the legitimacy of a punishment when failure to comply with an order is the result of factors outside the subordinate's control. Such questioning does not necessarily imply rejection of authority, merely a question about its exercise in any particular case.

'Authority' may also refer to the extent of an individual's knowledge, as in 'She is an authority on European health and safety legislation.' This implies that the person in question knows a great deal about that legislation and should be listened to accordingly. Such an expert may have neither the 'power' nor 'authority' to enforce the legislation in a particular company, because she is in a junior position, or indeed because she does not hold the appropriate position in the relevant regulatory agency with the necessary powers.

The distinction between power and authority in organizations

This distinction is important to an understanding of behaviour in organizations since it is so often taken for granted that:

☐ power and authority are synonymous;
☐ the existence of the one implies the existence of the other;
☐ they are located at the same point in the hierarchy.

A formal hierachy is evidence of the assumption that power and authority are located at the same points in a structure. However, this is not necessarily the case, and can only be established by empirical investigation of specific cases. (If you are unclear about this, refer back to the discussion of the 'formal' and 'informal' organizations in Chapter 3.)

compliance. Managers undoubtedly have the right, within limits set by statute, to sack people, but they may not always have the power.

The establishment and maintenance of social order, in society at large and in an organization, is dependent upon the transformation of power into authority because the exercise of power always has a cost. Resources have to be martialled, and opposition identified and dealt with, in some way. Social order is possible because this expenditure of effort and resources does not have to be continuous.

KEY CONCEPT 5.7

REBELS AND REVOLUTIONARIES

The distinction between rebels and revolutionaries is important in terms of evaluating the appropriateness or acceptability of responses that are seen as challenging the exercise of power and authority. Rebels do not seek to establish a different political or social system – either at the level of society or the firm. They do seek to re-establish the standing and authority of an 'office' in the bureaucratic sense, or of an ideal. They believe that the current occupant is failing to live up to the ideals demanded of the office holder, or is in some ways demeaning the office itself. A departmental manager is seen as 'incompetent', for example, or even if competent is thought to behave inappropriately in some way. A revolutionary, on the other hand, **is** concerned to change the system and to establish a different one based upon different values and interests.

Social order exists when subordinates obey superiors not because they feel compelled by the possibility of the use of force, but because they expect to get instructions concerning their work activity; such instructions may even be welcomed because that is what superiors are expected to do. Unreasonable instructions may be contested or ignored, but this does not imply a questioning of the right to give instructions. One may confront rebels, but not revolutionaries, as explained in Key Concept 5.7.

In the context of industrial relations, for example, the general response from the media is to view the manifestation of conflict not as part of a 'game' that is being played, but as a direct threat to the authority of management and hence to the basis of social order as we know it. The game player is not perceived even as a rebel, but is perceived as a revolutionary. What was intended as a strategy in a game is elevated into a direct threat to the system. When discussing industrial relations at their own plants or firms the vast majority of managers and union officials will describe the process as a 'game'. Offers are made and refused, demands are made and rejected not with the intention of undermining the system but in order to get a slightly better deal out of it. The important distinction between a game, a fight and a debate is set out in Key Concept 5.8.

Power is a characteristic of **social** relationships. Someone or somebody has power in relation to some other social actor(s). Power is relationship or context specific as Pfeffer (1981) puts it. This aspect is of considerable importance in terms of the exercise of power in organizations since the exercise of power may not conform to the hierarchical model of the formal organization. The formal structure is intended to be a representation of both power and authority in an organization. Whether either of these are in fact distributed in accordance with the formal structure is a matter of empirical investigation.

Rueschmeyer (1986) shows how power is related to the division of labour since the division of labour is a manifestation of the exercise of power. Complex organizations are characterized by the allocation of tasks between different departments and functions which are not likely to be equally powerful. Thus power is a structural phenomenon arising out of the division of labour and departmentalization. Changes in the product market

In his examination of conflict and the form it may take, Anatol Rapoport (1974) uses a classification of conflicts around the notion of games, fights and debates. The distinction between these forms is centred upon the ways in which an opponent can be perceived.

A **game** is characterized by the perceptions of the participants of each other in terms of a situation and of other situations that are seen as the outcomes of decisions taken by the participants. Typically these decisions are seen as rational in terms of the development of a strategy that is consistent with the rules. The opponent is bound by the same rules – by definition in a game – and the relationship proceeds according to strategies adopted by either opponent. The continuation of a game requires that the parties cooperate in terms of the shared acceptance of the rules as rules and by only adopting strategies consistent with the rules.

The opponent in a game is a necessary feature of the situation, someone who is to be outwitted as opposed to destroyed or subjugated. The latter is what happens in a fight.

In a **fight** the opponent is seen as an 'enemy', that is as someone who is not simply to be outwitted, but rather someone who is imbued with negative attributes and who is to be destroyed. In a fight, attention is focused on the enemy rather than rules, and emotional and value-laden characterizations of the enemy limit the exercise of rational analysis. This is most clearly seen in the efforts to dehumanize enemies by using pejoritive expressions or classifications to refer to them. This of course is the point of the saying 'One person's freedom fighter is another's terrorist.' One side's war hero (because of the success of the operations for which he was responsible, i.e. many of the enemy were killed) is the other side's war criminal.

A **debate** is different again. Here the objective is to convince or convert, rather than to outwit, eliminate or destroy, the opponent. Debates are essentially exchanges of verbal stimuli either to change the outlook of the other person/side, or to demonstrate to one's own side that their interests are being well represented and pursued.

'In short, the fight is dominated by affective, that is emotional, components of conflict, the game by rational ones, and the debate by ideological ones' (Rapoport, 1974).

---

may shift the location of power between departments, when for example the problem changes from that of 'making what we know we can sell' (when production is in command) to that of 'selling what we know we can make' (when marketing takes over).

A similar situation may arise with staff who are perceived as possessing new and crucial knowledge. Key individuals may be able to flout instructions and organizational mores as regards time-keeping and standards of dress because they are thought to be indispensable. While it may be true that no one **is** indispensable, some are more dispensible than others! Here again, authority to give orders is unquestioned, but power to ensure compliance may well be lacking. Indeed, resorting to a crude exercise of power may be seen as undermining authority by illustrating that power is problematic; it is better perhaps to ignore transgressions that do not affect the individual's or group's ability to meet targets.

We have so far suggested that the activity of management in organizations may usefully be regarded as a political process. This assumption provides a means of linking observed features of an organizational environment with the structural and behavioural aspects of an organization in some causal chain based on the exercise of choice, hence power. Having discussed power, and its relationship to authority, we now move on to examine the basis of power in organizations.

The basis of power in organizations

What is the basis of power in organizations? What is it that makes one group more powerful than another? The answer is important in understanding behaviour in organizations, not just in individualistic terms, but also in terms of relationships between groups and departments. Such relationships come under scrutiny, for example, when assertions are made about the relative importance to business success of the marketing function rather than the finance function . . . or of both in relation to the personnel or production departments.

Where does power come from? Why are some people or some departments usually able to have their definition of problems and solutions accepted? Why are some questions asked and others never surface onto an agenda? Why are some alternatives rather than others considered? Upon what basis is power in organizations exercised?

In order to establish the basis of power in organizations it is necessary to remember that organizations are made up of a number of specialized activities grouped by function into, for example, departments. It is also necessary to remember that such a grouping is designed to facilitate coping with complex problems or issues by reducing pressure on information processing activities. The division of labour and the creation of specialist functions creates the possibility that not all the activities involved will be equally important in terms of organizational objectives at any given moment in time. Some departments or individuals will be, or will be perceived as being, more 'important' than others.

An answer to the question 'What is the basis of power in organizations?' is set out in Key Concept 5.9. What exactly is meant by 'uncertainty' in this context? The human situation is one characterized by uncertainty due to the fact, mentioned earlier, that while information may reduce uncertainty, collecting and interpreting that information itself has a cost. Also, organizing the collection of affordable information presumes that we know what information is relevant. If the situation is genuinely new, then we may have our hunches as to what is relevant, but we are not – by definition – in a position to be certain. Duncan (1972) provides a three-part definition of uncertainty which is set out in Key Concept 5.10.

The major functional areas of business are identifiable by reason of the grouping together of all activities related to particular sources of

What determines differential influence? What is the basis of group or departmental power in an organization? The most useful, and succinct answer to this question is: 'the perceived ability to cope with uncertainty (Duncan, 1972).

A number of factors are important in this answer. Given that an organization is made up of interrelated departments and sections within departments, the coping activity of a department or section will be related to its power by virtue of the extent to which the activity of that department (or section) is central to the activities of other departments and sections. Important also is the extent to which a department's coping can be carried out by some other unit in the organization. A third factor contributing to power is the speed with which a failure on the part of that department or section to act would be felt elsewhere in the organization. These three key features of a department's or section's location within an organizational power structure have been described by Hickson *et al.* (1974) as:

☐ Workflow pervasiveness;
☐ Substitutability; and
☐ Immediacy.

KEY CONCEPT 5.9

THE BASIS OF POWER IN ORGANIZATIONS

Uncertainty is defined by Duncan (1972) by reference to three factors:

☐ A lack of information regarding environmental factors associated with a given decision-making situation. The situation cannot be clearly understood because, quite simply, not enough is known about it.
☐ Not knowing the outcome of a decision in terms of how much the organization would lose if the decision were incorrect. While enough is known about the situation to formulate a decision, not enough is known to make it possible to calculate the cost of a mistake.
☐ An inability to assign probabilities to the effect of a particular factor on the success/failure of a decision unit in performing its function.

KEY CONCEPT 5.10

UNCERTAINTY

uncertainty that may confront those running a commercial enterprise. Thus the accountancy and finance function deal with crucial questions concerning the 'profitability' of the enterprise and the acquisition of funds for future investment. Marketing is concerned with coping with the uncertainties that may arise as the competition develops or as the population changes in terms of age or status distribution, for example. Production is responsible for ensuring that output meets requirements of quantity, quality and cost, while the personnel department attempts to ensure a ready supply of suitably qualified and trained employees and purchasing ensures a ready supply of adequate materials. The implications of this situation for the basis of power in organizations are elaborated in Case Study 5.6.

CASE STUDY 5.6

COPING WITH UNCERTAINTY AS THE BASIS OF POWER

☐ Crozier's (1964) study of manufacturing plants in the government-run French tobacco industry provides an illuminating insight into how coping with uncertainty provided a power base for a group of workers. The work routine of the plants Crozier studied was highly regulated and about the only unpredictable event which could disrupt production was a machine breakdown. Such an eventuality gave the maintenance engineers their chance. They were the only people who could cope with a problem that was central to the organization's activities and which affected those activities rapidly. Not only that, but the engineers trained new recruits to their department informally, without the use of written procedures and manuals. Consequently no one else could easily carry out repairs because there was no documentation. Thus the validity of the saying 'knowledge is power' was once again demonstrated. It is demonstrated also when professional occupations claim control over the process of defining the needs of clients and how they should be met, e.g. doctors, lawyers, social workers. The use of jargon, while it undoubtedly facilitates communication within a group, is also a means of keeping knowledge within a specific social group by preventing others from understanding what is said.

☐ Around the time of the 1971 Industrial Relations Act, the present author was carrying out research into public-sector industrial relations. One organization interviewed saw itself very much as a 'professional' body, and while taking part in national collective bargaining machinery nevertheless kept a rather low profile and distanced itself from the trade unions with which it was associated on the national bargaining machinery. This concern on the part of the senior members of the organization to be seen as 'different' and apart from unions was reflected in the small number of industrial relations staff, two people, and their location in the basement of the headquarters building. The reality was that the presence of the organization on the national bargaining body made very little difference, if any at all, to negotiated outcomes and so the staff involved could be virtually ignored.

On a subsequent visit to this organization, after the legislation had passed into law, it was discovered that the numbers of industrial relations staff had increased considerably and were now housed in very imposing offices on the upper floor of the building. The legislation had actually put at risk the trade union functions of many so-called 'professional bodies'. The result in this and other similar organizations which nevertheless aspired to carry out, if only minimally, trade union type representation of their members' interests was the realization that the person responsible for industrial relations was very important indeed!

Under the 1971 legislation an organization which wished to retain a trade union role in terms of representing members as employees had to comply with certain features of the legislation and establish a formal system of representation in the workplace. In other words, 'shop stewards' had to be formally elected and recognized by the organization. This new-found importance of the department dealing with negotiating pay and conditions derived from the fact that the new legislation represented a source of uncertainty: one particular group of people were seen as able to cope – suddenly they were listened to, and rewarded!

The perceived ability to cope with uncertainty

It is important to remember that a department's or individual's ability to exercise power as the result of a perceived ability to cope with uncertainty is influenced by the three factors outlined in Key Concept 5.9 associated with the division of labour in an organization. The perception that an individual or group can cope with a source of uncertainty is enhanced the greater the extent to which that individual's or group's work pervades the organization, that is the extent to which other departments rely upon it. Second, power will depend upon the extent to which the work of a department can be replaced or dispensed with altogether. Finally, the power a department may exercise is a function of the speed with which a malfunction will affect the rest of the organization, assuming maximum pervasiveness and minimum substitutability.

It is the **perception** by other people that an individual or sub-unit can cope that is significant in determining the power of that individual or sub-unit. what is important in determining the location of power, and crucial to the ability of an individual or department or group to impose its definition of what the problem is and how it may be resolved, is the fact that others **believe** that a particular individual or group **can** cope with the perceived source of uncertainty. Whether they can or not, or whether they can cope better than some other group, is a separate question. What matters is that others **think** they can cope. If the group or department does appear to cope, that is things turn out 'right' as far as the organization is concerned, then the power of that group or department will be enhanced. Only the envious will attempt to argue that inaction would have produced the same result, or that it was factors outside the control of the department in question that changed to produce the desired outcome, i.e. that it was all luck! However, should the prescription of the department in question fail, or appear to fail, then power will evaporate.

The approach to identifying the basis of power taken here not only accounts for why particular groups are able to exercise power or not at any one time, it also accounts for why the location of power varies over time within the same organization and between different organizations at the same time. Importantly, this approach to power can also account for why 'power' as distinct from 'authority' does not necessarily reside at the same point in the hierarchy, why superiors may from time to time have to concede the demands of subordinates.

An important aspect of the examination of power in organizations is the distinction between 'power' and 'authority'. While having authority to tell someone else what to do, or to sanction financial expenditure, may itself be a source of power, those in authority do not necessarily have power in terms of controlling the behaviour of others. A manager may well have authority to exercise sanctions against workers who habitually take over-long lunch-breaks, but if the manager – and his subordinates – know that all they have to do is walk down the road to another or even better job, then exercising that authority in a tight labour market may well be counter-productive. In other words, the manager has authority, but little power.

It is also important to note that the implications for personal manner, style or presentation are equally significant. Since power is at least in part a matter of perception, **appearing** to have the answer to a problem, or knowing where such an answer may be found, is very important.

As we will see when we discuss the international comparisons in Chapter 10, the concern of British business with relatively short-term issues related to profit and price, as opposed to market share or non-price competition for example, places accountants in a much more powerful position than, say, production. This is reflected in significantly higher pay and status.

It should be borne in mind that there is a sense in which the success of a group in coping with uncertainty may be self-defeating. The more the group copes with uncertainty, the less threatening becomes that source of uncertainty in the perception of others. If the perception of what is uncertain changes, along with who can cope, then other groups may emerge as powerful. Thus the perceived ability to cope with uncertainty may coexist with political activity to maintain that perception.

Forms of power

While considerable attention in the literature on behaviour in organizations has been focused on the examination of power, there are at least two reasons why this has not always been particularly helpful in explaining behaviour in organizations. First, it is often not in the interests of those who hold power to admit to it. Societies characterized by ideologies of equality and consensus are not the places to set about examining the nature of power, how it is acquired, upon what it is based, or the ends for which it is exercised. Such an exercise may well identify areas where the rhetoric of those who support the status quo could be shown to be self-serving.

Secondly, and specific to the context of organizations, much published material has focused on the **forms** the exercise of power may take. Attention has been focused on the **way** in which one group determines the behaviour of another, rather than on **why** one group is able to determine, in whatever manner, the behaviour of another. What happens is that the **form** the exercise of power takes in action is confused with the **basis** of power.

The confusion between the form and basis of power can be illustrated by referring to one of the most frequently quoted examinations of social power, that of French and Raven (1959). French and Raven identified five so-called 'sources' of power, set out in Table 5.2, and all are seen as

Table 5.2 French and Raven's 'sources' of power

☐ **Reward power:** based upon the control of resources with which to reward others, e.g. pay, promotion.
☐ **Coercive power:** based upon the ability to inflict punishment and instil fear.
☐ **Legitimate power:** based upon the internalized values of those who accept the exercise of power over them (see the discussion of authority above).
☐ **Referent power:** French and Raven argue that this form of power derives from the wish to be identified with those exercising power, whether or not rewards are available. This is similar to the Weberian notion of charismatic authority (see Chapter 4, p. 96).
☐ **Expert power:** depends upon having the correct credentials, and the extent to which others perceive the expert's skill and knowledge as relevant.

Source: French and Raven (1959).

particularly applicable to organizations. The problem with the classification by French and Raven is that it does not offer a satisfactory account of the **basis** of power. It does not answer the question 'Where does power, exercised in the above-mentioned ways, come from?' What it does tell us, however, is some of the **forms** the exercise of power may take.

This question-begging aspect of the French and Raven account can be avoided by turning to the idea of the perceived ability to cope with uncertainty as the basis of power, whatever the form in which it is exercised may take. Consider 'reward power' for example. The ability of a manager to influence behaviour by offering subordinates a reward depends upon the subordinate seeking such a reward in the first place. If the subordinate does not depend upon the current employer for meeting material or psychological needs, then being offered more pay, or status, does not constitute 'reward'. If the employee is confident of being able to get a similar or better job down the road, at the same or better level of pay, then the present employer will not gain compliance simply by offering more money.

The same goes for all five of French and Raven's categories. In the absence of uncertainty none of these forms of power would have any significance at all. In so far as they are significant it is because of the prior existence of uncertainty in the minds of those over whom power may be exercised, and the assumption or expectation that the present employer is most likely to reduce that uncertainty. Remember, the point is that a particular group or individual is **perceived** as able to cope with uncertainty; that perception may turn out to be erroneous, but until such time as it is demonstrated to be so then it will operate to locate the source of power.

Power itself is of course its own reward. Being powerful is a very effective strategy for reducing uncertainty since the powerful can exercise control over significant material resources.

Strategic contingencies

The emphasis upon the perceived ability to cope with uncertainty as the basis of organizational power is consistent with the application of a

KEY CONCEPT 5.11

STRATEGIC CONTINGENCIES

For a definition of 'strategy' see Key Concept 5.1.

'Contingencies' refer to features of the environment within which a business strategy is developed, which influence the formulation of that strategy, and with which it is designed to cope.

Strategic contingencies are of two types and operate at two levels. First, there are those that operate at the macroeconomic level and so affect most if not all industries, though not necessarily to the same degree, e.g. the rate of economic growth, exchange rate and monetary policies of the government of the day, and rates of product and process innovation. Secondly, there are those contingencies which operate at the level of specific industries or firms, e.g. size and scale of operations, position in the market (e.g. high price, high quality and low volume, or the opposite), and skill levels and potential for enhancement.

contingency approach, specifically a strategic contingency approach (see Key Concept 5.11), to understanding behaviour in and of organizations.

A 'contingency' approach implies, as we saw in Chapter 4, that organizations will be structured and function in an attempt to cope with particular environmental factors or contingencies. Thus operating in a mass market where consistent standards are required in the production of high volumes of relatively low cost items will put different pressures upon organizational structures and management than if operating in a low volume, high quality and high price product market. One of the differences between such environments can be described as pressure to operate 'down to a price' as opposed to operating 'up to a standard'. One aspect of the competitive advantage of Japanese motor manufacturers, for example, is that they are able to **combine** these two distinct approaches. The term 'contingency' is appropriate because the demands placed upon management are not common to all managements, or indeed to the same management at different times. Demands will vary as product market conditions vary. How an organization and its management actually operate will be contingent upon what they perceive to be the prime sources of competitive pressure and available means of coping with them. This is the lesson of the research of Burns and Stalker discussed in Chapter 4.

The notion of strategic contingencies is related to the issue of power within organizations since, as we have seen, responding to environmental contingencies involves the exercise of choice by those who direct the organization. For example, someone, at some point, decided where in the market the firm was positioned. It may have been simply that the son of the founder continued 'the family business', or it may have been that after exhaustive analysis it was decided to stay with what they knew. The point remains that at some point choice was exercised. The nature of some possible choices in the context of the labour market are illustrated in Case Study 5.7.

At the simplest level the strategic contingency approach can cope with the fact that in different organizations, not only may the structure be different, but different departments may be the powerful ones and that

We will discuss international comparisons in more detail in Chapter 10, but for the moment it is relevant to point out that one of the major problems perceived by government and managers in the UK to be affecting the competitive performance of British industry is the uncompetitive nature of labour markets and the consequent high price (relatively) of labour. This view is held despite evidence that British pay rates are, by international standards, low, and that individual employment rights and security is greater in major European competitors.

Part of this emphasis on labour cost as a source of competitive disadvantage derives from the fact that the problem is perceived as being one of **price** competition. That is, British goods fail in international and domestic markets because they are too expensive, and this is due to labour costs rather than, say, the way stocks and materials (which can comprise up to 60% of total costs) are handled. However, expense, in price terms, is always relative, relative to quality, after-sales service and delivery in particular. If competition is not actually about price, but about quality, delivery and after-sales service, then focusing on ways of reducing labour costs might be missing the point. What is more, concentrating on reducing the relative cost of labour might actually bring about a situation where, because it is perceived as cheap, labour has relatively little invested in it: It is not thought worth training staff or personnel. If, in addition to this, the cost of laying off labour is relatively low by international standards in terms of the obligations placed upon employers, then this acts as a disincentive to invest in a highly trained labour force. A vicious circle results.

> An economy which is based on low pay is essentially an economy with limited incentives. Firms are provided with less incentive to compete through innovation in production methods or seeking new markets. Rather, competition is based on the cutting of already low wages while obsolete technology remains in use.
>
> (Brosnan and Wilkinson, 1988)

A number of conversations held with American managers operating in Europe has elicited the information that they actually prefer to operate in Britain because it is cheaper and easier to shed labour than elsewhere in Europe!

As we will discuss further in Chapter 10, (see also Neale and Haslam, 1989, Chapter 3), British employers concentrate their efforts on reducing labour costs almost to the exclusion of other sources of costs. So process innovation or the installation of new technology is invariably justified by the associated reduction in labour costs as a result of the reduced demand for labour given the productive potential of the new machinery. An alternative – increasing, as opposed to merely maintaining output and launching an attack on market share – is rarely envisaged. However understandable, this is a matter of choice; it is not inevitable.

This point has been forcefully expressed by Wilkinson: 'There is **no** inherent logic in microelectronics which demands that tasks become ever more mundane; nor does the technology **demand** that skills be

CASE STUDY 5.7

LABOUR MARKETS, CONTINGENCIES AND CHOICE

Continued over page

Continued from previous page	increased . . . The way in which work is organised . . . is a responsibility which managers cannot shirk by reference to the notion that everybody has simply to adapt to technology's demands' (1982, p.40, emphasis added).

within the same organization the same department may not be powerful at different times. Organizations and departments within them will face different contingencies, and hence sources of uncertainty, as a result of the strategic choices that have been exercised. Different contingencies, or differing perceptions of the same contingencies, may produce changes in the distribution of power within the organization in so far as different sources of uncertainty are perceived as threatening the organization and different individuals or groups will be perceived as best able to cope.

Power and the exercise of choice

The consideration of power in organizations is closely connected with the exercise of choice. There are a number of grounds for arguing that those managing an organization may in fact be faced with the possibility of

CASE STUDY 5.8 **THE POLITICS OF TECHNOLOGICAL CHANGE**	The extent to which technology has political as well as merely technical implications has been a focus of interest to writers examining both historical and contemporary instances of technological change. The 'political neutrality' of technology is brought into question, for example, by the argument that the part played by technology in the Industrial Revolution was determined by a desire to organize and control work, a desire which preceded in some cases both the invention and application of technological innovations (see Dickson, 1973, for example). In his article 'Do artifacts have politics?' Winner (1985) points out the explicit and/or implicit political purposes represented by the work of architects and city planners. The 'grands boulevards' of Haussmann's Paris were the direct consequence of a policy to reduce the incidence of street fighting and barricades which erupted during the revolutionary activities of 1848 by giving the police and military clear lines of fire. It is, after all, much easier to block a narrow street than a very broad one! The assumption that technological changes are introduced to increase efficiency is, sometimes at least, problematic. Winner refers to the study by Robert Ozanne (1967) of the labour relations history of McCormick and International Harvester, the manufacturers of agricultural machinery. In the foundary at the Chicago reaper plant in the 1880s, pneumatic moulding machines were introduced. These machines were largely untested and produced low quality castings. The cost of their introduc-

tion was put at about five thousand dollars. However, these machines could be manned by unskilled labour and were introduced by Cyrus McCormack in order to weed out the men responsible for organizing the National Union of Iron Moulders in Chicago. Within three years this labour relations policy had succeeded, the union had been broken and the machines were abandoned.

More recent evidence from the UK has been used to identify at least two distinct approaches to the management of labour which are relevant in the context of strategic contingencies, namely the 'direct control' and 'responsible autonomy' approaches (Friedman, 1977). These approaches are associated with the debate over deskilling (for which see, for example Wood, 1982) as well as with the implications of the predominance of the functional type of organization in Britain in comparison with Germany and Japan (e.g. Child *et al.* (1983), discussed in more detail in Chapter 10).

'Direct control' in Friedman's terminology refers to a strategy of control over labour which reduces the autonomy of the worker by the precise specification of the tasks to be carried out and the manner in which they are to be carried out. Very little discretion (if any at all) is left with the labour force. 'Responsible autonomy' on the other hand relies on the informed exercise of discretion by the worker, who is assumed to be capable of acting responsibly and knowledgeably.

Both of these approaches reflect the exercise of strategic choice. The use of unskilled labour on grounds of cost implies that being untrained, such workers will not have (even if it is assumed they are capable of acquiring) the skills or knowledge necessary for the exercise of informed discretion. On the other hand, a decision to opt for 'responsible autonomy' implies that not only must skilled and trained workers be recruited in the first place, but that continued training will be necessary in order to take advantage of product and process innovation.

Wilkinson (1983) provides examples of such strategies in action. He studied a number of enterprises which installed similar CNC tools but which adopted different strategies. Some separated out the programming functions into white collar departments, even if they staffed such departments from among the skilled workers. The result was that those left on the machines became not much more than 'minders', and had in effect been 'deskilled'. Other companies, however, trained the machinists to do the programming, thus enhancing the skills of those concerned. These cases provide a classic example of how a choice by management produced different structures although the technology was similar. 'De-skilling strategies were, however, more dominant than others, and it would take something of a shift in political stance among managers to change this situation' (Wilkinson, 1983).

The political nature of the process of strategic choice is illustrated by Wilkinson's examples of how in some cases work groups had to some extent succeeded in keeping control of skills, and had even developed new ones by training themselves to edit programs prepared off the shopfloor.

alternative courses of action. While size, market or technology may place constraints on the choices that are available, a real choice may nevertheless still be exercised.

The strategic intentions of management are more important than the technology in terms of the conflict that results from technological change and its impact on the labour force. A comparison of innovation in a number of industries in the USA and UK showed that '... conflict emerged from the desire to cut labour costs at all stages of the process: the technology merely offered assistance' (Willman, 1986). The political aspect of technological change is illustrated in Case Study 5.8.

Taking v. making decisions

The selection of corporate goals, and the means of achieving them, present an opportunity for the exercise of strategic choice. Such choices may involve, for example, the selection of the following: What specific rate of return on investment? Or what specific market share? Low-price high-volume, or high-price low-volume sectors of the market? Certainly once these choices have been made certain consequences may follow as day follows night, but this should not be allowed to conceal the fact that some strategic **choice** has been exercised.

The process of technological change is significant in illustrating the existence of strategic choice since the introduction of new technology is clearly a matter of strategy, that is the determination of goals and the allocation of resources to achieve them. The decision to introduce process or product innovation is a feature of the response to the product market environment by those who control the enterprise. In response to product market pressures the firm may develop new products or vary the price, quality or quantity of existing products. Or a decision may be made to identify a specific market niche, or to abandon the market altogether. The management of an organization, or group of organizations, may even bring about or prevent changes in the market. Advertising, lobbying, the activity of industry-financed pressure groups such as the Road Transport Federation, the Office of Health Economics and the Food Research Council may all have a part to play in mediating developments in the market.

A consideration of the choices which may be available to those who control organizations directs attention towards those groups or individuals who can exercise the power to **make**, even if they do not actually **take**, key decisions. This distinction is an important one and can be illustrated by considering the role of an expert advisor. Advisors are in the position of being able to present decision parameters based upon their expertise. That is, they can dismiss some alternatives as just being unworkable for a variety of reasons. As an advisor an expert will not have the authority to actually *take* the decision, but by virtue of the advice given will have been influential in at least narrowing down the range of options for the decision-taker(s) such that the eventual outcome may be inevitable. The expert then may well have **made** the decision although he or she did not actually **take** it. Of course, the recipient of such expert advice may ignore it, but there is then the problem of defending such action should the eventual decision not turn out favourably. Pettigrew's classic study, *The Politics of Organizational Decision-making* (1973), explores the nature of organizations as political systems and the role of power in decision-making as well as the significance of the decision-making and -taking distinction. A key figure in Pettigrew's case study was a manager whose structural location within the organization kept him in touch with the department which would operate a new computer, the board which would ultimately take the decision as to which machine to purchase, and the sales staff of the potential suppliers.

The decision to hire the services of consultants in cases such as that examined by Pettigrew is often not because the requisite knowledge and experience are not available internally, though that may at times be the case, but because of intra-organizational politics. As 'outsiders', consultants can be used as independent advocates for a course of action that those in control of the organization wished to undertake anyway. The converse can also apply; consultants can be used to justify not doing something which those in control had no wish to do in the first place.

A politics of decision-making

Having considered the nature and basis of power, and recognized that choices may indeed be available, it is then useful to consider the behaviour of those managing an organization in terms of political processes. Wildavsky (1964 and 1979) has demonstrated how the process of budgeting can be viewed not just as a social process, but as a political one. Since resources are scarce and have alternative uses it is necessary to undertake some considered examination of how they should be allocated – to whom, how much, for how long, for what return. In such a process differing points of view and interests (based upon departmentalization and the division of labour) will operate to produce conflicts that will require resolution if the enterprise is to function coherently, as an integrated unit.

One of the reasons for the status and influence of accounting may well derive from its role as a means of changing the nature of discussions about issues such as objectives and strategies and their implications for the exercise of control. By appearing as simply a technique, accounting creates the impression of objectivity and rational calculation rather than of political horse-trading (see Hopwood, 1983 and 1984). Those who do not understand the technical aspects, but nevertheless wish to contest the outcome, will find themselves at a considerable (political) disadvantage. 'The task of political language and symbolic activity is to rationalise and justify decisions that are largely a result of power and influence, in order to make these results acceptable and legitimate in the organization' (Pfeffer, 1981, p. 184).

Who are the politicians?

The most obvious groupings, perhaps analogous to political parties, are departments. Organizational departments are groupings which share a common situation and will perceive the world in a particular way. The interests of different departments are therefore likely to be different. For example, marketing will argue that either they should be given a larger budget for advertising, market research or even bonuses to motivate sales staff, or that more effective management of the production process is what is required. Production on the other hand will argue that more investment in process plant is necessary. Within departments there may also be factions who are influential in determining what strategies should be adopted in the competition for resources and how those resources should be utilized once they have been allocated.

While functional departments may be obvious political entities there are other possibilities. As we saw earlier, departmentalization by function is just one of a number of strategies available to organizational designers; another one is divisionalization around products or geographic areas, for example. Those who are employed by an organization, however it is structured, can also be categorized according to other attributes: age, sex, race, length of service, social and educational background, any of which may serve as a basis for coordinated action.

Exercise

Take as an example the department in which your course is located. Is it in fact located in a Department of Business Studies, or is it located in some other administrative unit within which groups of academic specialists are located? If it is located in a Department of Business Studies, does that department contain specialist staff (accountants, sociologists, economists, psychologists, marketing and personnel specialists, etc.), or do these specialist subjects get taught by 'servicing' arrangements with Departments of Accountancy, Sociology, Economics?

What is the relative influence upon the teaching, design and organization of your course of those who lecture on it as opposed to those whose role is mainly administrative?

Spend some time identifying what the influential groupings are. You can always ask student representatives on the various committees for their impressions.

It should be possible to identify categories of 'political' actors. What is required is some clustering around opinions, preferences and values which relate to what are regarded as important issues within the organization at the time. 'What the analyst wants to do is to identify groupings which are as inclusive as possible and which are internally homogeneous with respect to preferences and beliefs on the issues being investigated' (Pfeffer, 1981).

It is useful to start by making use of the groupings and the labels used by the organization since socialization by departments or expert groups has a powerful effect upon individual members. Being accepted as a member will require that an individual accepts (more rather than less) the frame of reference of the grouping to which they are attached.

Some of the possible groupings will suggest that, as in the wider society, individuals may have cross-cutting ties or attachments to a number of groups. An accountant employed in a business studies department may also have contacts with the Department of Accountancy; members of this department may influence the individual's approach and attitudes towards the courses upon which he or she teaches. Even within a department there may be sub-groupings based around shared values and expectations – say about the criteria for promotion, teaching responsibilities, research output, administrative duties.

Dominant coalitions and their role: a negotiated order

The possible diversity of interests within a single department in an organization, let alone between departments, suggests the further utility of viewing organizations as systems of coalitions. This idea was first put forward by Cyert and March (1963). It is consistent with the political analogy as it implies some negotiation between those whose interests, while not necessarily coinciding, are not necessarily mutually exclusive either. That is, 'you support me on this, and I'll support you on that' type

---

Cyert and March (1963) developed the concept of the 'dominant coalition' in the context of strategic choice within organizations. A dominant coalition is that coalition of interests which is able to impose its definitions of current problems upon others, and is also able to get its selection from among the available solutions accepted and implemented. The idea of a 'dominant coalition' is an abstraction in the sense that the identification of a coalition and the extent to which it may be dominant must be the result of empirical observations. An observer may be able to identify individuals as forming a coalition of interests as a result of their contribution to a debate. By recording the progress of the debate, the formulation of assertion and counter-assertion, it may be possible to identify the dominance or otherwise of a coalition.

As already implied in discussion of the formal and informal dimension to organizations, a dominant coalition may not be synonymous with the groups holding formal authority; secondly there may be a number of coalitions vying for dominance at any one time. Nevertheless, the concept of dominant coalitions is useful because it concentrates attention on the identification of powerful groupings and hence facilitates the examination of their influence upon strategic decision-making. It can account for changes within an organization over time as the dominant coalition changes in response to changing sources of uncertainty, and it can also cope with differences between organizations which are facing different sources of uncertainty. Understanding the behaviour of and in organizations can be enhanced by utilizing concepts from politics since this makes it possible to develop coherent and consistent accounts of what is going on and why it is going on. Failure to do this has been one of the major weaknesses of theories of organization and technology up to and including the 1970s and is largely responsible for the sometimes conflicting and often confusing volume of published research data on the relationship between organizational size, technology and structure.

KEY CONCEPT 5.12

DOMINANT COALITIONS

of negotiation – what the Americans call 'log-rolling'. The notion of a 'dominant coalition' is defined in Key Concept 5.12.

As a result of the division of labour and consequent specialization, organizations are very much systems of interdependent units. That is, in

---

CASE STUDY 5.9

ESTABLISHING A COALITION

Peter Smith was the manager of a medium-sized plant producing packaging cartons for a wide range of customers. He had been installed as 'managing director' of the unprofitable plant when it had been taken over by a national producer of packaging materials from the family who had founded it nearly 100 years ago. Smith was marked out for rapid promotion in the national company, and this was his chance to show what he was capable of. He had been given three years to produce a turnaround in profitability and had managed it in two. Part of his strategy had been based on the realization that an important aspect of the purchase of packaging material by his customers was storage. Companies using his products wanted to draw off small amounts at a time, and the ability to do this rather than store it themselves influenced their attitude to his prices. However, producing in 'small' batches added to Smith's costs, given the way his superiors designed and operated their quantitative control systems, because of the setting-up times involved.

It dawned on Smith soon after his appointment as he was doing one of his daily tours around the plant that he actually had available considerable storage space on site. This was a large hanger-like building which the previous owners had acquired when they purchased an adjoining site for expansion which had never materialized. Smith realized that he could utilize this space for storage thus meeting both his customers needs and his own.

With his commercial and sales managers he worked out pricing structures which, combined with the relatively small take-up sought by many of the larger customers, would enable them to expand their share of a very tight market, and meet the profitability targets set by head office. All went well until an accountant at head office, undertaking a review of property values, realized that Smith's site was much larger than required for the existing operation and consisted of a block of land upon which was a large warehouse and which could therefore be sold for development at a considerable cash profit.

When Smith heard about this he lost no time in telling his customers that he would be prevented from meeting their requirements as previously. He pointed out that their interests and his coincided on this point and they should support him against head office. His customers wrote to Smith letters which he sent on to head office, pointing out that in a highly competitive market they would be forced to take their business elsewhere if they could not rely on the service Smith had been offering. The potential loss of major customers in a highly competitive regional market persuaded head office both to delay selling the area in question until adequate storage was available on the main site and to provide funds for the provision of a replacement store.

order for one department or section to be able to attain its targets, the cooperation of at least one other department is necessary. This may create either conflict or cooperation. Cooperation will result where the realization develops that both groups can achieve satisfactory results if they collaborate while neither will be successful if they oppose each other. Organizational politics may then result in coalitions both within and without the organization as illustrated in Case Study 5.9.

It has been argued by Strauss *et al.* (1964) that organizations are in fact 'negotiated environments'. The situation in the mine in Goulder's study of the gypsum plant provides an example of a 'negotiated' order. That is, managers had at least turned a Nelsonian eye to some of the practices of the work group in exchange for 'acceptable' levels of output. The new management disrupted a previously negotiated order and attempted to impose a new one without much negotiation. The miners responded by working to rule, and eventually resorted to the strike weapon.

One of the features of bureaucratic records is that they serve as an 'organizational memory' which may facilitate negotiation by providing a 'record' of what has happened in the past and why. The existence of bureaucratic records facilitates negotiation in so far as they provide a basis for negotiation by setting out the basic framework for subsequent meetings. It is for this reason that whoever writes the minutes of a meeting can exercise considerable . . . 'influence' . . . over subsequent negotiations!

The idea of organizational order as 'negotiated' reflects the operation of factors which may limit or at least constrain the exercise of power. Individuals and departments will be less closely supervised to the extent that they are seen as 'successful' and consequently 'trusted'. Minor and even major infringements of organizational rules may be tolerated by superiors if the superiors are confident that targets will be reliably attained. The autonomy which success in the organization's terms brings an individual or department frees a superior to concentrate on those areas of activity which remain problematic in the organizational context.

It is important to note that the formation of a coalition does not imply that those forming it are equally influential. Indeed it can be presumed that the less powerful will be the more anxious to establish a coalition with a more powerful grouping in order to compensate for their own lack of power. Providing a service is a way of making another, to some extent, dependent upon you. Even if power is, as is usual, unequally distributed, there will be areas or issues which will redress the balance between groupings even if only for the duration of a particular issue. The work of Stewart and Mintzberg provide examples of how the behaviour of managers is oriented towards a concern to establish allies both within and outside their own organization. Observation of managers which the present author has undertaken provided numerous examples of managers making efforts to help another manager, even one in a customer's organization, simply in order to be able to call on that support at some later date, or to gain an ally in a current issue.

Sponsorship and the selection of protégés represent other forms of relationship that can be influential in exercising, gaining or increasing power. The sponsorship of senior managers is often crucial to successful innovation as well as the furtherance of individual careers. A characteristic of apparently successful managers, at least in terms of their personal careers, is the extent to which they seek, and more importantly, maintain personal contacts. It is important of course to make sure that your contacts are amongst those who are themselves successful!

As has been mentioned several times, one factor in the structuring of an organization is the problem of handling information. Organizational structures are information handling structures and so are likely to be influenced by the availability of cheap information technology. This presents another opportunity for strategic choice since the technology can be utilized either to centralize information flows and so enhance the ability of those at the top of the hierarchy to exercise control, or it can be used to disperse information more widely throughout the organization which is likely to increase the apparent autonomy of other groups. The information component of the model of business linking this volume with others in the series will be explored next in Chapter 6.

Summary

In this chapter we have considered an approach to the range of factors which may influence the design of organization structures that focuses upon the exercise of choice by dominant coalitions and the ability to impose that decision choice on others.

Such an approach requires the examination of the nature and basis of power and by whom power is exercised. In organizational terms this suggests the utility of the concept of dominant coalitions, whose power derives from the perceived ability to cope with uncertainty and their structural location within the organization in terms of the pervasiveness and immediacy of their tasks for the organization as a whole. The processes of intra-organizational life should then be understood in terms of a political framework. The management of organizations, the identification of strategic goals and the allocation of resources of the means of achieving them should be viewed as political processes involving the exercise of choice, albeit a constrained choice on occasions.

In this way the inference of causal relationships between what were previously just statistically correlated (and taken for granted) variables is possible. Also, not only is the issue of power directly addressed, but variations in structure and decision-making over time within the same organization and between different organizations at the same time can be explored and understood.

The discussion of power and its exercise by dominant coalitions is important in understanding behaviour within organizations. Regarding organizational processes as political avoids the methodological problem of reification – literally 'thingification' – which is treating an organization as though it is independent of the people who compose it and control the allocation of resources (see Key Concept 4.10). Organizations do not have 'needs' – people do. To talk of the needs of an organization is to resort to an ideological ploy to persuade others of the objective validity of what is only a particular point of view.

In Chapter 6 we move on to consider the role of information in organizations in the context of organizational structure and power. Information was always a major business resource long before information technology (IT) created the contemporary concern and interest in the competitive advantage that sophisticated information handling can provide. The demands of information processing make their own impact upon organizational structures and behaviour within them as we shall see.

Study questions

1. Why, as Mark Twain is reputed to have said, is there nothing quite so practical as a good theory?
2. Upon what basis may it be argued that management is a political process?
3. What is the basis of power in organizations?
4. How is 'power' distinguished from 'authority'?
5. What is meant by 'strategic choice'?
6. How does the concept of strategic choice enhance understanding of the impact of environmental factors on organizational structure?

Further reading

Child's (1972) paper provides a very succinct account of the role and nature of dominant coalitions and their role in strategic choice; Child (1984) gives a fuller account. Also, Pfeffer (1981) gives a very full treatment of power in both business and academic institutions – it sometimes makes amusing reading! A more philosophical or theoretical (but still very accessible) examination of power is offered by Lukes (1974).

References

Bachrach, P. and Baratz, S. (1962) Two faces of power. *American Political Science Review*, **56**, 947–52.

Baritz, L. (1975) The servants of power. In Esland, G., Salaman, G. and Speakman, M.-A. (eds) *People and Work*. Open University Press.

Brosnan, P. and Wilkinson, F. (1988) A National Statutory Minimum Wage and Economic Efficiency. *Contributions to Political Economy*, **7**, 1–48.

Buchanan, D. and Boddy, D. (1983) *Organisations in the Computer Age*. Gower.

Campbell, A., Currie, W. and Warner, M. (1989) Innovation, skills and training: microelectronics and manpower in the United Kingdom and West Germany. In Hirst, P. and Zeitlin, J. (eds) *Reversing Industrial Decline? Industrial Structure in Britain and Her Competitors*. Berg

Child, J. (1972) Organisational structure, environment and performance: the role of strategic choice. *Sociology*, **6**, (1), 1–21.

Child, J. (1984) *Organisation: A Guide to Problems and Practice*, 2nd edn. Harper & Row.

Child, J. *et al*. (1983) A Price to Pay? Professionalism and Work Organization in Britain and West Germany. *Sociology* **17**, 1.

Crozier, M. (1964) *The Bureaucratic Phenomenon*. University of Chicago Press.

Cyert, R.M. and March, J.G. (1963) *A Behavioural Theory of the Firm*. Prentice Hall.

Dickson, D. (1974) *Alternative Technology and the Politics of Technical Change*, Fontana.

Donaldson, G. and Lorsch, J.W. (1983) *Decision Making at the Top*: *The Shaping of Strategic Direction*. Basic Books.

Duncan, R. (1972) Characteristics of organisational environments and perceived uncertainty. *Administrative Science Quarterly*, **17**, 313–27.

French, J.P. and Raven, B. (1959) The bases of social power. In (D. Cartwright, ed.) *Studies in Social Power*. Ann Arbor, Mich.

Friedman, A. (1977) Industry and Labour: class struggle at work and monopoly capitalism, Macmillan.

Gerth, H.H. and Mills, C. Wright (1964) *From Max Weber*: *Essays in Sociology*. Routledge and Kegan Paul.

Hayes, R.H. and Jaikumar, R. (1988) Manufacturing's Crisis: New Technologies, Obsolete Organisations. *Harvard Business Review*, Sept/Oct, 77–85.

Hendry, D. and Ericsson, N. (1983) Assertion without empirical basis: an econometric appraisal of monetary trends in the United States and the UK: *Bank of England Paper (22)*.

Hinings, C.R., Hickson, D.J., Pennings, J.M., and Schenk, R.E. (1974) Structural Conditions of Intraorganisational Power. *Administrative Science Quarterly* **19**, 22–44.

Hopwood, A.G. (1983) On trying to study accounting in the contexts in which it operates. *Accounting, Organisations and Society*, **8**, (2/3), 287–305.

Hopwood, A.G. (1984) Accounting and the pursuit of efficiency. In Hopwood, A.G. and Tomkins, G. (eds) *Issues in Public Sector Accounting*. Philip Allen.

Lukes, S. (1974) *Power*: *A Radical View*. Macmillan.

Luthans, F. (1973) The contingency theory of management: A path out of the jungle. *Business Horizons*, June, 58–72.

Mintzberg, H. (1973) *The Nature of Managerial Work*, Harper & Row.

Mintzberg, H. (1983) *Structure in Fives*: *Designing Effective Organisations*, Prentice Hall.

Mintzberg, H. (1989) *Mintzberg on Management*, Free Press.

Mulkay, M.J. (1972) *The Social Process of Innovation*. Macmillan.

Neale, A. and Haslam, C. (1989) *Economics in a Business Context*. Chapman and Hall.

Ozanne, R. (1967) *A Century of Labour–Management Relations at McCormick and International Harvester*. University of Wisconsin Press.

Perrow, C. (1972) *Complex Organisations*, 2nd edn. Scott Foresman.

Peters, T.J. and Waterman, R.H. (1982) *In Search of Excellence*. Harper & Row.

Pettigrew, A.M. (1973) *The Politics of Organisational Decision Making*. Tavistock.

Pfeffer, J. (1981) *Power in Organisations*. Pitman.

Rapoport, A. (1974) *Conflict in a Man-Made Environment*. Penguin.

Rueschmeyer, D. (1986) *Power and Division of Labour*. Polity Press.

Stewart, R. (1985) *The Reality of Management* 2nd ed. Heineman.

Stewart, R. (1976) *Contrasts in Management*, McGraw-Hill.

Stewart, R. (1982) *Choices for the Managers*, McGraw-Hill.

Strauss, A., Schatzman, R., Bucher, D. *et al.* (1964) *Psychiatric Ideologies*. Free Press.

Wildavsky, A. (1964) *The Politics of the Budgetary Process*. Little Brown & Co.

Wildavsky, A. (1979) *Speaking Truth to Power: The Art and Craft of Policy Analysis*. Little Brown & Co.

Wilkinson, B. (1982) Managing with New Technology. *Management Today*, October, 33–37.

Wilkinson, (1983) *The Shopfloor Politics of the New Technology*, Heineman.

Willman, P. (1986) *Technological Change, Collective Bargaining and Industrial Efficiency*.

Winner, L. (1985) Do artifacts have politics? In Mackenzie, D. and Wajcman, J. (eds) *The Social Shaping of Technology*. Open University Press.

Wood, S. (1982) *The Degradation of work? Still, deskilling and the labour process*, Hutchinson.

6 Information and decisions in organizations

In this chapter we build on material from Chapters 4 and 5 to undertake an examination of the ways in which information technology may influence behaviour in a business context. In doing so we will consider the nature of human decision-making in general, rather than in terms of individual psychology. The context for the present chapter is the examination undertaken in previous chapters of factors which influence the structuring of organizations and the exercise of power within them. As we saw, dominant coalitions exercise strategic choice in developing different structures to cope with environmental constraints. The amount of information to be processed as a result of changes in the environment can be regarded as an important form of environmental constraint. Aspects of strategy which relate to the material covered in this chapter are to be found in Chapter 4 of Needle (1989).

There are at least two aspects to the central role of information in business behaviour. Not only is information required concerning the external environment of the firm, but information is also required concerning the responses of the various sub-units of the organization as they cope with the demands placed upon them from inside and outside the organization.

The implications of research into the contingency approach to organizational structures are that the processes by which the decision-makers in an organization receive and process data concerning organizational and sub-unit performance must match the organization structure and its environment. It is an important aspect of competitive advantage that management acquire and respond to both internal and external data more rapidly than can competitors. Similarly, the quality of the data is also crucial to competitive advantage. While this is not the place for a major investigation into information systems as such (Davis and Olson (1984) is a useful source, for example), it will be necessary to consider briefly some examples. In doing so, we will be moving into the central area of the business in context model which provides a focus for this and companion volumes in the series.

In this chapter we will be focusing on just-in-time methods of operation. Such methods, as well as representing a growing trend in modern organizations, are illustrations of the interactive nature of businesses, their activities and their environments and the vital role played by information.

Just-in-time methods of operation

Just-in-time methods manufacturing

Consider the often quoted 'just-in-time' (JIT) production systems pioneered by Japanese car firms and currently much in vogue in the United Kingdom. Such a system delivers components to the manufacturing site, and then to the workstation, immediately before they are required in the manufacturing process. 'Immediately' here means just that – not days, but at most hours before the component is required in the production process. The goal is to reduce production lead times (the time from the arrival of the component or raw material at the first stage of production to when the finished product leaves the production line) but anything up to 90% (Foster and Horngren, 1987). The characteristics of JIT systems are set out in Key Concept 6.1.

The idea of JIT centres around the elimination of waste. The continuous elimination of waste brings about changes in every aspect of company's activities:

☐ Eliminating work-in-process by reducing batch size – ideally to one;
☐ Eliminating raw material inventories as suppliers deliver direct to the shopfloor just in time to be incorporated in manufacture;
☐ Eliminating scrap by emphasizing total quality control;
☐ Eliminating finished goods inventories by reducing lead times such that all products are made to order;
☐ Elimination of material handling costs by redesigning the shopfloor so that materials flow directly between adjacent work stations.

KEY CONCEPT 6.1

JUST-IN-TIME PRODUCTION

Crucial to the operation of JIT systems is the collection and dissemination of information. The absence of buffer stocks means that information about the functioning of the various components of the production, supply and sales systems must be accurately and readily available to all involved. This extends to the operations of the suppliers and their production and sales systems on the one hand, and to machine operators on the other. In the case of operators, knowledge and information is required to mimimize the likelihood, and negative consequences of, machine or tool failure.

The production line under JIT conditions is operated on a 'demand-pull' basis. A workstation early in the process responds to demands from stations later in the process. In this way, the stock at a workstation is reduced to a minimum, ideally one item. Demand for warehousing is also drastically reduced, perhaps to a size sufficient to cope with no more than three hours' production.

The reduction of work-in-progress, inventory and buffer stocks in this way places great emphasis upon quality, of the raw materials and components received from suppliers, and of the work from each workstation to the next. With no buffer stocks, a below-standard component or subassembly results in the production line stopping. There are no buffer stocks to keep workstations active while re-working is carried out.

These consequences of JIT place considerable pressure upon those responsible for the various systems involved. The stress on managers, supervisors and operators requires that careful consideration be given to the structure and organization of work, and to information flows. For example, the need to feed back information about quality has resulted in systems which place responsibility for quality upon operators, rather than some other organizationally located individual or group. This also has implications for training to ensure that operators can cope with the responsibility, and, inevitably, for pay systems.

Just-in-time methods in retailing

Similar pressures affecting information flows and availability operate in retailing. Supermarket chains expect their managers to be able to order overnight for delivery within twenty-four hours, probably inside twelve. Competition between food processors/manufacturers is then not just in terms of products, but also in terms of the standards of their information systems so that they can participate in electronic data interchanges with their customers, particularly the major supermarket chains.

In the travel and tour operator business, the ability of a package tour operator to keep travel agents informed as to what seats are available upon which tour may well provide a competitive edge that can overcome price differentials. Tour operator X may be more expensive, but if the agent has up to date information which is lacking for other operators, then X may well clinch the sale.

The operational implications of JIT for manufacturers are set out in Case Study 6.1. Remember that similar influences will operate in the service sector.

CASE STUDY 6.1

JIT AND LEAD TIME TO WORK

The nature and significance of JIT can be illustrated by considering the operation of the system on a relatively small scale, what has been termed 'micro-JIT'.

If you look around the shopfloor of a manufacturing company, you will observe machines, say metal-working machines like milling, boring or turning machines, organized in some sequence. By each machine will be a stock of parts awaiting to be turned or milled etc., and another stock of parts that have been treated by that machine and are awaiting transfer to the next workstation. Evidence from the USA suggests that in conventional manufacturing processes (i.e. pre-JIT), the amount of time occupied by processes that add value to the material or item amounts to 0.5% of the time the material spends in the total production process. The remaining 99.5% is taken up by storage, moving, waiting, inspecting, re-working and so on. Over a three to five year period it is estimated that continuous improvements can increase the proportion of time spent in value-adding processes to around 15% (NEDO, 1988).

Consider a single machine or workstation. There will be a pallet or container of some sort from which parts will be taken by a human operator or a robot or mechanical system, placed on the worktable of the machine and then machined as required. After machining, each component or part will be placed in a container for transfer to the next process or machine. The container(s) from which the unmachined parts are drawn will be refilled from time to time.

Let us say that at any one time there are forty items in the container awaiting machining. Suppose those forty items are worth £10 each at that stage. That is the equivalent, at just that one workstation, of £400 lying around waiting for something to happen – work-in-progress at that machine is therefore £400. For the next machine in the sequence, of course, the value of WIP is even higher since the workstation we are considering will have added yet more value to each item by carrying out that operation. If the number of parts awaiting the next operation is also forty, but each is now worth, say, £12, then WIP is £480 at that workstation, and so on throughout the workshop.

There is another way of looking at this problem, by considering 'the lead time to work' content. Let us assume that each item awaiting machining takes six minutes to be machined. This means that with forty items awaiting machining at any one time the fortieth item will have waited 40 × 6 minutes, i.e. 240 minutes (4 hours), for six minutes (0.1 hours) work. That is a lead time to work content of 40:1.

The ideal ratio JIT would be 1:1, i.e. six minutes of lead time for six minutes work time. This would be achieved by having each part arrive just as the machine was ready to take it – no queueing at all. This ideal can perhaps be relaxed to a ratio of 2:1, with perhaps 3:1 still being considered acceptable. Anything above 5:1 should be considered very poor.

JIT will require the removal of 'buffer stocks' of WIP at each workstation by ensuring that parts flow directly from one machine to the next, arriving just in time to be worked on. This will require the harmonization of the speed at which the various machines involved in the process carry out their operations in order to avoid a build up of parts after the faster machines or before the slower ones. However, JIT is much more than the improvement of flows on the shopfloor; it is a pervasive philosophy that requires the integration of **all** aspects of the company's activities including job design, staff training and flexibility, purchasing, scheduling, marketing and selling.

Information and control: JIT and work organization

The type and degree of pressure placed upon work organization by JIT methods raises once again the question of the control of work and the role of information. In manufacturing, the emphasis upon quality which is integral to JIT requires that work organization in the assembly plant as well as in suppliers' plants is rigorously scrutinized. Human motivation (see

Chapter 7) is an important factor in attaining and maintaining high quality work whatever the industry or level in the hierarchy occupied by employees. In manufacturing, the minimal buffer stocks characteristic of JIT require that workers undertake a range of tasks, such as routine maintenance, fault-finding and setting-up, previously allocated to specialist groups of workers. This is because variations or problems have to be coped with immediately, rather than being left until a member of a specialized group which is allocated the responsibility arrives. Flexibility in this sense extends to the ability to work at a number of stations or processes. Once again, as in the first industrial revolution, what is significantly 'new' is not so much the technology (the components of which have been around for some time), but the way in which work is organized to take advantage of it.

Superior manufacturing performance does not depend upon investment in highly complex equipment, but upon the detailed examination of the whole process of manufacturing, not just the actual process of machining and assembly, but all the other activities which surround it. That the emphasis should be on process and not technology is shown by the fact that inventory reductions of up to 40% can be obtained in less than a year. This suggests that the examination of current procedures is all that is necessary in order to obtain considerable savings. There is no necessary requirement for technological change.

A major feature of successful competition is the efficiency with which organizational systems and practices operate (Depaoli *et al.*, 1986; Rushton *et al.*, 1986). Describing changes in the British car industry, Marsden *et al.* (1985) wrote that while major reductions occurred in the proportion of assembly workers and labourers (and clerical and secretarial staff), the major impact upon assemblers was not automation but changes in working practices on the line and improvements in car design which eased assembly.

A comparison of the American and Japanese car industries suggested that about 60% of the productivity differential in favour of the Japanese over the American industry was the result of the **organizational abilities** of companies in the areas of production process and personnel. The majority of this 60% advantage was due to a low rate of faults, reductions in processing time, increased working time due to plant reliability, maintenance practices and materials control procedures. About a third of the advantage was thought to be due to differences in job structure and responsibilities where Japanese workers experienced wider job profiles requiring more expertise and greater involvement in programming and controlling operations. This resulted in fewer management layers in the hierarchy (Abernathy *et al.*, 1981). The effectiveness of Japanese factories is argued to have more to do with the skills and responsibilities of workers than with the numbers employed, which may be larger than some British plants (Campbell *et al.*, 1989).

The philosophy associated with JIT can be compared to that which is known as 'just-in-case'. With the latter approach there is a back-up system to keep production going whatever may go wrong. The most common form of such a 'back-up' system is that of an inventory: there is always a stock of raw materials and components, part-finished and finished products, labour and machines just in case something unexpected happens. Machine breakdowns, for example, are accommodated by work-in-progress at the other machine stations, and extra demand is met by stocks of finished goods and raw materials, labour and machines, all of which may spend long periods unused or underutilized.

It is important to note that JIT production does not imply a rapid reduction in stocks, stoppages and interruptions to the manufacturing process. What matters is that there is a widely shared philosophy of **continually** improving performance towards an ideal of where the time required for parts to travel from goods inwards to despatch to customers is only as long as the time required for all the value-adding processes in manufacturing. The point is to seek continuous improvements, not to achieve dramatic, once and for all advances. It is in this context that information flows and availability have an important part to play in establishing competitive capability and advantage.

Information and organization

The implementation of JIT systems implies not only changes in the way information is collected and used, but also by whom it is collected and how and by whom it is used. For this reason information systems and organizational structures exist in a symbiotic or reciprocal relationship. Information systems can exert influence upon the structure of the organization and existing structures can influence the design and implementation of an information system. It appears that the information, knowledge and skill enjoyed by Japanese workers is an important component in achieving process efficiency. As discussed in previous chapters, there are choices to be made.

A common prediction at one time was that information systems would lead to increasing centralization. It was argued that improved access to information would allow managers to control even more activities more closely than they had previously. At the present time, and consistent with the discussion in the previous two chapters, it is considered that information systems are not **necessarily** causal in terms of structure. Depending upon strategic choices concerning goals and strategies, information systems may either increase or decrease centralization. For example, Robey (1981) found that of eight organizations he studied no less than five displayed no change at all in their formal structures. Furthermore, the changes that were made in the remaining organizations tended to reinforce, rather than alter, existing structures, as illustrated in Case Study 6.2.

To understand the impact of information technology in and on organizations it is necessary to build upon the two previous chapters. Such a foundation is necessary in order to understand the implications of the nature of human decision-making for the design and implementation of information systems, and their relationship with organization structures and behaviour. The following sections examine three models of human decision-making which have been influential in the study of behaviour in business, and move on to consider the significance of forms of uncertainty for decision-making in business.

CASE STUDY 6.2

INFORMATION SYSTEMS IN A MAIL-ORDER COMPANY

The information system was primarily intended to cope with the processing of routine orders, using remote terminals to handle customer service and the entering of orders. As a result these two processes were decentralized with decision-making taking place at lower levels than had previously been the case. The result was an increased speed of service and a reduction in costs. In addition an increased volume of business was now capable of being processed. However, while decision-making was decentralized, the effect of the computerized system was to enable management to keep in touch with what was going on and so avoid any loss of control over the operation. Nor did they lose any power.

However, the situation in the area of purchasing was very different. The data from the ordering system was used for centralized statistical analysis. The nature of purchasing decisions is that they are less routine than is the case with the handling of orders. Since an important component of success in a mail-order operation depends upon purchasing and pricing decisions, it is not surprising that these are centralized whether a computer is used or not. The case of mail-order suggests that the question of centralization or decentralization may well depend upon function, and that both processes can occur at the same time within the same organization. What appears to be the case is that even where change does occur as a result of installing a computerized information system, such changes reinforce existing structures and are consistent with either managerial objectives or political strategies, or both.

Source: Robey (1981).

Models of human decision-making

There are at least three models of human decision-making which are closely related to the organizational context: the rational economic man model (REM), the administrative model and the behavioural model. Each will be briefly examined in turn.

Rational economic man

This model derives from the theories of classical economics and belongs to the category of models referred to as 'normative'. The model is more concerned with how a decision **ought** to be made than with how it is actually made. The normative aspect derives from the fact that using the term 'rational', the model implies that failure to observe the precepts of the model is 'irrational', or at best 'non'-rational. The decision rule, the criterion for selecting amongst available alternatives, is the 'maximization' of some outcome.

The prime objective of this model is not so much to **predict** or **explain** the observed behaviour of decision-makers, but to establish an optimal choice

The main components of the 'rational economic man' (REM) model are:

☐ All possible outcomes are known;
☐ All relevant information is available;
☐ The decision-maker seeks to 'maximize' the return.

KEY CONCEPT 6.2

'RATIONAL ECONOMIC MAN'

when the alternatives are well known. The decision-maker is assumed to desire the maximum return, either in terms of profit or some other benefit or utility. The validity of this type of model, the elements of which are set out in Key Concept 6.2, is dependent upon the identification of an unambiguous objective and an equally unambiguous understanding of the variables involved. Such a model may be considered to underlie financial procedures for example.

A moment's reflection will show that under the conditions set out in Key Concept 6.2, there really is no 'decision' as such to be made. The decision-maker does not have a problem in the sense of having to choose among alternatives (i.e. 'make a decision'). This is because under the three conditions stated, a simple calculation is all that is required to identify the maximizing course of action. Since no 'choice' is required, no 'decision' has to be made. The decision, so called, is one taken under 'certainty'.

It is possible to modify the first component of the REM model in so far as probabilities may be attached to outcomes. While all possible outcomes may be known, the likelihood of one outcome rather than another occurring cannot be known with certainty. This is known as decision-making under 'risk'. If the decision-maker has sufficient information to allocate probabilities to each of the outcomes, then a 'rational' actor can still maximize expected value. Examples of such normative procedures are game theory, linear programming and various statistical techniques associated with management science.

A major problem with the normative approach of rational economic man is the assumption of perfect information. Not only is it assumed that all relevant information is knowable, but that actually knowing it does not involve any expenditure of resources such as time, money and effort. In other words there is no 'opportunity cost'. In the context of the human situation this is untenable except, possibly, in the **very** short term.

The human condition, markets and individuals

The human condition is one in which it is not possible to have all relevant information. In the short term it may be easier to identify what is relevant and to achieve a high degree of confidence concerning the proportion that is actually known and the quality of the known information. However, if one is making a decision for which the outcome is at some point in the future then problems concerning relevant information, its acquisition, cost and quality, multiply. The typical business decision is going to be one in which certainty is at a premium. The number of variables that may change over, say, a five year period in the technical or market spheres are too numerous to allow certainty, as are the sources of such variation.

Given a number of a variables that could change, and variability in the manner in which they could change, the problem becomes the cost of identifying and acquiring the information, such as it is, that might be relevant. The opportunity cost of information then becomes important. The expenditure of effort and resources on information involves foregoing some other possible investment. Once information is not costless, then perfect information is not logically possible. Some individuals or firms are more likely to be able to meet the cost of acquiring the information than others. Since resources are not evenly distributed, then neither will information. If information is unequally distributed then some individuals or organizations will be at an advantage over others. This is a key factor in the failure of market mechanisms which will be examined in more detail in Chapter 8.

At the individual level one has only to consider the situation of someone who is trying to decide what model of car or hi-fi to purchase. Magazines are referred to, the relevant edition of *Which?* is studied, advice is sought from friends and retailers perhaps. In the end, though, a decision is required. Further information begins to increase rather than reduce doubts, and the sheer time occupied by searching becomes intolerable.

It is because information is not a costless resource, as the REM assumes, that separate markets may come into existence. For example, two retail outlets stocking the same range of goods but at either end of a street may be able to offer differing prices. The extra effort and time (i.e. opportunity cost) incurred by potential customers as they trudge up and down the street to identify the lower price may be such that the number of people who prefer to settle for the price they know, and so do not continue the search, enables the two enterprises to achieve 'satisfactory' results. Is this 'irrational' behaviour on the part of either the shopkeepers or the public?

The administrative model of decision-making

This model was developed by Simon (1960) in his book *The New Science of Management Decision*, based upon an examination of how business people **actually** went about their decision-making. It is therefore a 'descriptive' model.

As a matter of observation, it is apparent that when people make a decision they are not necessarily attempting to 'maximize' some outcome or utility. We have already discussed (in Chapter 5) that it is not possible to maximize profits unless the time period can be specified, and that an important question remains whether profit is an end in itself or a means to achieving some strategic objective.

It is also a matter of empirical investigation that decision-makers do not consider **all** possible outcomes. They concentrate on achieving one or two of a relatively small number of outcomes. Neither do they have all the information or even an awareness of its availability. In fact, human decision-makers are caught up in a complex and at best only partially known environment. The phrase 'bounded rationality' is used to describe this situation as explained in Key Concept 6.3.

Under this 'descriptive' model (descriptive because it describes what people actually do, rather than what they 'ought' to do), it is argued that

The essential features of the administrative model of decision-making are:

☐ Only some outcomes are known;
☐ Only limited search takes place, on the basis of partial information;
☐ 'Satisfactory', not maximized, outcomes are sought.

What happens is that decision-makers are 'rational', i.e. able to justify what they did, within limits. The limits are set by their perception of available alternatives and scarce resources which have alternative uses. This is what Simon refers to as 'bounded rationality', the bounds being set by resources, experience and perceptions of alternatives.

KEY CONCEPT 6.3

THE ADMINISTRATIVE MODEL OF DECISION-MAKING AND BOUNDED RATIONALITY

decision-makers conduct a limited search amongst **known** alternatives. They accept an alternative which 'satisfies' the constraints they face. They will not go on searching until an 'optimal' alternative is identified. The administrative model assumes 'satisficing' rather than 'maximizing' behaviour. The dangers for business in this situation are illustrated in Case Study 6.3.

A canning company which held nearly 65% of the market for its main product persuaded the board of the parent group to invest several million pounds in a new automated factory. The basic assumption was that the pre-eminence of the main product, a premier brand at a premium price, would continue and so the calculations assumed long runs of a standard item at a relatively high selling price.

However, while the new plant was being built a number of features of the product market and the wider environment began to change. These changes concerned food processing technology, international trade in fruit and vegetables, and changes in the operation of the retail sector brought about by the growth of supermarkets and 'own-brands'.

After the removal of restrictions on the availability of tinplate in the 1950s, a number of small canning companies had established themselves to take advantage of a growing international market in imported fruit. This trade was basically seasonal, and so the canning companies were always on the look out for alternative products during the 'off' season for fruit.

The growth of popularity of quick-frozen food in the United States had a side effect of making available a sudden increase in the supply of vegetables which while of too low a quality to be frozen were suitable for canning. These were released onto world markets for cattle feed at very low prices. This happened because freezing requires constant standards of produce which cannot be easily maintained, so substandard crops (by the standard of quick-freezing processors) became available in considerable quantities at irregular intervals.

CASE STUDY 6.3

Continued from previous page

These crops were imported by the small canners at higher than animal feed prices, but still relatively low by normal canning standards, so as to keep their plants operating in the intervals between fruit harvests.

While the lower cost competition developed, and frozen foods began to encroach into the market share of the premium brand, the introduction of own-brand labels by the developing chains of supermarkets gave the small canners an opportunity to obtain bulk orders for their relatively cheap product. Not having any demand for expensive brand image advertising and so on, they were able to undercut further the previous market leader, Within three years the own-brands supplied by the smaller canners had gained nearly 50% of the canned vegetable market.

The new factory could not be redesigned or modified to cope with the new conditions, and as it happened the company had neither the human nor financial resources to undertake the product and market research necessary to develop new products for the new market conditions that could be produced by the new factory.

A capable management had not been able foresee that a number of separate changes were coming together to create a very different environment. By the time they had realized that significant change had taken place, not only were they hampered by inappropriate plant, but their initial efforts centred on regaining their previous market position with the old product.

Eventually the senior managment team became split over whether or not to enter the cheaper market sectors, and the group head office stepped in to resolve the matter by management changes and the establishment of a new strategy.

Source: Emergy and Trist (1965).

The behavioural model of Decision-making

Building upon Simon's administrative model, Cyert and March (1963) explained the behaviour of decision-makers in an organization in terms of coalitions whose members may have differing goals, influence and power. The key features of this model are set out in Key Concept 6.4.

The behavioural model of decision-making is important in understanding decision-making behaviour since if the decision-maker is operating under some uncertainty – as is normal – then there will be a trade-off between the value of an expected outcome and the degree of certainty attaching to it. A (rational) decision-maker is more likely to accept an 85% chance of gaining £1000 than a 10% chance of gaining £10 000. A lower expected outcome will be exchanged for a reduction in uncertainty. We can expect to see, therefore, examples of decision-making when the criterion is not an **increase** in the value of the outcome, but a **reduction** in the uncertainty of attaining a given outcome value.

Important concepts in this model are:

□ problemistic search;
□ incremental decision-making;
□ uncertainty avoidance.

Problemistic search describes a situation where the search for suitable alternatives is limited by the perception and formulation of a problem in the first place. Solutions are selected in terms of problems. A situation may not accord with expectations, but until such a discrepancy is perceived as a 'problem' no effort will be expended in searching for a solution. Threats and opportunities have to be actively identified. After the event of course there might well be general agreement that 'there had been a problem waiting to happen'.

Incremental decision-making is the situation where large changes are likely to be resisted in favour of smaller ones. In an organization changes will reflect a consensus around problem definition and the suitability of alternative solutions. Such a process is more likely to characterize decision-making in large organizations since such organizations will be composed of coalitions of interests in some political (i.e. power) relationship. A criterion for choosing decision outcomes is likely then to be 'consensus' in the interests of ongoing relationships. A small organization is less likely to be constrained by such issues since negotiations involve fewer people/groups and so less divergent interests.

Uncertainty avoidance is easy to understand. We are anxious, nervous, worried by change, because we are no longer sure that we can cope; decision rules we thought we understood and could rely upon are no longer appropriate. So tension increases, palms of the hands begin to sweat – all the usual signs of stress, just like after an awkward question at an interview ... or on the examination paper! So there will be a tendency to stick with the familiar, and this too will reinforce the tendency for change to be incremental.

Sources of uncertainty

An approach to decision-making which centred upon two key sources of uncertainty was described by Thompson and Tuden (1959). Decision-making is dependent upon the nature or source of uncertainty involved and these may cover either or both of the following:

□ Uncertainty over the causal relationships between phenomena;
□ Uncertainty over the preferred outcomes.

Using these two dimensions of uncertainty it is possible to construct a fourfold typology of decision-making environments as in Figure 6.1. Cell 1 is where the causal relationship between variables is understood and unambiguous but there are conflicting views as to the objectives to be

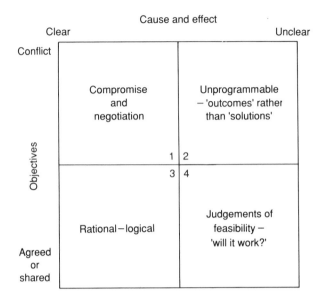

Figure 6.1 Types of uncertainty by source (derived from Thompson and Tuden, 1959).

pursued. Given the degree of certainty concerning causal relationships there is the possibility that bargaining may take place over the objectives or preferred outcomes. For example, in a particular sector of a market it may be well known that increasing advertising expenditure results in increased sales. However, even when this relationship is widely appreciated and understood there could still be disagreement about whether attempts to increase sales of existing products, rather then directing effort and resources to developing new products, is the appropriate stratgey.

Cell 2 covers those decisions where there is neither certainty over causal relationships, nor over the preferred outcomes. Here it is preferable to talk about 'outcomes' rather than 'solutions' to a decision-making situation. An example here could be a situation where there is disagreement over whether profit rather than market share is the appropriate objective and there is uncertainty over how, exactly, to go about either increasing profit **or** market share. The decision process is inherently unprogrammable and will be dependent upon inspired hunches or intuition (unanalysable search procedures in Perrow's terms – see Figure 4.7), or the exercise of power (see Chapter 5). Further examples of this type of problem can be found in those takeover situations where there is disagreement over whether breaking up a conglomerate ('unbundling') is the best way of realizing shareholders' value, or whether dividends should be reduced in order to finance investment and research in product and process innovation to fight off competition. Obviously the different timescales involved are an important aspect of the disagreements, as well as the uncertainties concerning the likely outcome of different strategies.

Cell 3 covers the situation where relative certainty or consensus over objectives exists alongside ambiguity over the causal relationships between variables. This is similar to Perrow's 'engineering' quadrant and involves feasibility judgements in response to the question 'will it work?' The emphasis is then upon practical rather than 'ideal' solutions.

Cell 4 equates with the decision-maker in a certain, unproblematic and known environment. As with rational economic man, no real decision is necessary. The problem is merely one of calculation.

The negotiated order in organizations: information and strategy

Following the discussion of organizations as 'negotiated' environments in Chapter 5, and given the interrelationships between sources of uncertainty described by Thompson and Tuden, it is important to remember that people think with **ideas**, not information. The ideas with which they think relate to their purposes and models of the world. Models of how the world ought to work, and perceptions of how it actually does work, impose meaning on data and transform it into information. Data then becomes a political resource – information and knowledge are sources of power. The distinction between 'data' and 'information' is set out in Key Concept 6.5.

Activities such as planning and decision-making must be seen as political processes, however formal (i.e. allegedly 'objective') the procedures used may appear to be. Organizationally located decisions will be the result of some more or less overt compromise or negotiation. Rarely will work processes be carried out exactly as specified since opportunities will arise for rules to be interpreted or re-interpreted.

Opportunities for negotiation or bargaining are more likely in hierarchical organizations since policy-making takes place at the top of the structure and implementation at the bottom. As we have discussed earlier, individuals or groups may occasionally exercise some influence (even if not

---

Information can be defined as 'Data arranged so it makes a difference to what we do' (Wildavsky, 1983).

'Data' is simply 'facts' – disordered or non-ordered items that require to be placed in some meaningful context. 'Information' is what is created when a theoretical and perceptual framework organizes data into meaningful patterns.

Wildavsky argues that automated information systems are likely to compound problems of decision-making since the existence of such a system is likely to increase the amount of data that is collected, but does nothing for the probability of it being organized into meaningful, 'useful' summaries.

As changing environments produce both more data and the felt need to acquire more data, executives are faced with a situation in which they are required to make more decisions making use of the increasingly available data. Not knowing quite what they need since the situation is changing all the time (consider the situation of the canning plant managers in Case Study 6.3), managers will demand more data since with automated systems there is less excuse for not 'knowing'. In other words, the number of decisions required goes up, but the time for assessing data and transforming it into information goes down.

KEY CONCEPT 6.5

INFORMATION AND DATA

actual power) by withholding information, effort or initiative, unless some reciprocity is forthcoming.

Efforts to include information from the lower levels of the hierarchy concerning the feasibility of decisions, and downward communication concerning intentions and options, may nevertheless result in implementation meeting counter-implementation strategies. The efforts of those further up the hierarchy to obtain information about how those below them perceive any proposed change may not necessarily produce a situation where intentions are either clear or shared. Indeed, the clearer subordinates are about what they think their superiors are trying to achieve, the more determined they may be to prevent them! The decision-makers then have to develop counter-counter-implementation strategies to overcome the strategies of subordinates.

For some time now there has been a growing realization, amongst management writers in the United States at least, that rational models at the strategic level are unhelpful. There is some evidence that sophisticated strategies fail their developers because it is not recognized that the formulation and implementation of strategy is a continuous process. There is a tendency for formulation to be regarded as distinct from implementation. Senior executives are surprised and hurt that their meticulously prepared plans are not received with rapturous enthusiasm when announced to an unsuspecting world. One study of senior managers in American corporations found that successful implementation of strategies resulted from an 'incremental' approach. These managers tried out partial solutions making use of slack resources available in the system. Such an approach involved seeking out and incorporating the views of people who were going to be affected by the strategy (see Quinn (1980) discussed in more detail later in this chapter). Similar views have been expressed by Hayes and Abernathy (1980).

Decision-making under ignorance

At the extreme of the continuum from certainty lies ignorance as a context for decision-making activity (i.e. extreme top right-hand corner of Cell 2 in Figure 6.1). Here, it is not even possible to know what outcomes are possible, let alone how they may be related in a cause and effect sense. If the situation in which a decision is required is genuinely new, then it is not possible to know what outcomes are in fact likely at all, let alone assign probabilities to them. This was the situation of the managers of the canning plant in Case Study 6.3 who failed to notice potential changes in the environment, or if they were aware of them, failed to see how they could interact with potentially disastrous consequences for their enterprise. What is the basis for a rational decision in such circumstances?

The search for error as rational behaviour

Collingridge (1980) argues that what is needed is a conception of rationality in which a rational agent is one who searches for **error** and responds willingly to its discovery. If this rule is applied fewer options will be found to have been closed off when the decision-maker is confronted

There are two essential aspects to such rationality: first, an ability to discover information which would show a decision to be in error; secondly, the ability to respond to such information. These two essentials then form the basis of a decision rule under uncertainty as follows:

  Choose that option that can be found to be in error, and corrected, quicker and more cheaply then can the alternative(s).

Under ignorance therefore there is a premium on 'corrigible options', those that are easy to correct. When making decisions under ignorance 'rationality' requires that the option chosen is that which minimizes the the following:

- ☐ monitoring costs;
- ☐ error costs;
- ☐ correction time;
- ☐ remedy costs.

Source: Collingridge (1980).

with error. This is known as a 'fallibilist' account of rationality, and is illustrated in Key Concept 6.6.

The point is that having made a decision, an individual or group will tend to seek confirmation that the correct decision has in fact been made. Evidence or information that might indicate error will be ignored while the search for confirmation continues. In this way a decision can be regarded as representing 'sunk costs'. By the time error is recognized the cost of correction may be prohibitive. Under ignorance, however, a rational decision-maker is one who willingly and thoroughly seeks to establish what was **wrong** with the decision. Then corrective action is taken. This is consistent with, though less risky than, the advice of Peters and Waterman (1982) who stressed the importance of trial and error, the importance of generating enough mistakes so as to ensure that the organization would be able to enjoy at least one great success.

Innovative behaviour

The constant search for error is of course uncomfortable to those trained in the 'old school' where being right is what matters! If organizations are going to be genuinely innovative then novel applications of novel technologies to novel materials are bound to throw up novel errors. Indeed, the errors will be essentially unknowable before they happen! When designers develop the instrumentation for a process they are concerned to represent to operators the development of events that have been identified as both possible and probable. The more rather than the less probable will be more closely monitored. What, then, about a sequence of events they do not think possible? Or so improbable that it is not worth the additional instrumentation?

In truly innovative situations it may not be possible to identify all possible or probable events. In this context another aspect of organizations as systems becomes important. This concerns the extent to which failure in one system or subsystem spreads to other systems and subsystems. The issue then becomes one of how closely subsystems and systems are linked or 'coupled'.

Tight and loose coupling

The idea of coupling applies to the coordination between systems or their components. 'Tight' coupling implies that two systems or components are so closely coordinated that failure in one rapidly affects the operatiion of the other. 'Loose' coupling implies the existence of some form of 'buffer' between the systems or subsystems. In this case a failure or departure from standard procedure will not immediately affect other components, thus giving time for remedial or recovery processes to be implemented before the system as a whole suffers a failure. Thus in the case of JIT close coupling is required if full advantage of the benefits are to be realized. This puts tremendous pressure upon control systems to ensure that nothing, but nothing, goes wrong, and is applied to the control of human as well as material resources. The coupling is so tight that failure in one area may immediately and dramatically affect the whole system. 'Tight coupling' in this context is defined in Key Concept 6.7.

KEY CONCEPT 6.7 **'A TIGHTLY COUPLED SYSTEM**	Perrow (1984) suggests six factors which would define a tightly coupled system: ☐ Delays in processing are not possible; ☐ The sequence of events cannot be varied; ☐ There is only one method of achieving the goal (the system has been designed that way); ☐ There is little slack allowed in the flow of raw materials; ☐ Any 'buffers' or 'redundancies' are built in at the design stage; ☐ Possible substitutions of supplies or equipment are also built in at the design stage.

A store of work-in-progress represents a buffer stock that enables other subsystems to continue functioning while the fault is corrected. In this case the system has been loosely coupled. 'Overmanning' – employing more people than are strictly required by the normally functioning system – is a form of loose coupling of production to the labour market. However, such buffers are very expensive, and can only be reduced by means of improved flows of information to facilitate rapid and continuous adjustment to the environment.

Loosely coupled systems are characterized by the possibility of delays and changes in the sequence of events. Alternative methods can be employed, if necessary, and there are additional resources that can be called upon. In addition to slack resources indicated by the existence of buffer stocks, further buffers or redundancies may be fortuitously available. This feature derives from the fact that stages in the process do not have to follow an invariant path and alternative raw materials may be available; in such situations 'jury-rigging' may well be possible.

A consequence of tight coupling is the premium that is then placed upon coordination and the subsequent demands for information. In the case of JIT systems in manufacturing and supermarkets the savings resulting from reduced inventories are countered by the extra resources required to process information in the interests of close coordination internally, and externally between the organization and suppliers and customers. Survival depends upon the rapidity with which information about changes in customer behaviour and preferences can be fed through to suppliers and the production process in order to defend, if not extend, market position.

The early applications of computing to inventory control resulted in considerably increased pressure upon shopfloor supervisors who found that the slack on which they had come to depend in managing the production process (buffer stocks of raw materials, part-finished and finished goods and so on) had disappeared. The system was now more tightly coupled. A failure in one subsystem rapidly affected others and soon the system as a whole. A machine breakdown that previously could have been coped with by calling upon buffer stocks while it was repaired now had to be dealt with immediately, or prevented if at all possible. Improved maintenance procedures and multi-skilled staff with delegated control are ways of coping with the demands of a tightly coupled system.

Tight coupling creates equally significant demands upon the performance of purchasing departments and suppliers in order to minimize variability in quality and supply. For this reason, organizations whose competitive advantage depends upon JIT methods invariably develop close contacts with their suppliers which have the effect of linking the supplier into the production process directly. Thus not only does the purchasing organization exercise considerable influence over the operating methods of suppliers in order to minimize variability, but a corollary is long-term contractual relationships. Thus both the purchasing and supplying organizations become closely linked.

This type of relationship has been established for some time by Marks & Spencers, for example, and poses both threats and opportunities for the parties. Companies like Sainsburys or Tescos may well have marketing information far superior to that obtainable by the manufacturers who supply them and this tilts the balance in the relationship even more in favour of the retailer. Considerable concern has been expressed for some time over the implications of the power that the major retailing chains can now exercise over their suppliers (Randall, 1987). Such tightly coupled systems as we have been describing may be the basis of competitive advantage, but as Porter (1988) has argued they may also be sources of competitive pressure.

Information and organization structure

It is important to realize that organizations are systems for collecting, formatting and manipulating information. Organizations are structured in order to undertake the transformation of data into a form that will make a difference to what people do. The structure of an organization has the effect of reducing data to manageable proportions. 'The very structure of organization – the units, the levels, the hierarchy – is designed to reduce data to manageable and manipulable proportions ... Organization necessitates selectivity' (Wildavsky, 1983, p. 29). What passes up the hierarchy of an organization from junior levels and departments to the senior management are 'data-reduction' summaries. A 'data-reduction' summary, with the emphasis on 'reduction', is what is required since the environment contains too much random 'data' and not enough ordered 'information'. Functional specialization is one way of dealing with this problem and of providing 'summaries' that can be used by senior management without overwhelming them with detail.

We saw in Chapter 4 that a functional form of organization was just one of a number of possibilities, others being divisions by product, region or customer. Each of these forms of organization represents an attempt to cope with data by reformulating it so as to represent 'information' in a manageable form in the pursuit of an objective. Considered in this way, organization structures would then vary according to the nature of the data handling and information processing problems confronting those controlling the organization. An important variable here is the nature of uncertainty facing those with responsibility for setting and achieving objectives.

Reducing complexity

One way of reducing complexity is to break the organization down into different units each dealing with its own activity or specialization. This not only decreases the number of interconnections but also has the advantage that operators can improve their performance because they concentrate on a narrower range of related activities. The result of such decomposition, whether of systems or people in an organization, is a hierarchy, as illustrated in Figure 6.2. It is possible to give a quantitative insight into the relationship between data, information and organization structure. Williamson (1970) gives the following formula to calculate the number of communication channels, N, required if operatives or subsystems must interact to complete a task:

$$N = \tfrac{1}{2}(M^2 - M)$$

where M is the number of interacting operatives or subsystems.

Using this formula it can be shown that increasing the number of interacting operatives or subsystems from 6 to 12 results in the number of connections or communication channels more than quadrupling from 15 to 66. Even going from 4 to 6 such interacting 'nodes' results in the number of channels increasing from 6 to 15.

Such a division of labour simplifies operations in that each task requires less knowledge and expertise than the whole. However, there is now the problem of coordination and control over the decomposed elements. This

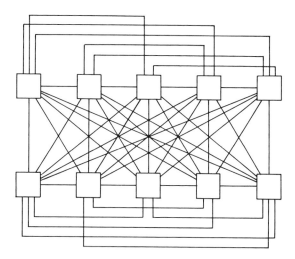

45 channels connecting 10 operating positions if all interact

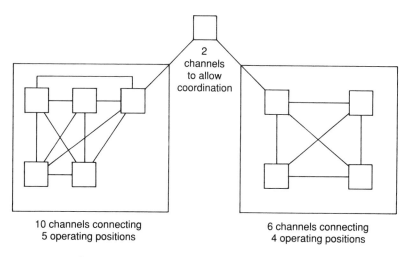

2 channels to allow coordination

10 channels connecting
5 operating positions

6 channels connecting
4 operating positions

By decomposing into specialist departments or function,
45 channels are reduced to 18 (10 + 6 + 2).

Figure 6.2 Reducing complexity.

applies to the development of the factory system of organizing work just as much as to the handling of information. The factory was a means of handling information about work – how it was done, at what rate and with what effort.

A timespan hierarchy

Coordination of activities subsequent to decomposition produces a hierarchy that reflects the differing types of decision behaviour required or expected of those occupying different levels in the hierarchy. This can best be represented by an inverted triangle reflecting different timescales over which decisions will operate and be evaluated, as shown in Figure 6.3.

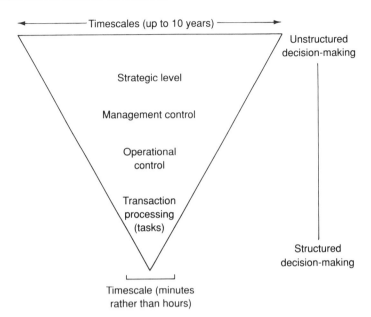

Figure 6.3 A timespan hierarchy.

Responses to information processing demands

There are a number of interdependent responses that can be made to demands upon information processing activities whether the processing is done by machines or people. Whether the system is manual or electronic, programmes or procedures have been worked out by people in terms of their perceptions of objectives and interests, and by use of their theoretical models of the way the world is thought to work (or ought to work). There are at least two strategies available for coordinating decomposed information and organizational structures:

☐ **Reduce the need for information processing** by, for example, the use of slack resources (decoupling), or the development of self-contained structures such as product divisions or groups or profit centres;
☐ **Increase the capacity for processing** either by improved hardware and software, or by opening up communication channels between previously unconnected subsystems.

The development of a coordinating mechanism reduces the need for information processing and so creates spare capacity to handle communication channels previously ignored or non-existent. Turning back to Figure 6.2, for example, it can be seen that after 'decomposition' each operating position has no more than four channels to monitor and activate, compared with nine prior to decomposition.

Power, information systems and decisions

Restructuring an organization will influence the distribution of power in so far as that reorganization represents a redesign of an information

processing system. Similarly, introducing an electronic information processing system will also influence power distribution in so far as access to the
new system is shared by more (or fewer) people, or governed by different
criteria from that which governed that previous system.

It is the relationship between information and power that causes
resistance to change in organizational structures. Given that organizations
comprise shifting coalitions, it is the implications of information technology for the exercise of power that cause resistance to change. While
resistance to change may be explicable in terms of the human need to
reduce uncertainty, or in terms of differing perceptions of interest, the
information handling characteristics of humans is also relevant. The main
factors in resistance to change, or 'social inertia', are set out in Key
Concept 6.8.

It is important to recognize that (a) decision-making is only partly
cognitive, and (b) human decision processes are remarkably simple. (See
the discussion of the behavioural model of decision-making and bounded
rationality earlier in this chapter). This is in large part due to the process of
socialization. The socialization of a human being provides or transmits
mechanisms for coping with the world without having to 'reinvent the
wheel'.

Ideologies also serve such a purpose by providing a mechanism for
rapidly interpreting perceptions of the world, indeed a mechanism for
perceiving the world. To 'perceive', to 'comprehend', is to format data into
information. Socialization and ideologies are programmes for perceiving
and interpreting, that is 'making sense of', the world.

The work of researchers like Rosemary Stewart and Henry Minztberg
(see section on Further reading at the end of the chapter) has shown that
managerial work is characterized by fragmentation, partiality and a desire
for current information. Managerial decision-making, like human decision-
making generally, is relatively simple. Information is discarded under
pressure. What worked in the past will be relied upon now and in the
future. Problems are simplified (decomposed) to the point at which they
become manageable by resorting to 'heuristics'. (Heuristics are rules of
thumb that are applied in preference to formalized decision rules.) This
process will be mediated by the models or theories available to the
decision-makers, the degree of threat they perceive, and the resources

---

There are at least four factors involved in the maintainance of social
inertia in organization. One of these we have discussed in some detail
already – that data and information are political resources. Other factors
are:

☐ Information is a relatively small component of decision processes
(see the earlier discussion of 'bounded rationality');
☐ Human information processing relies to a considerable extent upon
past experience and is based upon simplification;
☐ The complexity of large organization results in change being
incremental or evolutionary rather than radical.

KEY CONCEPT 6.8

*SOCIAL INERTIA AND
RESISTANCE TO
CHANGE*

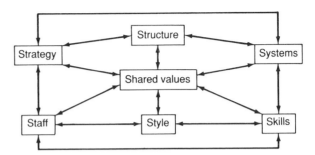

Figure 6.4 The 'Seven Ss': a framework used by McKinsey's consultants.

available to them. This is the process implied by Wildavsky's idea of 'data-reduction' summaries.

The nature of the problem confronting decision-makers is a function of their location in the organizational hierarchy (as in Figure 6.3), since the variation experienced is a function of the timescale involved. The longer the timescale the greater the complexity and the likely degree of uncertainty that will be experienced.

The complexity of large organizations is illustrated by the framework used by management accountants McKinsey: the 'Seven Ss', illustrated in Figure 6.4. With these interrelating factors, the complexity of the structure is considerable since change in one factor will have some (but what?) impact on other factors, and that impact will in turn influence the original factor . . . and so on. Stability, as with so many things, will be relative.

Incrementalism and strategic change

Under these conditions it is likely that change will be incremental since coalitions will have to be mobilized in support of change and the complexity will reduce the ability of decision-makers to be sure about possible outcomes. Decision-making will then be limited to those areas where uncertainty is relatively less and where frequent reviews of relatively short-run decisions are possible.

'Because of their familiarity, older options are usually perceived as having lower risks (or potential costs) than newer alternatives' (Quinn, 1980). In his article from which the foregoing is an extract, Quinn examines the methods adopted by executives seeking to introduce change into their organizations. He argues that they consciously create slack time and create discussion forums to allow others in the organization to work out the implications of new solutions. Such forums and slack time may also be necessary to enable those involved to gather relevant information. Quinn argues that there are too many uncertainties in organizational environments to allow managers the luxury of controlling all events likely to occur following major changes in strategy. This is of course consistent with Collingridge's 'fallibilist rationality' (Key Concept 6.6) discussed earlier.

Partial decisions

What happens is partly a function of the interactions between actors who hold varying amounts of power according to their information resources or organizational location. Since it is likely that no one actor can rely on holding the balance of power indefinitely, actual outcomes may differ from what any of them may have intended. As a result there tends to be a stream of partial decisions on limited issues made by constantly changing coalitions of the key power centres. Quinn makes the point that such a process is not piecemeal, it is incremental. What should prevent it being piecemeal is that in well-managed organizations there takes place constant reassessment by senior managers in order to integrate actions into a coherent strategic whole.

The development of incremental outcomes may be particularly appropriate for certain types of problems. Maier (1970) has identified two major problem types (see Cells 2 and 3 in Figure 6.1):

☐ Type I problems are those for which high quality standards are applied to solutions. Acceptance of the solution is forthcoming from those who have to apply it because of the standards applied to selecting it.
☐ Type II problems are those for which the solution is accepted as a result of bargaining processes. Such problems may not be amenable to the kind of examination that enable high quality solutions to be developed since the nature of the problem itself may not be amenable to precise formulation.

Decisions concerning the strategic plan of a business involve time periods and variables which prevent precise formulation. General statements of where the organization should be in ten years' time, what its 'mission statement' will be, and what tactics should be adopted are all amenable to more than one interpretation. The accuracy of any particular interpretation will not be known for some considerable time. Even then any variance may well be put down to environmental factors not present at the time the decision was made.

Take as an example the measures of performance in a company quoted by Nash (1983) shown in Figure 6.5 – no less than 31 different measures in total! This gives some idea of the complexity with which senior decision-makers will have to contend just to identify the criteria to be applied to their performance. In addition to such quantitative criteria, there may also be qualitative criteria relating to public relations issues: 'to be the leading company in the field' or 'to have the most progressive policies on staff conditions and promotion policies relating to women and ethnic minorites', to name only two.

From the discussion so far it is apparent that dealing with problems in organizations is not just a matter of technique in the sense of applying rules, but importantly is a socio-political process. Even at relatively low levels in the hierarchy, where the timespan over which the decision will operate before feedback is obtained is limited, alternative solutions or responses may be available and a choice made. What determines this choice may be political rather than technical considerations.

While it is important to remember that **outcomes** may be politically influenced, it is also equally important to recognize that the **formulation** of the problem in the first place is also crucial and subject to political influences. The way in which a problem is formulated will influence what are perceived as appropriate solutions. Problem formulation may well be

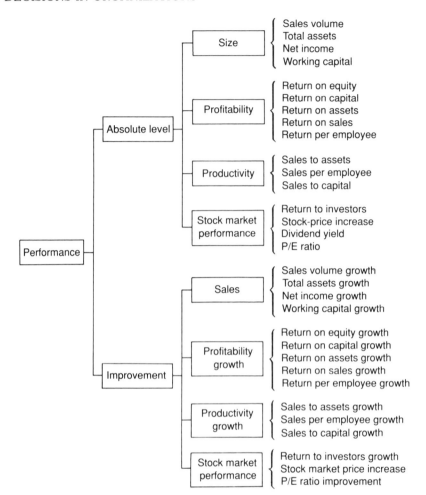

Figure 6.5 Measures of performance in a company. From Nash (1983).

largely a social and political process even though the language is couched in technical terms.

For example, falling market share may be unambiguously demonstrated – but what is the problem?

☐ Increased competition?
☐ Poor quality?
☐ High price?
☐ Poor delivery?
☐ Use of inappropriate outlets?
☐ Poor servicing facilities?

Each of these possible causes of falling market share can themselves be further broken down. Is poor quality the result of:

☐ Old machines?
☐ Poorly trained workers?
☐ Poor quality materials from suppliers?

If, as is often the case in British industry, it is assumed that high price is the cause of the problem, there is still the question of what factors are responsible for high prices:

☐ Powerful unions demanding high wages?
☐ Restrictive practices?
☐ Badly designed products?
☐ Out of date equipment?
☐ Poorly designed plant layout and workflows?
☐ Poorly qualified management?
☐ Poor procurement policies?

Aids to problem and solution formulation

Given the potential of information technology to open up genuinely new opportunities, both in terms of new value-added activities as well as in new methods of carrying out existing activities, the stimulation of creative thinking is important. This requires that the organization is structured so that the generation of ideas is linked to the examination of the assumption which underlie them. It is important to ensure that those involved should be able to free themselves as far as possible from conceptual or perceptual strait-jackets while at the same time retaining positive aspects from past experience. At least two questions require answering:

☐ Can those involved transfer what they have learnt in the past to current problems?
☐ Is what has been learnt in fact transferable?

In their examination of 'excellence' Peters and Waterman (1982) list a number of factors which appeared in successful companies and relate to the ability to generate and evaluate new ideas. Peters and Waterman stress the following:

☐ that both autonomy and entrepreneurship should be aimed at so that independent thinking can be subjected to competitive examination;
☐ that being 'close to the customer' is crucial in order to pick up potential threats or opportunities arising in the market-place;
☐ that employees know what the objectives are; and
☐ that employees have confidence that they will share in any rewards.

These precepts suggest senior managers need to foster a climate in which the central values of the enterprise are pursued via the toleration of idiosyncrasies on the part of individuals and groups. Such idiosyncrasies may well facilitate the achievement of shared goals. If this type of atmosphere is to develop, then there are implications for organizational structure which reflect the information processing functions of structure. Three problem-solving approaches are examined in the following paragraphs.

Approaches to problem and solution formulation

In their review of decision aids in problem formulation, Schwenk and Thomas (1983) list three procedures which may facilitate both problem formulation and outcome selection: brainstorming, devil's advocate and what Schwenk and Thomas refer to as 'dialectical enquiry'.

Brainstorming

This is the process of getting a small group of people to produce as many ideas as they like about how a problem could conceivably be resolved. Initially there should be no concern about the feasibility of the solution in terms of accepted or current practice, but a concentration upon any way at all that might be available to achieve the desired results. In this way, people are encouraged to think 'outside' what may have become a limiting framework of ideas or possibilities.

The group's ranking of what they think are the 'best' ideas is then the basis of developing strategies for implementation. One considerable advantage of this process is the cohesion of the group in seeking acceptance of its ideas. The implications for the organization are that such a group has to feel that its ideas will be taken seriously and that resources will be available for implementation. This kind of involvement is in part at least what lies behind and effectiveness of 'quality circles' where work groups identify possible methods of increasing the quality of their output.

For such group activities to be effective in changing behaviour, however, those involved must feel in control and that they will themselves, as individuals or as a group, benefit.

The devil's advocate

This approach is directed at key aspects of creative thinking, namely the identification of assumptions, the challenging of those assumptions and consequently the managing of conflict or tension within or between decision-makers. Conflict here refers simply to the process of generating alternative assumptions and challenges. The exercise of creative thinking has structural implications since those involved will require information as well as time to carry out their activity.

The devil's advocate method requires that one individual or group prepares a plan and presents it. Another group or individual (the devil's advocate) then criticizes the plan in as 'nit-picking' a style as they wish – criticism does not have to be 'constructive' when emanating from a devils' advocate! The devil's advocate concentrates on putting forward reasons why the plan as proposed should not be adopted. The plan and criticism then form the basis for a revised plan.

Dialectical enquiry

This addresses the same aspects of creative thinking as the devil's advocate method but centres upon groups. The process involves a debate between the advocates of two opposing plans based upon differing interpretations of the same data. This feature of the process will cause those observing the debate to concentrate their attention upon the evaluation of the assumptions underlying the two plans. Once assumptions have been changed, the new assumptions form the basis for a new definition of the problem and a

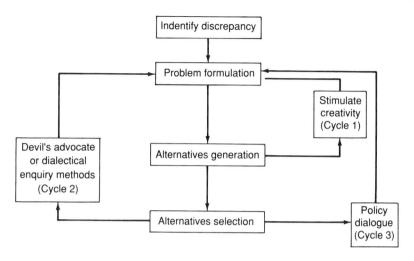

Figure 6.6 Techniques for identifying, formulating and resolving problems. From Schwenk and Thomas (1983), p. 251.

more effective solution – thus establishing a pattern of thesis, antithesis and synthesis.

It is important to remember that this discussion of decision-making and formulation has been constantly placed in the context of change, of new problems arising when old solutions no longer appear to work. Referring back to the discussion of rational economic man as a decision-maker and the alternative models proposed by Simon, it is clear that for highly structured problems in stable environments the discussion in this section is inappropriate. What has been under examination are techniques for identifying, formulating and resolving problems when the environment is unstable. Figure 6.6 offers a diagrammatic representation of the discussion in this section.

The potential conflict between traditional methods of problem and solution or outcome formulation, and contemporary issues concerning strategic and operational decision-making, are illustrated by Case Study 6.4. Aspects of this issue are taken up in the following section of the chapter.

Information, strategies and structure

The significance of managerial assumptions and their impact upon managerial style, organizational structure and strategy is evident in two studies concerned with the relationship between decision-making and structure in British industry: Senker (1984) and Wong *et al.* (1987). Further discussion of this and related issues concerning business strategy can be found in Chapter 4 of Needle (1989).

Senker makes the point that the use of procedures such as discounted cash flow for investment decision-making encourages the development of projects which promise relatively quick returns. This is because benefits accruing after several years will be heavily discounted. He also points out that the adoption of a 'profit centre' control system, combined with the fact that managers may be moved from profit centre to profit centre during their careers, will inhibit them from entering into long-term projects which may be crucial to future competitive advantage.

Senker's research into the adoption of computer-aided design (CAD) and its implications for management illustrates the importance of the relationship between strategy and organizational structure. Calculating the benefits of new technology cannot be an exact science since realization of the benefits depends upon structural factors that enable opportunities to be grasped. One particular feature of decision-makng in this context is an emphasis on labour-saving since this is an area where relatively quick cost reductions can be gained: 'I tell that to the directors – that it will save in labour costs – in order to get the money for the equipment. That's the only thing the Board understand . . . ' (quoted in Baldry and Connolly, 1986). In a later study, a payback period of only three years had been specified for a CAD system (McLoughlin, 1989).

In both Britain and the United States one of the major selling points used by those marketing CAD systems was the reduction in labour costs achievable with the technology. This of course, not surprisingly, meant that the labour relations consequences of the innovations were important factors in the smoothness of the transition. Management, however, underestimated the time required to overcome these problems and this led to considerable delays in reaping the expected benefits from cost reductions.

The emphasis on labour-saving also meant that attention was diverted from strategic considerations concerning the nature of the market in the

---

CASE STUDY 6.4

COMPUTER INTEGRATED MANUFACTURING

Computer integrated manufacturing (CIM) systems provide an example of a decision-making situation where there is apparent conflict between the need to introduce new techniques of manufacturing and traditional methods of justifying resource allocation to new capital projects. Two articles appeared in the *Harvard Business Review* in 1986 which examined this problem: Kaplan (March/April) and Jaikumar (November/December).

Kaplan sought an answer to the question whether CIM could only be justified by faith. He examined the apparent inability of traditional techniques such as discounted cash flow to justify investment in CIM. The problem was illustrated by reference to a Japanese company which had reduced the number of machines from 68 to 18, empolyees from 215 to 12, occupied floor space from 103 to 30 thousand square feet, and average processing time from 35 to 1.5 days. According to Kaplan the 'problem' was that the project's rate of return was less than 10% per year while many American companies set target rates of return at 15% or more.

Concentrating on just the consequences of higher quality products as a result of CIM Kaplan identifies a number of tangible benefits that need to be incorporated into the capital justification process. It is possible to achieve five to tenfold reductions in defect rates with CIM technology with all that implies for a reduction in scrap and re-working costs. In addition there are benefits to be gained from the reduction in human inspection requirments and warranty expenses. For example, General Electric found that the service call out rate fell by 50% when dishwasher production was automated.

Improved raw material flows can affect the number of fork-lift trucks required, and consequently their servicing and manning. There is also the competitive advantage that can be gained by a quality reputation in the market-place. If competitors are going to be utilizing the new technology can a firm avoid using it too? Mere presence in the market-place in ten years' time, let alone an increased share of the market, may hinge on the application of this kind of technolgoy.

Further advantages are to be gained from the flexibility which characterises CIM. Not only does flexibility mean reduced inventories, it also means that opportunities can be grasped that were not foreseen at the time the equipment was originally purchased. This means that shifts in the market-place can be met more quickly and without additional expenditure. Here we are considering **revenue enhancement**, Kaplan argues, not **cost reduction**, and the former is harder to capture in conventional procedures. As Kaplan concludes, valuing improved flexibiltiy, rapid customer service and market adaptability may not be exact mathematics but it does help put a meaningful price on the intangible benefits of CIM.

Jaikumar examines the same issue as Kaplan on the basis of a detailed comparison of the utilization of CIM in American and Japanese companies. He concludes that American managers, still hidebound by Taylorist assumptions, treated the new technology as though it was just a sophisticated version of conventional mechanization, just another set of machines for high-volume standardized production. As a result not only was the flexibility inherent in the equipment ignored, but so was that inherent in the operators. Skilled machinists were replaced by operators, and they had less discretion than when working on the previous generation of CNC stand-alone machines.

The failure of American firms to benefit on the same scale as the Japanese companies studied by Jaikumar derive from factors relating to assumptions and structures. There is no magic, he asserts, 'just an intelligent process of thinking through what new technology means for how work should be organised' (p.72). The operators in the Japanese companies were highly skilled engineers responsible for writirig new programs for subsystems as well as the system as a whole. As with the designers of the systems, the engineers worked in small teams, and Jaikumar goes on to argue that the new role of management in manufacturing will be to manage intellectual capital, not equipment. So instead of concerning themselves with routine problems of quality and production schedules, managers will have to concentrate on the selection of projects and the creation and management of intellectually powerful teams to work on them. This has considerable implications for decision-making, organizational structures and managerial styles, strategies and assumptions.

CASE STUDY 6.5

INFORMATION, STRATEGY AND STRUCTURE

In an examination of the marketing strategies adopted by a sample of British companies and the UK subsidiaries of major Japanese competitors, Wong *et al. (1987)* considered the relationship between strategy and structure and the implications for information processing. Although the sample was relatively small (15 Japanese and 15 British companies) the findings are illustrative at least. It is important to note that the Japanese subsidiaries were 'overwhelmingly run and managed by local personnel **who do not differ in age, experience or background** from those of the British competitors' (emphasis added).

The significance of structure for strategy is illustrated by the relationship between structure and information processing in the companies included in this study. The majority of the Japanese companies were organized on the basis of product lines and markets. The British companies relied upon traditional functional structures. The signifiance of this difference lies in the fact that under functional organization structure few managers felt totally dedicated to the performance of key products. According to Wong and her colleagues, few of the British companies had budgeting or information systems which provided information relating to the market for each product line. The systems were apparently 'designed to show factory or production profitability'.

The Japanese companies on the other hand were organized around the product market in terms of structure as well as information. The managers in the Japanese companies therefore had a clearer idea of the basis upon which their products competed in the market. They could then take steps to occupy developing sectors of the market as well as fend off competition in existing sectors. They were able to take advantage of opportunities as well as take steps to reduce potential threats. Their counterparts in British-owned firms were so concerned with financial and production data that their response in the marketplace was not only slower but tended to concentrate on relatively short-term issues of defending financial objectives.

'Marketing, planning and implementation should not be seen as separate from other functions in the company. The Japanese take a holistic view of marketing, seeing it as a conceptual framework for integrating the entire management process from product development to manufacturing, selling and after-sales service, and then back to product development' (p.62).

Source: Wong *et al.* (1987).

future and where the firm would and could place itself in that market. Consequently the full potential of the new technology was never explored or realized and did not figure in strategic thinking which was 'piecemeal' rather than 'incremental'. The relationship between information, strategy and structure is highlighted by the study of Wong and her colleagues which is examined in Case Study 6.5.

Summary

In this chapter the discussion has been based upon material dicussed earlier in the book in order to examine the factors which influence decision-making in business. We have not gone into great detail about individual decision-making, but have concentrated upon general issues governing human information processing in general and in terms of management in particular. The point has been to demonstrate that an 'organization' is an information system and that changes in the demands that are placed upon information systems as a result of changing environments and product markets will impact upon organizational structure. Such impact will then have implications for the way in which people react to changes as well as how they perceive changes – if indeed they perceive them at all. The point of the discussion in the last section of the chapter was to illustrate how structures may hinder perceptions of threats and opportunities by focusing attention upon methods of processing and evaluating data that are no longer appropriate to contemporary conditions.

There is the danger that the technical rationality of an information system, implying as it does an emphasis upon quantifiable criteria, may reduce the adaptability of an organization. Human adaptability based upon judgement, intuition and creativity may be ignored in favour of problem and solution formulations that most easily fit the information processing technology. As Abraham Maslow once wrote: 'If the only tool you have is a hammer, you tend to treat everything as though it were a nail' (quoted by Hoos, 1981).

The issue of control is highlighted by questions of decision-making in the context of new technology. As we saw with the discussion of JIT at the beginning of the chapter, the pressures upon workflow require that human beings are fully integrated into the production process – whether the end-product is a manufactured artefact or a service. The tendency of management to cling to ideas of work organization and job design associated with the scientific management of Taylorism in terms of simple quantitative measures of productivity improvements and increased control over fragmented jobs represents the application of nineteenth-century solutions to what are now twenty-first century problems (Burnes, 1988; Willcocks and Mason, 1988; McLoughlin, 1989).

The question of control is further complicated by the fact that, as the examples in the final section of the chapter showed, control and information systems such as accounting procedures have to be modified for the new technology. This will require that accounting information systems are measuring relevant variables, including human behaviour. Payment systems will have to be scrutinized to ensure that they are rewarding relevant behaviour. Not only does this require that quality **and** quantity are rewarded, for example, but that the effects of machine downtime on the subsequent workstations are also included. It is no use recording information on just one machine if the failure of that machine rapidly impacts upon subsequent processes.

The control issue will remain at centre stage because it is likely that in future the work activity of many people will not so much emphasize the carrying out of tasks, but the supervising and monitoring of control systems. 'Work' will become the controlling of control processes. This will have major implications for the selection, training, motivation, development, supervision and rewarding of people. If company managements are serious about improving competitive performance, and see a role for information technology in achieving that improvement, then they must realize that new technology, whether represented by information systems or machine tools, is only a solution if it is used by a skilled and motivated labour force (Burnes, 1988).

In the next chapter, we will examine issues associated with the selection and motivation of people in the light of the demands placed upon managers and their subordinates by competitive pressures. This will be followed up in Chapter 8 by examining the implications of the discussion in Chapters 4 to 7 for the development of appropriate organizational structures and strategies for the future.

Study questions

1. What is meant by 'bounded rationality' and how does it relate to decision-making in organizations?
2. Describe the three procedures suggested by Schwenk and Thomas (1983) that may help with problem formulation and the selection of outcomes or solutions. Why might each be useful?
3. How are organization structures and the coupling of information systems related?
4. How may organization structure be related to strategic decision-making?
5. What are the main attributes of human decision-making?

Further reading

A very comprehensive introduction to the issues raised by the design and implementation of information systems is that by Davis and Olson (1984). This work includes material on both the organizational and psychological aspects of decision-making. It also considers the implications of the operation of information systems for the power structure in organizations.

Two researchers who have made considerable contributions to understanding what managers actually do, and how they go about doing it, are Rosemary Stewart and Henry Mintzberg. Stewart's work concentrates on British managers and includes public sector managers in its coverage. Mintzberg deals with North American managers and tends to concentrate on more senior executives while Stewart covers a wider range of the managerial hierarchy. Stewart (1985) and Mintzberg (1980) are both worth looking at.

David Collingridge (1980) sets out a very useful account of decision-making under uncertainty and ignorance in terms of public policy on such issues as the formulation of science and technology policies and policies intended to increase the rate of the diffusion and take-up of innovations. The approach advocated by Collingridge is also applicable to business decision-making when the innovative combination of new processes, structures and materials makes it increasingly likely that novel (i.e. unforeseeable) errors are likely. The more closely coupled are systems of production, the more potentially devastating are errors it is not possible to predict.

References

Abernathy, W.J., Clark, K.B. and Kantrow, A.M. (1981) The new industrial competition. *Harvard Business Review*, **5**, 68–81.

Baldry, C. and Connolly, A. (1986) Drawing the line: computer-aided design and the organisation of the drawing office. *New Technology, Work and Employment*, **1**, (1), 59–66.

Burnes, B. (1988) New technology and job design: the case of CNC. *New Technology, Work and Employment*, **3**, (2), 100–11.

Collingridge, D. (1980) *The Social Control of Technology*. Open University Press.

Campbell, A., Currie, W. and Warner, M. (1989) Innovation, skills and training: microelectronics and manpower in the United Kingdom and West Germany. In Hirst, P. and Zeitlin, J. (eds) *Reversing Industrial Decline? Industrial Structure and Policy in Britain and Her Competitors*. Berg.

Cyert, R.M. and March, J.G. (1963) *A Behavioural Theory of the Firm*. Prentice Hall.

Depaoli, P., Fantoli, A. and Miani, G. (1986) *Participation in Technological Change: The Role of the Parties Concerned in the Introduction of New Technology*. European Foundation for the Improvement of Living and Working Conditions, Dublin.

Davis, G.B. and Olson, M.H. (1984) *Management Information Systems: Conceptual Foundations, Structure and Development*, 2nd edn. McGraw-Hill.

Emery, F. and Trist, E. (1965) The Causal Texture of Organisational Environments, *Human Relations*

Foster, G. and Horngren, C. (1987) JIT: cost accounting and cost management issues. *Management Accounting*, 19–25.

Hayes, R.H. and Abernathy, W.J. (1980) Managing our way to economic decline. *Harvard Business Review*, 11–25.

Hoos, I. (1981) Engineers as analysts of social systems: a critical enquiry. In Open University Open Systems Group, *Systems Behaviour*. Open University Press.

Jaikumar, R. (1986) Postindustrial manufacturing. *Harvard Business Review*, 69–76.

Kaplan, R. (1986) Must CIM be justified by faith alone? *Harvard Business Reiew*.

McLoughlin, I. (1989) CAD – the 'Taylorisation' of drawing office work? *New Technology, Work and Employment*, **4**, (1), 27–39.

Marsden, D., Morris, T., Willman, P., Woods, S., *The Car Industry* Livestock.

Maier, N.R. (1970) *Problem-solving and Creativity in Individuals and*

Groups. Brooks/Cole.

Mintzberg, H. (1980) *The Nature of Managerial Work*, 2nd edn. Prentice Hall.

Nash, M. (1983) *Managing Organisational Performance*. Jossey Bass.

NEDO (1988) *Strategy for Success*. Three NEDO Workshops, London.

Needle, D. (1989) *Business in Context*. Chapman and Hall.

Perrow, C. (1984) *Normal Accidents*: *Living with High Risk Technologies*. Basic Books.

Peters, T.J. and Waterman, R.H. (1982) *In Search of Excellence*: *Lessons from America's Best Run Companies*. Harper & Row.

Porter, L.W. (1985) *Competitive Advantage*. Free Press.

Quinn, J.B. (1980) Managing strategic change. *Sloane Management Review*, 3–9.

Randall, J. (1987) Who needs brands? *Thames Business Papers*. Thames Polytechnic.

Robey, D. (1981) Computer information systems and organisational structure. *Communications of the ACM*. October, 679–87.

Rushton, D., Hodgkinson, G., Broughton, T. and Winstoned, J. (1986) *A Guide to Manufacturing Strategy*. Institute of Production Engineers.

Senker, P. (1984) Implications of CAD/CAM for management. *Omega*: *The International Journal of Management Science*, **12**, (3), 225–31.

Simon, H.A. (1960) *The New Science of Management Decision*. Harper Bros.

Schwenk, C. and Thomas, H. (1983) Formulating the mess: the role of decision aids in problem formulation. *Omega*: *The International Journal of Management Science*, **11**, (3), 239–52.

Stewart, R. (1985) *The Reality of Management*, 2nd edn. Heinemann.

Thompson, J.D. and Tuden, A. (1959) Strategies, structures and processes of organizational decision. In Thompson, J.D. *et al.* (eds) *Comparative Studies in Administration*. University of Pittsburgh Press.

Wildavsky, A. (1983) Information as an organisational problem. *Journal of Management Studies*, **20**, (1), 30–40.

Williamson, O.E. (1970) *Corporate Control and Business Behaviour*. Prentice Hall.

Willcocks, L. and Mason, D. (1988) New technology, human resources and workplace relations – the role of management. *Employee Relations*, **10**, (6), 3–8.

Wong, V., Saunders, J. and Doyle, P. (1987) Japanese marketing strategies in the United Kingdom. *Long Range Planning*, **20**, (6), 54–63.

The individual and behaviour at work 7

In this chapter we will consider aspects of behaviour associated with individuals as individuals. So far we have considered work-related behaviour in the context of social groups subject to the impact of forces that may be thought to minimize the role and importance of the individual. The model of business upon which this and companion volumes in the series are based does not specifically identify individual behaviour as an element, but the effectiveness of organizations in the achievement of the goals they are established to pursue (and the formulation of those goals) relies heavily upon people and their motivation.

Current and future changes in the office and factory (in private and public sectors of the economy) emphasize the importance of the personal qualities of employees at all levels in the organization. Technological developments represented by computer integrated manufacturing (CIM) and flexible manufacturing systems (FMS), as well as process developments such as JIT, require committed and motivated employees able to cope with the demands of jobs under the new regime. The continuous search for cost and quality improvements is dependent upon the quality of staff as much, if not more so, than on technology itself. The success of a competitive strategy based upon continual improvements in quality and productivity is crucially dependent upon employees who are as committed to, and rewarded by, the success of the enterprise as are their managers. This has implications for the management of staff, how they are rewarded and how they are to be recruited and trained.

These issues are of particular importance to British management at the present time as they attempt to reach the standards of capability displayed by their competitors in Europe and the Pacific regions. The establishment of the Single Market in 1992 in effect puts a time limit on the process of adjusting managerial approaches to the management of human resources. Further aspects of this question will be discussed in Chapter 9 when we discuss property rights and industrial democracy, and Chapter 10 when international comparisons are studied.

The issue of human motivation, the selection of motivated people, and the maintenance and rewarding of their motivation, emphasizes the extent to which management is about 'getting things done through people'. This is illustrated by the fact that when managers talk about their problems those concerning people come to the fore. There is always a 'problem' about some combination of the quantity, quality, commitment, motivation, demands, expectations and reasonableness or understanding of what is at other times referred to as 'our (sic) most important asset – our people'.

These issues have been at the centre of a debate over the nature and extent of changes in British industrial relations during the 1980s, and the reassertion of the right of managers to manage. The identification of a 'sense of realism' amongst trade unions and their members, and the concept of 'macho-management' have been widely discussed in both the academic press and mass media. The debate revolves around the highly publicized changes in organization and strategies developed in a number of industries faced with severe product market problems; automobiles, engineering, steel, coal and newspapers for example. These developments are alleged to have had a profound impact upon methods and styles of people-management.

The traditional staff-specialist roles of the 'personnel' and 'industrial relations' functions are seen to have played a relatively minor part in changes which were predominantly developed and initiated in accordance with senior management strategies, even though these have had profound consequences for the way people are managed. This was due in part to a process of making line management responsible for the management of people as part of the reassertion of managerial prerogative.

Associated with, if not directly the result of, these developments has been the wide acceptance of the term 'human resource management' (HRM) in place of 'personnel' or 'employee relations'. HRM, as described in Key Concept 7.1, signifies an approach to people management which empha-

---

KEY CONCEPT 7.1

HUMAN RESOURCE MANAGEMENT

While the term 'human resource management' is not particularly new, it has recently become very fashionable in the United States and the UK. Its popularity can be seen to derive from a number of factors. Perhaps one of the most important influences has been the success of books such as *In Search of Excellence* (Peters and Waterman, 1982) and *The Winning Streak* (Goldsmith and Clutterbuck, 1984), in conjunction with numerous commentaries on the reasons for the Japanese resurgence in manufacturing. This kind of material suggests that in part at least competitive advantage 'has something to do with the way people are managed.

Another factor has perhaps been the reappraisal of the role of personnel managers. This has come about as the response to new competitive pressures domestically and internationally has forced a review of traditional management strategies. The result has been an emphasis upon the management of human resources as something central to the activity of management and not something to be hived off to a specialist function. In the UK this can be associated with a perceived decline in the power of trade unions following changes in legislation and growth in unemployment. The last two factors have arguably reduced the uncertainty with which personnel managers were hired to cope. The perceived decline in the power of trade unions and a reassessment of the role of the personnel function combine to reduce the significance of industrial relations as a strategic issue.

Key elements in the HRM approach are the search for flexibility (in contrast to narrowly demarcated skills and tasks), performance-related pay, and direct communication with the workforce which bypasses (or deliberately ignores) existing procedures involving trade unions.

> The aim in managing that (human) resource is no longer merely containment and compliance but the far more ambitious one of competence and commitment ... Commitment ... is seen as achievable through winning the hearts and minds of individuals rather than striking deals with collectives and their representatives.
>
> (Storey, 1988, p.25)

Once more, the problem is one of control. The nature of new technology, and the competitive strategies that appear to be associated with it, place renewed emphasis upon the need to control the behaviour of human beings.

The concept of human resource management is clearly associated with those firms like Hewlett Packard, Marks and Spencer and IBM which attempt to create a distinctive culture which focuses on the commitment of all personnel to the shared goals of the enterprise. Such firms invest heavily in recruitment, selection and training to ensure that employees are socialized in the appropriate fashion (see page 247 later in this chapter for a fuller account of socialization). The socialization process is supported by a style of management, a communication system, a reward system and a working environment that is not only aimed at maximizing employee satisfaction but which stresses commitment to the stated organizational goals. Commentators such as Peters and Waterman see clear links between HRM techniques and company performance. As we have already suggested in our discussion of theory in Chapter 5, cause and effect in organizational behaviour is often difficult to establish. It is true that companies such as IBM, Hewlett Packard and Marks and Spencer have been successful when measured in several different dimensions, but it should not be forgotten that their distinctive 'culture' may be a product of their success rather than its cause. A further discussion of this and related issues can be found in Chapter 3 of the companion volume *Business in Context* (Needle 1989).

sizes **commitment** as the key issue, and which integrates the selection, appraisal, rewarding and development activities of the personnel function with the process of strategy formulation and implementation.

In this chapter we consider aspects of psychological and social-psychological research intended to illuminate the behaviour of individuals in a work environment. This research provides a basis for techniques used in the selection, assessment and development of employees. The topics to be discussed have been, and continue to be, the subject of considerable research effort and publication. Further and more detailed accounts can therefore be found in the specialist literature, particularly introductory texts in social, organizational or occupational psychology, organizational behaviour texts such as Luthans (1981), and relevant journals. No attempt to replicate that kind of coverage is attempted here, so there is no treatment in this chapter of such topics as intelligence, learning, perception and attitude formation. This chapter sets out only to give an overview of the subject.

Approaches to the study of individual behaviour at work

Arguably, the difficulties faced by managers in their relations with those they manage have been multiplied by the number of approaches adopted by researchers. Approaches to the study of individual human behaviour at work have focused at various times on the issues of leadership, attitudes, personality, motivation, selection, job design and payment systems. The result has been that different theorists and researchers have tackled basically the same problem from different angles, thus producing partial answers. This tendency has been exacerbated by managerial pressure for the development of relatively simple tools which rapidly acquire the standing of panaceas.

A panacea is an idea or technique that is regarded by those who apply it, but not necessarily those who developed it, as being the key to **all** related problems. For example, as a result of studies of group behaviour and leadership carried out prior to and during the Second World War mainly in the United States, considerable emphasis was placed upon supervisory training in human relations skills in British management as the key to improvements in productivity and industrial relations. Unfortunately this emphasis overshadowed a range of other factors which were, and still are, far more important to the process of raising productivity levels in British industry. Such factors include rate of machine utilization, plant layout, and the lack of interest and investment in vocational education and training.

The fact that the 'people problems' of business have been explored via a number of approaches has resulted in a variety of prescriptive advice. Much, if not most, of this advice has not proved particularly effective or long lasting since it is derived from partial or fragmented views of human beings. A complex problem (the understanding of human behaviour in its various manifestations) has been approached from a number of directions – the whole has been broken down into parts and attention directed at selected parts. Not surprisingly, many solutions turn out to be partial too. The result has been a number of different literatures available to managers which should be regarded as different aspects of the same one (Watson, 1986).

The topics to be discussed in this chapter are listed below in the order in which they will be considered. This order reflects neither an assumption about relation importance nor the weighting accorded each in the chapter. They have been selected because they are central to current concerns which are encapsulated in the idea of ' human resource management', as well as having quite a lengthy history in the academic community if not among managers. The role of payment systems in influencing human

motivation goes back to the origins of scientific management for example.
Topics to be discussed in this chapter are as follows:

☐ personality
☐ motivation
☐ job design and orientations to work
☐ selection and recruitment
☐ payment systems.

Personality

This concept is perhaps a good one with which to start since it is closely associated with the essence of individuality and is taken to be a useful explanatory factor. Personality is considered important when selecting people for particular tasks or jobs. For example, salesmen and women are thought to require 'extrovert' or even 'aggressive' personalities.

The idea of 'personality' is persuasive since it can be linked to, and appears to explain, intuitive ideas about individual differences and people in general. When required to account for a particular action on the part of someone we know, it *feels* like an explanation to say 'Yes ... well ... John has an aggressive (or submissive, or extrovert, or strong, or weak) personality.' All such a statement really does, however, is to offer a shorthand expression for the kind of behaviour that has been observed. It is not an explanation as such, but it sounds reassuringly like one since it tells the observer that in John's case such behaviour is 'normal' or 'usual '. It is descriptive rather than explanatory. The term 'personality' is explained in Key Concept 7.2.

One way of demonstrating the potential variability of individual personality is by reference to what is known as the Johari window (so

Continued over page

KEY CONCEPT 7.2

PERSONALITY

'Personality' is, like other words that are very influential in everyday speech, what is called a 'motherhood' concept. 'Democracy', 'freedom', 'management' – even 'business' – are other examples. Every one is in favour of them and uses them as though they have precise meanings, but experience great difficulty when asked to define them. So it is which 'personality'.

Pleasant/unpleasant, good, cheerful, strong, weak, shy and so on can all be used to describe an individual's personality. Luthans (1981) suggests there are more than four thousand words appearing in the dictionary that can be used to describe personality in this way.

Over fifty years ago Allport (1937) attempted to define personality as: '... the dynamic organisation within the individual of those psychophysical systems that determine his unique adjustments to his environment.' However, this failed to achieve wide acceptance. Amongst academics the use of different theoretical frameworks to study the phenomenon resulted in disagreement, and lay people tend to use just

Continued from previous page

one apparently dominant characteristic to fix an individual's personality type, e.g. pleasant or unpleasant, strong or outgoing.

Problems with the idea of personality arise for two main reason. First, it has roots in both scientific and commonsense efforts to account for (i.e. explain) and so predict, differences in human behaviour. Secondly, an individual's personality is not invariable either over time or as perceived by different people. That is, human beings do not behave in the same way under different situations, one does not behave in quite the same way at work as one does when at home. Also, different people view the same individual differently even when in the same situation. Variations in the perception of an individual's 'personality' are due to the interaction between individuals and their environment. To add to the confusion, there are also biological or physiological explanations of personality which focus on how biological processes influence behaviour as a result of chemical changes in the brain.

For the lay person, personality tends to be a shorthand way of describing the 'typical' behaviour pattern of an individual. For the scientist, personality refers to the way in which people affect others, how they see themselves, and the pattern of measurable traits (see below) whether expressed in behaviour or not.

	What you know about me	What you don't know about me
What I know about myself	Self known to you and me	Self known to me but not you
What I don't know about myself	Self known to you, but unknown to me	Self known neither to you nor me

Figure 7.1 The Johari window.

named after its developers *Jo*seph Luft and *Har*ry *I*ngham), illustrated in Fig. 7.1. This diagrammatic representation by which an individual's personality may be considered uses two dimensions, 'me' and 'others'. Each of these is divided into those aspects of personality that are known to the individual and others, and those that are unknown.

This model is used in training exercises for people whose work requires them to understand how, and possibly also why, they are seen differently by different people and differently from how they see themselves. In this way, skills associated with social interaction can be enhanced and developed. This makes the idea of the Johari window relevant to managers and their subordinates since the vast majority of work situations require individuals not only to 'get on with' superiors and subordinates, but also with fellow workers.

Exercise 7.1

Take a sheet of paper and fold it in two: on one side write down no more than six, and no less than three, adjectives (one word each) describing how **you** see yourself: on the other side do the same for how **others** see you.

When you have your lists, arrange yourselves in groups of two or more and swap lists. Compare each individual's idea of how others see him or her with how you (and others in the group if it contains more than two people) see that person.

The measurement of personality

There are a number of ways in which different personality types have been identified or defined and the strength of a tendency typical of an individual measured. One well-known approach is that developed by Hans Eysenck which is concerned with the attributes of individuals measured along a continuum such as, for example, introversion–extraversion. These dimensions can be easily associated with the demands or requirements of particular jobs or work situations, but there is the methodological problem that the use of continua precludes any clear cut typologies. People will vary along the continuum, and the variation will be in part a function of the situation in which they are required to operate.

Another and perhaps more useful approach to the ordering of a typology of personality types is that based on traits. A personality trait is some attribute of an individual that appears consistent over time and situation.

One of the best known personality profile questionnaires, or inventory, is the Cattell 16PF (Sixteen Personality Factor). This particular inventory is compiled by applying factor analysis to the results obtained by asking a large number of people to respond to a large number of questions or

Table 7.1 Cattel's 16 personality factors

Reserved	Outgoing
Concrete thinking	Abstract thinking
Emotional instability	Emotional stability
Submissive	Assertive
Prudent	Impulsive
Expedience	Conscientious
Shy	Venturous
Tough-minded	Dependent
Trusting	Suspicious
Practical	Imaginative
Open	Calculating
Confident	Apprehensive
Conservative	Experimental
Group-dependent	Self-sufficient
Undisciplined	Controlled
Relaxed	Tense

Source: R.B. Catell, How Good is the Modern Questionnaire? General principles for evaluation. *Journal of Personality Assessment,* **38,** 115–29.

statements designed to indicate response tendencies or traits. Cattell identified sixteen factors (listed in Table 7.1) which he argued represented 'source traits'. A source trait is one that underlies observable patterns of behaviour that are consistent with the typologies of personality used by lay people in day-to-day conversation.

McKenna (1987) reports two studies that were carried out at two management colleges which attempted to identify personality trait differences between functional groups of managers. In one of these studies comparing managers with accountants, the accountants preferred to make decisions on their own, sticking to the rules and to take time. Managers on the other hand tended to be impatient, would bend the rules if it would help achieve objectives and were distrustful of others.

In the second study the accountants were found to be more critical and precise than other managers, and appeared to be less competitive – a trait they apparently shared with bank managers.

In this second study, engineers were found to be unsentimental, self-reliant and concerned with objectivity and practicalities rather than exploring imaginative ideas. Sales managers (of course) were found to be outgoing, adaptive, cheerful, sociable, unconventional, but also competitive. Finally, personnel managers were found to display traits associated with adaptability and sensitivity. They tended to slow the process of decision-making in committees, but were more imaginative than other managers.

Projective tests

Another method of identifying and measuring personality types is that based upon the use of what are called 'projective tests'. A projective test uses an ambiguous stimulus scuh as a scene in a picture or even in one case ink-blots (the Rorschach ink-blot test) to provoke responses from subjects. The subject is required to tell or write a story based upon the scene in the picture (what has happened, what is happening, and what is going to happen), or to say what image the ink-blot conjures up in their mind. Subjects are then assessed in terms of the themes that appear in their stories about the people in the picture or the images conjured up by the blots. For example, taking cues from the setting, action portrayed, clothing, and so on, attributes will be assigned to the people in the picture. This attribution, or projection, will be taken as an indication of the propensity for certain responses which underlies the subject's likely behaviour pattern. Providing large enough groups are studied, it appears possible to identify distinctive types of response which can then be given an appropriate label. It is then possible to create a questionnaire intended to identify individuals belonging to these response groups.

However, when companies are concerned to reduce the uncertainty inherent in the employee selection process it is probably less useful to identify an apparently predominant personality type, than to identify the personality profile or range of potential behaviour likely from prospective employees. While it may be possible to identify personality traits and even types, the association with job success may be more problematic. For example, personality types associated with good performance during

Table 7.2 The pros and cons of psychological testing

Advantages
1. Tests allow individuals to be compared on the same criteria.
2. Tests allow individuals to be compared over time; records of test results can be used to establish if individuals did perform as predicted.
3. Tests give less ambiguous, more precise responses than do written references.
4. Tests are more likely to be fair because they eliminate favouritism and the operation of 'old-boy' networks.
5. Tests are comprehensive, covering all dimensions of personality and behaviour.
6. Tests are scientific.

Disadvantages
1. Tests can be faked. 'Lie' scores are built in to some.
2. Accurate reporting of feelings and behaviour requires self-insight that may not be present.
3. Stress, fatigue, pain may result in unreliable answers.
4. Tests do not in fact measure what they claim to: scores do not predict over time.
5. May be able to measure some dimensions, but not key ones like trust, or likely absentee rates.
6. Those being tested must be both literate and articulate.
7. Since most tests were developed in the USA, subjects must be familiar with American jargon.
8. Absence of guidelines for the population as a whole; comparing subjects with US psychology students may not be very useful.
9. Danger of bias against ethnic minorities.
10. Interpretation of results requires skill and expertise that may not be available or is expensive.

Source: A. Furnham, 'Personality Faces the Big Test', *The Sunday Times*, 21 August 1988.

training may not be associated with desired standards of future perform-ance.

The relationship between personality types and job types is not always straightforward, if only because there are relatively few accurate job descriptions that would enable one to identify the relevant personality type. Even if there were, it is always possible that the job itself, or the context in which it is performed, might change and so require modifications to the behaviour of the job holder. Also, the demands of a particular job or job type might be compatible with a variety of personality types among those recruited for it. Some possible advantages and disadvantages of psychological testing are listed in Table 7.2, taken from an article appearing in *The Sunday Times*, 21 August 1988.

Job-related inventories

In order to overcome some of the problems arising from the potential variety of personality types suited to a particular job, attempts have been made to construct job-specific measures or inventories. These are similar to, and based upon, the Cattell type, but are constructed and framed in terms of actual job types and the demands they make. Such inventories are

Table 7.3 The 15 traits of the OPQ profile

Influence
Socially confident
Empathy
Gregarious
Imaginative
Conservative
Planful
Detail-conscious
Social desirability
Relaxed
Phlegmatic
Optimistic
Contesting
Active
Decisive

Source: P. Swinburn (1985) *Personal Review*, **4**, (4), 29–33.

specifically intended to be used in the selection and training of job applicants. One of these, for example, the Occupational Personality Questionnaire (OPQ), is a battery of tests based upon a large-scale study of work organizations and concentrates upon four aspects of work-related personality. These are:

☐ relationships with people,
☐ thinking style,
☐ feelings and emotions, and
☐ what is termed 'vigour'.

The components of the 15 traits of the OPQ are listed in Table 7.3.

One attraction for busy recruiters is that the OPQ can be administered by personal computers such as the Apricot, but this raises important questions concerning the extent to which those interpreting the results have been adequately trained. The problem is that the results are open to interpretation by stereotypes. The OPQ questionnaire does not use psychological language or jargon to the same extent as the Cattell 16PF, and this makes it more accessible to non-specialists. Since 'high scores' on a dimension tend to be seen as 'good' and low scores as 'bad', thorough training is required to avoid such stereotyping (Swinburne, 1985). Moreover if the results of questionnaires such as the OPQ administered by computer are stored on an electronic information system, then the subject has the right under the Data Protection Act 1984 to see the results.

An important aspect of assessing the utility of such questionnaires is of course to retain the results and compare them with future performance. However, this will not tell the recruiter how well those who were rejected have done subsequently, nor will it confirm that those recruited would not have done as well even if they had not been assessed in this way. The relationship between the demands of a job and the personality of the job holder is discussed in Case Study 7.1.

The matching of job types to personality types is important if psychologically based tests are to be at all useful. This is an aspect of the problem of personal development and career planning that has been of concern to management trainers for some time. Stewart's (1976) work looking at the different demands of managerial jobs grew out of the realization that a manager's performance in his or her current job was no necessary guide to performance in the next job up the hierarchy. The demands of the new job might require very different talents which would have to be identified and developed if the individual was to succeed.

This is the foundation of the 'Peter Principle' which states: 'a person will be promoted to the level of their incompetence'. That is, John is recruited and does well. On this basis he is promoted and does well in that post. He is promoted again, and again performs successfuly. This leads to yet further promotion. At this point he is unable to cope, so there he remains. The consequence is that many people are doing the job they are doing because they are not competent enough to be promoted out of it! This is not necessarily a comment upon the limited ability of John and others like him, but upon the competence of those responsible for his training, development and appointment.

The American approach to selection tools like the OPQ concentrates on assessing the requirements of jobs as a prerequisite to the matching of personality types. Consultants Saville and Holdsworth who market the OPQ in the United Kingdom carried out such an investigation at Rank Xerox. They studied two different types of sales jobs. Those which required staff to 'cold call' on customers, and those who dealt with large corporate customers.

The jobs that involved cold-calling not surprisingly required people who could take being given the brush-off by harassed and abrupt potential clients and still keep on working. The next call will produce the big order! . . . or the next . . . definitely the one after that!

The second group of jobs, dealing with large corporate customers, had very different requirements. In these jobs with an emphasis on the long-term development of relationships, more emphasis was placed on the ability to be sensitive and open in the expression of feelings. The kind of thick skin exhibited by the cold-callers was not required and indeed the type of behaviour required of cold-callers would make them quite unsuited for the other jobs.

(*Source:* Paul Fisher, *Guardian*, 3 November 1988 for the account of Rank Xerox.)

CASE STUDY 7.1

JOB DEMANDS AND PERSONALITY

Physical Attributes

In addition to tests designed to identify personality types and traits that may be relevant to the work situation, it is also possible to test for physical attributes and potential as well. Such tests relate to manual dexterity of the type required in assembly work at benches and on production lines where work is moving first towards and then away from the worker. This type of test is used as a predictor of trainability and those currently in use have norms for both men and women in particular jobs. The Industrial Training Research Unit at Cambridge has developed more advanced tests for trainability based upon norms established by previous testing. In this way indications of the suitability of applicants in terms of their trainability may be established (Lyons, 1988).

Problems associated with trait theories

While trait theories of personality, and the tests and inventories derived from them, have acquired some popularity among recruiters, they have been subject to mounting criticism over the last twenty years. Theories such as Cattel's and Eysenk's assume that behaviour is independent of situations, that the same person will display the same traits whatever the situation or people with whom they are dealing. That is, traits are assumed to be consistent over time and situation.

It is also important to note that attributing traits to individuals is a matter of language. Traits are terminological devices for describing other people. To say 'Jean is an extrovert' is to give a very concise account of how I think Jean tends to behave. Use of such a term may, however, say as much about me, in terms of what I regard as 'extrovert' behaviour, than it says about the consistency or characteristics of Jean's behaviour. Does Jean behave in the same way with **all** her friends/acquaintances? Does she behave the **same** way in front of her boss as she does when with friends, or with subordinates? Would **everyone** who met her regard her behaviour as 'extrovert' rather than, say, merely 'lively', or 'friendly', or 'confident'?

Traits are a carefully established but nevertheless 'shorthand' way of defining or cataloguing behaviour based upon relatively limited experience or evidence. General tendencies are identified as characteristic of an individual's behaviour after only few (relatively) observations. Also, since questionnaires form the basis of the process of identifying traits, the existence of traits is derived from the answers people give to questions concerning their own likely behaviour in hypothetical situations.

One of the earliest, and most trenchant, critics of trait theory has been that of Mischel, starting with *Personality and Assessment* in 1968. Mischel's response to the trait theorists was to emphasize an aspect of behaviour that underlies the approach taken in this book: that is, the situation in which people find themselves and what that situation means to them is crucial in understanding why people display the behaviour pattern/s that they do. This, if you recall, was the form of the explanation offered in the opening chapters to account for the managerial nature of the Industrial Revolution, and of the responses of working people to that revolution.

In subsequent publications (Mischel, 1973, 1981) Mischel responded to criticism of his original emphasis on situation by suggesting that instead of regarding people as bundles of traits, they should be viewed as a combination of the five variables set out in Table 7.4.

The approach to individual behaviour implicit in Mischel's five variables is consistent with that taken by, for example, Max Weber in his examination of rationality (see Chapter 4). The approach is also consistent

Table 7.4 Mischel's five personality variables

1. **Competences:** that is, abilities and skills.
2. **Constructs:** the frameworks people use to think about their surroundings.
3. **Expectancies:** what people have learnt to expect based on past experience of the people around them and of particular situations.
4. **Values:** how people evaluate features of their environment in terms of preferences as well as in terms of some moral code concerned with ideas of 'right' and 'wrong'.
5. **Strategies:** as a result of having goals, of being purposeful, people develop plans of action which to some extent at least determine their preferences and behaviour.

with the explanation that was offered in that chapter for the phenomenon described by Robert Merton as the 'trained incapacity' of junior bureaucrats. If you remember, junior members of an organization are dependent upon the evaluation of their performance by superiors. One of the ways in which subordinates can demonstrate their competence in a manner superiors find reassuring is to stick to the rules – thus demonstrating their reliability by virtue of their knowledge of the rules and willingness to apply them.

It is important to remember that social situations, those where an individual's behaviour takes account of the existence of others (whether favourable or unfavourably) are generally rule governed. Knowledge of the rules is socially acquired – that is, it is learnt – so how an individual behaves will generally be governed by such rules. 'Competent' behaviour in a social situation will then be a factor of which rules any particular actor has learnt, how well they have been learnt, and how accurately an individual can identify which are the appropriate rules for any given situation.

The process of determining which rules apply in a situation involves the attribution of 'meaning' to that situation. The meaning a situation has for an individual will in part be a consequence of experience and expectations as well as values. Harre (1979) suggests that an individual's behaviour involves a cognitive as well as a motivational aspect.

The cognitive aspect or input to the situation made by an individual relates to their competence in handling the relevant concepts and constructs. Competence is necessary in order to negotiate with others, that is to establish if others share the interpretation of the situation made by the individual, and if not, how such interpretations differ. Social skills are required as well as technical skills relating to the specific tasks involved. Social skills of negotiation are required because different individuals may well have different experiences and expectations, as well as differing competences, so that the same meaning is not immediately attributed to the situation by all involved.

To conclude this discussion of personality, there is no universally accepted theory of personality at the present time, though one of the most frequently used and discussed frameworks for the understanding of human behaviour is the psychoanalytic one associated with Sigmund Freud and which was adapted and extended by, for example, Jung, Adler and

KEY CONCEPT 7.3

THE PSYCHOANALYTIC VIEW OF PERSONALITY

☐ **The 'id':** This is the concept used by Freud and his followers to refer to the basic, primitive, instinctive drive behind human behaviour. The id is the core of the unconscious and strives for gratification and pleasure. This is manifested through sexual and aggresive urges or impulses. As individuals mature they learn, to a greater or lesser extent, to control the id.

☐ **The 'ego':** This concept refers to the logical or reality aspect of human behaviour. It is the 'conscious' which attempts to control the 'unconscious' of the id. The ego keeps the id under control by the application of reason. Thus ideas about appropriate behaviour between adolescent males and females, about marriage and the family, as well as the rules of warfare, represent rules developed to control the primitive instincts of the id. The id and the ego are often in conflict because while the id demands immediate gratification, the ego counsels deferred gratification to more appropriate times and places.

☐ **The 'superego':** The ego is aided in its struggles with the id by the superego which can be conceived as 'conscience'. The superego provides norms as to what is 'right' or 'wrong'. The superego develops by absorbing the cultural values and mores of society. However, conflicts can occur between the ego and superego when the ego's search for a reasoned reality flouts the values of the superego.

The struggles between the id, ego, and superego form the basis of observable human behaviour.

Fromm. The basis of the Freudian framework is the assumption of an unconscious conflict between the three concepts of the id, the ego and the superego, as described in Key Concept 7.3.

The work on personality type and trait theories has not succeeded in developing an overall theory of personality because they attempt to characterize personality by fitting it into discrete and discontinuous categories. Such efforts produced useful descriptive accounts, but these are not helpful in an analytic sense. Any unified personality theory would have to account for cultural, social (including family), situational and biological factors.

Table 7.5 The immature – mature continuum of Argyris

Passive	–	Active
Dependent	–	Independent
Limited behavioural repertoire	–	Extensive behavioural repertoire
Superficial interests	–	Developed interests
Short timespan	–	Long timespan
Subordinate situation	–	Superordinate situation
Not self-aware	–	Self-aware

An interesting and potentially useful approach to personality as far as behaviour in organizations is concerned was that put forward by Argyis (1957). This approach is based upon the idea of a seven dimensional continuum from immaturity to maturity as shown in Table 7.5. It can be seen that the characteristics of the left-hand or 'immature' end of the continua are those of the human infant, while those on the right accord with ideas of adulthood. People will vary according to their position on the various dimensions at any one time since not all will move along the continuum at the same rate on all dimensions.

The implication of this approach is that, to allow for mature behaviour, organizations must facilitate active rather than passive behaviour, independence rather than dependence, long rather than short time perspectives, and so on. Failure to do so will result in mature individuals becoming frustrated and so in conflict with the organization. Thus there may well be a basic contradiction between the requirements of contemporary approaches to the organization and control of work, and the requirements of mature individuals.

The issues raised by Argyris's approach are crucial to the question of motivation in the development of competitive advantage as companies strive to exploit technological and process innovation. The motivational input from an individual relates to that individual's goals, which may well be different from those of others sharing the situation, as well as being subject to change over time. The same person may not have the same goals at different times or in different situation. Bearing this in mind, let us now move on to a consideration of human motivation.

Motivation

Motivation is a term that shares aspects of personality since it not only has widespread acceptance in everyday talk, but is a key factor in the determination or categorization of personality types. In the same way that 'personality' is used to account for the behaviour patterns displayed by individuals, there are also widely shared views about what motivates people, what makes them 'tick'. One widely held view is that money is what motivates people at work, and as we saw when discussing the work of Taylor, this idea has been very influential. Piece-rate and payment-by-result systems are derived from this idea of motivation. However, Nealey and Goodale (1967) found in a study of worker preferences that extra holidays were the preferred option from a number of proposals for additional time off, with a 2% pay rise being fifth of seven compensation offers, six of which were various methods of shortening working time. That a 20% pay rise might have been ranked differently does not **prove** that people are motivated mainly by money. While everyone may have their price, what that price is at any particular point in time requires investigation, thus demonstrating the true, but essentially trivial, nature of the old saying.

Power and the exercise of power is also widely held to be a major motivating force in the lives of business people, particularly those who strive to reach the highest levels in the largest organizations. After all, in popular thought, 'With the kind of money they earn, another hundred grand is not going to make much difference' – apart from anything else it is all alleged to go in taxation anyway! Self-aggrandizement, social recognition, status, prestige, all can – and do – motivate people. In the same way that the term 'personality' can be seen to explain everything and so in fact nothing, everything can be argued to motivate everybody at some time or another. As Wernimont and Fitzpatrick (1972) show, money means different things to people with different backgrounds of training and experience. The question is, who is motivated by what, when are they motivated and how are they motivated?

Individual performance

An individual's performance in a job or task is a function of two variables: ability (can do?) and motivation (will do?). Performance will not be simply the sum of these variables, but the product. To improve performance (however measured), a manager will have to identify two categories of people. First, those whose motivation is fine, but whose skill or ability needs developing, and second, those whose ability and skill levels are fine but who lack motivation. It is the motivational problem that is likely to be the more difficult to deal with.

Motivation as an aspect of the study of human individual behaviour is concerned with how behaviour originates, how and why it is maintained once initiated, how it is guided or directed and how and why it ceases. Motivation concerns the reasons why people adopt particular courses of action and continue with them over a period of time even when confronted with difficulties or obstructions.

The issue of motivation is important in a business context because, for example, identifying an individual as having certain attributes relevant to a job or task (as measured by the Cattell 16PF or the OPQ inventories for example) is only part of the problem from the point of view of the recruiter and the potential employee's future superiors. The candidate may have all the right attributes in term of intelligence, ability to give attention to detail, to get on with people and so on, but he or she may fail to live up to such expectations. Such a failure may have nothing to do with aptitude or ability, but may be the result of a lack of motivation.

If you look around your class you will probably be able to identify someone who is undoubtedly bright and very capable, but just does not seem to bother with the work. Such an individual may, however, be very active in a club, union affairs, or in the bar, (No, the last two are not synonymous though you perhaps might be forgiven for thinking so on occasion!) Equally if you consider the staff: there will be those you might identify as being very capable teachers, administrators and academics but appear to be content with their situation and not actively in search of promotion. You may, if you are really unlucky, even identify one or two who match your capable but unconcerned/unmotivated student colleague! Conversely of course, there are people who would perhaps attain only a mediocre score on any ability measure, but nevertheless appear to put tremendous effort into what they do. This may not necessarily result in any improvement in performance, but in some cases it might well do so.

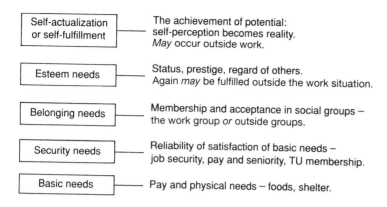

Figure 7.2 Maslow's hierarchy of needs and its relationship to behaviour in work organizations.

The question of motivation is bound up with the role of needs in organizing human behaviour. **Needs** arising due to deprivation are prior to **drives**, 'directed deprivation', which in turn help to identify **goals**, associated with the reduction of drives. Theories of motivation based on needs and associated drives and their reduction are known as 'content' theories of motivation. One of the earliest and still very influential of such theories is that of Abraham Maslow, first published in 1943 and illustrated in Figure 7.2.

In Maslow's theory, the basic needs have to be met first before the individual will be concerned with the next level of need, and so on up the hierarchy. Once a given level of need has been met, those needs no longer motivate the individual. Subsequent behaviour is motivated by drives associated with the next, 'higher', level of need.

This notion of Maslow's has been very influential even though there is very little research evidence to support it. However, it does make managers aware of the range of human needs, and aware of the implications of the fact that such needs may be legitimately met outside work organizations. In many cases of course, the fact that human needs can be met outside work is just as well since management strategies on job design and control over work may preclude any but basic needs being met by, or in, the work situation.

The basic problem with Maslow's notion is that while the assumption that a hierarchy operates is plausible, and has been very influential, in the final analysis it is just that – an assumption. Further criticism of the approach of Maslow, and the so-called 'human relations' approach to behaviour at work, can be found in Watson (1986).

Motivation is central to the job design and job enrichment strategies which have been advocated as solutions to the problem of low productivity and poor quality associated with 'alienated' workers. Closely associated with job design are payment and reward policies which also have a role in enhancing both the quality and quantity of output. Most recently these include profit-related pay and employee share ownership plans. (ESOPS), which will be considered in the final section of this chapter.

In the next section we will consider two approaches to the study of motivation and relate them to issues of job design and reward systems later.

The two-factor theory of motivation

The two-factor theory grew out of a study by Frederick Herzberg in Philadelphia during the 1950s. He used what is known as the 'critical incident' method of collecting data on work and motivation by asking his respondents to report on a time when they felt particularly good, or particularly bad about their job, and to say why this was.

The answers fell consistently into two groups. Those reporting on periods when the job holder felt particularly good about his job (since this work was carried out in the 1950s among engineers, the sexist terminology is possibly accurate!), tended to concentrate on job content and job experience. Reports of bad times and feelings consistently referred to aspects of the job **context** rather than the job itself. The two sets of factors are set out in Key Concept 7.4.

KEY CONCEPT 7.4	Herzberg identified two distinct sets of factors that affected work performance.
HERZBERG'S TWO FACTORS THEORY OF MOTIVATION	☐ Those factors that appeared to result in the expression of satisfaction at work were labelled **motivators,** and related to the work itself. Motivators according to Hertzberg were such things as a sense of achievement, recognition for good work, the interest of the work itself, the exercise of responsibility and the preferment that was a consequence of recognition for good performance. ☐ Those factors that were associated with bad feelings about work and which focused on the job context were termed **hygiene factors.** Hygiene factors were catalogued by Herzberg as, for example, company policies, the quality of supervision, salary levels, working conditions. An undoubted advantage of Herzberg's work was that it concentrated the minds of managers by pointing out that their usual response to problems of 'motivation' was to develop fringe benefit packages, better pay scales and more attractive workplaces, i.e. 'hygiene' not 'motivating' factors. Management had become fixated on hygiene factors – satisfiers – and ignored motivators.

Herzberg's theory is very attractive to common sense. However, despite his own original note of caution about the conclusions, it has come in for considerable criticism. Such criticism has, however, been the basis upon which subsequent and more theoretically sound, hence useful, theories of motivation have been based. The main criticisms levelled at the two-factor theory focus on the method used in its development.

The methodology of the two-factor theory

It is likely that when people set out the good things about work they will record factors which reflect well upon themselves; when they record the bad aspects, they note the shortcomings of other people. Also, since two types of question were used to bring out what made people feel good or bad about their work (later categorized as hygiene and motivation factors), it is not surprising that two sets of answers were forthcoming. Different research methods have produced results different from that which the two-factors theory predicts, and even when Herzberg's own method was replicated the study produced different results (Schwab, DeVitt and Cummings, 1971). However, in general, methods similar to those used originally by Herzberg tend to produce compatible results, whereas different methods produce conflicting results.

Apart from methodological criticisms, the Herzberg approach shares a feature with much of the earlier human relations and Taylorist studies. That is, it is criticized for 'psychological universalism'.

'Universalism' describes an approach which implies that everybody will respond in the same way to the same stimulii since they share the same needs. As Goldthorpe (1968) and his colleagues pointed out in their study of the (then) highly paid workers in the car plants at Luton, the commonly assumed alienating aspects of production-line work did not detract from the desirable aspects of the job. Those migrating to the plant were actively and consciously seeking the high financial rewards that were available.

What is termed an 'instrumental' orientation to work also could confound the predictions of a theory of motivation like Herzberg's. In addition, as Daniel (1973) points out, employees will have different priorities at different times. They will not express satisfaction when they are in the process of negotiating with employers, but having achieved what at that time is regarded as a satisfactory outcome then acknowledgement will once again be granted to the 'satisfactory' aspects of work.

Very few people are going to feel that they do not deserve their last pay rise either because they consider that they work hard (certainly harder than some they could mention), or because the organization made bigger profits, or the cost of living has risen, or that people doing similar or even lower level work in other organizations earn more than they do. A pay rise may therefore be thought of as no more than an individual's due, and not the basis for greater effort on their part.

The issue raised by the charge of psychological universalism relates to the earlier discussion in Chapter 2 concerning the social role of work. A sense of achievement and recognition are doubtless important for the vast majority of human beings, but that is not to say that such motivators can only be found in work. Even cursory reflection is likely to lead to the conclusion that many jobs, because of the way they are organized, are unlikely to provide a sense of achievement and recognition. These will have to be sought elsewhere – on the playing field, in the pub or in the community outside work. Thus what motivates people at work will be influenced by the orientations they bring into the workplace as Goldthorpe *et al.* argued. These orientations may vary during the period of employment due to factors internal and external to the work organization, as Daniel (1973) and Watson (1980) suggest. Factors external to the work situation may be as diverse as the demands of a growing family, or the pay and conditions offered in other firms or industries for similar work skills.

Geography and age may prevent individuals moving to take advantage of higher rewards for similar skills.

It is important to recognize that while there may well be advantages for management in applying notions of a universalistic kind in so far as turnover and absenteeism may be reduced, this is not necessarily the same as increased productivity and is crucially dependent upon the state of the labour market generally.

The issues we have been discussing in this section do at least encourage managers and their advisors to recognize that workers are surprisingly similar to managers in terms of what interests and needs they seek to satisfy. The problem is that not everybody has the same opportunities to satisfy such interests and needs. What is required is a theory of, or at least an approach to, motivation that allows for the variability and complexity of human beings and that of the organizational, social and political environments in which they have to operate. This suggests a 'process' approach to motivation, and one of the most fruitful is that known as 'expectancy theory'.

Expectancy theory of motivation

The first formulation of an expectancy theory was by Vroom (1964), a major critic of the work of Herzberg and of 'content' models of motivation involving notions of self-actualization, responsibility and personal growth.

Vroom's original formulation has been extended by others, e.g. Porter and Lawler (1968), but was nevertheless a significant advance since it recognized the complexities of human motivation in a way earlier theories did not. As originally formulated by Vroom, however, it did not offer much practical help to managers. Luthans (1981) has suggested that the expectancy model is analogous to marginal analysis in economics; no one expects a businessman to calculate marginal revenue and marginal cost, but such notions are useful in the theory of the firm.

One of the major problems underlying the treatment of motivation, performance and satisfaction has been the assumption that satisfaction necessarily results in high performance. As we pointed out earlier, a highly cohesive work group can resist management pressure just because it is highly cohesive. Satisfaction with one's work situation and rewards does not imply that one is motivated to increased effort. One is only getting one's due, as a reliable employee, after all.

A second point that needs recognizing is that increased effort on its own does not necessarily result in increased performance. Skill (as opposed to effort) is also necessary, as is an improvement in the flow of work to the worker. The significance of Porter and Lawler's modification of Vroom's model is that they provide a useful understanding of the relationship between satisfaction and performance by **reversing** the direction of causality – performance results in satisfaction, not the other way round.

The role of expectations
While individuals may not sit down and work out the consequences of particular actions in terms of payoff as a matter of course (though they will on occasions do just this), nevertheless people do weigh up the

attractiveness of alternative outcomes. They do attempt to estimate the likely results of particular actions in terms of those outcomes (Porter, Lawler and Hackman, 1975). Individuals' effort at work will be a function of their expectations concerning (a) the likely rewards for extra output and (b) the probability that extra effort will result in extra output. Such expectations involve an assessment by the individual of how available rewards may assist in the achievement of particular personal goals. A model of the expectancy approach to motivation is shown in Figure 7.3. The Key components of the model are described below.

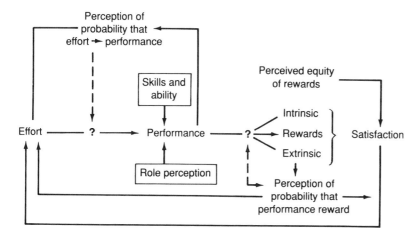

Figure 7.3 Expectancy model of motivation.

☐ **Effort** is a function of the perception which individual workers have of their own roles and of themselves as a person. These perceptions will influence the 'valence' or strength of the importance, significance, preference, or value of a particular outcome. 'Effort' simply means the energy that has to be expended or exerted by the worker – it does not imply 'performance'.

☐ **Performance** refers to some objectively measurable outcome. The emphasis should be on 'objectively measurable' since in many work situations this may not be easy given the nature of the product or the technologically influenced relationship between individual effort and output. That is, it may not be possible for an increased effort on the part of individuals to be reflected in increased output if the flow of work is not under their control.

☐ **Rewards** may comprise any or all of, for example, pay, promotion, recognition, praise, belonging and achievement. An important point about rewards was noted by Porter and Lawler (1968) when they established empirically that rewards should be divided into intrinsic and extrinsic types. Although there is some doubt as to the utility of this distinction, and of the extent to which it is possible to operationalize it, the basis of the dichotomy is set out in Key Concept 7.5.

Equity and rewards

The significance of whether or not rewards are perceived as equitable was examined by Adams (1965). He argued that a major factor in the

KEY CONCEPT 7.5 *INTRINSIC AND* *EXTRINSIC REWARDS*	☐ **Intrinsic** rewards are those which are mediated by individuals themselves and stem directly from performance. In the work setting they can be the acquisition and exercise of skill(s), achieving a target or level of performance, recognition, personal growth. ☐ **Extrinsic** rewards are those which are mediated by someone else and form part of the job situation, for example money or promotion.

relationship between performance and satisfaction was the extent to which the balance between individual inputs and outcomes was seen to be equitable or 'fair'. Inputs were such factors as age, sex, education and effort. Outcomes were rewards such as pay, promotion, status and the intrinsic interest of the job. A perceived imbalance between inputs and outputs will result in efforts to reduce it. Such efforts may or may not be functional for the organization.

Luthans (1981) reports some empirical support for Adams's equity approach and the likely impact on peformance. For example, both hourly paid and salaried workers who see themselves as overpaid tend to increase ouput as a means of reducing the imbalance. There is support for the hypothesis that overpaid piece-rate workers will increase quality and reduce output as a means of reducing perceived inequality. Not surprisingly, salaried and hourly paid workers perceiving themselves to be underpaid will reduce output, while piece-rate workers wil increase output but reduce the quality of that output. It is worth noting that Adams himself was aware that an incongruity between pay and performance, where pay was greater than justified performance, could be tolerated if that imbalance was seen as due to luck. In a market-oriented economy a bargain is a bargain and if the employer is not aware of the mismatch, or apparently ignores it, well . . . Jack (as they used to say) is 'all right'!

The utility of the expectancy model

The advantage of the expectancy approach is that it provides a framework for analysing the context of job design as well as providing an assessment of the operation of reward systems on the basis that workers are rational individuals whose rationality is not so different (if indeed at all) from that of managers. The approach copes with the development of output restrictions by work groups in terms of a rationality shared by workers and managers. If increased output has resulted in piece-rate changes and quota increases or lay-offs in the past, then current managerial exhortations will fall on apparently deaf ears. The expectancy approach illustrates the fact that motivation is a process, since account is taken of an individual's experience and what is learnt from that experience.

If past increases in effort have not resulted in increased output then a rational individual will calculate a reduced value for the probability that effort results in performance. Similarly, if an organization is not thought to have rewarded past increases in performance, then the probability that performance will produce desired rewards is discounted.

The approach can also handle the fact that not everybody is necessarily after the same rewards, or values available rewards in the same way. Rather than making assumptions about what motivates workers in general, it might pay managers to establish what motivates their employees as individuals. This is obviously significant in terms of the design of reward systems and jobs, and for the proponents of profit-sharing and employee share ownership schemes.

Developing competence – training

The availability of training, often the first activity to be cut in a recession, can also be seen as central to improvements in performance. There are two aspects to this. First, the nature of intrinsic rewards suggests that enhanced skills and the opportunity to practise them are significant inputs to effort. Secondly, as mentioned earlier, effort will only produce performance if the worker has the knowledge and skills necessary for enhanced performance.

The role of training in motivation has implications for the simplistic notion that people do not like, or will not welcome, change. If the installation of new equipment is perceived as creating the opportunity to acquire up-to-date skills which are well regarded in the community, then change is welcomed. Only when change is seen as unrewarding or threatening is it resisted or regarded with suspicion. In this respect managers are no different from their subordinates. If one has been well trained in up-to-date techniques then the prospect of entering a buyers' market for labour will be less daunting than otherwise. It may even be welcomed as an opportunity for personal growth.

This is not to say that well trained employees will want to leave their present employer. Satisfied workers are likely to stay with their current employer. The point is that if change in the product market does put pressure on employment levels then resistance to such changes may be reduced, so facilitating a more rapid process of adjustment at minimal cost to all concerned. (See the discussion of the work of Willman (1987) in Chapter 8.)

Implications for management

Expectancy theory has practical implications for management, particularly at a time when British industry is seen to face severe competition from highly skilled and motivated workers in well organized factories and offices which utilize the latest technology. Well motivated employees will be prevented from performing well if their work is badly designed, if they lack the necessary skills, or if the rewards for preformance are either inaproppriate or non-existent. Capable employees will become disillusioned by poor management, facilities and organization. Output will stagnate and labour turnover may well rise as (the best) employees join the competition.

Job design and orientations to work

Lawler (1969) argues that job design changes can have a beneficial effect on motivation (from the organizational viewpoint) since such changes can result in changes in an individual's assessment of the probability that a given reward will result from a given increase in effort via increased performance. Also, job content is a key factor in motivation since it is related to intrinsic rewards associated with a sense of achievement and esteem. 'It is precisely because changes in job content can effect the relationship between performance and the reception of intrinsically rewarding outcomes that it can have a strong influence on motivation and performance' (Lawler, 1969).

Lawler goes on in his paper to list at least three factors, listed in Table 7.6, which a job must have if it is to support the expectation that increased performance will lead to intrinsic rewards. These three attributes of jobs are closely related to what Turner and Lawrence (1965) call the Requisite Task Attribution Index (RTA) which includes the following characteristics:

- □ variety
- □ autonomy
- □ skill
- □ feedback
- □ responsibility
- □ interaction.

Significantly, in the context of our discussion of the merits of the expectancy model, when testing the RTA index Turner and Lawrence found a positive correlation between satisfaction and reduced absenteeism amongst those whose jobs contained the RTA factors. However, this relationship appeared to be mediated by socio-cultural factors related to geographic location and religious affiliation. While the correlation was positive in small towns where the subjects were mainly protestant, in urban areas amongst mainly catholic groups it was inversely related to satisfaction and absent altogether in the case of absenteeism.

Subsequently, Hackman and Lawler (1971) after adapting the RTA index in the light of the expectancy model, found that while performance and attendance was enhanced by jobs possessing the attributes in question, the relationship was mediated by the strength of individuals' need for growth. Need for growth may in fact be influenced by religious affiliation due to differing emphasis upon the nature of expected rewards – those of this world, or of the next.

Table 7.6 Factors influencing the expectation of intrinsic rewards

---

1. The individual receives meaningful feedback on performance. This may mean that individuals have to evaluate their own performance and even determine the nature of the necessary feedback. This implies that the job involves working on a complete product or significant part of the complete product.
2. The tasks making up the job must require the exercise of skills and abilities that the individual values. Such a valuation will be influenced by the valuation in the community outside the work situation of those skills.
3. The job holder must experience considerable control over the setting of goals and the methods of achieving them. Only in this way can an individual experience 'success' as a result of increased performance.

Table 7.7 Criteria for the design of jobs

1. Optimum variety of tasks
2. Meaningful pattern of tasks
3. Optimum length of work cycle
4. Scope for setting standards of quality and quantity
5. Inclusion of preparatory and auxiliary tasks
6. Tasks included in the job should include degree of care, skill and knowledge worthy of respect in the community
7. Job should make perceptible contribution to the utility of the product for the consumer

Based on studies in the UK, Norway and the USA and reported by E. Thorsrud, Work Research Institute, Oslo.

A more detailed breakdown of the factors those designing jobs should take into account resulted from research on job design in the UK, the USA, and the Work Research Institute in Oslo. These factors are set out in Table 7.7.

Two points should be noted when considering questions of job design. First, given the significance of the social role of work discussed earlier, jobs are more than just a matter of design from the point of view of the job holder. Second, while the job might be the most significant organizational reference point for the individual, it is not necessarily the appropriate focal point for job-design exercises.

The phrase 'work structuring' is sometimes used of indicate a focus upon the work group and its task rather than individual tasks. This suggests that job design is a key aspect of the organization of work and this in turn implies that designers have to pay attention to the design of the organization as a whole. The model of the determinants of pay satisfaction developed by Dyer and Theriault (1976), set out in Figure 7.4, reinforces

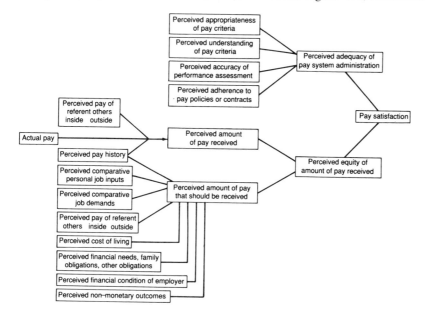

Figure 7.4 The determinants of pay satisfaction. From Dyer and Theriault (1976).

this last point in a manner consistent with the expectancy model of motivation.

This is particularly important when, for example, firms attempt to install quality control and assurance systems. The current concern with 'total quality' in at least some sectors of British industry, and the need for companies to install the relevant British Standard 5750 covering quality assurance, requires that **all** aspects of organizational life are considered together. Installing 'total quality' systems requires that the following aspects of work organization are scrutinized in relation to each other:

☐ organizational structure
☐ job design
☐ payment systems.

Failure to appreciate the extent of the interaction between these elements will result in only partial success at best. Complete failure is the more probable result. The failure to appreciate the interations involved in work restructuring and job redesign is the major reason for the majority of efforts in this area failing (Child, 1984).

The need to treat as variables requiring investigation just what needs, and how strongly they are felt, individuals seek to satisfy in their work was incorporated into an approach to job design developed by Hackman and Oldham (1976) and set out in Figure 7.5. These researchers considered the contribution job characteristics made to the creation of psychological states which were critical for subsequent outcomes given the influence of an individual's need for personal growth. The causal process implied by the arrows in the figure is mediated or influenced by the strength of the individual's growth needs.

While much has been written about job design, enrichment and enlargement, the actual impact of more than twenty-five years of research and experimentation has been relatively limited. The concern with the quality of working life which motivated government programmes of

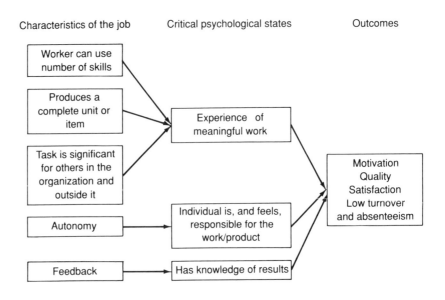

Figure 7.5 The Hackman-Oldham model of job characteristics and motivation. Adapted from Hackman and Oldham (1976).

industrial democracy and job design in Scandinavia in the 1960s was never developed on a similar scale in Britian.

Much of what is talked about in the context of job enlargement and enrichment relates in the majority of cases to just one or two firms. Even in these cases the initiatives were not extended to the total labour force. A number of reasons why attempts to redesign jobs have failed outright or over a period of time (the majority) have been suggested by Child (1984). These reasons include the failure to develop adequate analyses of existing jobs and working methods, and failure to establish the significance and implications of existing, as well as the redesigned, jobs for the workers, supervisors and managers involved.

Supervisory and managerial attitudes to changes in job design appears to depend on the extent to which changes may be seen to undermine authority and status by making workers responsible for tasks previously carried out by supervisors and managers. This concern for authority and status may be indicative of a less technocratic approach to management which is reflected in the different behaviour of managers in Britain compared with those in Germany and Japan, for example (see Chapter 10). Hackman himself suggests that the manner of implementation is the most frequent cause of failure in implementing job redesign. The factors involved in implementation which contribute to failure are set out in Table 7.8.

Table 7.8 Manner of implementation as the most frequent cause of failure of job-redesign

1. Inadequate diagnosis of existing jobs
2. Failure to assess receptiveness of employees to job enrichment
3. Failure actually to change jobs at all
4. Unexpected side-effects, e.g. supervisory resistance
5. Lack of systematic evaluation leading to project being discredited in management's estimation
6. Inadequate education of managers and staff responsible for project
7. Reassertion of bureacratic procedures

Source: Hackman (1975).

The way in which the significance and nature of motivation is regarded is the major shortcoming of job-design theory, since work performance can only be understood once motivation is displaced from its position of pre-eminence according to Kelly (1982). Kelly bases this conclusion on, amongst other things, the fact that numerous empirical studies of the operation of incentive payment systems show that poor motivation has relatively little to do with restrictions on output. Far more important is a lack of trust between management and workers which fosters the belief amongst the labour force that management will exploit any improvements in productivity for their own advantage.

A second factor identified by Kelly as a reason for minimizing the significance of motivation is the impact of the technology that is used. A major influence on output in production-line situations is the flow of parts to the workstations and the problems of coordination. It is these factors, rather than the motivation of workers, that have a major influence on output. Such influence is even greater in continuous process situations, although groups of workers responsible for key stages in the process may be able to exercise considerable control over output.

Thirdly, any improvements from the managerial point of view as a result of job-redesign exercises could equally well be explained by those aspects of design associated with changes in payment systems, work methods, reductions in labour inputs (in terms of both quality and quantity), and improved managerial control. These aspects are of course associated with the scientific management approach of Taylor which the human relations approaches were trying to humanize.

The approach to understanding worker behaviour, including performance, which considers the orientations of workers to their work situation is consistent with both the expectation model of motivation as well as with Kelly's valid assertion that, to date, job-redesign theory has suffered from the lack of an adequate theory of organization. This is not necessarily because such a theory has been non-existent, but more because available theories of organization have been ignored by job-design activists and publicizers. Several of these issues can be seen to be present in what is perhaps the most frequently quoted example of job-redesign, the case of the Volvo car company in Sweden described in Case Study 7.2.

CASE STUDY 7.2

THE VOLVO EXPERIENCE

The Volvo company is one of the best known that has attempted to develop an approach to the organization and design of jobs that includes most if not all the approaches that have been developed over the last fifty years or so.

The project was initiated by Pehr Gyllenhammar after he took over as chief executive of the company that was Sweden's largest employer. One of his major concerns as chief executive was with the rate of labour turnover and absenteeism that prevailed. The problem was seen to be one which derived from the conflicting demands of automobile manufacturing technology – the assembly line – on the one hand, and social values which supported demands for more meaningful work, better job security and higher standards of living.

Basing their strategy on the socio-technical approach, Gyllenhammar's team decided to adapt the technology to reflect the changing expectations and demands of the work force. Autonomous work groups were formed so as to reflect a form of work which could be considered more 'natural' in the non-alienating or anomic sense than was the production line.

Autonomous work groups consisted of a maximum of twelve workers who nominated their own supervisor and organized, scheduled and inspected their own work. Payment was based upon the output of the group and all received the same share of the group payment with the exception of the supervisor who received a differential. This policy was initially implemented in a rather *ad hoc* manner as and when it became possible. However, the construction of a new assembly plant at Kalmar (population 50 000) on the east coast provided the opportunity to construct a plant which incorporated the socio-technical approach from the very foundations.

The plant began production in 1974 replacing the moving conveyor belt of an assembly line by work pieces which were moved in sequence through each of 25 workstations and groups of workers by a computer-controlled battery-powered carrier guided by magnetic strips buried in the floor. Each work group , now numbering fifteen to twenty people, worked on complete subassemblies or modules: drive chain, interiors, electrics, chassis, steering and brake systems, etc. Each group could organize their work as they saw fit, including the scheduling of rest periods, but had to meet agreed production targets. Facilities were provided for work groups to stockpile work, thus enabling them to exercise some control over the work consistent with output targets.

Further environmental aspects of the quality of working life were also included by designing the plant layout to be light, airy and with relatively low noise levels. Rest areas were carpeted and well-equipped changing rooms were provided.

Too much should not be read into this, or other examples, even though the response from the workforce was positive. Kalmar covers a relatively small proportion of the total assembly work of Volvo (only 8 per cent of total production by 1980 according to Francis (1986)). Gyllenhammar himself has said that they would not have gone ahead with the programme if they had not been confident that benefits to management would accrue: 'We wouldn't invest in dock assembly if we couldn't see economic as well as social justification for it' (P.G. Gyllenhammar, quoted in the *Harvard Business Review*, July/August 1977).

The improvement in the quality of working life which undoubtedly resulted from the Volvo plan was not the **objective**, but a **means** of facilitating the achievement of managerial objectives relating to competition in the market-place.

The tasks actually carried out by workers were little different from those carried out by workers in other plants, and managerial control still prevailed over production targets and methods – the speed at which the carriers moved between workstations was centrally controlled for example. While the work group could themselves arrange the distribution of tasks within the group, the nature of the tasks themselves were not so very different from what they had been. However, there was some enhancement, since inspection was now the responsibility of the group.

No systematic investigation of the programme has been carried out, and many observers have noted that the identification of a causal relationship between the changes and improvement in labour turnover, absenteeism and performance is extremely difficult since **everything** was changed. Indeed, the rising trend in absenteeism was not halted, although alleged to be lower than average for Sweden as a whole, and no clear indication of relative cost benefits are available (Francis, 1986). Continued over page

Continued from previous page More recently *The Financial Times* has carried a report of yet another new plant being built by Volvo to accommodate further developments in assembly processes ('Volvo Plans Big Changes in Car Assembly', 22 April 1988). The new plant is sited at Uddevalla, eighty kilometres north of Gothenburg which is the main production centre for Volvo in Sweden, and will contain thirty fixed workstations and associated work groups or teams, each of which will produce four cars per day. Each car will move only four times during the assembly process and spend up to two hours at each assembly point or workstation. It would seem that this plant is, like Kalmar, concerned with final assembly only.

The Uddevalla plant will employ between one thousand and one thousand two hundred workers which Volvo now consider the ideal number for any one site. However, while the new assembly process will mean the performance of even more complex tasks than was the case at Kalmar, Volvo no longer allocate responsibility for inspection and quality control to the work teams. It is suggested that this will be only a temporary feature, but no indication is given as to why this change was adopted nor for how long it is expected to operate. It is reported, though, that Volvo have intitated a project to involve production workers more closely in maintenance and workload planning at some point in the future.

Orientations to work and their significance

The study of orientations to work has its origins in the work of Weber and the assumption that human beings are on the whole rational, although the form of rationality might differ amongst different people and groups, and at different times for the same person or group. This approach encompasses the idea of a 'negotiated order' existing in organizations and avoids some of the problems associated with the definition and attribution of needs implied by the discussion of 'higher' and 'lower' order needs in the human relations tradition. A categorization of needs into higher and lower ranks is not necessarily unhelpful or inaccurate, but it does tend to beg the question of just which needs are felt by which workers at any particular time, how strongly they are felt, and how such needs influence behaviour.

A demand for higher wages does not necessarily reflect the pressure of basic needs, though it may do on occasions. It could equally reflect needs, wants or preferences which, while not 'basic', still require money for their satisfaction. Foreign travel, family outings and holidays, for example fall into this category and do undoubtedly play a very important role in the basic quality of life.

Furthermore, the demand for such activities may well be stoked by advertising in so far as this may increase a sense of relative deprivation. If yours is the only family amongst those you know not taking two holidays a year, then the feeling that you are underpaid may develop – particularly if those against which the comparison is made are not obviously better trained, harder working or doing clearly 'better' jobs. As Wernimont and

Fitzpatrick (1972) put it: 'Material comfort in terms of basic needs and material comfort as an indicator of status or esteem appear to be two very different things, both of which, though, are associated with the concept of money.'

One of the earliest, and important, applications of the orientation approach was that, mentioned earlier, of Goldthorpe, Lockwood *et al.* (1968) in their study of the impact of affluence on the behaviour and outlook of manual workers in the car industry. They argued that it was not possible to explain the behaviour of those workers in the face of what was widely (and not inaccurately) seen as the alienating conditions of the automobile production line without asking what it was that brought those workers to that job. What was it they were looking for when they took what they knew were repetitive, narrow jobs? The problem for 'need' theorists was that the workers interviewed in the Luton studies expressed satisfaction with the job and the employer!

The approach adopted by Goldthorpe and his colleagues produced a result which is consistent with expectancy theory since what workers were seeking on the production lines in Luton was high wages. They had what is termed an 'instrumental orientation' to work. This had been adopted on the basis of a calculative rationality which recognized that given their relative lack of skills a certain standard and quality of life outside work could only be supported by undertaking a particular type of work. That is, relatively high paid, at best semi-skilled, repetitive work on automobile production lines.

The significance of non-work factors

While the orientation approach is consistent with the expectancy theory, it goes further since it locates the expectations which influence workplace behaviour in the family and social network **outside** the workplace. It is this aspect of behaviour which is involved in the Turner and Lawrence studies on the RTA index which produced different results for workers located in different religious and social environments. The influence of factors outside work can account for the fact that orientations, expectations and even needs will change over time, as will behaviour. For example, at different periods in the life cycle (i.e. single, married, married with children, married with grown-up children who have left home), expectations will differ, as will needs, wants, preferences and behaviour.

Equally important can be changes in the work situation itself. Changes in job design may or may not be consistent with the orientations of the workers and so may be rejected if they offer rewards not sought by the people concerned.

Watson (1980) develops the distinction between 'prior' orientations to work which may be derived from past experience, family, education and so forth, and the notion of 'dynamic' orientations which derive from the experiences in the workplace itself and the impact of non-work factors. A reduction in strike activity, for example, or an apparent willingness to accept previously rejected changes in working practices may be the result of pragmatic adjustment to changed labour market conditions rather than a fundamental change in outlook. An important idea here is that of the

KEY CONCEPT 7.6

THE WAGE-EFFORT BARGAIN

On the basis of expectations and orientations derived from past experience of work and of socialization, a worker establishes some notion of 'balance' between effort (input) and the offered wage (output). Factors which change the wage-effort bargain or ratio will induce changed behaviour as the worker tries to re-establish the old ratio or establish a new one. Thus changes in job design even if they are accompanied by extra pay and more enriched jobs may well radically disturb the wage-effort relationship. The fact that many job-redesign exercises are often associated with increased payments for some workers at least means that there are two possible explanations for a subsequent increase in output – the satisfaction derived from the new job, or the desire to earn the new pay rate.

'wage-effort bargain' or 'wage-effort ratio' developed by Baldamus (1961) and described in Key Concept 7.6.

Selection and recruitment

The approaches to personality, motivation and job design discussed so far have important implications not only for the management of human resources, but also for the recruitment of employees. It is to the process of recruitment and selection that we now turn.

It is important to recognize that the process of recruitment is not a one-way or one-dimensional activity. Recruitment is two-dimensional since (consistent with the expectancy model of motivation) the process of recruitment implies not only that the organization is selecting an employee but also that an individual worker is selecting an employing organization. Of course, the nature of the labour market (in terms of the availability of certain types of jobs and of certain types of potential workers) will mediate the balance of such a two-way process.

From the assumption that recruitment involves a selection process by both the employer and potential employee, it follows that selection methods must be considered from two perspectives:

☐ their ability to identify required attributes amongst applicants, and
☐ the explicit and implicit signals to the applicant about the organization.

The second perspective is important because when, for example, expectations raised during the selection process are subsequently frustrated by organizational characteristics, dissatisfaction may result. Such dissatisfaction will result from the appointed individual calculating a low probability that performance will result in a valued reward. Conversely, failure to inform a potential employee of what rewards are available may result in the loss of a highly motivated and able worker to the competition.

The most widely used methods to select employees are interviews, biographical data and psychological tests. While virtually all organizations will interview applicants (however perfunctorily) and require the completion of an application form which asks for biographical data (age, education, qualifications, hobbies/interests, marital status, schools/colleges/universities attended, previous work history and so on), not all organizations will additionally apply psychological tests for personality, needs and aptitude, though these are becoming increasingly common.

Interviews

Porter *et al.* (1975) report a number of studies that provide an empirical basis for questioning the efficacy of interviews. Evidence has accumulated over more than eighty years of the poor reliability of interviews in selection processes. There are at least six reasons for this unreliability which are set out in Table 7.9.

Table 7.9 Factors affecting the unreliability of interviews

1. Unless the interview is well structured, it is likely that material will not be systematically covered.
2. Different interviewers are likely to assess the same information differently.
3. When an interview is unstructured the interviewer tends to make an assessment early in the interview before all relevant information is to hand.
4. More emphasis is placed upon negative information than on positive information.
5. Interviewers rank applicants against a stereotype which may not be used by all interviewers, and which may anyway be inappropriate.
6. The quality of prior interviewees may negatively influence the rating of subsequent interviewees.

An over emphasis on negative factors may well result from the fact that in many cases for many jobs there is a surplus of potential applicants. This will put pressure on the selectors who will look for what are known as 'cheap screens'. In their desire to reduce an unwieldy list of possible applicants amongst whom it is difficult to choose, selectors may well pick on a negative feature of a candidate and ignore other positive ones simply to reduce the pressure imposed by a long 'short list'. The type of school, college or university attended, the course studied, age, sex or race, and marital status may all function (legally or not) as cheap screens. So too can personal features such as dress and hair style and whether or not a male candidate has a beard! A few years ago at the annual conference of the Institute of Personnel Management a lively debate was precipitated by two personnel managers who held opposed views about the use of postcodes by job applicants. One announced that he did **not** short-list those who failed to use the postcode since this indicated a slip-shod, disorganized approach. A second then anounced that he never short-listed people who **did** use the postcode since they were likely to be finicky, nit-picking and narrow-minded!

While the interview is a notoriously unreliable selection method when used in isolation, it is not suggested that it be abandoned since, as pointed out earlier, the process of selection is two-way. An advantage of the interview is that it enables applicants to collect information relevant to their decision as to whether or not to accept any job offer. Such information is not restricted to data about the job, pay, fringe benefits and so on, all of which could be accurately recorded in an information sheet. More importantly such information will relate to the social climate of the organization, the type of people employed, the atmosphere between management and subordinates, and the social rewards likely to be available. The personality and presentation of the interviewer are therefore important, as is the opportunity to meet future colleagues, as part of selection process.

Effective interviews

After reviewing published research on the effectiveness of interviews Mayfield (1964) suggested six factors that enhance the validity of interviews:

☐ Trained interviewers who are familiar with the job and organization involved.
☐ Structured interviews to ensure relevant information is acquired.
☐ Interviewers to be informed of what constitutes favourable or unfavourable information in the context of the job being applied for.
☐ Interviewers to concentrate on collecting information rather than 'attracting' the applicant.
☐ The interview to be used in conjunction with tests.
☐ More than one interviewer, either at the same time or sequentially.

Implied here, particularly by the third factor listed above, is the existence of a clearly stated list of required qualities or attributes derived from an adequate job analysis and specification. The basis for forming such a list is provided by Rodger's seven-point plan (Rodger, 1970) which covers the following aspects:

☐ physical
☐ attainment
☐ general intelligence
☐ specific aptitudes
☐ interests
☐ disposition
☐ personal circumstances.

Selection tests

Some of the tests available to those involved in staff selection were discussed in the earlier section of this chapter when discussing personality. Tests are particularly useful when it is necessary to identify the extent to which applicants possess aptitudes or abilities that are differentially distributed amongst the population. The problem here is to establish whether the applicant already can do the job in question, or can learn to do it. Manual dexterity and intelligence tests come into this category for example, as does the Technical Test Battery (TTB). This is a series of tests that focuses on the mental skills required in particular jobs – for example engineering and computing – and covers verbal, spatial, mechanical and diagrammatic reasoning and comprehension.

When assessing the validity and utility of psychological tests it is necessary to distinguish between those that will indicate the applicant's maximum performance from those that will indicate likely 'typical' performance. Following the discussion of theories and models of motivation, three separate but related issues should be noted. While a test may indicate that an applicant is capable of delivering a particular **level** of performance, equally important are the conditions under which the individual will **attain** and subsequently **maintain** that level of performance.

Following the earlier mention of biographical data it is worth noting in the context of tests that when such biographical data is correlated with similar data from existing personnel files valid predictions can be made concerning how individuals with particular attributes are likely to perform. Lyons (1988) reports that in the United States the use of 'biodata' has been extended and developed to the point where application forms have become in effect personality and aptitude tests. A number of organizations in the United Kingdom, for example the major banks, are now adopting this approach.

This development was commented upon by Porter *et al.* (1975) in their reference to research that attempted to analyse reasons for the effectiveness of application forms containing questions the answers to which were weighted on the basis of their relationship to performance criteria. In America these forms include questions directed at individual achievements, family experience, and changes in social status. Porter and his colleagues emphasize that while the validity of these methods has been quite good, it is not clear why they predict so well.

Before rushing to adopt such processes in other cultural situations, the UK for example, management should recognize that a balance has to be struck between selection methods and processes that will at the same time prove useful to the employer while not disenchanting potential applicants. The selection process is two-way since the methods used, or not used, will also tell applicants something about the organization they have applied to join.

Too much probing into an individual's background may lead applicants to feel that their personal privacy is under threat and to question just how such information may be used in terms of their future promotion chances. Will an honest answer about an unfortunate episode be held against the individual? Or will the event be considered 'water under the bridge'? Close investigation of this type may be tolerated if the job market is very tight, or the chances of getting the desired job with a sought-after organization are perceived as good. If not, however, potential applicants may be discouraged from continuing with their application.

Equal opportunities

An even more significant issue concerning selection tests and the role of biodata than those discussed in the previous paragraphs concerns the problems of equal employment opportunities. It is known that some tests used in selection processes produce different results for the two sexes and also for different ethnic groups. This produces the danger that such a difference can be used to justify discrimination. The fact that different groups produce different scores may be used to justify a prejudiced decision on the part of the selector, whether or not the difference is significant in terms of the job in question.

However, there is considerable research evidence that aptitude tests, which cut across social, ethnic and religious boundaries, are fairer and more valid than other forms of assessment used in selection. They can provide opportunities that would otherwise be lost to particular social groups. In the case of computing for example, it is argued that the introduction of aptitude tests provided opportunities for rapid advancement and high earnings to people previously ignored by recruiters.

Since tests used in recruitment can be described as part of the process of deciding who should be offered employment they come under the authority of the Sex Discrimination Act 1975. This means that employers can be required to justify the nature and use of tests in the selection process if there is a higher rate of rejection for one group. The technical and legal aspects involved have yet to be examined in any detail in the United Kingdom where there are no regulatory guidelines at present. This contrasts with the situation in the United States where since 1971 employers have been required to justify the use of tests whenever the rejection rate for one group was higher than for another.

By 1978, US employers were required to conform to strict procedures for validating the tests they used. Since many of these procedures were of considerable sophistication only the larger firms could comply with the requirements of the United States Equal Employment Opportunities Commission. The result has been that many employers decided not to use tests at all. While a general reduction in the amount of testing has taken place, that which does continue is on a sounder basis though still the subject of controversy on occasion.

Recently published research by the Equal Opportunities Commission in the UK, (Pearn *et al.*, 1988) suggests that test publishers are not providing the level of practical guidance required by employers. Employers felt there was insufficient information on the following:

☐ gender differences in test performace;
☐ the gender composition of the groups used to establish test-related norms;
☐ the interpretation of gender differences in average performance.

It would seem from this research that many employers (probably most) do not bother to validate the tests they use because validation is both time-consuming and demands high levels of statistical analysis. It was just such a lack of validation that resulted in many US companies being taken to court in the 1970s and the subsequent stringent guidelines on employment testing now in operation.

It should also be noted that similar issues are involved in the context of race discrimination.

Adaptation

Once an offer of employment has been made and accepted, there commences the first stage in the employment relationship which can be seen as one of adaptation. This process is also two-way in that while the individual has to concede (some) autonomy to organizational superiors and interests, organizational superiors also have to come to terms with the individuality of their new employee or co-worker. Expectancy theory is important here too since, as a result of the selection process, both sides will have formed expectations about the other's future performance which will influence motivation and effort.

Apart from the problem that questions and answers used and produced in the selection process may themselves be of questionable validity (to some degree at least since it is difficult and expensive to exclude totally the possibility of error whether deliberate or unintended), there is the possibility that the competitive nature of the selection process may add to the validity problem for both parties. The potential employee will be in competition with other potential employees, and the firm will be competing with other firms engaged in recruiting similar staff. It is possible therefore that either by accident or design one or both sides may form erroneous expectations.

The process of adaptation will be looked at from two sides in the following paragraphs, that of the organization which will be concerned with the process of socialization, and that of individual employees who will be concerned to achieve their own goals and to establish or maintain their self-identity or individuality. It is important to recognize that there is a tension at the heart of the employment relationship in western societies in so far as the ruling ethos is that of individualisms, of individual effort, determination, grit, ambition, ability and so on. Yet the context for most work situations is that of a group of some kind where at the very least individual effort has to be coordinated to some degree with that of others.

Socialization

This topic was first introduced in Chapter 2 and is discussed further here. The process of human socialization starts from the very first moments of life when the midwife announces the sex of the new baby! It continues through the medium of the family and education and, in industrial societies, includes preparation for the world of work. Information about work in general and particular occupations will be derived from the experiences of family members as well as from contact with the employees of organizations with which individuals come into contact, e.g. shops, banks, teachers.

One of the reasons, for example, that many employers hesitate to take on school-leavers, preferring to recruit people who already have work experience, is that the problem of socialization is likely to be greater when the individual is entering a work organization for the first time. While the truly remarkable fact may be the smoothness with which the school-to-work transition is effected in the vast majority of cases, the process is obviously one that requires very careful consideration by all concerned. Subsequent career changes may be less dramatic given the build-up of experience, but even so new organizations and new jobs involving promotion will require a period of socialization.

The initial period with a new organization will require that the individual 'unlearn' old ways of acting, and even thinking, and learn new ones. This period may be quite fraught if the changes expected by the organization are considerable or are regarded as unreasonable or unnecessary by the new job holder. To overcome such resistance the organization will operate reinforcement, that is some reward will be offered in exchange for compliance. The prestige attaching to employment with a high status organization may in itself be sufficient to overcome any overt objection on the part of the employees to the new methods or demands imposed upon them.

Expectancy theory is relevant here because a crucial factor in the effectiveness of the socialization process will be the extent to which it is consistent with the expectations about the new job and employer that led to joining in the first place. This will influence the effort put in by the individual which will in turn influence the perception of the employer.

Assuming that socialization proceeds reasonably smoothly, the individual will acquire and develop the attributes of an organizational member in terms of ideas and behaviour. This involves the acquisition of new values, relationships and a self-image. Much of the socialization process will be informal in that it will be carried out as a result of day-to-day contact with peers, subordinates and superiors in addition to any formal training and induction process. This is important because as a result of these informal processes the newcomer may learn what the organization is **really** like and so may modify expectations with subsequent impact on performance. Such socialization may or may not be consistent with the interests of the organization and management.

The individual

As individuals, new employees will be concerned to ensure that the organization will assist in the attainment of their goals at the same time that management are attempting to ensure that the individual will facilitate the attainment of their goals. The concept of 'organizational culture' may be important in this context, as described in Needle (1989), Chapter 3.

The process by which the individual seeks to secure personal interests can be crucial for the survival and adaptability of the organization. This is because the process may well result in innovation which is functional for organizational survival. If individuals did not attempt to pursue individual interests it is possible that the organization would atrophy as it came to be characterized by an unchanging set of ideas and behaviours. Organizations require a modicum of what Richard Hoggart, in *The Uses of Literacy*, has called 'responsible disobedience'. While Hoggart was examining the role of disobedience in social and cultural change, the notion can be applied to people who, while accepting the essential norms and values of the organization, nevertheless reject or at least question many less central ones.

Such people are potential innovators and hence of vital importance for organizational survival. An organization that cannot tolerate such behaviour will lose the potential for adaptation as innovators seek more rewarding employment with the competition. It is possible to argue that many organizations need more, not less, dissatisfied workers, just as long as they are dissatisfied about the right things!

Expectations

The issue of adaptation on the part of individuals and organizations is relevant to what many see as a problem of recruiting young people, graduates in particular. It is widely held that graduates (and particularly post-graduates like those holding an MBA) go into employment with unrealistic expectations about what they will be doing and how rapidly they will be promoted.

This is particularly likely to happen when there is a shortage of suitable applicants (actual or perceived) which leads recruiters to make promises they cannot possibly keep, or to describe the work new recruits will be undertaking in unrealistic terms. Indeed, the failure to impart realistic accounts of the work and promotion chances may itself create the illusion of a shortage of qualified recruits. This will happen as new employees become dissatisfied and frustrated with the type and level of work they are required to do after appointment, and resign.

As soon as they reasonably can, having acquired an acceptable minimum of experience as far as their CV is concerned, they will leave. This means that the organization has continually to attempt the recruitment of qualified workers, with harassed recruiters prone to put their problems down to the personal inadequacy of recruits or the inadequacy of supply. Recruiting graduates and then putting them to do the work that someone less well qualified could do, or where promotion is likely to be much slower than their contemporaries enjoy, will create frustration.

The fact that a relatively small proportion of the relevant age group in the UK attend education after eighteen years of age is likely to raise expectations amongst what is a fairly select group by definition. Recent graduates and diplomats may not be as good as they think they are, but they obviously are to some extent 'special' . . . at least 'different'!

There is some, but not very recent, research evidence that presenting recruits with accurate information, as compared with concentrating on the most favourable possible outcome concerning the work and promotion prospects, does not necessarily reduce the number of applicants, but does reduce turnover in the early phases of the employment relationship. The factors leading one major company to assert the existence of a 'shortage' of graduates in relevant disciplines and how this shortage was dealt with is described in Case Study 7.3.

In the final section of this chapter, we will examine the role of payment systems and their impact on behaviour.

The role of payment systems

Whatever the role of intrinsic rewards in motivating behaviour, pay is undoubtedly important for all grades and level of workers from the most

CASE STUDY 7.3

**A SHORTAGE OF
ELECTRONIC
GRADUATES**

A major company in the domestic and defence electronics field was constantly concerned about the difficulty experienced in recruiting an adequate supply of graduate electronics engineers. Representatives of the company, like many others, constantly complained about the supply and quality of graduates, and of the failure of universities, polytechnics and the government to do anything about it.

After some time, a survey was carried out to assess the company's policy on graduate recruitment in the light of what it could find out about its competitors' policies. This was done in part by way of contacts in competitor companies and comparing advertised details, partly by asking those who did not accept offers of jobs what they thought of their treatment by the company during the recruitment/selection process, and partly by questioning those who did accept jobs. This last group were interviewed shortly after appointment and, if necessary, when they left the company.

As a result of this exercise it was established that at least part of the problem was due to lower initial salary offers, but more significant was the way in which applicants were left to make their own travel and accommodation arrangements for their interviews. Competitor companies arranged hotel accommodation the night before interviews for those who required it, and then sent a coach to take applicants to the interview location. Matching this level of courtesy, and raised starting salary levels, produced an immediate improvement in recruitment.

However, the improvement in actual recruitment then focused attention on another problem associated with the alleged shortage of electronic specialists. Turnover of newly recruited graduates was unacceptably high. Having recruited the targeted numbers for three years, the recruiters were still having to recruit just as hard to keep the number of employed graduates up. Once again an investigation was undertaken, this time into retention.

Again, contacts in other companies were utilized, and particular attention paid to the reasons why people were leaving. It soon became apparent that two factors were important, one which had been picked up on the previous survey but then ignored, and one which had not before been examined.

The factor identified in the previous survey concerned the apparent failure of recruiters to establish what the individual was seeking for their career, and how the applicants envisaged their career developing. This then highlighted the second factor. The company was recruiting very highly qualified graduates but then insisted that they start their employment by carrying out tasks that could have been done by people with an HNC/D. The problem was not the arrogant assumptions of the recruits, but the very pragmatic fear that if they spent too long at that sort of task at that stage of their working life, they would fall behind their peers who had gone to other companies. Since many new recruits kept in touch with friends from university and polytechnics, it soon became apparent they were being used for lower grade work. After two years, they started looking for other jobs.

junior member of staff to the chairman of the board. Current interest in employee share ownership and profit-sharing plans as well as the various share option schemes for senior management testify to the importance of the pay-effort bargain, and attempts to gain the willing cooperation of employees.

While Oscar Wilde may have regarded a cynic as someone who knew the price of everything and the value of nothing, even Frederick Hertzberg is reputed to have admitted that money helped him sort out his priorities! Apart from the fact, mentioned earlier, that money may be required for the satisfaction of other than basic needs, money is central to the operation of a market economy in so far as such an economy attempts to put a price on practically everything. Even when there is no overt intention to do so, the fact that choices have to be made amongst possible allocations of scarce resources in an environment in which all organizations are accountable for the use of resources implies that, for example, a price will be put on a human life. Of relevance to organizational behaviour is that it is easier to put a money value on some outcomes than others. Just how do you value an 'intrinsic' reward, for example?

We have already noted some of the factors which might influence the importance of pay for individuals or groups, and employers may have little control over them – stages in the lifecycle for example in so far as people are 'expected' to establish stable relationships with members of the opposite sex, to have childern, and for those childern to leave home at some point.

In the context of motivation and performance it is important that management are aware what it is they are rewarding through the pay system. It is no good management demanding high quality output if the pay system rewards quantity at the expense of quality. Equally, it would be wise to accept that an attempt to change the system to reward quality is likely to be viewed (at least initially) with suspicion on the part of the workforce since this will create uncertainty over the level of future earnings.

How rapidly that suspicion is overcome will depend upon the past behaviour of management and the quality of the discussions that take place concerning the change. Such discussions should take into account the implications of expectancy theory and the factors determining the orientations of the workforce.

Dyer and Theriault's model (Figure 7.4) of the determinants of pay satisfaction includes the extent to which employees perceive congruency between the criteria they think **ought** to be used in establishing pay, and the criteria they see as **actually** being used by the employer. It is important, these authors argue, that employees actually understand the criteria used in pay systems, and that they perceive any performance appraisal system to produce accurate results.

Types of payment system

There are six basic types of payment system in general use. These are set out in Table 7.10. Combinations of two or more of these basic systems may be established.

Table 7.10 Basic payment systems

---

1. **Flat time rate:** given level of pay for specified number of hours of work.
2. **Output incentive:** pay related via a formula to level of output.
3. **Merit rating:** pay dependent upon assessment by superiors (may be subjective).
4. **Measured day work:** pay determined by the consistent attainment of production 'norms'.
5. **Negotiated productivity and flexibility:** pay negotiated along with changes in work processes and rules involving task flexibility.
6. **Profit-sharing:** pay levels dependent on profit achieved by the organization.

Adapted from Child (1984), p. 191.

The six types of payment system encompass four distinguishing characteristics:

☐ What is actually rewarded.
☐ The inclusion, or not, of an incentive element.
☐ The frequency of payment.
☐ Individual or group effort as basis of payment.

All of these can be seen to be important in so far as each of these characteristics may affect the way in which an individual's expectations are actually rewarded or not. It might, for example, be better to have bonuses paid twice yearly rather than annually, since the reward may be too distant from the effort with the longer period. Similarly, if payment is related to group output the effect on individual effort may be mediated by the perceived ability of any one individual to influence the group result by their own efforts.

Current efforts to increase the functional flexibility of the labour force are also related to payment systems since if flexibility is to be accepted with some degree of willingness, then expectations about pay have got to be protected. A payment system that in effect punishes workers for changing jobs because different rates are applied, or because performance criteria take time to achieve, will not facilitate the smooth operation of functionally flexible work systems.

There is considerable debate about the advantages and disadvantages of various payment systems, and a considerable literature providing guidance and assistance to management for the design, implementation and operation of payment systems. The factors we have been considering in this chapter are relevant to current attempts to engage employee interests and involvement in their employing organizations by such strategems as employee share ownership plans (ESOPs) and profit-related pay (PRP), which are discussed in the following paragraphs.

Employee share ownership plans and profit-related pay

The debate over payment systems and their role in creating greater involvement and interest on the part of workers has been given an impetus in recent years. This has come mainly from the publicity given to ideas designed to deal with the problem of creating flexible pay systems in the context of the socially and politically desirable objective of increasing employment without increasing inflation.

An important aspect of these proposals has been the concern to develop employees' participation in the success of the enterprise. While a profit-related bonus, paid in cash, is a well-established method of involving workers in success (and relative failure), there are potential problems. One of the problems about profit-sharing is that profit itself is an arbitrary concept that depends considerably on decisions taken in the past, and secondly there are current accounting conventions. These factors can have unpredictable effects on the variability of bonus levels and may be outside the control of current mangers let alone employees. There is also the problem that the desire to pay out cash bonuses may be affected by investment demands for new equipment and products. This is likely to result in equally fraught negotiations over the bonus as over pay rates.

Employee share ownership plans

One solution to problems that may arise with cash bonuses is to pay a profit-related bonus in shares under an Employee Share Ownership Plan (ESOP). The 1978 Finance Act established Approved Deferred Share Trusts which entitles both employers and employees to tax concessions if shares are bought for the benefit of employees and held for two years. A variation on this theme was established by the Chancellor in 1980 when it was further enacted that employees could gain tax concessions if they used the proceeds of a Save as You Earn (SAYE) Plan to buy shares in their employing organization.

The extension of employee share ownership has of course been given a boost in some cases by privatization, the National Freight Corporation, British Telecom, British Gas and British Airways being perhaps the best known examples. However it is worth noting that the circumstances of the major flotations of the privatization programme have occasioned widespread concern that the conditions of sale provided a risk-free (initially at least) investment. It is difficult therefore to draw too many firm conclusions about just what the implications of the extension of employee share holdings means.

A major criticism of ESOPs is that they in effect require workers to put all their eggs in the one basket by investing in their employing organization. If it fails, not only is the job likely to go but so will the value of the shares. In terms of the earlier discussion of motivation, it is also necessary to consider what the expectancy model would suggest about the behaviour and responses of an outside investor in a company's shares in comparison with those of employees who regard their shareholdings as a reward for past inputs.

Poole (1988) provides evidence showing a close link between the adoption of ESOPs and profit-sharing schemes, and managerial attitudes to industrial relations. This survey suggests that companies which already engage in sharing information and employee involvement in decision-making, a consultative decision-making style, are more likely to adopt successfully forms of employee share ownership and profit-sharing.

This is consistent with evidence from the United States also (*Employee*

Stock Ownership Plans in the United States, Partnership Research, London, 1987). However, in a firm where workers who were strongly committed to the firm were no more likely to take part in the SAYE linked ESOP than those who were not, it was found that workers favoured participating on the basis of a positive attitude to such schemes in general, rather than on the basis of their feelings about the employing organization (Dew, Dunn and Richardson, 1988). The question of external factors influencing orientations is relevant here, and will perhaps be tested further as the study by Dew *et al.* will follow the fortunes of this particular scheme over a period of time. The share price had already tripled by the time the 1988 article was written.

Profit-related pay

In his 1986 Budget speech the Chancellor of the Exchequer introduced the notion of profit-related pay (PRP) and a Green Paper followed in July. Relevant legislation followed in the Finance Act 1987. In the context of the requirement for job creation without stoking inflation, the idea had been propounded for some time by Professor Martin Weitzman of MIT and involves the idea of a lower basic wage with the balance made up from profit-sharing. The rationale is that workers will only be taken on if their marginal contribution matches the cost of employing them. If a proportion of earnings was made up from profits, and basic pay reduced, any additional workers would have to contribute at a lower marginal rate. This would mean that more workers would be taken on.

Stated like this of course the idea look like a scheme to cut pay! Weitzman argues that providing a 'critical mass' of employers go over to such a scheme the economy will expand without inflationary pressures so that even if employers do try to expand employment via lower pay, labour market pressures will prevent them from doing so. The proponents of the idea argue that such schemes not only increase employment prospects for those currently unemployed by reducing the cost to companies of taking on labour in good times, but they also incease security of employment since they provide for reductions in the total wage bill in bad times (by reducing the profit-related element) without resort to redundancy. These aspects are seen as crucial to efforts to improve industrial efficiency and so enhance competitive performance.

As with ESOPs, the impact of such schemes is difficult to judge and the motivational aspects are also unclear. An Institute of Personnel Management Study (Bell and Hanson, 1987) suggests that companies with profit-sharing schemes do in fact perform better than those without. Significantly the study emphasized that the successful operation of a profit-sharing scheme required a general approach to employee involvement which means that profit-sharing is just one, albeit significant, factor in improved economic performance. An investigation by Income Data Services argues pessimistically that profit-related pay schemes are unlikely to result in either greater pay flexibility or higher employment. The companies surveyed felt that the potential for flexible pay would have little impact on employment, and that while morale may be enhanced by a successful scheme, the link between effort and reward would be hard to establish in some companies and departments (IDS, 1987). A subsequent report showed that while 674 companies had joined the scheme since September 1987, involving 100 000 employees (an average of 148 per scheme), two companies accounted for 15% of the total membership. Not only were the participating companies relatively small, but they had better paid employees anyway (IDS, 1989). IDS argues that on the evidence so far, and it is relatively early to be conclusive, PRP is '. . . the icing on the cake rather than part of the rations'.

The motivational aspect of these schemes is implicitly considered in so far as they have tax concessions attaching to them. These currently (1989/90) allow tax relief on schemes which involve £3000 or between 5% and 10% of total pay (whichever is the lower) being profit-related and the relief applies to half the amount received as a share for the profit.

The insider v. outsider problem

A major aspect of both types of scheme that we have been discussing and which relates to motivation and expectations is that presented by the different interests of those in employment (insiders) and those not in employment (outsiders). This problem also exists in the case of cooperatives and other forms of employee participation (see Chapter 9).

Benefits from an expanding market share or improved market situation could be taken by those already in employment rather than distributed through job creation to those unemployed. Existing workers will do overtime and benefit from a share of increased profits rather than opting for an expansion of employment which will have the effect of reducing the per capita distribution of profits and so total earnings.

The problem has been conceptualized as that of establishing agreement to operate a two-tier payment system, with newer employees benefiting at a lower rate than existing employees. American Airlines have operated such a system for some time. One of the most widely discussed proposals of this type in the United Kingdom is that put forward by Professor James Meade of Cambridge. Meade (1986) proposes a 'discriminating labour-capital partnership' in which new workers receive lower entitlements in terms of fewer shares or profit fractions than established workers. Subcontracting, franchising and hiring self-employed workers are alternative ways of establishing a two-tier payment system.

Summary

We started this chapter by looking at the notion of personality and how it may be measured. Some time was spent examining the trait theories of personality associated with various inventories that have been used to identify personality types by recruiters. The major problems with such trait theories is that they assume;

- [ ] it is in fact possible to measure personality by means of questionnaires; and
- [ ] that once identified, a response pattern will remain sufficiently constant to make the exercise worthwhile.

Critics of trait theory argue that not sufficient account is taken of the perception by individuals of the situation in which they find themselves, the meaning the situation has for them, and how this may influence behaviour patterns.

Of particular concern to employers is the problem of motivating employees. We examined a very influential theory of motivation, the Herzberg two-factor theory, and found it wanting for a number of reasons associated with the methodology used in its development, and the fact that it was universalistic, assuming everyone was motivated by the same things at different times. People are motivated by different factors at different times – finding out what motivates particular people at a particular moment in time is crucial. Performance is not just a question of ability, but also of motivation.

The expectancy theory of motivation was seen to be able to handle some of these issues be taking account of the variability that characterizes human motivation. An important aspect of the expectancy approach is that it reverses the simplistic notion that satisfaction leads to performance and concentrates on ensuring that desired rewards are in fact achievable as a result of additional effort. This requires management to give as much (if not more) attention to the design of the work flow as to individual needs.

We then turned to recruitment and the subsequent process of adaptation. The post-recruitment stage was characterized as one of adaptation and socialization on the part of the employee as well as employer. Expectations were again seen as important in this process in terms of their influence upon individual performance and satisfaction.

Job-design and motivation were then linked with a sociological approach which considers the orientations to work employees bring with them. The design of work has important implications for performance and requires that the total organization is considered, including pay systems. How an individual employee reacts at work will be significantly influenced by their orientation to work. This will be influenced by factors internal to the organization, such as the perception that increased effort will be rewarded by desired rewards, as well as factors external to the organization, such as the stage in the lifecycle currently occupied by the individual.

Payment systems have an important role to play in establishing performance since an important influence on an individual's orientation to work will be the perception that relevant criteria are being used in the determination of pay levels. It is important that the pay system actually rewards desired behaviour patterns, and that those rewards are desired by employees. It is perhaps rather too early to make a judgement upon schemes relating pay to profits, or rewarding employees with shares in the employing enterprise. Such schemes are intended to increase employment without stoking inflation by attempting to deal with the insider/outsider problem through the establishment, in effect, of a two-tier payment system.

The crucial issue is, as always, how are the benefits of increased profitability, as well as the necessary investment costs, to be shared amongst employees, managers, the non-employed and shareholders? This issue will be further examined in Chapter 9 when we consider forms of ownership and employee participation.

In the opening paragraphs of this chapter reference was made to the term 'human resource management'. This is the term that is increasingly being used to refer to what previously had been called 'personnel' or 'industrial/employee relations'. At the present time there is some debate about just how significant a change in the management of the employment relationship the new terminology represents.

It is the case that a number of organizations, especially but not necessarily always associated with the establishment of greenfield sites, have adopted quite radical (by historical standards) approaches to the management of employee relations which have tended to go beyond the more traditional personnel or industrial relations functions. It is also the case that many of these organizations have seen themselves as responding to extremely threatening environments: Austin Rover, Ford, Lucas, and even British Rail. In all such examples a number of common features of the approach to employment relations can be identified. These include performance-related pay, bypassing the trade union machinery to communicate with employees, a concern with the commitment of employees, and functional as well as numerical flexibility.

In addition, the ever-present perceived threat from Japanese competitors has had the effect of turning management's attention to what are considered to be the key features of the Japanese employment system. The media coverage of the employment relations policies and practices of Japanese companies who have invested in greenfield sites in the UK has, not surprisingly, resulted in them being constantly examined for ideas as to what may be considered 'best practice'. The impression given by such examples – and that of other companies such as Hewlett-Packard – representing a very small proportion of all established enterprises in the UK, is the development of a new and sophisticated model of employee relations management. The general features of this presumed model include, in addition to a central concern with commitment and reward systems, an emphasis upon the integration of selection, appraisal and development into the processes of corporate planning and strategy formulation and implementation.

To add a little 'edge' to this particular development in the management of organizations, it is often discussed in terms of the impact of government policies since 1979, and to what extent any changes that have been observed in the approaches of both employers and unions can first of all be explained as a consequence of government policies, and secondly, just how long lasting or fundamental such changes, where they may have occurred, will turn out to be.

In Chapter 8 we go on to explore the implications of the discussion in this and preceding chapters for future developments in the organization and control of work in terms of the strategies and structures organizations may have to display in the future.

Exercise

Mr Rivers is 50 years of age, the oldest of five supervisors in the packaging department, and has been with the Penn Paper Company for 23 years. He left school at 16 and completed an electrical maintenance apprenticeship with a City and Guilds certificate. He has no other formal qualifications. He worked for Penn Paper as an automobile electrician for 12 years, followed by two years as a work study engineer before moving into the packaging department. After five years he was promoted to a supervisory position.

The holding company of which Penn Paper is part has been putting the Penn management under pressure to increase profits despite a declining market for its main product.

As a result of declining sales, Penn rationalized its operations and one consequence of the rationalization was a reduction from five to four supervisors in the packaging department. It was Mr Rivers' position that was redundant. Given his record with the company, and a 'no redundancy' policy for supervisory staff, he was informed that every effort would be made to find him an alternative position within the company. The personnel manager told Mr Rivers that he should apply for positions as they became vacant through the usual internal procedures.

Having been rejected for the position of technical advisor, for which he considered himself eminently suitable, Mr Rivers contacted the personnel manager to find out what had gone wrong and what he, Rivers, could do about it.

The personnel manager informed Mr Rivers that he had not been thought as well qualified for the technical advisor's position as the person appointed. However, the personnel manager reiterated that every effort would be made to find Rivers a suitable position within the company. It was suggested to Mr Rivers that he consider a wider range of alternative positions than he had so far, and it was pointed out that it was usual in cases such as his to seek the advice of an occupational psychologist concerning the range and type of jobs that would suit him and for which he would be suited.

Mr Rivers readily accepted this advice, and his attention was drawn to the departments operating in the company: marketing, sales, production, administration, management services, personnel, training, finance and technical services.

A month after his discussion with the personnel manager, Mr Rivers attended a test session run by a consultant occupational psychologist. He completed an intelligence test, an interest inventory and a personality test. A week later, Mr Rivers met the consultant to discuss the test results and to discuss what direction his career could take in the future.

The following report was then fed back to Mr Rivers in a subsequent meeting with the consultant.

Intelligence and abilities

The intelligence test measured two attributes, verbal and non-verbal intelligence. Rivers was in the top 20% of the population on verbal intelligence, and within the top 10% on the non-verbal intelligence scale. This latter scale measures the ability to reason logically using shapes and diagrams and is particularly relevant to practical/mechanical/technical understanding of how things work.

Interests and motivation

Rivers was in the top 5% of the general population on practical/mechanical activities, and well within the top 20% on administrative interest. He was also within the top 20% of the population in terms of interest in people in so far as this related to a desire to influence them. His interest in people as individuals was below average though not unduly so. Rivers was below average in scientific, artistic and verbal interests.

Personality

Mr Rivers is marginally above average in extroversion, shown by his sociability and gregariousness. The latter is his most marked extrovert characteristic. Being accepted by others is important to him. He is a little below average in anxiety and so above average in terms of self-assurance and self-control. He is within the top 10% of the population on self-control. Rivers is about average in emotional stability, timidity, suspiciousness and tension, and clearly above average in conscientiousness – well within the top 20% of the population. He is persevering, and will follow rules without being too rigid.

Self-reliance and realism are indicated by his slightly above average score in tough-mindedness, and he is above average in imagination which suggests a liking for playing with ideas. A tolerance of traditional difficulties is indicated by his above average score on forthrightness and slightly above average on conservatism, though a willingness to change is apparent.

Conclusions

Given his interests and abilities, Mr Rivers should be in a position which utilizes his technical experience. His strongest interest is in this area and his non-verbal intelligence is very high. His interests and abilities, coupled with his conscientiousness and work motivation, also suggest an administrative ability.

His interests, abilities and personality suggest someone who is capable of managing others effectively; he enjoys influencing others and is not excessively extroverted. The potential to handle people in a mature way would be beneficial in an advisory role as well as a managerial one.

Of three possible career paths, technical services would be the most appropriate, followed by district sales manager – provided a suitable induction programme is developed, while personnel would be the least appropriate area for Mr Rivers.

After receiving this report, the personnel manager offered Mr Rivers a position as administration manager in the personnel department.

It soon became apparent that Mr Rivers was not coping in his new position and after three months he and the personnel manager met for a critical evaluation of the situation. Mr Rivers acknowledged that he was not coping, he worried constantly and was having problems sleeping.

The personnel manager considered the problem was that Mr Rivers was unable to cope with a lack of structure and guidance in his administrative post, he had had to deal with a workload he could not handle. He was faced with the need to prioritize, and was having to leave work at the end of the day with tasks uncompleted. None of these aspects of work had been experienced by Rivers before, and he was greatly worried by them.

At the interview, the personnel manager encouraged Rivers to apply for the recently advertised post of refrigeration equipment repair controller. Rivers' application for this post was successful, and he underwent two months' training.

Six months after being appointed to the repair controller post Mr Rivers had a follow-up interview with the psychologist. He said that after the eight-week training he felt ready for his current job, and actually enjoyed the administrative component which was a relatively minor part of the work and came as 'light relief'. Rivers thought that his present job would have been a useful precursor to the administrative job in the personnel department. He was currently enjoying running a small team and particularly liked the technical aspect of his work.

Rivers put his failure in the administration job down to a lack of adequate induction. This meant that he had continually to interrupt people to ask for help. He had felt increasingly unable to do this. Consequently he made mistakes which slowed up the work which in turn meant that he took work home.

He had been frustrated by the fact that the job of administration manager had meant that he could not carry out tasks because other people were not available, and he found it difficult to cope with a number of currently uncompleted tasks. This characteristic of the administrative job put a premium on allocating priorities and this he had found difficult.

Some time after this follow-up interview, the personnel manager wrote to the psychologist expressing the view that people like Mr Rivers were not retrainable. The personnel manager was influenced by the fact that Mr Rivers had, from very early on in the administration job, displayed a failure to grasp fundamentals and to understand principles and interpret concepts. Yet the evidence of the intelligence test that he took suggested, wrote the personnel manager, that Rivers was bright enough at his age to cope with a different level and type of task.

Source: Adapted from Case 1 in Poppleton and McGoldrick (1988).

Questions
1. Were you surprised to find that Mr Rivers was not happy as administration manager? Why?
2. As the personnel manager of Penn Paper, can you justify the appointment of Mr Rivers to the administration manager's position in the personnel department?
3. What factors concerning assessment, and its use in redundancy situations, are raised by this case?

Study questions

1. What factors influence individual behaviour at work?
2. Outline the main features of the expectancy model of motivation.
3. What are the characteristics of a reliable interview procedure?

4. (a) What factors should be taken into consideration when implementing schemes which link worker's earnings to measures of corporate performance such as profit or share prices?

   (b) How could a similar exercise be carried out in a non-profit organization?

Further reading

The psychological literature on the topics covered in this chapter is considerable, as is the sociological material. A number of textbooks on organizational behaviour are American, but those like Luthans (1981) do provide a very comprehensive and accessible source of information. Also useful is Chell (1987). A very useful account of the practical and theoretical developments in the study of work related behaviour is Rose (1988) McKenna (1987) provides a comprehensive introduction to the application of psychological research in the business context, while Francis (1986) offers a very accessible account of some of the major issues confronting employers implementing new technologies.

References

Adams, J.S. (1965) Inequality in social exchange. In Berkowitz, L. (ed.) *Advances in Experimental Social Psychology*. Academic Press.

Argyris, C. (1957) *Personality and Organization*. Harper.

Baldamus, W. (1961) *Efficiency and Effort*. Tavistock.

Bell, W. and Hanson, C. (1987) *Profit Sharing and Profitability: How Profit Sharing Promotes Business Success*. Institute of Personnel Management.

Cattel, R.B. (1965) *The Scientific Analysis of Personality*. Penguin.

Chell, E. (1987) *The Psychology of Behaviour in Organizations*. Macmillan.

Child, J. (1984) *Organization: A Guide to Problems and Practice*, 2nd edn. Harper & Row.

Daniel, W.W. (1973) Understanding employee behaviour in its context: illustrations from productivity bargaining. In Child, J. (ed.) *Man and Organization: The Search for Explanation and Social Relevance*, Allen and Unwin.

Dewe P. Dunn, S. and Richardson, R. (1988) Employee share option schemes: why workers are attracted to them. *British Journal of Industrial Relations*, **26**, 1–20.

Dyer, L. and Theriault, R. (1976) The determinants of pay satisfaction. *Journal of Applied Psychology*, **61**, (5), 596–604.

Francis, A. (1986) *New Technology at Work*. Oxford University Press.

Goldthorpe, J., Lockwood, D., Bechoffer, F. and Platt, J. (1968) *The Affluent Worker: Industrial Attitudes and Behaviour*. Cambridge University Press.

Hackman, J.R. (1975) On the coming demise of job enrichment, In Cass,

E.L. and Zuhimer, F.G. (eds), *Man and Work in Society*, Van Nostraud Reinhold.

Hackman, J.R. and Lawler, E.E. (1971) Employee reactions to job characteristics. *Journal of Applied Psychology*, **55**, 259–86.

Hackman, J.R. and Oldham, G.R. (1976) Motivation through the design of work: a test of a theory. *Organization and Human Performance*, **16**, 250–79.

Harre, R. (1979) *Social Being*, Blackwell.

Hoggart, R. (1958) *The uses of literacy:* aspects of working class life with reference to publications and entertainments, Penguin.

Income Data Services (1987) *Profit Related Pay and Profit Sharing*, IDS Study 397.

Income Data Services (1989) *Employee Share Ownership Plans*, IDS Study 438.

Kelly, J. (1982) *Scientific Management, Job Re-design and Work Performance*. Academic Press.

Lawler, E.E. (1969) 'Job design and employee motivation'. *Personnel Psychology*, **22**, 426–35.

Luthans, F. (1981) *Organizational Behaviour*, 3rd edn. McGraw-Hill.

Lyons, P. (1988) In Cowling, A.G., Bennet, R.D., Curran, J. and Lyons, P. (eds), The individual at work. *Behavioural Science for Managers*, 2nd edn. Edward Arnold.

McKenna, E. (1987) *Psychology in Business: Theory and Applications*. Lawrence Erlbaum Associates.

Mayfield, E.C. (1964) The selection interview – a re-evaluation of published research. *Personnel Psychology*, **17**, 239–60.

Meade, J. (1986) *Diffferent Forms of Share Economy*. Public Policy Centre.

Mischel, W. (1968) *Personality and Assessment*. Wiley.

Mischel, W. (1973) Toward a cognitive social learning reconceptualisation of personality. *Psychological Review*, **80**, (6), 730–55.

Mischel, W. (1981) *Introduction to Personality*, 3rd edn. Holt Rinehart & Winston.

Nealey, S.M. Goodale, J.G. (1967) Worker preferences among time-off benefits and pay. *Journal of Applied Psychology*, **51**, (4), 357–61.

Needle, D. (1989) *Business in Context*, Chapman and Hall.

Partnership Research (1987) *Employee Stock Ownership Plans in the United States*. London.

Pearn, M. Kandola, B. and Mottram, R. (1988) *Selection Tests and Sex Bias*. HMSO.

Poole, M. (1988) Factors affecting the development of employee financial participation in contemporary Britain: evidence from a national survey. *British Journal of Industrial Relations*, **26**, 21–36.

Poppleton, S. and McGoldirck, J. (eds) (1988) *Business Case File in Behavioural Science*. Chapman and Hall.

Porter, L.W. and Lawler, E.E. (1968) *Managerial Attitudes and Performance*. Irwin.

Porter, L.W. Lawler, E.E. and Hackman J.R. (1975) *Behaviour in Organizations*. McGraw-Hill.

Rodger, A. (1970) *The Seven Point Plan*. NIIP.

Rose, M. (1988) *Industrial Behaviour*, 2nd edn. Penguin.

Scwhab, D., DeVitt, H. and Cummings, L. (1971) A test of the adequacy of the two-factor theory as a predictor of self-report performance effects. *Personnel Psychology*. Summer, 293–303.

Turner, A.N. and Lawrence, P.R. (1965) *Industrial Jobs and the Worker*. Harvard Graduate School of Business.

Vroom, V. (1964) *Work and Motivation*. Wiley.

Watson, T.J. (1980) *Sociology, Work and Industry*. Routledge and Kegan Paul.

Wernimont, P.F. and Fitzpatrick, S. (1972) The meaning of money. *Journal of Applied Psychology*, **56**, (3), 218–36.

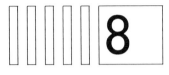

8 Organizational structures and strategies for the future

This chapter examines the implications of the material covered in previous chapters for the structure and functioning of organizations in the future in the light of expected changes in the nature and organization of work. Given that electronic technology has at least the potential to encourage innovative behaviour, there are major implications not only for the way in which organizations are structured and workflow organized, but also for the way in which people adapt to their work surroundings. These implications concern the management of workers in the near future and the demands that will be placed upon managers as they cope with the management of workers whose primary tasks will be centred around the control of control processes. This implies not only considerable skill levels, but also commitment by workers. We will focus on the way organizations attempt to meet changing product and labour markets and changes in technology. We will examine such concepts as the entrepreneurial organization, the flexible firm, organizational development and 'Theory Z' organization and management.

It was suggested at the end of Chapter 6 that the information-processing demands of work organizations based around JIT type processes, in the context of constant pressure to maintain competitive advantage, would require managers to turn their attention to the management of what in effect will be intellectually powerful teams of workers. Chapter 7 considered some of the psychological and social-psychological research that has been done which relates to the selection, motivation and adaptation of workers. The management of intellectually powerful teams of people will require different approaches to the organization and control of work from those developed to date.

Having worked our way from the outer ring of the model of business towards the centre in Chapters 1 to 6, in this chapter we start working outwards again in order to consider organizational structures and strategies of relevance for the future development of work organizations and behaviour within them. We will then move on in Chapter 9 to examine the implications of different forms of ownership for behaviour in work organizations. In Chapter 10, when examining what lessons can be learnt from major international competitor economies, we will explicitly and implicitly by considering the role, if any, of culture in explaining superior economic performance as opposed to differing organizational and managerial strategies.

At this point in the book it is perhaps worthwhile reminding readers that in the introduction it was pointed out that the question of behaviour in business as far as British management was concerned had to be seen in the context of relative economic decline. A major feature of the competitive environment facing British business is the apparently greater ability of managers in other economies to obtain the (more) willing compliance of highly trained and better qualified workers.

The material in this chapter is based upon an approach to the problem of the management of work organizations developed in the United States due, in part at least, to that country's problems with competition from the 'Pacific Rim' economies as well as West European economies like Germany. It is important to note, as will be explored further in Chapter 10, that many of the objectives sought by writers quoted in this chapter may be obtained in Germany, France and the Scandinavian countries, for example, by a legislative system which guarantees workers (not necessarily trade unions) rights of participation, information and training which are crucial to the establishment of willing cooperation by a highly trained workforce.

The approach taken in this chapter is based upon that developed by Williamson (1975), and in a number of publications by Ouchi and his collaborators (1978, 1980, 1981). While Williamson was not the first to investigate the relationship between markets and organizations, his work did provoke an examination of the forms that organizations might take in the future. The subsequent debate illustrated useful typologies of organizational forms. Such typologies, of which Ouchi's is an example, are consistent with the view that organizational structure and human behaviour are influenced by the need to acquire, process and interpret information.

The chapter starts with an examination of Williamson's account of how markets fail as mechanisms for allocating scarce resources (such as labour), and how this gives rise to organization. We will then move on to examine what happens when bureaucracies fail, some of the causes of which were discussed in Chapter 4, and the idea of the 'intrapreneurial' organization as a response to bureaucratic failure. This in turn leads to a consideration of the notion of the 'flexible' firm. The discussion is centred around the problem of establishing willing commitment from employees in the work organizations of the future. The chapter concludes with a consideration of an organizational form derived from an examination of key features of American and Japanese organizational types which is considered to promote commitment. This is the 'Type Z' organization, so named by Ouchi in deference to McGregor's 'X' and 'Y' typologies of behaviour in organizations.

Market failure and the rise of organization

The market failure approach to the study of organization is based upon the assumption that in certain circumstances the market as an allocating mechanism will fail. Remember, **any** society, whatever form it takes, must solve economic problems, problems arising from the fact that the human condition is one where scarce resources that have alternative uses must be allocated among a number of important activities. However, a market may not always be an appropriate mechanism for the allocation of such scarce resources. The necessary information may not be available to all actors in the market-place, or the necessary medium of exchange through which choice is expressed (i.e. money) may not be distributed such that 'efficient' allocations result. Self-interested action may deteriorate into sheer opportunistic behaviour where opportunities are exploited for immediate and usually short-term gains in a manner inconsistent with long-term survival.

In a market transaction 'information' may relate to the prices at which commodities are being traded, or it may relate to information about the quality of the commodity itself. This is a problem which has long been recognized with the increasing technical complexity of goods available to mainly non-technical consumers. It becomes increasingly unreasonable to maintain the dictum 'buyer beware' when the buyer is in no position to acquire the technical knowledge necessary to evaluate the product but has to rely instead upon the assurances of the manufacturer or retailer.

The central notion of the market failure approach is that of 'transaction costs', defined in Key Concept 8.1. In a perfect market, price is the mechanism which mediates the transaction. The reputation of a trader or product is based upon value for money and the availability of information concerning products and prices enables prospective purchasers to identify items offering appropriate 'value for money' characteristics. However, by itself price may be insufficient to satisfy the demand for information. This may be because of the nature of the product or service (e.g. technical complexity and the inability of the customers to judge for themselves) or because of a lack of trust between the parties to the transaction.

In such a situation, further efforts have to be made to check on the quality of the product or service and the reliability of the supplier. These efforts represent transaction costs. Transaction costs can often be reduced by resorting to bureaucratic rules as with trading standards and their enforcement (e.g. weights and measures legislation and public health

---

KEY CONCEPT 8.1

TRANSACTION COSTS

A transaction cost is the cost of determining the value of the item or service that is being traded. In order to ensure that the value given and received in an exchange is in accordance with the expectations of the parties to the exchange, some means of monitoring are necessary. The process of monitoring a transaction will involve some cost, and that cost is a transaction cost. So the time spent checking up on relative prices and quality standards by studying *Which?*, for example, is a transaction cost, as is hiring the AA to run a check on the second-hand car you are thinking of buying. In other words, a scarce resource with alternative uses (time, money) has to be allocated to ensure the value of the transaction.

inspectors), factory inspectorates, and the licensing arrangements for professional services provided by lawyers, doctors and accountants for example. Recently (June 1989) proposals governing the standards to be observed by estate agents have been published. Some of the earliest attempts, historically, to ensure that markets did not fail related to efforts to ensure the validity of coinage and attempts to control the adulteration of food. Concerns over insider-dealing in deregulated financial markets also illustrate the problems of maintaining equity between all operators in a market.

How are transaction costs to be minimized?

The significance of the factors which may underlie market failure is that 'organization' can be seen as developing out of the need to contain the costs associated with transactions in the market-place. In other words, bureaucratic rules come to replace price as a mediating mechanism in the process of assessing value given and received in a transaction. The argument is that organizations come into existence because they can mediate economic transactions at a lower cost than can a market mechanism. It was after all Adam Smith who suggested that a meeting between two people engaged in business will always end in some agreement to defraud the public.

Consider the labour market as an example. The features which lead to the failure of market machanisms in this context are outlined in Case Study 8.1.

Hiring workers to work in a situation where they must coordinate their activities with others makes it difficult to assess the value of each individual worker. The interaction required will make it difficult to identify just how hard any one individual is actually working and why. The development of work rules governing the behaviour of each individual, when not only is team working necessary but the worker must also interact with machinery, stems from attempts by employers to monitor the effort expended by individuals when monitoring cannot be carried out via price (market) mechanisms because of the fear (justified or not) that workers will behave opportunistically – that is, take advantage of something they know that management does not so as to reduce the effort expended or increase the income earned.

An additional problem for market-based mechanisms arises from the fact that workers who already are in employment at a particular job will have acquired knowledge that gives them an advantage over others who have not been employed at that particular task. They know the work, whereas a new employee has to learn or be instructed. Not only do existing workers have an advantage over other possible workers, but they will have acquired knowledge about the task that will not be known to potential employees or even to the employer. The work group may have developed working methods which enable them to achieve output

CASE STUDY 8.1

LABOUR MARKETS AND TRANSACTION COSTS

Continued over page

Continued from previous page

targets with less effort than is assumed by management. In this case either all may work at a slower pace than management are paying for, or members of the gang take it in turns to have unofficial 'rest periods' – which amounts to the same thing.

The point about such actions is that they are usually designed to bring some order into what otherwise are relatively disordered (from the workers' point of view) situations. Dock work, for example, was characterized by a hiring system which required people to report, some times twice a day, for work and then be selected on the basis of popularity with the foreman. In the days before liner cargo services (i.e. regularly scheduled arrivals and sailings between named ports, as opposed to 'tramp' services where a ship travels between any number of ports as and when cargoes are available), employers and work groups could not be sure when the next ship would arrive or how long it would take to load and unload. 'Casual' hiring on a daily or even half-day basis made some economic sense for employers who wished to avoid paying when there was no work to be done. Similarly, working arrangements which shared out the available work made equal sense for employees. Such sharing could be achieved by unofficial rules governing the number of men in a gang, or by strategems which slowed down the workrate to ensure there would be work tomorrow.

Piece-rate systems are notorious for producing behaviour on the part of employees which is heavily criticized by employers. The constant skirmishing between work-study engineers and production workers is the result of low levels of mutual trust. Workers fear, with some justification, that if they meet bonus rates of production too readily, the rates will be raised. Managers are afraid that any weakness on their part will be rapidly exploited by workers. There is also the problem that irregular flows of material to production workers on piece-rate systems of pay may have dramatic effects on earnings, but are quite outside the control of those affected.

A classic method of overcoming the impact on earnings of variations in workflow and market demand is illustrated in Roy's (1952) account of what in American factories was known as 'gold bricking'. This was known in British factories as 'doing one for the back of the book'. Methods vary, but the principal remains the same: when workers on piece-rates find themselves with a job that allows them easily to meet the bonus target, they will not 'book' all their output on that shift. If they did, management might feel that the bonus rate was too low and so raise it. When the rate is 'easy' or 'loose' workers will keep back a ticket recording work done, and submit it when they are faced with a job which has very 'tight' rates, i.e. a job on which it is very difficult to meet bonus targets, or the ticket will be used when there is an interruption to the workflow in order to maintain earnings. The effect is to maintain a predictable level of earnings over time. Management's attempts to control this kind of activity will produce greater efforts by the employees to conceal from the rate fixers exactly how easy or difficult a particular job is in order to ensure stability of earnings.

Opportunism

In a market it is assumed that individuals are acting in their own best interest. Individuals act, and indeed are only required to act, in a self-interested manner. If this is the case, how can one ensure that either party to the transaction is not taking advantage of their particular knowledge and experience with the result that information is available only to a few? Implicit in the state of affairs described in Case Study 8.1 is the idea of 'opportunism', described in Key Concept 8.2.

Opportunism refers to behaviour which is not merely self-interested, but which is engaged in with the explicit intention of maintaining or gaining an advantage by exploiting knowledge or information not generally available. For example, one party to the transaction may have more up-to-date or accurate information than the other and acts to retain that advantage.	*KEY CONCEPT 8.2* *OPPORTUNISM*

Just taking the labour market example we have two of the major features of market failure. First, unequal distribution of information and resources, and second, opportunistic behaviour. These are sufficient conditions for the existence of a bilateral monopoly. That is, both parties to the transaction have vested interests in trading with each other rather than seeking to establish new trading relations since the problems of selection, training and retraining are avoided. That is transaction costs are lower for both employer and employees if they continue to deal with each other rather than re-enter the labour market as buyers and sellers. In these circumstances opportunism will be unchecked since potential alternatives (for employers or employees) are seen as incurring even greater risks than continuing with the current arrangements. This is the 'devil you know' syndrome, or the problem of 'small numbers' to use the language of the market failures approach, because each party deals only with those they already know, present employer or employees, and ignores other potential employers or employees.

Limits on opportunistic behaviour

There are at least two possible responses to this state of affairs. Either steps can be taken to ensure that rigidities in the market are removed, which will necessitate a regulatory body of some sort (i.e. bureaucracy) or rules can be formulated and put into operation to control behaviour more closely, again establishing a bureaucracy. Either way, 'organization' or 'bureaucracy' (rule-bound administration) is introduced to minimize the costs of ensuring value in exchange. Put this way, it can be seen that one person's attempt to contain opportunism by establishing rules is someone else's market rigidity. The recently abolished Dock Labour Scheme, introduced to combat the worst excesses of casual dock labour, is an example.

Organizations can be said to exist, therefore, because in certain circumstances they provide a means of mediating transactions at a lower cost than could be accomplished through the market mechanism. The inefficiencies of a bureaucracy may incur lower transaction costs than would a market. If one considers for a moment the characteristics of a bureaucracy discussed in Chapter 4, then it can be appreciated that the existence of a framework of impersonal rules applied in a judicial manner may engender an atmosphere of trust more readily than could a market relationship where there is uncertainty over the value that is given and received in an exchange. Where trust prevails, a reduced likelihood of opportunistic behaviour will entail a reduction in costs due to the reduced need to monitor performance.

The nature of what is traded

An important factor underlying the market failure or transaction costs approach to behaviour in organizations is the nature of what is traded. Some products and services are easier to monitor than others. The customer goes into any shop to buy washing-up liquid; the transaction is completed there and then; no relationship has to exist between the shopkeeper and the customer since both can rely upon the existence of branded goods, marked prices and legal tender to ensure that both are getting a fair deal irrespective of any differences that may exist as to their respective goals. If the customer realizes that he or she was actually charged over the odds, well, the washing up needed to be done and there was no time to go to the usual shop where the price was lower. The customer may well not go back to that particular shop again . . . but if that is the only one in easy reach at ten o'clock at night, well perhaps the higher prices are worth paying. The point is that with certain goods or services the purchaser is little concerned about the reliability of the provider, or the product, since there is little ambiguity over the quality of what is provided.

However, underpinning the transaction illustrated above are two considerable bureaucracies. First there is that bureaucracy represented by the legislation concerning weights and measures and the display of prices. This will come under the responsibility of the local authority. Secondly, there is the bureaucracy represented by the manufacturing organization and its brand management activities. These ensure that products are standardized wherever they are traded.

It is important to remember that not all goods and services fall so easily into such unambiguous categories. This issue is one of those at the heart of debates about privatization for example. Is the provision of services like public transport, clean water, health, education, electricity, and prison administration, for example, amenable to the same methods of allocation as groceries, banking, newspapers and motor vehicle manufacture?

The concern over salmonella and other forms of food contamination during 1988/89 illustrates precisely the problem of transaction costs. Rather than risk infection, the public boycotted the product, whoever was responsible for its production and retailing. The cost of monitoring the transaction of purchasing half a dozen eggs would have been considerable in terms of the expertise required to test for salmonella. If one did not test and a member of the family was poisoned, then the cost would also have been high, possibly fatal. The readiness with which the public purchase mass produced items (or not) is in very large part due to the presence (or not) of an organized framework of rules and the resources invested in their enforcement.

Similar problems arise with certain occupations and the services they provide. The power and status of professional bodies like those responsible for doctors, lawyers and accountants is due in part to their assurance of the quality and integrity of the practioners for whom they are responsible. One of the major contradictions at the heart of the debate over professionalism and its relevance is because occupations which claim to regard the interests of the client as paramount actually use that claim to justify considerable rewards. The major professional bodies came into existence because of the difficulties of ensuring that 'quacks' were prevented from misleading the public. Contemporary discussions over the regulation of the professions implicitly involves the market failure thesis, as does the debate over how the health service should be operated and managed.

The significance of transaction costs and their role in determining the form of organizations can be summarized as follows. Markets, and their associated price mechanism, are effective when there is little ambiguity over performance and the parties can readily evaluate the quality of the service provided. They can then tolerate relatively high levels of opportunistic behaviour, or conflicting self-interested objectives, since competition will ensure that the terms of the exchange are equitable.

When there is ambiguity over performance, that is ambiguity as to the quality of the service or product, and the goals of the parties are incongruent, then a bureaucracy will help to reduce transaction costs because of the perceived legitimacy of rules governing the performance standards required of both parties. However, if the degree of ambiguity, goal incongruence and opportunism increases, the development of yet more rules (and their enforcement) will consume so much effort at higher levels in the hierarchy that the consequent over-loading may result in a decline in the quality of decisions. At this point bureaucracy too fails.

Bureaucratic failure and the 'intrapreneurial organization'

As was discussed in Chapter 4, when the activities are such that clear and unambiguous rules can be formulated and applied with a minimum of ambiguity then bureaucracies 'work'. When tasks or environments are no longer amenable to the unproblematic formulation and application of rules, then the costs of bureaucracy rise.

When bureaucracy fails what can replace it? A 'commonsense' (one might almost say 'knee-jerk') reaction is to reassert the advantages of markets: to break down a monolithic organization into smaller, more manageable units that are 'closer to the customer' and with which individuals can more readily identify. Profit centres or some form of divisionalization are examples. Another alternative is to be found in the form of organization that was described by Burns and Stalker (1961), and discussed in Chapter 4, Case Study 4.6. The essence of the 'organic organization' is that discipline is maintained not through a contractual obligation to follow rules with an associated emphasis on hierarchy, supervision and enforcement or policing, but through the belief that individual interests are best served by the attainment of the interests of the group as a whole. Ouchi (1980) has used the term 'clan' to describe this form of organization. The 'clan' form of organization is characterized by the operation of implicit rules which are dependent upon socialization and which may therefore offer lower transaction costs. This notion captures the essence of Durkheim's idea of 'organic solidarity' as a means of recreating the moral character and cultural significance of work, and so of overcoming anomie (see Case Study 3.3 in Chapter 3).

The 'intrapreneurial' organization

Some time ago the editor of *The Economist* developed the idea that in order to overcome the deadweight of bureaucracy the principles of entrepreneurial activity should be applied within, and not just between, organizations. What was termed the 'intrapreneurial organization' is described in Key Concept 8.3.

The basic idea behind this proposal is not new. Many services are already provided within organizations on the basis of internal prices and cost centres, the so-called 'internal market'. A product division will purchase services from the marketing department and the price will have to come out of the product division's budget and be a contribution to the budgeted profit or surplus the marketing department is required to produce. Similarly with the personnel, design, cleaning, catering, training, data processing and transport departments, and all the other activities required in the course of getting a product to the market and final

KEY CONCEPT 8.3 ***THE INTRAPRENEURIAL ORGANIZATION***	The basic assumption underlying this approach is that the flair and initiative required if new ideas are to be developed also requires that opportunities for profit-seeking behaviour be created on a large scale. Such an extension of profit-seeking requires, it is argued, a reduction in the scale and influence of bureaucratic ideas and policies. Since an organization is made up of departments that in effect service other departments, this relationship should be the basis of contracts for the provision of services between the component departments of the organization. The typing pool, for example, would set itself up as a service agency offering skills to whoever could be persuaded to buy. The assumption is that if, say, the marketing department could get its word processing done more quickly or to a higher standard outside the organization then it would be free to do so. The same principle would apply to all departments, ensuring that innovation would be encouraged while competition would provide assurances concerning the reasonableness of prices, effort and quality. In this way the suffocating tendency of bureaucracy would be avoided and enterprise would flourish.

consumer. In some cases these services are already bought in or subcontracted as a matter of routine in organizations – the 'make or buy' decision.

The logic behind the policy of 'contracting out' is that services can be acquired more cheaply, with less risk of opportunism as a result of the 'small numbers' phenomenon, than when the organization incorporates the supply and consumption within its boundaries. A factor in this type of decision is the identification of activities representing the central business activities of the organization. Answers to the question 'What business are we in?' are derived from an examination of the activities undertaken by the organization in order to identify what the core activities are – what Peters and Waterman term 'the knitting'.

Another approach to the problem of adapting organizations and their employment policies to the competitive environment of the 1990s and beyond is that which focuses on what is termed the 'flexible' firm.

The flexible firm

The Institute of Manpower Studies developed the idea of the 'flexible firm' as a model to describe and account for changes in employment practices that are said to derive from the reassessment of strategy by management. The model revolves around the notion of 'core' and 'periphery' workers and is an extension of the dual labour market framework developed by Doeringer and Piore (1971). Interest in this approach is prompted by the need to respond to economic recession and overseas competition by concentrating on labour costs and the perceived rigidities affecting the utilization and hiring of labour.

Numerical flexibility

The notion of the 'flexible firm' involves two types of flexibility. The first, numerical flexibility, relates to the ability of a company or department to adjust the numbers employed in response to changes in the product market. This may imply hiring temporary, part-time or contract workers to meet increased demand. Contracting-out activities or services has this effect. The firm does not have to maintain a payroll whose numbers are determined by peak demand, which results in some workers at least being 'underemployed' from time to time.

A variation of this form of flexibility may be established by varying the hours worked in a week or month within a total established for the year. That is, workers are contracted to work for a given number of hours per year, but not for a standard number of hours per day or week. Under this arrangement workers are paid a standard weekly/monthly sum, for an agreed minimum and maximum number of hours, but the actual hours worked within that range will be determined by product demand. In this way fluctuations in take-home pay are minimized, but the employer can call upon extra hours of work without having either to increase the number of employees or pay out overtime at premium rates.

Casual labour, as existed at one time in dock work for example, has the disadvantage already noted in Case Study 8.1 that in the face of uncertain demand for labour, workers are tempted to devise schemes to share out what work is available. This is likely to result in restrictive practices which employers are unable to resist when market demand increases. The point about 'intrapreneurialism' and the 'flexible' firm is to achieve numerical flexibility without the social and economic consequences of casualization.

Functional flexibility

Another form of flexibility which is currently of major interest in terms of competitive advantage is known as 'functional' flexibility. This refers to the number of skills or tasks mastered by an individual employee, which may be utilized in at least one of two ways:

☐ First, the fact that workers can carry out more than one task enables product market fluctuations to be accommodated by switching workers from one set of tasks to another as the need arises.

☐ Second, the fact that workers are multi-skilled means that they can carry out tasks previously the preserve of a number of other skilled or occupational groups.

In manufacturing industry, for example, the existence of distinct occupational categories of machine operators and skilled maintenance workers has tended to inhibit flexibility due to the operation of demarcation rules. If, as is often the case, machine operators are not able to reset the machine themselves because of lack of training or demarcation rules, they have to wait until a qualified person is available. This further extends machine 'downtime'. Also, if lack of training or demarcation rules prevent operators from carrying out routine or preventative maintenance, this may result in more frequent breakdowns and extended stoppages while operators await the arrival of the maintenance crew.

To make up for this lost time, long runs of each item are often scheduled. There is no point in setting up a machine to deal with a number of components below some minimum number. The result is that parts or products are produced which are not needed for some time – in other words 'producing for stock'. Multi-skilled workers can reduce the negative impact of machine downtime by getting on with the required changes themselves or by carrying out routine and preventative maintenance in unavoidably slack periods. Minimizing downtime in this manner reduces the length of production run required under conventional accounting systems. This in turn will not only reduce buffer stocks, and hence the sum invested in inventories, but will also enable the company to respond more quickly to product changes.

However, while the 'flexible firm' model which concentrates on numerical flexibility has achieved some popularity, its utility as either description or prescription has been questioned (Pollert, 1987). The basis of the criticism is that the empirical evidence adduced in support of the model ignores the fact that many industrial sectors have traditionally used 'flexible' labour and such a strategy appears to vary even between firms in the same sector. A further irony is that where 'flexibility' as a strategy does appear to have been recently developed, in the public sector, this sector is ignored by the proponents of the model.

A feature of the emphasis on numerical flexibility in the model of the flexible firm is an emphasis on the role of labour costs in competitive advantage. This emphasis in part derives from the concentration on price as the basis of competition which has characterized the approach of British management. As Eatwell (1982) pointed out, the decline in the British share of world and domestic markets probably has less to do with price than the quality, delivery and design of manufactured products. Very few of the finished manufactured products imported into the UK have acquired their market share by being lower priced than domestically produced items. Consumers of domestic as well as industrial products are prepared to pay a premium for well designed products which are delivered on time, are reliable and supported by an after-sales service. It is 'value for money' that counts, not just price.

There is an inherent tension between mass production techniques as a means of reducing unit costs, and worker involvement and training as a means of raising the quality standards applied to the product. The significance of technological developments in manufacturing processes is that competition is increasingly based around the production of relatively customized items on a mass production basis. This appears to put a premium on the willing commitment and multi-functional skills of employees. This in turn has implications for the way work is organized and structured.

For example, Rubery et al. (1987) suggest that on the basis of a sample of manufacturing firms wage costs amount to 15% of sales revenue, and that if wage costs were to fall by 20% the average British firm could secure at best a relative price advantage of some 3%. The point is, as we have stressed earlier, competitive advantage has to consider factors such as delivery, quality and service in addition to simply price. In addition, long-term survival of the enterprise will depend on developing new markets or larger shares of existing markets and this requires an emphasis upon the design and development of new products and production processes to meet changes in the product market. Evidence from a study of the BL incentive scheme (Towse, 1982) suggests that increased output generates greater gains for the company than cutting wage costs by reducing manpower. Revenue from the additional output outweighs savings in wages at constant output.

Willman (1987) points out in his examination of Austin Rover that:

The goals of productive efficiency can be served by machine pacing of work, intensive supervision, output related payments and an attempt to keep trade union activity out of the plants. On the other [hand], requirements of high-quality output and production uninterrupted by disputes imply individual employee involvement, some form of team organization, and problem solving activity by shop stewards.

The key problem, and one which is addressed by those considering how organizations should be structured in the future, is that of motivating people when they are not sure that the distribution of benefits and costs reflects the distribution of effort – as discussed in the relevant sections of

Chapter 7. Motivation is problematic when there is ambiguity over what rewards are likely to be forthcoming in return for a given effort on the part of the employee. In such a situation the 'effort bargain', the ratio of reward to effort, is unclear. The concept of the effort bargain is central to the exercise of control over work as both employers and employees are concerned to ensure that any transaction (effort v. reward) is consistent with expectations. There are two distinct concepts of efficiency, suggests Willman. One is based upon the approach of industrial engineering as exemplified by Taylorist work-study methods, while the other considers the motivational factors which influence attitudes and behaviour and consequently the quality and quantity of output.

Product markets and the organization of work

In a comparative examination of the consequences of computerized machine tools for manpower and skill utilization in British and West German manufacturing companies, it was reported that firms were increasingly being forced to cater for smaller market niches rather than for homogenous mass markets (Hartmann et al., 1983). One of the implications of competitive pressure deriving from increasingly fragmented product markets is the demands made by small batch production on machine setting in terms of the frequency of re-setting and the time involved. The more the company has to meet demands for small runs of an increasingly large number of product variants, then the greater is the cost implication of machine changes.

Coping with the frequent re-setting of machines implies increased demands upon work groups directly involved since, as Hartmann and his colleagues point out, this cannot be met bureaucratically by simply increasing the complexity of the division of labour. This has implications for the argument that microelectronics is likely to result in 'de-skilling'. In so far as de-skilling is likely, then this could well be the consequence of a managerial response which is focused, one might say 'fixated', on reducing labour costs to the exclusion of other factors relevant to the nature of competition. This is the industrial engineering approach mentioned by Willman and attempts to cope by concentrating on the division of labour.

However, the utilization of microelectronic technology places demands

---

CASE STUDY 8.2

RE-EXAMINING THE ORGANIZATION OF WORK

The aspects of the application of new technology in production highlighted by Willman (1987) and Hartmann and his colleagues (1983) emphasize the need to re-examine the organization of work. At Ford, for example, the consequences of the pressure on work organization can be seen in the development of semi-autonomous work teams grouped under 'area' foremen who in effect become managers on the shopfloor rather than merely enforcers of rules. Each team is supervised by a team leader recruited from among manual workers and will include sufficient skilled workers to carry out the maintenance tasks in their area (*Financial Times*, 6 November 1987 and 20 February 1988). At Ford's engine and chassis plant in Sharonville, Ohio, work teams will be responsible for setting production schedules, planning training and determining a pay structure based on qualifications and flexibility (*Financial Times*, 20 February 1988). Ford is said to be aiming at removing not just the distinction between skilled and unskilled workers, but also that between production and maintenance workers and blue-collar manual and white-collar supervisory staff.

Developments similar to those reported in Ford are explored by Willman and Winch (1985) at what was British Leyland, and for Austin Rover by Willman (1987). It is argued that the attempt to develop the team concept illustrates the changes that technological and product market conditions impose upon firms while they are at the same time attempting to achieve committed cooperation from their employees. A major block to what Willman calls 'consumate cooperation' on the part of the workforce has been the past strategy of employers who respond to product market changes by way of the labour market. That is, reductions in demand result in reductions in pay or in numbers employed. Increases in demand are similarly met by increased pay (overtime) and/or increases in numbers employed. When the market demand is growing, employers are vulnerable to opportunistic behaviour of workers as they demand higher pay. When market demand is contracting of course, employees are similarly vulnerable to the opportunism of employers. The reliance of employers upon the labour market to cope with product market changes not surprisingly makes empolyees suspicious of change since they cannot be sure how, if at all, any benefits of change will be distributed between shareholders, managers and employees. One way employees can protect themselves is by maintaining distinctions between tasks – demarcation rules. This is done in the hope that it will maintain the coherence of skills in a situation where they expect to be forced to re-enter the labour market at frequent, if not regular, intervals during their working lives. Both Austin Rover and Ford hope that the work team, rather than some occupational identity, will become the focal point of the individual's attachment to the company.

upon traditional demarcation lines since the maintenance of electronic equipment requires preventative action on the part of the operators. While this may be the case with mechanical machinery too, the flexibility required by fragmented markets (including minimal buffer stocks), plus the cost of the electronic machinery itself, places a premium on preventing break-downs and dealing with them rapidly if they occur. This in turn puts pressure upon traditional distinctions between 'skilled' maintenance and 'unskilled' production workers as illustrated in Case Study 8.2.

Key problems

The significance of the demands raised by the new technology are further considered by Hartmann *et al.* (1983) when they point out that the key problems with the latest generation of electronically controlled machine tools involve 'materials, feeds, speeds, faults and breakdowns'. Handling these problem areas requires skills derived from actually operating the machine. This implies the continued development and even extension of craft skills based upon the shopfloor rather than the development of specialized planning and programming departments away from the shopfloor.

The implications for the management and organization of work are highlighted by the Hartmann study and that undertaken by Steadman and Wagner (1987) for the National Institute for Economic and Social Research (NIESR) which compared the manufacture of kitchen furniture in Britain and Germany. These studies highlight aspects of British industry which have been a cause of concern for some time: the lack of investment in, and low levels of, training, and the blue/white collar distinction. The significance of these factors is brought out in Case Study 8.3 which describes the Steadman and Wagner study.

Consideration of the developments in motor vehicle and kitchen

---

CASE STUDY 8.3

TRAINING AND COMPUTER-CONTROLLED MANUFACTURE IN BRITAIN AND GERMANY

In German industry generally shopfloor workers are better trained than is the case in British industry in terms of the numbers who have acquired technical qualifications and the general level of those qualifications. In kitchen furniture manufacturing Steadman and Wagner (1987) report that in the firms they studied 90% of shopfloor workers in Germany had undergone a three-year training course whilst only 10% of their British counterparts had vocational qualifications. German foremen are re-quired to qualify as *Meister* in addition to their basic craft training and this can take several years' additional study at night school as well as attendance on training courses. Associated with this disparity in qualification is the degree to which the programming and planning functions are separated from operations in the two countries.

In the German case, programming CNC machines was the nucleus around which managers, engineers, planners, foremen and operators were integrated. While planning and programming appear to confer white-collar status in Britain this is much less common in Germany.

The greater emphasis on training in German companies was matched by greater investment in technology and the combination resulted in differing approaches to production strategy. The British manufacturers of fitted kitchens manufactured for stock using relatively cheap machinery which was re-set manually once a batch of about 1000 panels had been produced. Under this system it would be difficult to justify the cost of computer-controlled machine tools because only the cost per unit of production is calculated. If the advantages of the flexibility available with CNC machines were included in the calculations then a different answer would be forthcoming. Producing batches for stock implies a rigidity (and very high lead time to work content ratio, i.e. buffers) which prevents rapid response to product market changes or surges in demand for a particular item or range. A response to such pressures may be possible, but not without disrupting normal production or arranging overtime working.

In the German industry, orders are fed into a computerized system which not only calls up the necessary materials but also provides a production timetable for the operations involved. The working day is divided into production periods, some as short as two hours, within which operators are required to produce a specified number of units or components. In this way the company is able to supply customized orders on virtually a mass production basis. This places considerable emphasis upon the quality and training of operators, planners, programmers and management.

The sophistication of the technology also emphasizes the need for maintenance skills amongst operators in order to minimize lost time due to machine failure and to carry out adjustments to machine settings without having to wait for somebody else to come and do it. This study found that the British manufacturers experienced considerable delays when machine failures occurred because of a lack of qualified staff, and that in fact machine failure was far more common amongst British production plants than was the case in Germany.

Researchers at NIESR have carried out a number of studies of the level of vocational qualifications held by German and French workers. This they argue accounts for the majority of the productivity advantages which industry in those countries enjoys over that in the United Kingdom.

Source: Steadman and Wagner (1987).

furniture production serves to emphasize the extent to which the organization and control of work will have to change in response to changes in the nature and characteristics of product markets, some of which, at least, will be the consequence of technological developments. The case of kitchen furniture is a further example of strategic choice based upon the recognition that competition may not be just about price. The ability to offer high quality products to customers' individual requirements enables a premium price to be charged. While this implies decisions concerning the marketing focus of the firm, it also has implications for the organization and control of work.

The future organization and nature of work

After an examination of potentially catastrophic failures such as malfunctions at unclear power stations, Hirschorn (1984) explores the implications of the nature of new technology, and the way it is utilized, for the future organization of work. This examination provides further insights which are consistent with those discussed in the context of kitchen furniture and motor vehicle manufacture in the previous section.

Hirschorn argues that work is becoming characterized by the exercise of 'second-order' control activities. Workers will not exercise control over processes so much as be responsible for controlling the control processes themselves. This kind of work, Hirschorn argues, is similar to that undertaken by development engineers.

Development work will become the model for factory labour because 'failure' increasingly becomes defined in terms of slippage in the quality of output. This is similar to the point Hartmann *et al.* (1983) are making when they refer to the crucial nature of problems concerning materials and the speeds at which they are fed into the latest generation of machine tools. Hirschorn points out that the flexibility of modern tools means that output variety is achieved not by adding new machines, or even complete plants, but by modifications to the control systems of existing machines. This requires knowledge of the interactions within the control system and between the control system and raw materials. These interactions require development behaviour on the part of workers as they monitor and modify the control processes to maintain the quality of output. This view of the nature of work also relates to Collingridge's (1980) observations (see Chapter 6) on decision-making under ignorance when it becomes necessary to seek out, and learn from, error. Automation would appear to require human intervention as a matter of course. The demands of this type of work are for a cognitive and iterative approach as workers move between observation and interpretation of data from the instrumentation to action based on that interpretation of the data in order to keep the process under control (Cavestro, 1989). Cavestro goes on to point out that the operators of automated plant work with symbolic representations of the process presented to them visually and aurally. Operators must learn how to

---

KEY CONCEPT 8.4	Hirschorn quotes a case study of the relationship between product mix and the design of jobs and work groups in Olivetti factories. In order to meet changing product market conditions for electronic office equipment designers and engineers enlarged the jobs of assembly workers. This was not for the workers' good, but in order to meet the quality standards and product differentiation demanded by the market.
DEVELOPMENTAL WORK IN THE OLIVETTI CASE	

By increasing the skill and knowledge requirements, the redesigned and enlarged jobs increased the workers' capacity to adapt rapidly to new assembly tasks. This facilitated rapid response to product variations when they were demanded by customers. The redesigned jobs had the effect of redefining the worker as '... someone who not only contributes muscle power or fine motor skills to a task, but also contributes learning to a process of adaptation and change. In this sense the workers at Olivetti performed developmental work.'

'Creating the learning organisation' is the subtitle of a book, *Dynamic Manufacturing*, by Hayes, Wheelwright and Clark (1988) in which the authors put considerable emphasis on the need for organizations to find ways of encouraging specialists of all skills to work together more rapidly and effectively if they are to be effective in the modern world.

decode the data and this accentuates the intellectual dimension of their work. The notion of 'development work' as applied to factory labour is illustrated in Key Concept 8.4.

Market failure, anomie and 'theory Z'

The first half of this chapter has approached the question of organizational forms for the future by way of the 'market failure' thesis. That is, markets as allocating mechanisms only work under certain conditions. When there is ambiguity over the value or quality of the product or service being traded, then the costs associated with a transaction may actually be reduced as a result of the development of rules, of an 'organization'.

However, increasingly complex product markets which may develop as a result of the application of flexible manufacturing systems may both reduce the advantages of traditional market responses concerning labour, for example, **and** the advantages of bureaucracy. The second half of the chapter looks at organizational forms which may be more appropriate for the twenty-first century than those taken for granted today, and issues which are central to the reorganization of work and control over it. In doing this, it will be necessary to bring together topics that have already been discussed in this book.

We will put forward a link between alienation and anomie and the market failure approach discussed in the first half of this chapter, and the perspective on organization development put forward by Ouchi (1981). The discussion of the expectancy model of motivation from Chapter 7 should be remembered as the discussion in this part of the chapter develops.

Cooperation v. opportunism

Before reading further, consider the points raised in Case Study 8.4. Lincoln's observations address the key issues faced by management when they seek the willing cooperation of employees, what Willman calls 'consumate cooperation'. Failure to consider these issues is what Durkheim would have recognized as the basis of the abnormal or 'anomic' division of labour. Such a failure would also be recognized by Marx as an aspect of 'alienated' labour.

Failure to observe Lincoln's advice also underlies the development of what Williamson (1975) called 'opportunistic behaviour' in the context of his market failure approach to transaction costs.

How to limit opportunistic behaviour

Willman (1987) suggests at least four conditions, set out in Table 8.1, which must exist if opportunistic behaviour is to be limited or constrained. These four conditions relate directly to the points made by Lincoln in Case Study 8.3 above, and are also the prerequisites for what Fox (1974) called

CASE STUDY 8.4

**THE LINCOLN
ELECTRIC COMPANY**

The Lincoln Electric Company is a manufacturer of electric motors and welding equipment founded in 1895 and remains one of the largest manufacturers in its field. James F. Lincoln was the younger brother of the founder of the company John C. Lincoln and joined it in 1907. Lincoln's strategy was to concentrate on continuous cost reductions as a result of improving manufacturing processes, and the benefits were passed on to customers through lower prices. As a result both market share and demand had increased and companies like General Electric had left the industry or sought more specialized markets.

All production workers were on piece-rate pay systems (at one stage even typists had been), and the incentive scheme produced annual bonuses which averaged 100% of annual earnings. The company view was that once a piece-rate had been set, it could not be altered just because a worker's earnings were several times his previous total. Piece-rates only changed when the method of work changed. Workers could challenge a piece-work price, but were expected to correct any defective work in their own time. In other words, they were responsible for the quality of their own work.

The company policy was to fill all positions other than initial entry ones by internal promotion. Apart from one or two cases where special skills had been thought necessary this policy had been adhered to. While they did have business school graduates on the staff (including some from Harvard), the numbers tended to be small because they offered lower starting salaries than was usual, and because they insisted that everyone who joined started by doing seven weeks in the welding school.

The following are extracts from James F. Lincoln's observations on management which appeared in the American *Journal of Civil Engineering* in January 1973.

1. Some think paying a man more will produce cooperation. Not true. Many other incentives are far more effective than money. Robert MacNamara gave up millions to become Secretary of Defense. Status is a much greater incentive.
2. If those crying loudest about the inefficiencies of labour were put in the position of the wage earner, they would react as he does. The worker is not a man apart. He has the same needs, aspirations, and reactions as the industrialist. A worker will not cooperate on any programme that will penalize him. Does any manager?
3. The industrial manager is very conscious of his company's need of uninterrupted income. He is completely oblivious ... to the worker's same need ...
4. Higher efficiency means fewer manhours to do a job. If the worker loses his job more quickly, he will oppose higher efficiency.
5. There never will be enthusiasm for greater efficiency if the resulting profits are not properly distributed. If we continue to give it to the average stockholder, the worker will not cooperate.

6. A wage earner is no more interested than a manager in making money for other people.

7. If a manager received the same treatment in matters of income, security, advancement and dignity as the hourly worker, he would soon understand the real problem of management.

8. The first question management should ask is: What is the company trying to do? In the minds of the average worker the answer is: 'The company is trying to make the largest possible profits by any method. Profits go to absentee stockholders and top management.'

9. There is all the difference imaginable between the grudging, distrustful, half-forced cooperation and the eager, whole-hearted, vigorous, happy cooperation of men working together for a common purpose.

10. Continuous employment of workers is essential to industrial efficiency. This is a management responsibility. Laying off workers during slack times is death to efficiency. The worker thrown out is a trained man. To replace him when business picks up will cost much more than the savings of wages during the layoff. The worker must have a guarantee that if he works properly his income will be continuous.

11. Continuous employment is the first step to efficiency. But how? First, during slack periods manufacture to build up inventory, costs will usually be less because of lower material costs. Second, develop new machines and methods of manufacturing; plans should be waiting on the shelf. Third, reduce prices by getting lower costs. When slack times come, workers are eager to help cut costs. Fourth, explore markets passed over when times are good. Fifth, hours of work can be reduced if the worker is agreeable. Sixth, develop new products. In sum, management should plan for slumps. They are useful.

12. Resistance to efficiency is not normal. It is present only when we are hired workers.

13. Do unto others as you would have them do unto you. This is not just a Sunday school ideal, but a proper labour-management policy.

14. An incentive plan should reward a man not only for the number of pieces turned out, but also for the accuracy of his work, his cooperation in improving methods of production, his attendance.

15. There are many forms and degrees of cooperation ... The worker's attitude can vary all the way from passivity to highly imaginative contributions to efficiency and progress.

Source: The Lincoln Electric Case. President and Fellows of Harvard College.

Table 8.1 Conditions limiting opportunism

1. Equity between employees
2. Strategies for responding to product market changes which offer security to employees
3. Disclosure of information (to limit uneven distribution)
4. Employee access to decision-making

KEY CONCEPT 8.5

HIGH- AND LOW-TRUST SYNDROMES

Fox (1974) identifies two sets of associated features of economic relationships which he refers to as 'syndromes', and which are labelled 'high' and 'low' trust respectively. The low-trust or discretion syndrome covers the following features:

☐ Supervisors regard subordinates as though they cannot be trusted to perform in accordance with the supervisors' values and goals.
☐ Consequently supervisors resort to systematic control based on specific and impersonal rules and close personal supervision.
☐ Open communication and interaction appropriate to more complex problem-solving situations is ignored in favour of tight coordination via standardized routines and schedules.
☐ Supervisors assume that failure to meet targets is the result of negligence or insubordination.
☐ Conflict tends to be conducted on a group basis between supervisors and groups of subordinates on the basis of bargaining over recognized differences of interest. Bargaining is conducted via threats and gamesmanship strategies.

The high-trust or discretion syndrome is characterized by:

☐ Supervisors assume personal commitment by subordinates to the goals and values identified by supervision. Effort and application are not based on some calculation of a specific return.
☐ Consequently, workers experience an absence of close supervision and detailed regulation.
☐ Open communication and interaction with supervisors who are seen as supportive colleagues.
☐ Communication from supervisors seen as advice, information and consultation rather than orders, instructions and directives.
☐ Problem-solving then seen as a process of mutual adjustment rather than taking the form of standardized and imposed routines.
☐ Performance shortfalls seen as the result of misjudgement rather than malevolence.
☐ Disagreement between supervisors and subordinates handled by 'working through' problems in the light of shared goals rather than bargaining on the basis of divergent or conflicting ones.

It does not require too great a leap of the imagination to see how these two syndromes are mutually reinforcing. The assumption by supervisors that their subordinates have certain characteristics will indeed produce

> just those characteristics in their subordinates! As Tom Peters often tells managers, if they look at what their employees do outside work in terms of commitment, enthusiasm and skill they will find that they only '. . . display characteristics of apathy, laziness, ignorance and so on during the eight hours they are working for YOU!'
>
> As Fox writes, 'In return for a specific extrinsic reward, in the form of a wage or salary, the occupant of the role performs certain services of a predominantly specific nature. Both sides . . . bring . . . expectations of a highly specific reciprocation. Hopes by either that the other can be brought to go beyond the prescribed terms without guaranteed reciprocation prove forlorn. **This makes it likely that mutual vigilance will increase rather than diminish** (emphasis added).'

the 'high-discretion' or high-trust syndrome in contrast to the 'low-discretion', low-trust syndrome described in Key Concept 8.5.

Willman argues that if employees are voluntarily to forego opportunistic behaviour rather than be disciplined into avoiding it, management must modify the degree to which information is unevenly distributed between management and workers and the extent to which workers are excluded from the decision-making process.

Modifications to the hierarchy of decision-making will be further discussed in the next chapter when considering forms of ownership, and in Chapter 10 when the German form of company structure and employment legislation are examined. For the present we will stay with the extension to the market failure approach undertaken by Ouchi and his associates (see Ouchi and Jaeger, 1976; Ouchi and Johnson, 1978; Ouchi and Price, 1978; and Ouchi, 1980).

Organizational development

The starting point for Ouchi and his colleagues is a conclusion derived from various reviews that have been undertaken of the effectiveness of methods of instituting change in organizations which are collectively referred to as 'organizational development', described in Key Concept 8.6.

It was the association of successful organizations and the existence in those organizations of relatively cohesive small groups that led theorists and practioners to adopt techniques for facilitating change based upon small groups. The intention was to develop social awareness and participatory and problem-solving skills of individuals in order to facilitate small group functioning and formation.

As always when noting correlations or associations, there is the problem of sorting out the nature and direction of the causal mechanism. In the case of organizational development techniques and change in organizations, it may well be that success itself facilitates, even if it does not cause, the appearance of cohesive small groups. Cohesive work groups and a team approach by employees may be the result, not the cause, of success.

KEY CONCEPT 8.6 ***ORGANIZATIONAL*** ***DEVELOPMENT***	Organizational development (OD) is a term used to describe a particular approach to the management of change. The basic features of this approach are as follows: ☐ OD is a long-term effort to change the beliefs, attitudes, structures and values of an organization; ☐ the emphasis tends to be on a collaborative management style; ☐ this involves the development of work teams and the contribution of a 'change-agent'; ☐ a 'change-agent' is a third party who comes from outside the organization and actively intervenes in the activities of the organization; ☐ the change-agent is usually engaged in 'action research' – that is actively participating in the resolution of practical problems facing the organization. The purpose of the change-agent is the establishment of a new system of organizational values and processes which integrate individual and organizational objectives. In other words, an increase in the opportunities for all concerned to develop their truly 'human' qualities.

The role of the group and *homo hierarchus*

A concentration on small groups and the development of a team approach to the well-documented problems of hierarchic organizations which typified the human relations approach was mainly the legacy of Elton Mayo who reacted to the perceived decline in the quality of American industrial society in the 1930s and 1940s by turning to the example of non-industrial tribal societies. Mayo argued that in such societies social cohesion was based upon each individual's link to a group larger than a family in the conventional sense but smaller than the tribe. This group was the 'clan'. In this respect Mayo was echoing Durkheim's typology of 'mechanical solidarity' where people are linked by their similarity, in comparison with 'organic solidarity' where cohesion results from differences, interdependence deriving from the division of labour.

While recognizing the importance of small group membership in maintaining psychological health, Mayo never satisfactorily confronted the problem that in large-scale industrial society 'hierarchy' has become not just a defining feature, but that without which 'industrial' production cannot be achieved. A return to forms of organization characteristic of non-industrial society is not a feasible proposition, the clock cannot be turned back. Another American psychologist of organizations, Chris Argyris, attempted to reconcile these apparently conflicting aspects of modern society (Argyris, 1964).

Like Durkheim, Argyris saw the tension between organization and the individual as the basis for a positive outcome. If handled in a humane manner the competition between the organization and the individual could help human beings fulfil their potential. The prime requisite for such an outcome was trust between superiors and subordinates. It is not difficult to see how success itself breeds the kind of climate in which individual and organizational goals are compatible, and in which conflict may be resolved with a minimum of psychological damage.

If an organization is successful, then those in authority have some leeway which may be reflected in greater autonomy for workers. The very fact of success suggests that workers are trustworthy and not trying to sabotage management's goals. An organization that is failing, or whose management is coping with threats by reducing the security and autonomy of workers, may well be confronted with a situation in which managerial action itself brings about precisely the outcome it is attempting to forestall. Less trust expressed towards the workers results in less commitment from them. This in turn lays the foundation for opportunistic behaviour in what has now become a threatening environment for all concerned.

The origins of dependency

While recognizing that hierarchical organizations were central to at least some of the goals of an industrial society, Argyris attempted to mitigate the dysfunctional aspects of organizational life for the individual by minimizing those factors which maintained the dependent situation of employees. The dependent situation of organizational members arises out of their exclusion from decision-making processes. This emphasizes exlusion from power and responsibility. Dependency for a human being of any age is the basis for anxiety, and if not handled in a manner which enables the individual to 'grow' will result in frustration and eventual aggression (refer again to Table 7.5 in the previous chapter).

Douglas McGregor was another writer who, like Durkheim, recognized that interdependence was a key feature of industrial society and had therefore to be the basis of human development. He also, as did Argyris, likened the dependent situation of the worker in an hierarchic organization to that of the human infant. Consequently a method had to be found which enabled people to develop as human beings and so avoid the physical and emotional traumas of dependency, with its connotation of infancy and immaturity.

Such a method, McGregor argued, was to be found in the development of the social skills of managers. The foundation upon which such skills could be developed was a philosophy of people management based upon

'T' (training) group or sensitivity training is designed to develop individual and group skills. Concentration is on 'process' rather than 'task'. That is, attention is directed at the way in which individuals and groups behave towards each other in the process of completing some task. The objective of this type of training is to make individuals aware of the emotional needs and reaction of others as well as their own. By paying attention to their own needs and those of others, participants are able to perceive and learn from the consequences of their actions.

KEY CONCEPT 8.7

SENSITIVITY TRAINING

assumptions about human nature (ontological assumptions) centred upon trust. This was the basis of his 'Theory Y'. McGregor's response to the need for the enhanced social skills of managers was the development of skills through the use of 'T' (training) groups and sensitivity training, described in Key Concept 8.7. The aim was to improve the effectiveness of work groups in the psychological sense. In turn this would be reflected in improvements in production related criteria.

This approach is similar to that adopted by the Tavistock Clinic under whose auspices some classic work has been carried out, in this country and elsewhere, and which formed the basis for the 'socio-technical' approach to organizational design. This concentrates on developing interpersonal skills and attempts to develop participative decision-making processes as the means of ensuring that both personal and organizational goals may be achieved.

Alternatives to hierarchy

Ouchi and his colleagues identify what they claim to be a critical omission in the work of the human relations approach to the problems of organization. Nowhere do any of the authors and researchers associated with the approach give 'any explanation of why hierarchy seems to be the inevitable response to industrialization' (Ouchi and Price, 1978). As mentioned earlier, the association of cohesive work groups with commercial success begs the question of the direction of causality. Without some idea of the crucial contribution hierarchy makes to modern industrial activity it is difficult to identify just how and why focusing on small groups will necessarily bring about fundamental alterations in the situation of organizational employees.

Following the market failure approach, Ouchi and his colleagues build on the fact that hierarchy is one of at least three ways of organizing coordinated activity amongst a number of individuals. The three methods are bureaucracies, markets and clans.

The basic method of coordination in a market is the price mechanism. Ideally no personal supervision or monitoring intrudes into the pursuit of self-interest since supervision and monitoring is the responsibility of the price mechanism. In a sense, in a perfect market there is no competition between suppliers because no one supplier can influence the situation in the market.

When the market fails to function, when transaction costs rise beyond a certain level, an alternative will be sought. Bureaucracy functions as one alternative since the rules fulfil the basic coordination need. In addition, the existence of rules applied in a judicial manner may assist in the development of trust between those engaged in transactions.

Clans on the other hand function on the basis of socialization and resulting homogeneity. Socialization has the effect of bringing about a merging of individual and organizational goals. This process is faciliated when recruits already share some of the same values as existing organization members as this avoids the need for radical re-socialization.

Whilst there are industrial organizations which approach the clan form of organization in the UK and USA, e.g., IBM Hewlett-Packard, Cadbury and The Body Shop, the most widely reported examples are perhaps Japanese companies.

In order to minimize the demands of the socialization process recruits are drawn from those who have received some 'anticipatory' socialization due to education and family background. This has been a very important factor in the role of the British educational system exemplified in the 'old school tie' syndrome associated with the public school system and which is still important in the higher reaches of British management and society. The public school displayed the 'total institution' form of complete socialization which is associated with the clan.

Forms of organization and individual involvement

Ouchi and his colleagues have developed a continuum of three 'ideal type' models of organization. At one extreme is the European/North American type, and at the other is the Japanese type. It is suggested that an intermediate form is developing and this is argued by Ouchi and his colleagues to be particularly suited to the Western world in general and North America in particular. This will be discussed later in the chapter.

Features of these organizational types at the ends of the continuum, referred to as Type A (American) and Type J (Japanese), are shown in Table 8.2. The atrributes of each are discussed below.

Table 8.2 Organizational forms: Types A and J

Type A (American)	Type J (Japanese)
1. Short-term employment	1. Life-time employment
2. Individual decision-making	2. Consensual decision-making
3. Individual responsibility	3. Collective responsibility
4. Rapid evaluation and promotion	4. Slow evaluation and promotion
5. Explicit, formalized control	5. Implicit, informal control
6. Specialized career path	6. Non-specialized career path
7. Segmented concern	7. Holistic concern

Source: Ouchi and Jaeger (1978).

The first three dimensions for each type are self-explanatory and require no elaboration except in the case of the first under Type J. It is important to remember that while this may be a significant feature of Japanese companies in comparison to Anglo-Saxon (even allowing for the examples quoted above), it is limited in operation even in Japan. Life-time employment operates in large companies only, and even then it applies to no more than one-third of employees. These will, however, tend to be the 'key' or 'core' workers.

The fourth dimension, rapid/slow evaluation and promotion, relates to the impact that evaluation and promotion have upon behaviour, attitudes and the development of interpersonal relationships. Rapid evaluation and promotion implies that individuals are forced to follow instrumental, and hence impersonal, strategies. The main thing is to get targeted results for this quarter or half-year, for example. Long-term matters are ignored, and the development of trust, mutual understanding and cooperation tends to be ignored, thus at least creating the possibility of opportunistic behaviour.

The fifth dimension, explicit/formal and implicit/informal control processes, covers the extent to which rules and regulations are formally stated and operated. That is, the extent to which rule books and operating manuals are relied upon.

The career path dimension refers to a well-known characteristic of Japanese recruitment methods which are not concerned with specialist, functionally oriented activities. Individual employees are not accountants or marketers first, and an employee of the company second. They are employees first, and then are allocated to whatever activities are appropriate as the career and the company develop. This has obvious implications for training within the company, and for the content of secondary school and college and university curricula where a generalist rather than specialist orientation will be required. As Ouchi and Jaeger (1978) put it: 'A specialised career path yields professionalisation, decreases organisational loyalty, and facilitates movement of the individual from one firm to another' (p. 309).

Finally, 'concern' refers to the extent to which the individual employee is regarded as a whole person by superiors, rather than as just a pair of 'hands'. Holistic concern is that associated in the West with paternalism. The supervisor or employer takes an interest in employees' lives outside the work organization and is concerned with the welfare of employees and their families. Segmented concern focuses upon the employee as worker, and those adopting this approach regard a lack of concern with non-work problems as appropriate to a society of individual market operators.

Concern, as a dimension, illustrates the extent to which the two patterns of organizational structure and involvement are associated with cultural contexts. The systematic nature of the two organizational types, in which each component is related to at least one other, represents cultural or environmental consistency. This does not mean that 'culture' is causal, only that these structural features are consistent with a particular cultural environment.

Type 'J' organizations are associated with cultural environments in which the collective is seen as of greater significance than the individual. Individual interests are to be achieved through the achievement of collective interests. Coordination is achieved as a result of incorporating the individual into the collective through socialization. Control is then implicit and internalized by the individual. Such a control system can be more reliable and adaptable than an explicit system based upon the formulation and supervision of specific rules. One result of such a system is that employees become experts on the organization itself, rather than becoming expert in some specialist function or activity. As a result, they can be relied upon to act in the interest of the organization with a minimum of supervision and explicit rules.

The Type 'A' organization is favoured where emphasis is placed upon individuality. Such an emphasis tends to be associated with individual social mobility and values of independence and self-reliance. Such values

can conflict with the need for cooperation and teamwork since coordination requires, to some extent at least, the subordination of individual
interest.

Disorder and opportunism

In the British case it can be argued that there is an inherent contradiction
within the A Type organization. The emphasis on 'teamwork' and being
a good team member to some extent conflicts with an emphasis upon
individuals self-interest. This feature may well account for what Maitland
(1983) identified as the basis of the 'disorder' he found in British as
compared with German industrial relations.

When there are two apparently conflicting value systems at work
uncertainty and subsequently suspicion become the norm. How does an
individual respond to superiors who at one time advocate the virtues of
teamwork, and yet at another time justify their decisions on the basis of
individual self-interest in the market-place? If an individual or group
cannot be sure of which rules their associates are playing by, sticking to just
one of a number of possible sets could be potentially damaging.

This is a certain recipe for opportunism. Maitland argued that in the case
of British industrial relations, it was not the case that no one could agree on
what, for example, represented a fair day's pay for a fair day's work. The
problem was that no one could be sure that such an agreement would be
consistently acted upon. It was not that there was no consensus, there was
simply no confidence that a consensus could be administered. There was
no confidence that if one group 'played the game' some other group (of
managers or workers) would not take advantage of them for doing so. This
is the problem of 'moral hazard' or the 'free-rider'. Many aspects of the
institutions of industrial relations, on the union and employer side, derive
from this problem. British trade unions have developed in response to a
management style and strategy that relies upon the labour market as a
means of coping with product market variations. Thus every change in
methods of work or terms and conditions of employment is an opportunity
to bargain.

National agreements on pay have been favoured by employers in the
past because such an agreement reduced the chances that they would be
undercut by another employer exploiting local opportunities to pay lower
wages. This worked in favour of unions also. However, when accidents of
market situation enable one employer to force down the rate of pay, other
employers will be anxious to be freed from the restrictions of national
agreements in order to take advantage of market forces: in other words
'opportunism'.

Type Z organizations

Research by Ouchi and his colleagues at Stanford University in the 1970s
appeared to unearth a third ideal type which encompassed aspects of both
'A' and 'J' type organizations. This is the Type Z organization (so named in
deference to McGregor's Theory 'X' and 'Y') which is suggested to

Table 8.3 Characteristics of Type Z organizations

Long-term employment
Consensual decision-making
Individual responsibility
Slow evaluation and promotion
Implicit, informal control with explicit formalized measures
Moderately specialized career path
Holistic concern, including family

Source: Ouchi and Jaeger (1978).

combine factors favourable to both economic and psychological success in the Anglo-Saxon world. Although not mentioned by Ouchi, the Lincoln Electric Company in Case Study 8.4 also illustrates the features of a Type Z organization which are set out in Table 8.3.

Based upon observations in the electronics industry in the United States the Type Z organization displays, Ouchi suggests, characteristics conducive to the development of long-term interests and relationships. It appeared that such companies stayed out of the most volatile markets and subcontracted tasks that fluctuated according to demand. In addition, while such companies also calculated the profitability of divisions, they did not operate strict profit-centre mechanisms replicating the market mechanism within the organization. This enabled decision-making to concentrate upon longer-term, corporation-wide objectives and reduced the emphasis upon more immediate and individually oriented performance measures.

Table 8.4 Hewlett-Packard corporate objectives

1. **Profit:** To achieve sufficient profit to finance our company growth and to provide the resources we need to achieve our other corporate objectives.
2. **Customers:** To provide products and services of the highest quality and the greatest possible value to our customers, thereby gaining and holding their respect and loyalty.
3. **Fields of interest:** To participate in those fields of interest that build upon our technology and customer base, that offer opportunities for continuing growth, and that enable us to make a needed and profitable contribution.
4. **Growth:** To let our growth be limited only by our profits and our ability to develop and produce innovative products that satisfy real customer needs.
5. **Our people:** To help HP people share in the company's success which they make possible; to provide employment security based on their performance; to ensure them a safe and pleasant work environment; to recognize their individual achievements; and to help them gain a sense of satisfaction and accomplishment from their work.
6. **Management:** To foster initiative and creativity by allowing the individual great freedom of action in attaining well-defined objectives.
7. **Citizenship:** To honour our obligations to society by being an economic, intellectual and social asset to each nation and each community in which we operate.

Source: Hewlett-Packard.

Ouchi and his colleagues suggest that Type Z organizations have to some extent replaced the control strategies of hierarchy with those of the clan. What this type of organization has done is to develop a philosophy or mission statement that is consistent with wider goals than mere profit. Consider, for example, the statement of objectives for Hewlett-Packard set out in Table 8.4.

'Profit' is mentioned, but very clearly only as a means to a number of ends, none of which specifically mention shareholders! Shareholders will undoubtedly benefit from the success of such a company, but this will be a by-product of the activities of the company rather than the sole or even a prime purpose. In such a climate it is possible to develop goals which are consistent with the achievement of psychological success on the part of company members.

As Wong and her colleagues (1987) found in their sample of British companies (described in Case Study 6.5), there is some evidence that functional specialization hinders a company's efforts to compete. The work of both Wong *et al.* and the NIESR researchers suggest that a concentration on profit may not be the most effective means of ensuring survival. Profit is a means to an end, not an end in itself (a point made many times in this volume!). This requires that considerable attention is given to identifying the most cost-effective methods of production since enhancing market share requires considerable investment in both people and machines. Such investment places a premium on the effective utilization of both. The surplus has to be sufficient to fund the investment necessary to meet the demands of the strategic objectives. The effective utilization of people and machines, in order to ensure the necessary surplus, requires consideration of the impact of the ways in which work is organized and controlled upon the commitment of managers and workers.

In attempting to explain why such philosophies are not more widespread Ouchi and his colleagues refer back to problems inherent in market mechanism, for example, 'externalities' as defined in Key Concept 8.8.

An 'externality' is an activity which has a cost, but that cost is not borne by those who undertake or benefit from the activity which gives rise to it. So, every time John Smith drives to work, or to the tennis club, he causes pollution; but this does not (yet) cost him anything. The cost is borne by other people who live along his route whether or not they drive or even own a car themselves. Similarly of course, Smith bears the pollution costs imposed by those who drive past his home. Legislation on exhaust emissions and the fitting of catalytic exhaust systems forces consumers to bear the cost of pollution.

The debate over fossil fuels in power generation is another case. To date the cost of acid rain and so on has been borne by those who are on the receiving end, not those who produce or consume the electricity. Again, international standards for sulphur 'scrubbers' in power station chimneys is a way of imposing the cost of pollution on those who benefit from the process which causes it.

KEY CONCEPT 8.8

EXTERNALITIES

Continued over page

Continued from previous page In the case of private industry and its impact on the environment the costs are borne by all taxpayers or members of society whether or not they share in the profits of the companies concerned. As the market mechanism may not, due to externalities, influence decisions about pollution, for example, legal rules have to be developed, supervised and enforced in order to ensure clean air or water.

Similarly, the failure of companies in Britain to engage widely in training is explained by the fact that an emphasis on market individualism results in trained people leaving once they have been trained. So, it is rational in market terms for companies to avoid the cost of training and recruit, or poach, trained people from other companies. In the long term this will rebound to the disadvantage of all companies, but in the short term the savings accrue to the company while the cost of not training is born by the population as a whole in terms of the consequences of relatively poor economic performance and reduced earnings. Markets may distribute the available skills around the economy in an 'efficient' way, but the market does not appear so far to have functioned to produce necessary skills in the first place.

The significance of externalities

One reason why Type Z philosophies are not widely developed is that there is no great incentive for organizations to integrate value systems. The problem is that of 'externalities' as described above.

In the same way that the market mechanism may not cope with all the costs incurred by an activity, so it does not recognize psychological success. While high labour turnover is readily recognized as a problem, it is perceived as a cost problem only. Unsophisticated costing systems ignore the costs of psychological failure and the benefits of psychological success.

A second factor explaining the absence of philosophies conducive to psychological success is that most managers are not in the happy position of starting their own firm and so implementing a philosophy from scratch. Most managers work for large organizations while many of the factors that facilitate psychological health are ascribed to small firms. In a small firm all employees can be known as individuals. All can recognize the contribution each makes even if that contribution cannot easily be measured in financial (market) terms. In a small organization it is likely by the nature of things that information will be more widely distributed. The personal nature of relationships also facilitates a wider participation in decision-making, even if that participation is informal rather than formal. However, for a critical evaluation of the reality of life in small firms, see Rainnie 1989.

A major problem facing those who manage and work in small firms is that of growth, not so much in terms of achieving it as in coping with the interpersonal and psychological consequences. As the numbers employed increase, it becomes more difficult to maintain the degree and nature of interaction that was possible when fewer people were involved. It is not possible to remember everybody's name let alone their personal worries. Managers have to spend more time in formal activities of monitoring and evaluating because such activities can no longer be carried out simply as a product of casual conversations as people move around the plant. Planning has to be put on a more formal footing since increasing complexity prevents coordination on the basis of *ad hoc* responses to product market changes.

The growth and success of a small business takes it into the league of medium-sized businesses. The atmosphere that management (owner) and employees enjoyed and valued may be lost, resulting in feelings of frustration, confusion and even betrayal. New methods have to be learnt, but under the pressure of economic growth the mechanisms for psychological growth are ignored. This is due to the lack of any conscious awareness amongst the participants of the processes at work in the first place, rather than an overt decision to ignore them. Consequently, what was a successful small business rapidly ceases to be such and develops into a mediocre medium-sized business. It is at least arguable that in terms of economic policy, resources should be targeted on the transition of successful small firms to successful medium-sized firms. This should be the focus of policy rather than the current emphasis on the start-up phase of small businesses.

Anomie again

The approach taken by Ouchi is interesting in so far as it consciously addresses the problems of anomie. In doing so it links the examination of market failure with established theories in social science. The approach is particularly concerned with anomie rather than with alienation. The two terms are linked by Ouchi almost as synonyms – as is often the case – but there is little recognition of the essential character of alienation as distinct from anomie.

The development of Type Z organizations is linked by Ouchi and his colleagues to changes in American society which affect the extent and forms of social integration. At one time, they argue, American society could tolerate a high degree of individualistic market-oriented behaviour because integration of individuals into society took place via the community and institutions such as the church. Sources of affiliation were outside the workplace. Achieving the very social mobility that was desired has resulted in the deterioration that many observers and politicians see as typical of modern society in both the UK and North America. This deterioration is perceived in terms of the decline in church attendance, increased rates of marital breakdown and broken homes, illegitimacy, rising crime rates, and the general malaise in moral life of which drug abuse and social disorder generally are seen as symptoms. This condition is represented by the bottom right-hand quadrant (cell 3) of Figure 8.1.

In this situation, affiliation through the work organization becomes not only possible but desirable. Such an affiliation was not previously possible because an individual who was fully integrated into his or her community would have been overloaded if they were also required to integrate fully into the work organization (cell 1). However, in the face of the break-up of traditional communities and industries, a low level of integration in the work organization results in individuals with unmet affiliation needs. 'They will experience "anomie", the sensation that there are no anchors or standards, and thus a feeling of being lost' Ouchi and Jaeger (1978).

Affiliation in the organization	Affiliation in society	
	High	Low
High (Type Z)	Overload　　　　1	2　　　Integrated
Low (Type A)	4　　　Integrated	3　　　'Anomie'

Figure 8.1 Focus of affiliation and its consequences. Source: Ouchi and Jaeger (1978).

A significant feature of the approach adopted by Ouchi and his colleagues is that it avoids explaining differences in organizational management by reference to 'culture'. This is consistent with the fact that most of what Japanese companies are noted for in terms of their human resource and market strategies were (and are) central to much material on industrial management published in the UK and North America. This is particularly the case with motivation and quality for example. While 'culture' might well have something to do with detailed arrangements in different countries, the basic problem addressed by Ouchi's Type Z organization has been the subject of concern for decades in the West. Perhaps the reluctance to implement, in the Anglo-Saxon world, precepts which originated there and have been adopted elsewhere has been due to accidents of history, for example the point in time at which a country industrialized or its fortune in war.

The significance of the distinction between early and late industrializers is explored in more detail in Chapter 10, but an example of the impact of military victory or defeat is worth noting at this point. In the United Kingdom a concern with the perceived superiority of German industry and education and training systems dating from the 1860s was undermined by Germany's defeat in the First World War. UK advocates of the German model were challenged by those who pointed to the Allied victory as evidence that the German system was not so superior, nor the British system so inferior, as had previously been thought. Even today, part of the confusion over the relative economic success of countries like Germany, France, Italy and Japan stems from the assumed consequences of their defeat or occupation during the Second World War.

Again, it may well be that the observed differences between Anglo-Saxon managers and workers in comparison with, say, those in Germany and Japan is due to the organization structures and procedures adopted in Germany and Japan, rather than reflecting some cultural phenomenon which causes those structures and procedures to be adopted in the first place.

This issue will be examined further in Chapter 10, but it is worth noting at this point that in terms of the problems that the UK and USA economies experience in competing with many continental European economies, let alone Japan, the attributes that Ouchi and his colleagues are concerned to develop by means of organizational structures are achieved in Germany and other EC countries by legal frameworks that not only affect organizational structure, but also endow workers with rights which facilitate cooperation, participation and commitment. Legislative means of achieving socially desirable ends are often regarded critically in societies such as the USA and the UK which place considerable emphasis on market mechanisms.

The sceptical, to say the least, approach by many UK politicians and business people to the Social Charter of the European Commission, and the concern of the current British government and business interests to ensure that the market for corporate capital (i.e. takeovers) is as 'free' throughout the EC as it is within the UK is significant in the context of the issues discussed in this chapter. The general willingness in other member states of the European Community to accept the provisions of the Social Charter and the relative underdeveloped markets for corporate capital are symptomatic of an approach to business which does not raise the goal of maximizing shareholders' returns above other goals. In such a context, especially where employee rights to consultation, participation and information are protected by law, the attainment of willing compliance, or 'consumate cooperation', may be a more easily attained objective.

In the next chapter we move on to explore the influence of forms of ownership over both the structure of, and behaviour within, organizations.

Summary

In this chapter we have been looking at some of the factors to be taken into account when considering the adaptation of organizational forms to the demands arising out of the development of electronic technology, its impact on product markets, and the implications for behaviour in organizations. The key feature is that, as has been recognized for some time, standards of quality, technical performance and design are more important factors than price *per se* in governing efforts to increase market shares and hence the growth of manufacturing industry (Panic, 1975). It is important to note that we are here talking about 'growth' of manufacturing industry in terms of market share, not in terms of numbers employed.

In such a situation, and given the nature of the technology itself as we saw in the case of the German kitchen furniture industry, what Willman calls 'consumate cooperation' becomes essential. How this may be achieved has been suggested by the work of those who have utilized the idea that markets are appropriate mechanisms for allocating scarce resources only under certain conditions. They may fail due to increasing costs associated with monitoring the value given and received in transactions. At the risk of repetition: if industrial societies really are experiencing radical, even if not revolutionary change, then it is necessary to question assumptions that have been taken for granted irrespective of how well they may have served up to now. Such questioning must be directed at conventional organizational forms since such forms have for long been regarded as not only obstructing the attainment of psychological health for those involved, but also inhibiting adaptation in the face of new demands.

As Hirschorn (1984) has suggested, modern technology requires that organizations are restructured to meet the demands arising from its utilization. These demands are not only technical but social and psychological as well. By continuing to insist on traditional organizational forms and employment relations there is considerable likelihood that nineteenth-century solutions will be imposed not only upon twentieth-century problems, but upon twenty-first-century problems also.

In the next chapter this discussion will be extended to an examination of forms of ownership and their significance for the attainment of 'consumate cooperation'. The question of the nature and form of ownership is likely to come to the fore, implicitly at least, in the debate over the Social Charter and the liberalization of the market for corporate capital markets in the European Community where the maximizing of shareholders' wealth is not considered the sole purpose of economic success.

Study questions

1. What role do transaction costs play in the determination of organizational forms?
2. What forms may 'flexibility' take and what are the implications?
3. How do Ouchi and his colleagues suggest 'anomie' may be overcome in the context of new technology and increased competition?
4. Evaluate the assertion that 'workers are market maximizers as are employers'.
5. What are the necessary conditions suggested by Willman for the limiting of opportunistic behaviour on the part of management and workforce?

References

Argyris, C. (1964) *Integrating the Individual and the Organization*. Wiley.

Burns, T. and Stalker, G.M. (1961) *The Management of Innovation*. Tavistock.

Cavestro, W. (1989) Automation, new technology and work content. In Wood, S. (ed.) *The Transformation of Work?* Unwin.

Collingridge, D. (1980) *The Social Control of Technology*. Open University Press.

Doeringer, P.B. and Piore, M.J. (1971) *Internal Labour Markets and Manpower Analysis*. Lexington.

Eatwell, J. (1982) *Whatever Happened to Britain?* BBC.

Fox, A. (1974) *Beyond Contract: Work, Power and Trust Relations*. Faber.

Hartmann, G., Nicholas, I., Sorge, A. and Warner, M. (1983) Computerised machine tools, manpower consequences and skill utilisation: a study of British and West German manufacturing firms. *British Journal of Industrial Relations*, **21**, (2).

Hayes, R., Wheelwright, S. and Clark, K. (1988) *Dynamic Manufacturing*: *Creating the Learning Organization*. Free Press.

Hirschorn, L. (1984) *Beyond Mechanization*: *Work and Technology in a Postindustrial Age*. MIT Press.

Maitland, I. (1983) *The Causes of Industrial Disorder*. Routledge and Kegan Paul.

Ouchi, W.G. and Jaeger, A.M. (1978) Type Z Organisation: stability in the midst of mobility. *Academy of Management Review*, 305–14.

Ouchi, W.G. and Johnson, J. (1978) Types of organizational control and their relationship to emotional well-being. *Administrative Science Quarterly*, 293–317.

Ouchi, W.G. and Price, R.L. (1978) Hierarchies, clans and Theory Z: a new perspective on organisation development. *Organisational Dynamics*, **7**, 25–44.

Ouchi, W.G. (1980) Markets, bureaucracies and clans. *Administrative Science Quarterly*, **25**, 129–41.

Ouchi, W.G. (1981) *Theory Z*. Addison-Wesley.

Panic, M. (1975) Why the UK's propensity to import is high. *Lloyds Bank Review*, **115**, 1–13.

Pollert, A. (1987) *The Flexible Firm*: *A Model in Search of Reality* (*Or a Policy in Search of a Practice*)? Warwick Paper in Industrial Relations, (19).

Rainnie, A. (1989) *Industrial Relations in Small Firms: Small Isn't Beautiful*, Routledge.

Roy, D. (1952) Quota Restriction and goldbricking in a machine shop. *Amer. J. Soc.*, **57**.

Rubery, J. *et al.* (1987) *Labour and Society*. January.

Steadman, H. and Wagner, K. (1987) *A Second Look at Productivity, Machinery and Skill Britain and Germany*. NIESR Review, February.

Towse, A. (1982) *The BL Incentive Scheme in Perspective*. Nuffield College, Oxford.

Williamson, O.E. (1975) *Markets and Hierarchies*: *Analysis and Antitrust Implications*. Free Press.

Willman, P. and Winch, G. (1985) *Innovation and Management Control*: *Labour Relations at BL Cars*. Oxford University Press.

Willman, P. (1987) *Technological Change, Collective Bargaining and Industrial Efficiency*. Clarendon Press.

Wong V., Saunders, J. and Doyle, P. (1987) Japanese marketing strategies in the United Kingdom. *Long Range Planning*, **20**, (6), 54–63.

Wood, S. (1989) *The Transformation of Work?* Unwin Hyman.

 **9** Organization structure: the effect of the nature of property

In this chapter we will examine the implications for behaviour of the structure and functioning of organizations in the context of what may be regarded as the fundamental organizing principle of Western market economies, that is the concept of property and the exercise of property rights. Variations in the limits placed upon property and the exercise of property rights form the basic distinguishing features between industrial societies in terms of the legal, political and social framework within which work is organized and controlled. Like other variations between countries these can be seen to arise from the different political and socio-cultural experiences associated with the process of industrialization.

It should be remembered that all attempts to legislate for the rights of employees at work, especially in terms of their participation in decision-making, sooner or later raise the question of the extent to which rights accorded employees as employees may contradict the rights of property owners to dispose of their property as they see fit. This is an issue in the United Kingdom just as much as in Germany where workers enjoy considerably more statutory rights in employment than is the case in the UK. It is also an issue which is much discussed in the context of the implementation of the European Social Charter after 1992, and the extent to which shareholders' interests should dominate the evaluation of takeover bids in the Community, as they do in the UK, rather than other and perhaps longer-term interests as tends to be the case in other European economies. These other interests include those of employees and those of the economy as a whole.

The role and nature of property rights are also central to the debate over how the 'intellectual property rights' of authors and computer program innovators may be best defended in the electronic age.

We are continuing our move out from the centre of the model of business as we consider the likely future development of business organizations. In this chapter we extend the discussion in the previous chapter of organizational forms for the future by addressing specifically the nature of ownership, and implicitly the role of the state in so far as it supports ownership and the rights attaching to it. The state also has a part to play in so far as the executive and legislative arms of government are involved in programmes which contain or limit the exercise of property rights by legislating about pollution, health and safety, and employment rights for example. So we will be covering issues falling under the organizational and environmental headings of the model.

The comparative aspect of the study of behaviour in a business context will be developed further in Chapter 10, but for the purposes of this chapter it is necessary to note that we are moving towards the outer ring of the model which informs this series. We are less concerned with what factors immediately and directly influence intra-organizational relationships in terms of interpersonal attitudes and behaviour, and more concerned with the macro-level framework within which these relationships operate.

As pointed out several times already in this book, all societies (if they are to survive) have to create, and to find some means of distributing, a surplus arising out of economic activity. The distribution must generally be regarded as legitimate if social order is to prevail. Economic activity is activity which involves the allocation of scarce resources to the range of activities necessary for the survival of the social group, whether that group is organized around the minimal group of the family or some larger entity such as a clan, tribe, organization, or even nation.

The social activity of creating and distributing a surplus requires that decisions be taken which ensure an allocation of resources (all with alternative uses) such that some satisfactory outcome is achieved. Satisfactory for whom, and upon what basis, is ultimately the outcome of political as opposed to economic considerations, although much ink has been spilt and debating effort expended in establishing the actual nature of the relationship between these two apparently distinct (i.e. 'political' and 'economic') activities! The key question in this debate concerns the extent to which being wealthy gives a person or group power, or whether being powerful facilitates wealth acquisition.

A significant role in the process of creating and legitimating the distribution of an economic surplus in Western industrial countries is played by the concept of **property**. Property, and the extent to which the exercise of the associated rights are constrained and defined by custom, policy and law, is crucial to the nature of employment relationships as experienced by owners, managers and workers. Such rights are central to the framework within which industrial relations institutions operate and to management's perception of its own role.

In the following sections of this chapter we will examine the notion of property, its impact upon social relations and the manner in which contemporary notions of property are related to the development of a market economy from the eighteenth century onwards. The extent to which contemporary conditions may be creating the conditions for a re-examination of property will then be discussed.

The chapter will conclude with a study of the cooperatives based on Mondragon in the Basque region of Spain as an example of an alternative basis for the organization and control of work, and the creation and distribution of a surplus. These cooperatives have been remarkably successful and have received considerable publicity. They provide evidence for the existence of alternative methods of organizing and controlling work to those currently dominant in Western industrial societies. The point is not that such a system could, or even should, be transplanted to the UK.

The significance of the Mondragon experience is to be seen in terms of the alternative ways in which the problems of motivation and 'consumate cooperation' that have been discussed so far in this book may be discussed.

Property, its nature origins and role

This section draws heavily on the work of C.B. Macpherson and especially his essay 'A Political Theory of Property', one of a collection first published by OUP in 1973 under the title *Democratic Theory: Essays in Retrieval*.

While unequal distribution of property is held to provide a necessary incentive to economic activity, concern is expressed even by property holders over the consequences of extremes of distribution. Concern over the distribution of property at either end of the political spectrum is fuelled by the perception that maintaining a social order which regards property as central implies that as large a proportion of the population as possible should have a property stake in society. The concept of a 'property owning democracy' is a policy moulding concept intended to spread the incentive effects of property while at the same time giving as many people as possible a minimum property-based stake in society. One consequence of this concern in the UK is the existence of a sophisticated financial system of loans for home ownership.

Property is another of those 'taken-for-granted' assumptions that mould and constrains thinking about everyday events and relations. In order to illuminate its role in the formation of behaviour in a business context, it is necessary to consider the development of the concept and its contemporary significance.

The development of the concept of 'property'

Like many other concepts taken for granted in contemporary society, property, as it is currently understood and defined, is very much a product of the Industrial Revolution. Current concern with the protection of new forms that property may take goes some way to supporting this assertion. Concern with intellectual copyright in the areas of computer software and audio recording and playback technology illustrates that what is considered 'property' has to be defined in accordance with the technological, social and economic criteria relevant to particular social groups at a particular time. Intellectual property has been protected by copyright law to date, but

KEY CONCEPT 9.1 **THE NATURE OF PROPERTY**	The property relationship is basically 'triadic'. That is, rights of ownership over some object or other structure the owner's relationship with those who do not own comparable objects, as illustrated in Figure 9.1. The ownership of objects *qua* objects is not itself significant. What is significant is the class of objects that are owned and how that ownership is distributed.

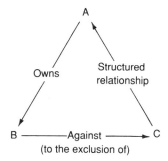

Figure 9.1 The triadic nature of the property relationship.

modern technology is increasingly seen to render current definitions and techniques of protection inadequate. The characteristics of the property relationship are set out in Key Concept 9.1 and Figure 9.1.

Private and public property

Contemporary notions of property are identical with that of 'private' property described in Key Concept 9.2. These characteristics of private property should not be taken to imply that there are no restrictions at all on the use or enjoyment of private property – far from it. Property owners cannot cause a nuisance or endanger the safety and enjoyment of other property owners by the way they use their property. Non-property owners are protected in their enjoyment of clean air, rights of access to the countryside and so forth by restrictions placed upon the operation of private property rights. One may wish to argue that such restrictions on property are not very effective or stringent, or that they are not enforced with any seriousness by the forces of law and order (dogs fouling footpaths in built-up areas or children's play areas in public parks, the integrity of public rights of way for example), but restrictions on private property rights do exist in some form.

The concept of private property, created by the guarantee that an individual can exclude others from the use or benefit of something, can be contrasted with the notion of 'common' or 'public property' described in Key Concept 9.3.

This concept of public property is of interest because the question of public rights of way, for example, raises the issue of the **collective**

The right of an individual or corporate person to **exclude** others from the use or benefit of something, some material thing. Property is an individual right in or to material things. Such a right is regarded as exclusive and 'alienable'; **exclusive** because the owner can exclude others and **alienable** because the owner can dispose of it in accordance with his or her wishes – it can be given away or sold.

KEY CONCEPT 9.2

PRIVATE PROPERTY

KEY CONCEPT 9.3	'Public' or 'common' property is created by the guarantee that an individual will **not** be excluded from the use or benefit of something. This can be interpreted as an individual right in the sense that the right not to be excluded is enjoyed by individuals. It is this right for example that the Ramblers Association try to protect or enforce by ensuring that rural public rights of way are kept open.
PUBLIC OR COMMON PROPERTY	

enforcement of what may be regarded as **individual** rights. That is, in order to maintain the effectiveness of the guarantee that an individual will not be excluded it may be necessary to combine, to organize, to protect what may well be enjoyed as an individual right.

This issue of the collective defence of individual rights lies at the heart of discussions about the nature of the employment contract and the role of law in industrial relations and the operation of the labour market. It also underlies policy-making in the area of product liability legislation, trading standards and consumer protection, and race and sex discrimination.

We will return to the question of the employment contract later. For the moment attention will remain with the origins of the contemporary notion of property and its association with private property. This is necessary in order to examine how the notion of private property may once again have to change in order to meet the demands of democratic society in an era of technological change.

Comparative factors are also important in this context. One of the major problems facing the pharmaceutical industry in the United Kingdom, for example, is the way in which weaker patent legislation in, for example, Italy enables manufacturers in that country to market highly profitable drugs without incurring development costs and with minimum licence payments. The strength of one country's patent laws may influence the speed at which an innovation is introduced since competitors may be prevented from entering the market with related products for a number of years. This enables the holder of the patent to approach the implementation of the innovation with less urgency than would be the case if the protection of the patent legislation was reduced, a factor illustrated in Case Study 9.1.

Closer to home, so to speak, how many readers are aware of the restrictions on photocopying from books and articles that currently exist? The availability of cheap and fast means of copying may have been a boon to the administrator – and the student – but have been a major source of concern over lost profits to authors and publishers.

To recapitulate, remember that the point of this discussion about property, its nature and role is related to the question of obtaining the willing commitment of organizational employees to the objectives pursued by management in a context where the market mechanism is regarded as the major legitimate means of allocating scarce resources. While the modern economic and technological environment may require changes to organizational structures, such changes may also require changes in the approach to the exercise of ownership, something implied by the Lincoln approach to management set out in Case Study 8.4. In order to discuss the

Some years ago the manufacturers of the 'Workmate' bench for the 'do-it-yourself' trade had a problem with someone who was plagiarizing or pirating their idea. The 'workmate' is an ingenious combination of a collapsible workbench in which the working surface of the bench doubles as the jaws of a long vice. This produced a very flexible piece of equipment. The whole contraption folded flat for transportation and storage, and was strong enough to take the weight of a person and so act as short step-ladder. Demand for this product rapidly outgrew the capacity for production.

As a result of this excess demand an entrepreneurial individual commenced manufacturing 'Workmates' in contravention of the patent which the original manufacturer had taken out. When this person's activities were discovered the manufacturer instituted legal proceedings against him.

As usual, such matters took some time to come to court and by the time they did so the counterfeiter had long since gone out of business and was in fact dead. Nevertheless the case went ahead.

When asked why they were bothering to persist with the case when the offender was not producing and was indeed dead, the original manufacturer said that they wished to demonstrate to others in their position that the patent laws were available for protection of products in short supply. The company had plans to expand production capacity but wished to do so at their own speed. They used the patent legislation to block other sources of supply.

In a country with strong patent laws, therefore, there will not be quite the same pressure on a producer to concentrate on the refinement of production methods as a defence against others entering the market for a highly successful product.

The Japanese company Brother report that when they produced the first portable electric typewriter they had about an eighteen months start over their nearest competitor. In 1988 they calculated that from the time they introduced a new product they had about four weeks before someone else produced a similar product at the same or lower price. This type of pressure concentrates their attention on product development, and on production methods in order to establish themselves in the market so as to raise the entry costs for a competitor.

(Further details of the 'Workmate' can be found in Case Study 5.2 in Needle (1989).)

CASE STUDY 9.1

THE 'WORKMATE'

implications of the approaches discussed in Chapters 7 and 8, it is necessary to spend some time examining the nature of property in the modern economy, and its influence on behaviour in work organizations.

The origins of private property and rights of access

In his 1973 paper Macpherson is concerned to make the point that the notion of property as identical with private property is a 'modern' development. It is central to the development of industrial society in that it not only legitimated the role of capital in the production process, but it also functioned as an incentive to labour.

The notion of private property was familiar to pre-industrial English society. MacFarlane (1978) has demonstrated the importance of private property for individuals and their families as far back as the twelfth or thirteenth centuries and probably earlier. Private property was not, however, the basis upon which society was organized in terms of social relationships.

For example, what was important in feudalism were property rights organized around rights to revenues from land, rather than the exclusive and alienable right to the land itself. The land was not **owned** by a feudal lord: what was significant were rights to the revenue from the land in exchange for the obligation to provide military (and other) support to a feudal superior. On the death of the tenant, the rights to a revenue from the land reverted to the person (as an 'office' holder) who had granted the right in the first place. The rights to future revenues might, or might not, be transferred to the deceased's heir. Macfarlane demonstrates that this system existed alongside one where private property also existed, but private property was not the basis on which social, political and economic relations functioned; it was not the 'organising' system of property.

The right of access

The significance of the feudal notion of property was that throughout the social hierarchy there existed rights of access. The serfs had the right to graze their own animals on 'common' land, and to take specified amounts of fuel or building materials from forests for example. This is the origin of common land open spaces today. It was these rights of access that were curtailed by the process of enclosing land in the interest of more efficient forms of agriculture in the sixteenth and seventeenth centuries, and the Highland clearances in the eighteenth. Clearances and enclosures in the interests of commercial agriculture added impetus to the growth of urban populations as well as to the development of the concept of private property.

Rights of exclusion

The idea that all property must be private property, since it consists of the enforceable claims of individuals, goes back no further than the seventeenth century, Macpherson argues. From as early as the sixteenth century (and even possibly earlier) land was increasingly becoming private property, and that form of property was being seen as an individual right to exclude others from the use or benefit of it.

The right to exclude others from the use or benefit of some material thing, like land, was also acquiring certain important characteristics. Such a right to exclude from use or benefit was:

☐ **unlimited** in terms of the amount which could be held;
☐ **unconditional** in that no social functions were required to be performed;
☐ **alienable**, i.e. regarded as being freely transferable by the owner.

Private property as the basis of markets

The notion of private property as described in the previous paragraphs is a *sine qua non* for a market economy. If the market is to take on the role of allocating scarce resources (including 'ideal' resources such as prestige), then there will be an increased emphasis on 'private' property.

The development of the market mechanism introduced the need to find means of legitimating the distributional consequences of market behaviour. Not only did industrialization mean that there were changes at the material level of existence, there were also changes at the ideological level. It was in order to deal with the ideological changes in terms of legitimation that private property developed its function as an incentive to labour.

Legitimation

Political philosophers of the eighteenth and nineteenth centuries were anxious to develop moral and philosophical justifications for the political institutions of industrial society. This required that everyone, from the highest in the land to the lowest, occupied a position the value of which could be measured in market terms. In addition it was necessary to be able to assert that all persons were capable of achieving their potential as human beings. This did not (and still does not) mean that all could aspire to the **same** levels of achievement, but that all would have the opportunity of fulfilling their individual potential. If all persons were to be considered equal in terms of their humanity, then there was a requirement for a property right that was open to all.

However, it was still assumed that resources like land and capital would never be distributed other than in basically unequal holdings. Thus it would not be possible to use land and capital as a basis of property open to all, even though all human beings had needs for which land and/or capital were the basic means of satisfaction. A form of property which was more widely distributed than land or capital was required to fulfil the legitimatory needs of a market economy. A solution was assumed in the property which each individual was held to have in their own labour. In this way land, capital and labour were all reduced to the valuation of the market; all were private, exclusive and alienable – in other words, marketable.

The future of property

Having established the origins of the modern notion of private property in the process of the development of capitalist market economies, Macpherson goes on to argue that changes in the nature of industrial society imply that the notion of property must change again. As Macpherson illustrates, it is not difficult to show that such changes have already occurred and why they will continue.

Contemporary shareholders, for example, are not particularly interested in the exercise of property rights over the physical assets of companies. They are more concerned with the financial return from their investment. This return is measured by dividends and capital growth, i.e. rising share prices, which can be realized in future sales or as collateral for loans. What is important for the modern shareholder is in fact a right to a revenue, rather than rights in or to material things. Modern shareholders are more accurately described as '*rentiers*' rather than 'owners' who exercise property rights over material items.

The development of the welfare state in modern industrial societies also represents the development of, or a return to, earlier definitions of property centred on the right to receipt of a revenue. The welfare state, by providing a basic income as of right, emphasizes the importance in a democratic society of the right to a revenue.

An aspect of contemporary society that illustrates changes which may have to occur in the nature of property concerns the consequences of changes in the proportion of people employed and unemployed. Contemporary levels of unemployment, while perhaps being largely the result of demographic changes (an increase in the number of school-leavers in the late 1970s and early 1980s for example), and changing competitive fortunes in the international economy, may nevertheless be influenced by technological changes as well. The implications are that while **present** levels of employment and unemployment may not be particularly influenced by technological innovations, attempts to reduce unemployment or maintain employment levels in the future may well be hindered by the labour-saving

---

CASE STUDY 9.2

GROWTH IN UNEMPLOYMENT AND THE IMPACT ON PROPERTY

A feature of a number of industries over a considerable time period indicates the possible source of pressure on contemporary notions of property. This source has three components:

- □ increased output;
- □ stable, or declining, numbers employed;
- □ increasing capital investment.

These three factors constitute the syndrome of 'jobless growth'. That is, an economy, industry or firm expands its share of markets, but this occurs without any significant growth in the numbers employed. This has been the experience in agriculture for some considerable length of time. Even the financial services sector had begun to display some of these characteristics. While the introduction of computers in banking and insurance, for example, during the 1960s and 1970s took place at the same time as increasing numbers were being employed in those industries, this should not be taken to indicate that technology is not labour saving. The problem in the 1960s and 1970s was that the demand for financial services was growing at such a rate that both more people and technology was required to cope.

With the market not growing quite so fast, financial services companies find that they no longer need to recruit as the same rate, or even retain the staff they have recruited. Given the potential of the new technology there is at least the possibility that any future growth in markets will be covered without employing more people – in other words 'jobless growth'.

The implications are that while new technology may not have caused unemployment, future growth in demand may well be met without increasing the numbers employed. While agriculture provides the classic example, there are others – car manufacturing and the steel industry are but two.

The significance of this situation is that, in a democratic society in which work has the social role discussed in Chapter 3, an important individual right must be that of access to capital – in other words, a job. The ability to participate fully in a society which is geared to and legitimated by the increasing consumption of material products, requires some minimum level of income – which suggests the importance of a right to a revenue. This is the problem that underlies policies designed to price people into jobs by administering minimal benefits on the basis of an obligation to take any job, or be immediately available for a job.

impact of modern technology on both the service and manufacturing sectors. This is explained in Case Study 9.2.

People who are unemployed are in effect excluded from participation in society even if only in the sense that the legitimation of their share of the surplus in the form of benefits is problematic. The effect of a means tested benefit system is to question constantly the legitimacy of the benefits received by those in need. The question of legitimacy is constantly kept in the forefront of the public consciousness – both for those in receipt of benefits and those who are not themselves in receipt but may be considered as 'paying' for the benefits others receive.

To be in receipt of 'charity' inevitably divides society into three major groupings: those who give to charity, those who are considered deserving of charity and those who are not considered deserving of charity. In this way society is stratified in terms of the deserving poor, the undeserving poor, and those whose wealth is considered to impose an obligation of aiding the deserving poor.

Access to capital

In contemporary industrial societies work is a major factor in the day-to-day experience of 'democracy'. If an industrial society wishes to maintain the claim to be a democracy, then one of the major features it will have to present is the availability of work to all. Such work will require features which enable the indiviual to play a full role in society. One way of expressing this is to assert the 'right to work' or the 'right to a job'. In the context of the nature of property, this can be reformulated as the 'right of access of capital'. If a person cannot mix their labour with capital for the purpose of earning an income (i.e. revenue), then property rights in labour are of very little use.

The right to a revenue

A formulation of a currently relevant definition of democracy is then one which emphasizes an individual's 'right to a revenue'. By virtue of being a member of society every citizen should be entitled to a revenue, derived from the surplus arising from the operation of the national economy. This revenue enables them to participate in society as full members. This implies that not only must there be a right to receive a revenue, but that such a right is to be regarded as legitimate.

What is implied here is that, for a society to retain the democratic label, the notion of property has once again to emphasize rights of access (to capital), and rights to revenue (income). Only in this way will all citizens be able to participate fully in industrial society.

The problem for contemporary democratic industrial societies arises from the fact that their continued survival and development both as industrial societies and as democracies requires that a new method of distributing the surplus created by economic activity be developed. Failure to do so will result in a significant proportion of the population being excluded from participating in society. This will have inevitable consequences for social order as it will call into question the relevance, for that proportion of the population who are excluded at least, of democratic values. This will have severe consequences for those responsible for maintaining social order.

A wider distribution of ownership

Spreading more widely the ownership of the productive capital present in society would be a means of securing the basic standard of living for all. This proposal, focusing on the need for a truly contemporary notion of property which emphasizes rights of access to capital and the right to a revenue in a democratic society, echoes Macpherson. Brittan (1986) a respected liberal economist and economics editor of the Financial Times, has argued against the privatization of public sector enterprises such as British Airways, British Gas, British Telecom and British Steel amongst others by means of selling shares. In his scheme, the revenues accruing from the utilization of such assets should be distributed to all members of society simply because they are members. If such a programme were to be followed, the returns from increased productivity would be distributed more widely, rather than only to those who still remained in employment or happened to own shares – as opposed to selling them as soon as possible to realize short-term and relatively small cash profits.

There are many facets to this issue, but it is important to remember that selling shares of nationalized industries and distributing them to those employed in those industries is not what Brittan has in mind. Part of the problem is that shareholdings in such issues tend to be relatively small and soon end up in the hands of large institutions as a result of people taking their profits. Given wide disparities in the size of holdings, is it possible to conclude that the interests of employees as shareholders, and those with much larger holdings who operate in the share markets of the world, are

Let us recapitulate the features of Brittan's suggestion. First, the existence of a surplus of labour, whether brought about by stagnant or slow growing markets or the utilization of modern technology, does not imply that there are no services or products the unemployed could provide. The problem is that many goods and services for which there is a need are not covered by the market system.

Second, even where goods and services are covered by the market system the conditions in the market-place may mean that those able and willing to provide labour cannot find employment at a wage that enables them to meet even modest levels of consumption. Equally, those in employment will resist a cut in pay if that will force them below a commonly accepted standard of living. The result is that the market mechanism is then blocked. The market will not 'clear'. Employers will have unmet demand for labour at the price they are willing to pay, while on the supply side, labour will be on offer at a price above that offered by employers.

Put simply, Brittan's solution is to provide a basic income to all by virtue of being a member of society. As a citizen, each individual will be entitled to a given level of income. This revenue will be derived from the economic activities of private and public enterprises in the same way as wages and salaries are currently, and will protect a basic standard of living for all, 'basic' here being synonymous with 'standard' rather than 'minimal'.

This is an answer to the question asked earlier that if the size of the cake increases, as is the case even in the UK since GNP does increase even if more slowly than in other countries, why should anyone get a smaller slice? Under Brittan's proposal, as the size of the cake increased, so all would get a larger slice. How much bigger the slice was would depend on how much GNP increased. Conversely, if it shrank, then so would all citizens' shares.

Having a protected material standard of living, individuals would then be free to seek additional income in whatever manner was available to them. Those lacking skills which were in demand at any particular time would be able to sell their labour at whatever price they could get for it. Labour markets would clear since those seeking additional income would not be seeking to defend a particular level of wages since their standard of living no longer depended solely on what they could command in the labour market, but was determined by the success of the economy as a whole.

Those who possessed skills much in demand, or who had foregone earnings in order to acquire skills that were in demand, could command higher rates of pay than those lacking such skills. Thus the incentive function of labour prices would still operate. Ambitious people could still work longer and harder than the less ambitious and so earn more, or rise higher, in their chosen activities.

As a liberal economist, Brittan regards this as an acceptable solution since it avoids what he would regard as 'illiberal' interference with the exercise of individual choice. Such interference is implied by policies

CASE STUDY 9.3

THE WIDER OWNERSHIP OF PRODUCTIVE CAPITAL AND THE RIGHT TO A REVENUE

Continued over page

Continued from previous page designed to share out available work by limiting the period over which people are allowed to work. Such policies include those favouring a reduction in the retirement age, for example, or reductions in the hours in the working week, or working weeks in the year (e.g. longer holidays).

Exactly how a system such as that suggested by Brittan would operate in practice is a complex but not necessarily insoluble problem. For example, membership of society – the status of citizen – is already dealt with by means of the franchise. Certain people are entitled to vote in national and local elections while others are not. The right to vote may be forfeited, for example, as the consequence of criminal activity. More arbitrary or contentious methods for defining a citizen operate in matters of nationality and acquisition of passports. In the same way as the PAYE tax code system operates to recognize the responsibilities and demands of the lifecycle (number of dependent children, mortgage, dependent relatives and so on) so basic entitlements to a share of the surplus produced by society could be established.

The point of the discussion of these issues here is not to work out exactly how such a system would operate, but to indicate the kind of problem that modern societies will have to face and how the nature and role of property is involved in any solution.

necessarily the same or even mutually consistent? The implications of Brittan's suggestion are further examined in Case Study 9.3.

Developments in the concept of property

In the remainder of this chapter we will consider a form of the organization and control of work which not only takes account of the type of issues raised by Macpherson and Brittan, but also involves consideration of factors which influence the nature of relationships between management and labour, and the extent to which a workforce may be persuaded to display commitment to the enterprise.

There is an important link here with the material covered in chapters 7 and 8. Lincoln's observations on management (Case Study 8.4 in Chapter 8) are based upon the idea that as human beings, management and workers have very similar concerns and aspirations. What distinguishes them is the extent to which those concerns and aspirations are recognized and achieved. This distinction arises from the operation of a system of property rights which forms the basis of the contract of employment.

The arguments put forward by Macpherson and Brittan presume changes in the nature of property and hence in the nature of the employment contract. It should be remembered that current arrangements concerning the organization and control of work were developed at a particular time in social, economic, technological and legal history. Thus there is nothing inevitable in current arrangements; they could be other than they are. It is likely that current problems will result in changes, so what might the organization and control of work look like in the future?

This is the question that Ouchi and his associates attempted to answer by considering the characteristics of organizations based around the notion of markets, bureaucracies and clans, as discussed in Chapter 8. If one considers this work, plus that of Hirschorn and the problems of obtaining 'consumate cooperation' discussed by Willman, then it becomes apparent that all are implicitly at least addressing the same question – that is the question of motivation and reward discussed in Chapter 7. How should workers be motivated and rewarded to ensure that organizational and individual interests are at least compatible, when such compatibility appears crucial to establishing and maintaining competitive advantage?

In order to develop at least one possible answer to this question, we will consider an extant example of an alternative method for organizing and controlling work, a method that does not rely upon private property rights, which distinguishes between the ownership of scarce resources and the exercise of control, and which sets out to involve all who are employed in the enterprise in the process of creating and distributing a surplus for the benefit of the community as a whole. This example, based upon ideas originating with the founders of the cooperative movement in Rochdale in 1844, forms the subject of the remainder of this chapter and focuses on the cooperative enterprises engaged in manufacturing, retailing, banking, education, research and housing which are centred upon the town of Mondragon in the Basque region of northern Spain.

Issues in the debate on cooperatives

The debate over the economic effectiveness of cooperatives has received considerable attention over the years. The major issues of the debate are centred around the question as to which of a number of alternative forms of ownership are likely to be most effective in increasing employment, efficiency and investment. Implicit in the debate is the question of whether the real problem is the rate at which wealth is created, or whether the problem is really about the way wealth is distributed. Is the problem the size of the cake and the way it is growing, or is it about the way the cake is sliced up? This is not the place to engage in a detailed analysis of wealth and income distribution, but it is necessary to identify one or two features of the debate.

Citizens as workers

Interest in the relative effectiveness of differing forms of ownership and control derives from the contrast between the rights of workers in a capitalist enterprise in comparison with their rights as citizens outside the enterprise. Interest in industrial democracy and worker participation has been sustained by concern over the mismatch between the internal and external power structures with which enterprises have to cope. This issue is at the centre of the dispute over the European Commission's proposals for workers rights to information (known as the Vredeling proposals after the

Commissioner who was responsible for formulating them) and the current debate over the Social Charter associated with the establishment of the Single European Market. The result has been to create a perceived need to develop some form of arrangement which will enhance the compatibility of the objectives of labour and capital. It is hoped to reduce, even if not entirely eradicate, perceived differences in interest between management, workers and shareholders.

All sides in the debate, labour and capital and their representatives, express the view that 'participation' is a 'good thing'. Disagreements centre around the form that participation should take and how it should be demarcated. Since all sides agree that increased participation is desirable, there is the need to ensure that all concerned are in fact talking about the same thing.

'Participation' and 'democracy' are rather vague concepts. They are 'motherhood' concepts because almost everyone expresses favourable views about them, without necessarily being able to specify precisely (and unanimously!) what defines them. It is the shared quality of vagueness, of indefinability, that renders the debate more fraught than would otherwise be the case. Can we be sure that all parties actually mean the same thing when they assert the desirability of 'participation', of 'consulation' and 'industrial democracy'?

Consider for a moment the right to be consulted. What can this mean? What expectations could be raised among members of the two groups (or more) that may be involved? Does it mean that management will not only inform the work group of what is going on but also seek their comments? Does it mean that such comments will be allowed to influence the decision-making process and outcome? Does it mean that those whose views are sought have a role in the actual decision-making process itself, other than simply submitting views? There is also the question of whether the process should be supported by statutory structures and rights (as in Germany for example), or should it be left to the goodwill of enlightened management as is thought appropriate in the UK?

Questions such as these indicate quite clearly the significance of the issue of control, especially in the case of the UK where labour has no constitutional right to strike (even a 'legal' strike involves a breach of the employment contract by strikers who are therefore liable to dismissal), or to information about management's intentions. Management may wish to establish what the views of employees are but ultimately it is they, management, who are held responsible and hence are held to have the right to exercise control – they have the final say.

Jarasalav Vanek (1975), who investigated the operation of the Yugoslavian system of workers management in the 1970s, categorizes socioeconomic systems in terms of two criteria: 'control' and 'ownership'. The question of control, what Vanek regards as the 'first-order distinction', addresses the issue of whether or not those who work in the enterprise exercise rights of control over it. If they do, then this would be an example of the 'self-managed' enterprise. The 'second-order' distinction concerns the question of capital ownership and Vanek suggests eight types ranging from the state through to private ownership as set out in Table 9.1.

From these distinctions derive at least four distinct types of organization

Table 9.1 Vanek's ownership types

1. State
2. National
3. Collective
   — Involving all participants
   — Involving some participants
4. Individual
   — Involving all participants
   — Involving some participants
5. Consumers or users
6. Labour union
7. Suppliers
8. Private

There is a distinction, generally regarded as crucial, between:

☐ labour-managed organizations, and
☐ worker-managed organizations.

Labour management occurs where working people regard the means of production as capital that belongs to society. For the use of this 'capital' they pay a scarcity rent. Worker management on the other hand is where the means of production are recognized as belonging to society, but workers do not have to pay a scarcity rent.

Worker-managed enterprises are found in Yugoslavia. Many of the problems associated with this form in the Yugoslavian experience arise, Vanek (1977) argues, because of the failure to develop fully fledged labour management, because of the impact forms of ownership and control have on decision-making. Put simply, it is generally asserted that workers' decision-making in non-capitalist owned or controlled enterprises will centre on maximizing the returns to those working in the enterprise and this may result in sub-optimal decisions for wider society. The likely danger is that workers will be tempted to appropriate a disproportionate share of any surplus to the detriment of future investment and the wider interests of society, which is what is argued to have happened in Yugoslavia.

There is also the distinction between:

☐ consumer cooperatives, and
☐ producer cooperatives.

The former are the most widely known in the UK and derive from the activities of the so-called Rochdale Pioneers. Producer cooperatives are less well established on any scale in the UK, though their numbers are growing. The issue of their effectiveness is tied up with the sceptical appraisal of the original Rochdale development, the efforts of Robert Owen centred on New Lanark, and more recent efforts during Wedgewood Benn's tenure as Minister for Trade and Industry which were criticized as 'social engineering'.

KEY CONCEPT 9.4

ALTERNATIVES TO CAPITALIST ENTERPRISES

which should be noted in the context of alternatives to capitalistic enterprises. These are set out in Key Concept 9.4.

Scepticism regarding cooperatives

The scepticism with which producer cooperatives are viewed in the UK is largely centred on questions concerning their profitability. This in turn derives from assumptions about the impact on decision-making if the rigours of a capital market are inoperative or ignored. In particular there is concern that cooperatives (where the enterprise is worker-managed and controlled) cannot overcome the 'free-rider' problem as effectively as capitalist enterprises. Raising the necessary capital for expansion or intial start-ups is difficult. However, it is perhaps worth observing that while the relative rarity, and small size, of producer cooperatives is put down to doubts about profitability and fund-raising, banks in capitalist societies do lend to nations with non- or even anti-capitalist ideologies, and profession-al partnerships of solicitors, accountants and architects can in fact be viewed as cooperatives (see the law volume in this series for the elaboration of forms of ownership available to enterprises in the UK).

Before going on to discuss the structure of the cooperatives of Mondragon as illustrative of an alternative method of organizing and controlling work, it is worth emphasizing that the significance of their existence and success is due to their relevance for two related issues in capitalist democracies at the present time.

These issues are, first, can efficiency and equity can be combined? Is it possible to have a system which is both efficient and equitable in the eyes of all those involved? It is certainly possible to have an enterprise that is efficient but not equitable, and one that is equitable but not efficient. The trick is to achieve high scores on both dimensions!

This is turn relates to the second issue, that of the problem of control. Can control be exercised in a way which allows full commitment on the part of those at all levels in the enterprise? If all are to commit themselves to the aims of the enterprise then there has to be some symbiosis between the interests of the enterprise and of those working in it. This implies some modification of control processes both vertically and horizontally.

'Consumate cooperation' requires that a workforce not only has some control over work processes but are also perceived to have some legitimate influence on the decision-making processes of management. Fundamental-ly, the question can be phrased as follows; 'Should the ownership of capital carry an entitlement to the receipt of a scarcity price only (i.e. interest), or should it also imply control?' It is to this question that the following examination of the Mondragon example is addressed.

The Mondragon cooperatives

Much has been written elsewhere about the origins of the Mondragon cooperatives, and what follows is but a brief account of the background.

The moving spirit behind the formation of the cooperative movement in the Basque region of Spain was the parish priest of Mondragon appointed in 1941, Don José Maria Arizmendi (1915–1976). He had entered a junior seminary in 1927, and interrupted his studies to act as a Basque army journalist and newspaper editor during the Spanish Civil War. He narrowly escaped execution for rebellion after being captured by Franco's forces and returned to the seminary to complete his studies. He was ordained in 1941 and spent the rest of his life working in Mondragon.

Arizmendi's work among the youth of Mondragon started when he took up teaching in the apprentice school of the main industrial company in the town. Attempts to persuade the management to increase the intake of students by enrolling others in addition to the sons of employees failed despite the fact that Arizmendi himself offered to raise the necessary funds. His concern for the whole community, as parish priest, resulted in a proposal to establish a technical school and he sought support from the local population. Some 10 per cent indicated support, including local firms, and twenty students were enrolled in 1943.

After graduation in 1947, eleven of these twenty students went on to further studies in the evenings at the Zaragoza School of Engineering while working during the day. Two years after graduating from Zaragoza, five of the eleven set up a limited company in 1954 which purchased a small workshop and a manufacturing licence for a paraffin cooking stove. After careful examination of the laws governing the establishment and operation of cooperatives in Spain over a two-year period, the original company known as ULGOR (from the intial letters of the names of the five founders) was reorganized as an industrial cooperative.

Arizmendi also made a close investigation of the factors which appeared to have resulted in the eventual failure of the original enterprise established by the founders of the cooperative movement in Britain, the so-called Rochdale Pioneers of 1844. Arizmendi was determined to avoid the mistakes made by the Pioneers in allowing those who invested in their cooperative, but who were not members, to exercise control rather than simply receive a scarcity price for their capital.

It is important to note that the motivation behind this project was social and political – a desire to develop a relatively deprived region that had suffered under the impact of the Franco regime, and to put into practice a set of ideas relating to the relationship between labour and capital. Social concerns, especially to create employment and reduce poverty, and the need to develop education and training, were paramount. Such concerns are the motivation behind the continued development of the cooperatives to this day, and represent the interaction of the various levels in the business in context model which informs this and the other volumes in the Business in Context series.

The structure of the Modragon cooperative is explained in Case Study 9.4. Membership of the Modragon cooperative system grew steadily during the 1970s to just over eighteen thousand in 1979 and to approximately twenty thousand by 1986/7. New cooperatives are created at an average rate of four per year, though the general impact of the world economy affects this figure. Sales increased tenfold over the decade 1972–83 from ten million pesetas to one hundred and nine million, of which 22% were exports.

The original enterprise, ULGOR, is now known by its trademark of

CASE STUDY 9.4

THE STRUCTURE AND OPERATION OF THE MONDRAGON COOPERATIVE SYSTEM

The contract of association, which is the basic document establishing a cooperative, covers five principles which underlie the Mondragon movement:

☐ Employment creation
☐ Capital ownership
☐ Earnings differentials
☐ Distribution of the surplus
☐ Democratic organization

These principles must be adhered to if those wishing to establish a cooperative wish to receive managerial, consultancy and financial support from the Caja Laboral Popular Savings Bank.

New members pay 800 000 pesetas to join. This entry fee can be paid over a two-year period, with 25% down-payment. Of this, 15% is allocated to the Cooperative's Reserves, 85% is allocated to the individual's capital account, as is the individual's share of the annual surplus or loss. Members are paid interest on their capital accounts at a rate no more than 3% above that operating for inter-bank loans.

Cooperators cannot realize the balance on their capital accounts, but the balance must be paid out within two years of retirement. Individuals who voluntarily leave a cooparative enterprise may forfeit up to 30% of their accumulated balance on capital account. This is discretionary and only likely to be imposed if the withdrawal of funds is likely to damage the enterprise.

While Cooperatives offer no guarantee of secure employment, the emphasis on job creation of the movement ensures that any adjustment that takes place as a result of product market conditions will not be through redundancies. Either new cooperative enterprises will be formed, or members will be redeployed to other enterprises. If neither of these possibilities are available, cooperators receive 'unemployment' pay of 80% of their salary for two years to assist in finding alternative employment. If this is not possible, they are assured of being reabsorbed. Bradley and Gelb (1987) suggest that structural unemployment is about 1%.

Initial responses to unfavourable market conditions are based upon resort to the reserves of the enterprise. If the situation continues, then pay will be reduced. But remember that all these decisions will require the approval of all members through the General Assembly, and will affect individual members in proportion to the salary differential. In other words, the response to market fluctuation will involve all members of the cooperative in proportion to their pay rate, and on the 'one person, one vote' procedure of the General Assembly. 'Since cooperateurs combine the labour and capital components of their enterprises and experience no informational assymetry, the wage-surplus decision is simultaneous. A cooperative can therefore be considered to operate as a single factor decision maker, whereas adjustment in the mixed economy is a dynamic game between capital and labour groups characterised by asymmetric information and low trust' (Bradley and Gelb, 1987, p.82).

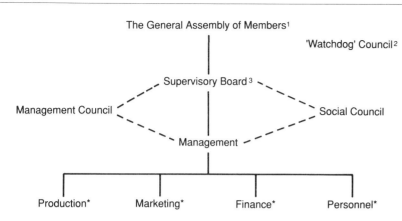

Figure 9.2 The structure of a Mondragon cooperative.

The structure of a Mondragon cooperative is outlined in Figure 9.2. Those labelled 1–3 are mandatory bodies under Spanish cooperative law, while those marked with an asterisk are for illustrative purposes only and do not indicate the actual organization of any particular enterprise. The main bodies are discussed further below.

☐ **General Assembly:** Meets at least once a year to examine and approve the accounts for the past financial year. Considers modifications to, or creation of, the rules for administering the cooperative. Each member of the cooperative has one vote.

☐ **Supervisory Board:** Consists of nine elected members and meets once a month. The chair of the Supervisory Board is the legal representative of the cooperative. Each member is elected for four years and half the membership stand down every two years. The management is appointed by the Supervisory Board and may attend Board meetings and take part in them, but they do not have a vote.

☐ **Management:** Has the executive function of running the cooperative. Responsible and accountable to the Supervisory Board and through the Board to the cooperators in General Assembly. Management's authority is derived from their ability to run the enterprise successfully, and from their demonstrated commitment to the values of cooperativism. Managers are appointed for a minimum of four years and can only be dismissed as a result of serious fault identified by the Supervisory Board. Their dismissal has to be sanctioned by the General Assembly. Management select candidates for subordinate roles.

☐ **Management Council:** This is an advisory and consultative body that meets at least once a month. Membership is made up of management and senior executives (heads of departments) plus outsiders who may be contracted for special experience and skills.

☐ **Social Council:** Representatives are elected for three years by workers at section level, with one-third stepping down each year. Each section representative is required to hold weekly meetings with his or her section. Once a quarter there is a general plenary session. The decisions of the Social Council are binding in such matters as:

Continued over page

Continued from previous page

— accident prevention;
— social security issues;
— wage levels;
— administration of the Social Fund;
— welfare payments.
☐ **'Watchdog' Council:** This body exists for the purpose of controlling and inspecting the conduct of management, Supervisory Board, and the Social Council. Comprises three members elected by the General Assembly for four years. It may seek expert advice from outside the cooperative.

FAGOR, and employs 6000 people in thirteen enterprises organized into three divisions: domestic electrical appliances, industrial components ranging from car parts to electronic equipment, and engineering and capital goods, including advanced production systems. It is the largest producer and exporter of domestic products in Spain with annual sales in 1986 of £246 million (*Financial Times*, 17 December 1986).

By 1983 the Mondragon cooperative group comprised a number of 'second-degree' cooperatives in association with 163 'first-degree' cooperatives. (A second-degree cooperative is one which comprises not only those working in it, but also has represented on the governing body other cooperative enterprises.) The first second-degree enterprise to be established was a savings bank in 1959, the Caja Laboral Popular – The Peoples' Savings Bank. Independent cooperative enterprises collaborated with each other to form this organization and are associated in turn with the bank through a Contract of Association. In 1983, 164 first-degree cooperatives

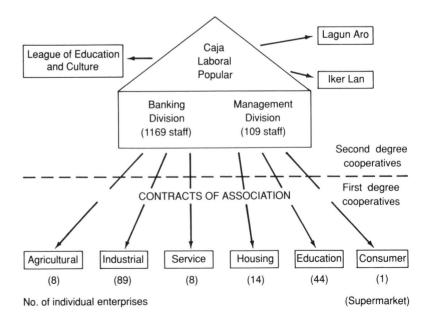

Figure 9.3 The structure of the Mondragon Group.

were linked in this way to the CLP. These were active in the areas indicated in Figure 9.3.

The function of the CLP was to act as a channel for the savings of the local population to be invested in established enterprises via loans, as well as to be available for newly created cooperatives. The commitment of local people to the Mondragon philosophy can be judged by the fact that in 1983 the banking division employed 1169 staff in 132 branches handling half a million accounts worth £435 million.

In addition to providing financial services to the cooperatives, the CLP also provides technical and social assistance. The management division of the bank provides technical and managerial assistance to existing and proposed cooperatives. The organization of the 109 staff of the Management Division is shown in Figure 9.4. They carry out specialized work including advising on, and executing, product promotion and the preparation of feasibility studies for new cooperatives.

The social assistance division of the CLP works closely with another second-degree cooperative, Lagun Aro, which concentrates on providing a social security and health care system. Cooperators are regarded as self-employed by Spanish law and so unable to benefit under the Spanish state social security system.

In addition to the CLP and Lagun Aro, two other second-degree enterprises operate: the League of Education and Culture which is concerned with schooling (43 cooperatives), and Iker Lan which functions as an extension of the educational effort by carrying out technological research for associated enterprises. There are also fourteen housing cooperatives.

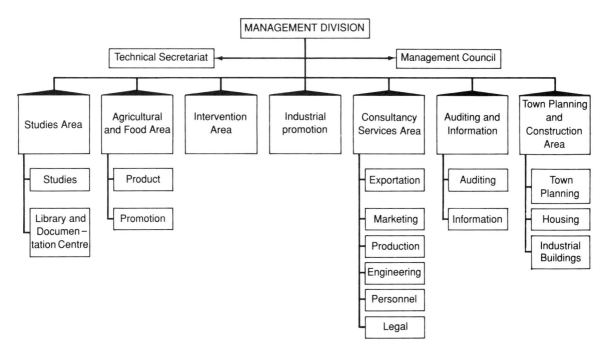

Figure 9.4 The structure of the Management Division of the Caja Laboral Popular.

For detailed, though by now dated, accounts of the operation of the CLP consult Thomas and Logan (1982).

The significance of Mondragon

So far we have merely **described** the organization of the Mondragon cooperatives and not provided any idea of how, or why, they work. The point of discussing the cooperatives is to illustrate an alternative form of organizing and controlling work to that found in capitalist enterprises. This is relevant since much effort is expended by management in capitalist enterprises in order to gain the willing and wholehearted cooperation of their employees, particularly at times of economic difficulty.

This effort concentrates on encouraging employees to see their interests as consistent with those of the organization. To develop this perception, management attempt to encourage workers to participate more fully. This is assumed to imply not only the establishment of channels of communication, but also the development of payment systems that more readily reflect the success – or relative failure – of the company via the pay-packets of those employed.

In the following paragraphs consideration is given to factors which might be considered important in the operation and success of the Mondragon cooperatives in terms of worker involvement and commitment.

Job creation

It has already been stated that the original objectives of the founders were social, political and economic. Job creation was one of their primary concerns and this is still the main item in the articles of association of any cooperative. Decisions at the micro- and macrolevel are still debated with this objective in mind. The socio-political objectives of the movement are, in part at least, motivated by feelings and philosophies shaped by the experience of the region economically and politically. As a culturally and linguistically distinctive group in Spain, the Basques have been engaged in a long struggle to maintain their identity, which has brought them into conflict with the central government in Madrid over many years. The confrontation was particularly difficult during the years of the Franco dictatorship and a reliance upon self-help based upon their own resources underlies the Mondragon experience. This reliance is fostered by a combination of political, economic, social, cultural and linguistic features which distinguishes the Basque region from the rest of Spain, let alone other parts of Europe.

The manifestation of these aspects of Basque experience is not only visible in the provisions of the Contract of Association, but also in the criteria adopted when recruiting new members. Not only are skill and educational qualifications sought, but so also is a demonstrable commitment to the ideals of the cooperative movement. New entrants have to demonstrate their social and ideological suitability (i.e. their acceptability) for employment. A six-month probationary period is served in which the individual is assessed for his or her suitability for membership of the enterprise.

In some ways this approach is not so dissimilar from that adopted by capitalist employers who are anxious to employ people upon whose loyalty they can rely. However, what is significantly different can perhaps be perceived most clearly in the attitude towards remuneration in the cooperatives and in the manner in which any surplus or loss is distributed.

Distribution of the surplus

Any surplus is distributed to three sets of accounts or funds:

☐ The Social Fund is, in accordance with Spanish cooperative law, credited with a minimum of 10% of any surplus.
☐ Reserves are credited with normally 20% of any surplus, but a feature of the formula used is that this percentage figure rises as the surplus grows.
☐ The remainder is distributed to the capital accounts of the cooperative members. Members receive interest on their accounts at a rate which cannot exceed 3% above the inter-bank base rate.

The distribution to individual accounts is in proportion to members' relative rates of pay which ensures that the wealth created is distributed on the same basis as pay – see Figure 9.5.

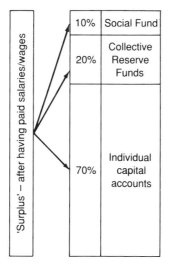

Figure 9.5 Distribution of surplus.

Pay relativities and pay as a share of the surplus

A key feature is that pay differentials are limited so that the highest paid member earns no more than three to four and a half times the lowest paid, and that pay rate is set at an average of the rate for the job in the region. The result of this distribution is that whilst workers are relatively well paid, those occupying management positions earn about half what they could earn outside the cooperative movement.

More important still than the ratio of highest to lowest rates of pay is that the pay of all members is regarded as an advance out of an anticipated surplus. Wages and salaries are not therefore regarded as a cost as they are in coventional profit and loss accounts. Consequently pay is not amongst those items to be minimized. Instead, being seen as a share of the surplus, pay becomes something any one would wish to see increased even if not maximized.

The effect of the formulae used for the distribution of the surplus means that around 90% of any surplus remains in the enterprise since it is distributed to the Reserve Fund and individual capital accounts. The significance of this for cash flow can be appreciated when one recalls that the payment of dividends, plus the tax due on them, can represent a severe strain on the cash funds of capitalist enterprises under pressure to maintain dividends in the interests of maintaining share price while at the same time making investments in technology and product development to ensure long-term survival.

The distribution of losses

Another crucial feature of the system is that losses are distributed according to a similar formula to that used for surpluses. The effect is to ensure that a distinction between management and non-management employees is not institutionalized in terms of income and wealth distribution since any 'failure' on the part of management in terms of the eventual level of surplus, i.e. a loss, can result in a manager's personal account being debited with three times (or more) the proportion of the loss that is born by non-managerial cooperators. It can be appreciated that the system operated by the Mondragon cooperatives achieves some of the objectives at the centre of the discussion over two-tier payment systems and profit-sharing discussed in Chapter 7.

Ownership v. control

The hiring of outside, i.e. non-cooperative, labour is minimal in the Mondragon case, though the going market rates will be paid for the acquisition of the services of individuals possessing scarce skills. Such people, however, will not be members of the cooperative in any way. Neither will those who merely lend funds to the enterprise. Those who invest in the enterprise by way of loans will simply receive interest on their loan. There is a recognized distinction between ownership of capital (financial or intellectual) and the right to exercise control. Capital, or the posession of a skill in short supply, merely entitles the individual to receive a scarcity price and implies no control prerogatives at all.

Does it work?

The most recent examination of the record of the Mondragon cooperatives to hand is that carried out by Bradley and Gelb (1987). The following comments draw on that article which takes the story on from 1979 which was the date at which previous English language accounts stopped. The significance of this date is that from the late 1970s the Spanish economy experienced a period of stagflation after having grown considerably since the 1960s.

One indication of the achievements of the cooperatives in terms of their major objective of job creation is that had cooperative membership fallen in line with employment in the region as a whole over the period 1976–83, membership would have been only 69% of its actual level in 1983.

On pay levels, the comparison does not appear quite so favourable since after rising faster than in the economy as a whole up to 1979, pay rates have fallen rapidly since then and the adjusted rates for the cooperatives is now some three index points below the national level. Adjustments have taken the form of reducing the actual rates of pay in member enterprises in relation to a scale established by the CLP. Variation across the group is now, according to Bradley and Gelb, between 80 and 110% of the CLP scale. This variation allows for differing rates of surplus creation, and the exact percentage of the CLP rate to be paid is determined by the General Assembly of each enterprise.

It should be noted that these adjustments in pay occurred in a system in which all, including management, were affected and in which differentials remained stable. Also, the capital accounts were at least protected in so far as reserves bear the initial impact of any loss. In one case, a cooperative initiated an 11% pay-cut which was effected by capitalizing two months' pay. That is, instead of paying out cash to cooperators, their capital accounts were credited with an equivalent amount.

While there are examples of workforces, both union and non-union, in capitalist enterprises accepting pay-cuts during periods of economic difficulty for the employer, the situation in the majority of capitalist enterprises is one where hourly paid staff bear the brunt of any deterioration in the market environment. Often this is because shift premiums, overtime and piece-rates make up a considerably greater proportion of hourly paid incomes than they do of salaries. A willingness to take a cut in pay is obviously facilitated when the reward system automatically feeds any improvement in the financial health of the enterprise into the accounts of the employees as a matter of course, and when all employees, including management, are affected in the same way.

It should be remembered that when the management group of a cooperative enterprise recommend some reduction in the amount paid as wages, not only does this proposal have to be agreed by the General Assembly, but it is a proposal which directly affects management's pay as well. Consistent with the philosophy set out by Hewlett-Packard (see Table 8.4), that company responded to a decline in market fortunes some years ago by requiring **all** employees (including management) to take two weeks' unpaid leave and stopped the provision of free coffee and biscuits! This was tolerated because of the confidence that **all** were hit equally, and because of confidence that when fortune smiled again **all** would benefit.

The speed and cost of adjustment

Bradley and Gelb (1979) suggest that the institutional arrangements of a cooperative enterprise enables it to adjust to adverse market situations with a time lag of not much more than one year. In the case of a capitalist enterprise, they suggest, the time lag may be from three to six years. This relates directly to the argument that Willman makes in his examination of institutional labour market factors and their impact on adaptation. Not only are cooperatives able to respond more quickly to adverse conditions, they can probably do so more cheaply as well.

Such rapidity of response may well be significant in the profitability performance of the cooperatives in comparison with that of the Basque or national economy. Profit rates in the Basque region declined below zero in 1976, a point not reached by the cooperatives until 1980, and reached a nadir of minus 11% in 1980 and rose to minus 9% in 1983. The cooperatives on the other hand saw their net surplus, after deductions of payments to internal capital, decline to minus 7% in 1981 and projected a return to breakeven in 1984.

All of this is not to say that the movement in Mondragon has had an easy ride or is without serious problems – far from it. Considerable effort has been expended in adapting the system to cope with adverse changes in the national and global economy in a manner consistent with the social and economic aims of the cooperators. Difficulties also arise from the need to invest in new technology, and to cope with the demographically induced rate at which cooperators will be retiring over the next decade or two. This will have major implications for the capitalization of the enterprises as the withdrawal of accrued savings on capital accounts takes place. This particular problem is already being worked on, and schemes are being developed which are consistent with Spanish law on cooperatives as well as with the interests of retired and existing members.

Is the Mondragon system transferable?

It should be stressed that the purpose of discussing the Mondragon example was to illustrate **one** alternative way of organizing and controlling work that appears to meet many of the objectives of writers in the UK and USA who urge the necessity for new forms of organizing and controlling work. Again, many of the advantages in terms of employee commitment which appear to operate in systems like Mondragon may operate in countries like Germany where the legal framework governing employment and company structures (to be discussed in Chapter 10) serves to create an atmosphere of common interest and security.

It is not suggested that the Mondragon system can be simply or easily transferred. Social, ethnic and ideological factors are important in explaining the success of the system, and in influencing the acceptability of such a system in other countries or regions. However, the system does illustrate that alternative means of organizing and controlling work do exist, and do involve important modifications of private property to emphasize rights of access to capital and the right to a revenue.

Summary

In this chapter we have examined two fundamentally different approaches to the basis upon which work is or could be organized and controlled. These approaches are, first, that based upon the notion of the exclusive and alienable rights of private property, and, second, the idea of property based upon the rights of access – the right not to be excluded – associated with cooperatives and any serious examination of meaningful participation in the running of the workplace. This examination has been undertaken in order to illustrate the way in which ideas about the organization and control of work can influence perceptions, and hence behaviour, of those who are controlled and those who do the controlling. This chapter should be read in conjunction with the ideas on management set out by J.F. Lincoln and which were detailed in Case Study 8.4.

The contents of this chapter are to be considered in the context of attempts by managers to encourage the workforce to take an active interest in the progress of their employing enterprises.

Upon what basis can people be expected to commit themselves to employing organizations? Is it reasonable to expect people dependent upon one employing organization for their daily livelihood to invest a proportion of earned income in that enterprise? Upon what basis may a workforce come to see increased profits as directly benefiting them? To what extent may it be argued that increased participation and involvement in the enterprise can only be assured if those expected to invest can exercise some control? Should employees be equated with shareholders in this respect? After all shareholders are not noted for their long-term commitment.

These are all questions which are fundamental to any serious attempt to increase the degree to which employees may participate in the management and control of employing organizations. Failure to consider these questions is likely to produce a cynical response to exhortations of management and politicians concerning 'participation'. There is a very real sense in which the term 'industrial democracy' is meaningless if the nature of property is ignored. What could industrial 'democracy' mean when the ruling notion of property is one centred on private property defined in terms of an exclusive, alienable right to exclude others?

A possible, and particular, answer to these questions was suggested by the examination of the Mondragon cooperatives. These organizations have to compete in a capitalist world with capitalist organisations. In so far as they have been able to do this with some success it suggests that there is at least one alternative to current ideas about the organization and control of work. In so far as these cooperatives have been successful, that success also offers some indication of what is required if employees are to perceive their interests as being met by, and identifiable with, the interests of the organization and its management.

It is important to note that it is not being suggested that the Mondragon experience suggests **the** answer to the problems of establishing 'consumate cooperation' on the part of the workforce, only that it suggests **an** answer. What makes it interesting is that it appears consistent with the ideas of writers as different in their outlooks and beliefs as Macpherson and Brittan. In addition, the view of wages or salaries as an advance payment of a share of the surplus radically alters the way in which cost reduction exercises operate. As we stated earlier, costs for any social enterprise in any situation of human development are to be minimized; surpluses are something all wish to see grow **if** it is perceived that the benefit flowing from that growth will be widely available.

This chapter has attempted to illustrate the way in which notions taken for granted like 'property' and 'organization' can mould the behaviour of individuals and groups. In order to understand social behaviour it is necessary to understand how such notions and assumptions can operate to produce such a regularity in behaviour that people, as individuals and as members of groups, come to be seen as acting in a consciously malevolent and obstructive way.

In the next chapter attention will turn to other examples which are accorded considerable significance because of the impression that somehow they have solved the problem of engaging workers' interests in the enterprise and its future. In the context of this chapter and the discussion of Mondragon, it is worth noting that in the case of Germany workers not only have a constitutional right to withdraw their labour (i.e. to go on strike), they also have rights regarding access to information and involvement in decision-making. These matters will be discussed in more detail in the next chapter. The question of what can be learnt by British managers from their peers in Germany and Japan will be examined not only to identify any specific answers, but also to illustrate the factors to be considered when making comparisons between societies.

Study questions

As individuals, or in groups, sketch out the requirements for a system of allocating a revenue derived from the productive potential of a society to each member of that society. Consider how membership is to be determined; what services would be provided individually or by the state/local authorities; how different needs would be catered for; and so on. **Do not** simply ascribe features of the present system as being due to or derived from 'human nature'!

Once you have sketched out the requirements, **then** you can debate whether you would prefer one or another of the proposed systems the groups have developed, or stick with the system that centres on the contemporary social role of work.

The exercise would require that you address, and therefore be clear about, the following questions:

1. What is the basis of the distinction between 'private' and 'public' property?
2. Of what significance is the distinction developed in 1 to contemporary industrial society?
3. Should the ownership of capital, or the possession of scarce skills, entail a right of control rather than simply a right to a scarcity price?
4. In the light of the discussion of payment systems and organization structure in Chapters 6 and 7, and the discussion about property and the Mondragon example in this chapter, how might 'consumate cooperation' be achieved?

Further reading and references

For a discussion on the role of property and ownership in England, and the differences between England and other European countries preceding the Industrial Revolution see:

Macfarlane, A. (1978) *The Origins of English Individualism*. Blackwell.
Macpherson, C.B. (1973) *Democratic Theory*: *Essays in Retrieval*. Oxford
    University Press.

The second contains the essay A Political Theory of Property upon which
the first half of this chapter relies. Also included, and of relevance to the
debate are essays entitled: Democratic Theory: Ontology and Technology
and Elegant Tombstones: A Note on Friedman's Freedom.

Samuel Brittan's ideas have been set out in a number of articles in *The
Financial Times* over the years, e.g. 'There Must Be a Better Way',
Financial Times, 20 November 1986, and are also presented in:

Brittan, S. (1985) *Two Cheers for Self-Interest*, The Sixteenth Wincott
    Memorial Lecture, Occasional Paper 73, Institute of Economic Affairs.
Brittan, S. (1987) *The Role and Limits of Government*. Temple Smith.

The account of the Mondragon cooperatives relied upon the following
sources:

Bradley, K. and Gelb, A.H. (1983) *Cooperation at Work*: *The Mondragon
    Experience*. Heinemann.
Bradley, K. and Gelb, A.H. (1987) Cooperative labour relations: Mon-
    dragon's response to recession. *British Journal of Industrial Relations*, **25**
    (1), 77–98.
Thomas, H. and Logan, C. (1981) *Mondragon*: *An Economic Analysis*.
    Allen & Unwin.

Further discussion about the issues involved in both cooperative and
labour managed enterprises is to be found in:

Bradley, K. and Gelb, A.H. (1983) *Worker Capitalism*: *The New Industrial
    Relations*. Heinemann and MIT Press.
Thornley, J. (1981) *Worker's Cooperatives*: *Jobs and Dreams*. Heinemann.
Vanek, J. (ed.) (1975) *Self Management*: *The Economic Liberation of
    Man*. Penguin.
Vanek, J. (1977) *The Labour Managed Economy*. Cornell University
    Press.

Also of interest is R. Dore's (1987) article, Citizenship and employment
in an age of high technology, in *British Journal of Industrial Relations*, **25**,
(2), 201–25.

10 International comparisons

In this chapter we will consider what lessons, if any, those engaged in business in the United Kingdom can learn as a result of an examination of the attitudes and behaviour of business people in industrial societies which are major competitors. While economies such as Germany, France, Italy, Sweden and Japan, to name five, have apparently performed better than the United Kingdom, we will limit our examination to just two – Germany and Japan.

Germany and Japan are selected since they are the most frequently quoted when Britain's relative decline as a manufacturing and trading nation is under discussion. The significance of the German case is based upon a number of factors: the recovery experienced by West Germany after 1945 (the original 'economic miracle' of the post Second World War period in Europe and which preceded those of France and Italy); the role that Britain as one of the four victorious occupying powers is assumed to have played in this recovery – particularly in the field of industrial relations; and the fact that the Federal Republic has a population not disproportionately greater than that of the UK.

France, while having a population similar in size to that of the UK, was not as heavily industrialized as either Germany or Britain until sometime after the Second World War. When General de Gaulle came to power in 1958 some 25% of the French population was still engaged in agriculture, while the equivalent British proportion was about 3%.

The case of Sweden is rendered possibly less relevant by the fact that the population is approximately that of Greater London, only about eight million.

Japan's apparently miraculous recovery from the devastation of war, including nuclear weapons, has been even more significant for British sensibilities emphasized by the impact upon major industries such as automobiles, shipbuilding, steel, and electrical and electronic goods. The fact that this economic domination has been achieved by a country with virtually no natural resources and a reputation for following (i.e. copying) rather than innovating has added to the mystique of the Japanese 'miracle'.

America does not figure in this chapter mainly because the United States is the one country to have suffered as badly (relatively) from European and South East Asian or 'Pacific Rim' economies (mainly Germany and

Japan), as the UK. Furthermore, some of the features of British management which can be seen as at least partly responsible for the relatively poor economic performance of British industry – the emphasis on financial techniques and the relative short-term concern with share price and profit for example – are associated with the popularity in the UK of American management methods. In part this is due to the dominance of American management literature in the UK, which in turn is one of the consequences of a shared language and ideology which emphasizes the maximization of shareholders' value.

The impact upon the consciousness of the British public of the rejuvenation of countries like West Germany, Japan, France and Italy has to be seen in the context of the assumptions and perceptions of the British people – or more correctly, the English people – and their political leaders. These assumptions and perceptions not only influence the reactions to the relative performance of competitor economies, but also provide explanations for the turn of events which has resulted in the 'first industrial nation', victor in two world wars, administrator of the largest empire the world has ever seen, and mother of democracy, sinking to a position in the bottom half of the league table of industrial nations.

Relationship to the series' model

By undertaking a comparative exercise of this nature we have arrived at the outer ring of the model of business around which this volume, and the others in the series, are structured. This chapter will be particularly concerned with the impact of social and cultural factors on the way in which business activities are perceived and performed. These factors are important in terms of the way in which labour and technology are related. This relationship is also influenced by the perceived role of the state in the management of an industrial society. The framework which social and cultural factors provide enables people to interpret and make sense of situations and events and so form responses to them.

Readers are reminded that in the introduction to this volume the context in which behaviour in business was to be examined was that of the relative failure of the British economy in terms of the share of world and domestic markets. The point of this chapter is to examine some of the institutional factors which it may be argued facilitate the achievement of 'consumate cooperation' in competitor economies.

Questions of method

Before proceeding to examine what might be considered important differences between, say, British and German or Japanese attitudes to management and managing, it is necessary to enter a caveat or two. If one is hoping to identify causal factors and relationships as a result of comparing two situations, then it is important to recognize that a number of discrete processes may be involved, each with their own methodological difficulties.

Comparing like with like

First, it is necessary to acquire or develop some means of identifying relevant empirical factors which are present in the two situations under study. If one is comparing a British company or industry with an equivalent German or Japanese one, for example, it is necessary to ensure that like is going to be compared with like. Does 'industry' mean the same thing in both cases? Is the degree of integration (vertical and horizontal) comparable? Do we mean 'company' or 'plant'? Are patterns of ownership, control and company structure well enough understood (and so translatable in the linguistic sense) to enable comparisons to be made? At a very basic level, can we identify comparable legal forms available for business enterprises? What are the features of the German equivalent of a 'partnership', of 'private' and 'public' limited companies? Is it possible to make assumptions about the the comparability of size (in terms of numbers employed, for example) of different legal forms in the two countries?

When talking about recruitment, is it possible to make comparisons between the groups that enter straight from school? Are they the same age? Have they studied 'similar' courses? Are 'graduates' comparable in terms of age at graduation and length and breadth of their courses? What proportion of the age group stay at school beyond the minimum leaving age or go on to university?

Relevance

Second, assuming it is possible to clarify meanings to such an extent that comparisons can be made between selected and allegedly similar factors, is it possible to be confident that these factors are indeed relevant for the purposes for which they are required? How could, or would, one know? It may be the case that engineers form a larger proportion of students in higher education in country A compared with country B, but so what? It is perhaps plausible that such a comparison is central to the superior economic performance of country A, but there is the danger that all that will be developed is a simple correlation. This leads to the third problem in comparative analysis: the identification of causal relationships and the nature and direction of chains of causality, as discussed in Chapter 5 where we examined the nature and role of theory for practical action.

Causality

Even if, for example, it has been possible to identify comparable and relevant variables, can it further be assumed that the chain of causation is itself unambiguously direct? This is the same point that was made when discussing the organizational characteristics of successful organizations; are they successful because they have the attributes which can be identified as attaching to them, or do they display those attributes simply because they are successful? How exactly does, say, the proportion of engineers in higher education explain superior economic performance? Or is superior economic performance reflected in the popularity of engineering as an undergraduate subject?

Even if it is reasonable in the light of the available evidence to assert with some confidence that the proportion of engineers is indeed a significant explanatory factor, there is still the question as to how that feature of the educational and industrial life of country A actually came about. Why do so many students opt for engineering? Are the courses intrinsically more exciting than in country B? Why? What sort of students choose engineering, i.e. from what type of social background do engineering students come?

Comparing policies

Similar issues are raised by observed differences in the policies implemented in different countries concerning science, technology, education, vocational training and innovation. The observed discrepancies between sums invested in research and development, for example, do not themselves explain very much. Important questions which have to be answered before conclusions are drawn include: What are the sources of the funds? (Government departments? Individual companies? Trade associations?) What does the term 'research and development' actually mean? For example, does 'R&D' refer to basic or fundamental research associated with the world of science? Or does it in fact mean research into production methods and techniques? What is the significance of military and defence research expenditure for a country's ability to compete in commercial markets?

Equally important are questions relating to the way in which government policies on research, development and the diffusion of innovations are implemented. Is there a state body, a ministry or department of central government that is responsible, or is it assumed that the private sector will develop the necessary procedures, projects and funds through the operation of market forces? What impact do different methods of financing and accounting have for the investment decisions taken by commercial organizations in the areas of training and product or process innovation? For example, in countries where company accounts are used to assist in national planning (as in France, for example), uniform and standardized rules are required, while in the USA and UK company directors are allowed freedom to decide how best to value assets subject to verification by auditors that the result is a 'true and fair' picture of the situation. In countries where representatives of major sources of finance (banks) and shareholder and worker representatives have formal representation on the supervisory board (as in Germany), there is less pressure to produce the kind of detailed information which is characteristic of British and American companies. This is because in such a situation the bulk of those interests entitled to such information are members of the enterprise by virtue of the legislative framework governing membership of two-tier company boards and the rights and duties of worker representatives. This aspect is discussed in more detail when examining the German situation later. Such factors will influence the emphasis that is placed upon profit as opposed to other aspects of the business (see, for example, Raimond, Hinard and Weitkamp, 1988).

A role for culture?

The questions raised in the previous paragraphs lead on to questions concerning the role and nature of cultural factors in the identification and explanation of differences in business behaviour and performance between two countries. A culture is a set of ways of thinking about, and reacting to, events and problems. It provides a framework within which experience of the world – in both physical and social dimensions – can be ordered so as to appear meaningful and amenable to action by individuals or groups. Culture not only tells people what is or is not a problem, it subsequently tells them how to cope with what has been defined as a 'problem'. In developing such a framework, history has a major role. Past experience and the manner in which it was perceived and coped with are powerful influences on the development of coping strategies – for individuals, groups and nations.

It follows that the attempt to carry out a comparative study between different cultures requires some mechanism for translating systems of meaning. It may be obvious that managers from country A react to, say, an unexpected production problem differently from those in country B, but if the observer is also from country B, upon what basis is it possible to assume that while the events are the same in both cultures, e.g. a machine breakdown, the **meaning** for the people involved is also the same or similar? And if they are similar, in what ways are they similar? For example, a machine breakdown in a society where there is strict demarcation between skilled maintenance work and semi-skilled production work may well be interpreted as another example of the detrimental consequence of powerful trade unions and their intransigence over demarcation. In other cases, a breakdown may not have these connotations and so provokes different responses.

Can lessons be learnt from comparisons?

All of these issues combine to throw some doubt on the utility of attempting to identify the lessons that can be learnt, or the practices and techniques transferred, from the experiences of other countries. At the very least, caution should be employed when identifying causes and implementing recommendations following comparative studies.

This is not to say that the comparative exercise is a waste of time – certainly not. Such studies may have the advantage of forcing a re-think of assumptions taken for granted even if relatively little is directly taken over from the country or system that is studied. The study of another system may make possible the identification of alternatives that are available within the observer's own system. Comparative study may so illuminate the seriousness of a situation that the political will and pressure to develop alternatives is encouraged.

The motivation for comparative studies

It is worth considering the motivation which underlies the attempt to identify the sources of economic success of another, particularly a competitor, economy. It is arguable that such motivation has much to do with factors that are rooted in historical and cultural factors.

The 'learn from Germany/Japan' bandwagon owes its growth in part at least to the fact that the success of these economies represents something of an assault upon the sensibilities and self-image of those countries whose business people and politicians (hence their academics and consultants) are most active in the area – Britain and the United States. It is of some importance that while Britain and the USA are the two major industrial economies to have fared the worse in the world economy since the period of the oil price shocks in the 1970s, they are also the two nations who see themselves as enjoying a special relationship in terms of scientific research and discovery, and as the major practitioners and defenders of an economic system argued not only to produce more and better goods than any other, but also to guarantee individual liberties more effectively.

Both countries have a history which is capable of being represented as serving the ends of material well-being **and** individual freedom. In the case of the United Kingdom the relationship has been encouraged by the fact that in two world wars it has been possible to render the processes and outcomes as instances of the 'bulldog' qualities of the English. To be overtaken in one's own game by two nations associated with the most horrific and notorious political parties the modern world has experienced, both of which were forced into unconditional surrender as a result of superior military and social qualities, produces a shocked reaction. 'Where have we gone wrong?' 'Where is, and how can we recreate, the Dunkirk spirit that saw us through the dark days of the blitz?' 'We would have been better off if we'd lost the war!' And so on.

This shock to a historically based self-perception initially produces studied unconcern. After all, the Germans had their manufacturing capacity destroyed by bombing and 'we' had to help them rebuild, thus resulting in more up-to-date equipment and institutions. The Germans are 'naturally' disciplined and amenable to bureaucratic rules. The Japanese only got where they are by copying everybody else's inventions – 'How many Nobel Prizes have **they** won?' 'Its all done by cheap labour.'

This last reaction, combined with ever more intrusive evidence of the superior performance of competitor economies, perhaps leads on to the search for scapegoats in some instances. One example of such scapegoating concentrates on out-of-date trade unions that have undermined the 'balance' of power between themselves and managers, and which demand 'unreasonable' pay increases and refuse necessary changes in work practices. A second example is perhaps the inappropriate educational values and standards affecting our schools. A third may be tax rates that are too high and so stifle innovative and entrepreneurial initiatives, and so on.

While in actual fact such alleged differences do not stand up to close investigation, any or all of these explanations *could* be true. The point is, how would the researcher establish their validity and identify actual causal mechanisms?

The advantage of attempting some comparative investigation may be that at least the result of the effort will establish which, if any, of the proffered explanations are worth following up further and which can safely be dropped straightaway.

Having entered the necessary caveats, we will now proceed with a very short exercise in comparative causation, looking first at Germany and then Japan.

Germany and the United Kingdom

> How can one hope to beat world-class competitors when one is small, has high cost labour, cannot easily lay off workers, enjoys few natural resources, and suffers from high debt ratios and low profit margins?
>
> (Limprecht and Hayes, 1982)

No, this was not written about the United Kingdom, but about West Germany!

What follows is in no way to be seen as a considered attempt to establish why the post Second World War Federal Republic of Germany has been so conspicuously successful in international markets. You will find a list of further reading at the end of the chapter to serve as the basis of such an exercise. What follows is simply an attempt to illustrate some of the material and explanations that have been offered, and are currently viewed as important factors in the relative decline of Britain as a manufacturing economy. It is necessary to bear in mind therefore earlier discussions in this volume concerning the importance of manufacturing industry in economic growth. Remember that what is of interest to us here is the extent to which different institutional and organizational frameworks may influence behaviour in business organizations.

One of the factors most frequently commented upon in explanations of the decline of manufacturing industry in the United Kingdom has been the relatively low status of engineering as an occupation in comparison with law, medicine and accountancy. The result is argued to be that the most gifted individuals, especially those from high status families, or those with status aspirations, opt for the 'City' or gentlemanly professions rather than manufacturing. So even if a career in industry – as opposed to commerce – is chosen, then ambitious young men and women will choose marketing, finance or personnel – not production.

The status of engineers

This issue is of interest for a number of reasons. Concern over it goes back as far as the presumed hey-day of British industrial hegemony before 1850, and is closely associated with the peculiarly Anglo-Saxon meaning associated with 'professionalism' as an indicator of social status.

Engineering was at the centre of developments in the role and significance of the professions for British society. Some engineers could more easily claim, and be accorded, the status of 'gentlemen' since they could claim some association with those who had built and designed fortifications as members of the King's army. Up to 1772 all military engineers, the Royal Engineers, were commissioned officers. Since officers are assumed to be gentlemen, those engaged in constructing civilian projects such as canals, railways, bridges and harbours were anxious to distinguish themselves from their military colleagues while at the same time laying claim to the status of gentleman. This was achieved by adopting the term 'civil' engineer.

When Telford became President in 1820 of the student's discussion group which was to become the Institute of Civil Engineers, he expressed concern over the allegedly low status of the engineer in terms that were not very different from those used by Sir Monty Finniston a hundred and fifty years later.

Mechanical engineers, originally known as 'machine engineers', had a much more difficult job to establish themselves as professional gentlemen, and to some extent appear not to have been anxious to link with the 'civils' via their organization centred in London. The history of engineering in the Royal Navy right up to the first decade of the twentieth century illustrates very well the class implications of the status of mechanical engineering. Engineers were first recognized as an occupational category in the Royal Navy in 1837. They were not commissioned and remained as civilians holding the Queen's Warrant, at this time being ranked below ships carpenters. They achieved commissioned status in 1847, although still as civilians, and were not fully recognized as naval officers with appropriate titles of rank until 1910 (Nicholas, 1988).

This link between class, status and engineering can be related to our examination of Germany by considering features of the English and German languages. Lawrence (1980) and Hutton and Lawrence (1981) offer some insight into the way linguistic factors can be argued to play a part in the status defining role of occupations and activities, as illustrated in Case Study 10.1.

Anglo-Saxon usage contrasts 'arts' and 'science' in a manner described by C.P. Snow in his reference to two cultures existing in Britain. This phenomenon was illustrated by the campaign of Lord Joseph, when as Sir Keith Joseph he was Education Minister, to change the name of the Social Science Research Council to 'Economic and Social Research Council' on the grounds that economics and sociology were not 'real' sciences. Sir Keith's concern was that subjects like economics and (especially) sociology, were not 'science' because they did not give numerically precise and invariable results. In addition of course, they were tainted by 'ideology', unlike the 'natural' sciences which are only concerned with the discovery of 'facts'.

This type of distinction, particularly in terms of 'two cultures', is not as well developed in the German language. This is not because Germans do not make a distinction between, say, sociology and physics, but because they make **different** distinctions. As a language, German groups formal knowledge whether concerned with arts, science or even the social sciences under one heading – *Wissenschaft*. This term implies a critical, objective and empirical approach to all knowledge. Formal knowledge in this sense refers to knowledge which can be represented by formal, i.e. testable, propositions. It is possible to make such propositions about the attributes of phenomena in the physical world of

CASE STUDY 10.1

LANGUAGE AND THE STATUS OF ENGINEERS

Continued over page

Continued from previous page

material things, e.g. chemical compounds, types of steel, behaviour of molecules and so on, and also about a piece of literature. It is after all possible to identify authors by close examination of literary style and techniques. Particular subjects in German are often designated by terms which are compounds of *Wissenschaft* – *Wirtschaftswissenschaft*, for example, translates as 'economics'.

The German term *Kunst* refers to 'art' in terms of the products of artistic endeavour – a painting, statue or concerto – not as a generalized sense in opposition to 'science' as in English. Perhaps the most important feature of the German language in the context of our discussion is that of *Technik*.

Technik is a term which overcomes the problem C.P. Snow was dealing with in his famous reference to two cultures. It refers explicitly to the knowledge and skill necessary for the manufacture of artefacts, in other words, manufacturing. Snow attempted to fit engineering into the two-culture model and achieved this by defining it as 'applied science'. The point about this is that such a terminological classification not only places engineering in a subordinate position to 'science', it also misrepresents the relationship and roles of science and engineering. As Fores and Rey (1977), put it: '"Applied science" as an alternative for TECHNIK fails because manufacturing cannot be well characterised as the application of scientific knowledge . . . . . The rate of technical progress in manufacturing cannot be equated with the rate of adoption of science.'

Science, engineering and social classification

An important aspect of the subordination of engineering in the English speaking world illustrated in Case Study 10.1 is that it also reflected a social classification. Science was an activity undertaken by 'gentlemen' (often of independent means) in their own studies or laboratories and was consequently perceived as a 'respectable' activity. Science was an acceptable activity for gentlemen since it was carried out in the pursuit of knowledge, was often refered to as 'natural philosophy' and was thus brought under the rubric of the elite classical education. It was not directly related to any commercial activity.

Engineering, on the other hand, particularly mechanical engineering, most definitely was associated with industry. Hutton and Lawrence (1981) suggest that the German concept of 'technik' represents '. . . an autonomous cultural rubric tending to dignify engineering and certainly serving to differentiate it from natural science.' This dignity is in an important sense represented and protected by the fact that the term 'engineer' can only be used by, or in reference to, people who have acquired specified qualifications and undergone specified training. In the UK (and also Japan by the way) the term engineer covers a very wide range of activities.

The significance of the role of 'technik' is reflected in the proportion of undergraduate students who study engineering and the prevalence of engineers in the management structure of German companies. As Sorge and Warner (1980) put it, '. . . engineering education in Britain seems to be more closely patterned on the model of science-education, whereas it is clearly recognised as following a pattern of its own in Germany.' The superior status of 'technic' is also evidenced by the fact that engineers in Germany appear among the better paid managers and certainly those in industry are better paid then engineers working in the public sector.

Market signals

It has been a point of some concern since the nineteenth century that in the UK bright students, if they do go into industry or commerce after graduation, tend to go into functions other than production, usually finance and marketing. This would appear to be a rational choice in response to clear market signals. The best jobs, the highest status, the best working conditions, the fastest promotions are all available in these activities. Handy (1987) observes that Britain has something like 120 000 accountants (the majority of whom will actually be employed in management although not necessarily trained as managers), in comparison with 6000 in Japan, and 4000 in Germany.

A survey on pay covering the three areas of finance, personnel and engineering found that out of seven hierarchical levels below board level, it was only on the lowest level surveyed that engineers were not worse off in terms of salary, bonus payments, cars, free fuel and holidays than their peers in personnel who, in turn, were worse off than those in finance. It was noted that geography may have had a part to play since 60% of personnel staff were located in higher paying areas of the country compared with only 40% of engineers. However, why personnel should be located in such areas was not explained, and anyway it was estimated that geographical factors accounted for only about half the observed differential (M. Dixon; 'Why ambitious engineers seek different work', *Financial Times*, 25 October 1989).

As a matter of empirical observation the kind of degree you have does not hinder your chances in non-production functions of business in the United Kingdom. Certainly if you have done a first degree in accountancy you may gain some exemptions in the professional exams, but by the time you have acquired the professional qualification, no one is particularly concerned about your first degree anyway.

A similar market process operates in Germany, but with different results. Germany has about one-sixth the number of students studying history as the UK, about one-third the number reading languages and half the number reading geography. Why? Market signals!

If you want to get on in business in Germany you study engineering, economics or law. That's how it is. If you read history, then it is because you want to teach it, not because you want to go on to become an accountant, marketer, personnel manager, banker, stockbroker or systems analyst. It is interesting to note in this context that the very considerable demand for places on law degrees in the UK is not because law students want to go into industry or commerce, but because they wish to enter the gentlemanly profession of law as solicitors or barristers. If they do eventually enter industry or commerce it will be as lawyers rather than as 'managers'.

The important point is that industry has a relatively high standing in Germany, reflected in the rewards that are available. This status is at least in part associated with the lack of a social class component to the arts/science distinction and to the autonomy of the 'technik' rubric. The result is that involvement in the manufacturing process is itself worthy of esteem in comparison with, say, staff positions in finance, marketing and personnel who in the UK service those with line responsibility for production.

Schooling and vocational education and training: Germany and the United Kingdom

The standing of manufacturing, of actually making things, is reflected in the role of technical schools (*Realschule*) in Germany which take about a fifth of the pupils of school age. In Britain of course, technical schools, although established by the 1944 Education Act, failed to make an impact. Something like them is having to be re-created by the City Technological Colleges, although how successfully is a matter of keen debate. It is also worth noting that social divisions in the German secondary or higher educational systems tend to be less sharply drawn than those in the UK represented by the public schools and Oxbridge divide. Attendance at a private school in Germany leads people to wonder what is, or was, wrong with you. That is, attendance at a private school is commonly assumed to indicate some learning difficulty rather than primarily attesting to wealth, status or ability. While German universities are grouped and ranked by size and age, of equal if not greater importance are particular courses or departments and institutes which are recognized as prestigious.

It is also worth noting that university degrees in Germany take a minimum of four years to complete, and the majority of students take even longer to complete their first-degree courses before commencing post-graduate studies. Undergraduate studies follow an 'A' level course, the *Arbitur*, taken by pupils who attend the *Gymnasium* (grammar school), which gives the right to attend university and does not limit the choice of degree subject. This last feature of the German system is not only of significance in terms of the time taken to complete a degree course, but is also related to the idea of a 'core curriculum' to be followed by those at secondary school.

English culture and the decline of the industrial spirit

This is the title of a study by Wiener (1981) in which factors relevent to our discussion are explored in the context of the absence of a developed system of technical education in England. Much of Wiener's case is based upon the gentlemanly qualities assumed to be associated with pure science and the negative attributes of engineering, especially in the context of manufacturing.

Maintaining a distance from the crude activity of making things to make money has for long been feature of professionalism in the English-speaking world. This resulted in what Glover (1988) refers to as 'arm's-length managerialism'. This refers to the extent to which a distinction between line and staff is central to the British perception of management. Management becomes an activity which is theorized about and for which courses are designed and sold on the basis that what is being managed is irrelevant. Management is perceived as a general activity associated with the offering of advice rather than direct involvement in the process of manufacture.

This is reflected to some extent in the popularity of the Master of Business Administration (MBA) among engineering graduates as a means of transferring to 'general management' from direct involvement with production. Such a standpoint of course is consistent with a generalist style of recruitment. That is, first-degree subjects are relatively unimportant, being a 'decent chap' is what matters, and social class background, secondary schooling and the university attended then become more significant than the subjects read.

Wiener's thesis is that the distinction of gentlemanly behaviour from the actual business of making things was associated with the absorption of the new class of manufacturers into an established, basically 'rentier' and pre-industrial élite. The English feudal and aristocratic élite was not destroyed or undermined by either revolution or military defeat as was the case in Europe generally. The desire on the part of the new 'middle class' for acceptance by an established, and basically pre-industrial, élite influenced the development of general and technical education in Britain, as did an emphasis upon laissez-faire on the part of the state. For example, when Liverpool University College was founded in 1881, £80000 was subscribed by local people. When government grants were established in 1889 Liverpool received £1500. Roderick and Stephens (1972) quote an 1859 minute from the Science Division of the Department of Science and Art: 'It is to be hoped that a system of science instruction will grow up among the industrial classes which will entail the least possible cost . . . on the part of the State.' The point is that technical education was seen as not just 'different' from a classical education, but as a 'lower' form, suitable only for the labouring classes.

The situation differed in Germany. There, a corporatist strategy resulted in government, employers and unions being involved in technical education from the beginning. The first laboratory for systematic research into chemistry was established in Giessen in 1826, and leading British chemists went there for training. When the Royal College of Chemistry was established in 1845 it was based on the German model. University College, London, was established in the same year as the laboratory at Giessen – it was modelled on the University of Berlin and the founders looked to Scotland in addition to Germany for their ideas. By 1902 there were seven English universities for a population of some 31 million, but Germany had 22 for a population of 50 million. By 1908 when 3000 pupils were at technical schools in England, Germany had 14 000 students at ten technical universities.

The legacy of this corporatist approach can be seen today where a major role is played by employers through obligatory membership of the

Industrie und Handelskammer, the Chambers of Commerce, and training and assessment organized by the Chambers. A similar system operates in France where since the early 1970s there has been established the obligation upon employers to pay a 'tax' based upon their total wages bill (currently 1.2%) for training. There is also a legal requirement for employers to consult with employees concerning the annual training plan via the works council or *comité d'entreprise*. This system of vocational education and training (VET) in France involves the local Chambers of Commerce, for which membership is obligatory, as it does that in Germany. It is important to note that the apparent antipathy towards technical education for workers was maintained by British employers during a period often thought to be the high point of this country's political, industrial and technological influence during the latter part of the nineteenth century. The new industry-dominated Training and Enterprise Councils (TECs) announced in a Government White Paper in December 1988 is the latest attempt to bring vocational education and training in Britain up to standards common throughout Europe.

Some of the consequences of the lack of concern with VET in Britain can be seen in the fact that while a number of major developments in steel-making occurred in this country none were actually implemented here. Even in the railways, where it is often assumed British engineering led the world, it is sobering to reflect that many of the advances in locomotive design associated with a major figure in this field (and a major company), Churchward of the GWR, derived from the importation of French locomotives before the First World War. The level of technical training received by French locomotive crews was noted in the late nineteenth century and is regarded as an important factor in the popularity and effectiveness of technically complex compound steam locomotives in France in comparison with their unpopularity and minor role in the UK. In the case of the electric telegraph, which was successfuly developed in the UK from the mid-nineteenth century and in which a lead was maintained for about thirty years, the first President of the Society of Telegraph Engineers was one William Siemans, a naturalized Prussian.

Vocational education and training

An important aspect of the comparison between training in Germany and Britain is illustrated by the role of apprenticeships. These form the basis of training for both industry and commerce in Germany and are very often the basis of a career that reaches the most senior level. This is possible because the provision is such that one level of training leads on to the next. Having an apprentice qualification is not only seen as relevant for promotion, but is the foundation for future courses and qualifications. It is not a 'terminal' qualification, to use the jargon. In this sense training in Germany is hierarchical. This means that the division between line and staff is less influential in Germany. Line officials have a training that enables them to carry out tasks or responsibilities that would be allocated to staff groups in Britain.

The structure of courses is established jointly by Chambers of Commerce, government and educationalists, and involves rotation round the jobs that are relevent to the trade, as well as attendance at colleges as a result of a statutory entitlement to day-release for those leaving school at the age of fifteen or sixteen and following a semi skilled or skilled training. For a skilled worker the apprenticeship lasts between three and three and a half years, and concludes with both practical and theoretical exams. Success results in the worker being formally qualified as a *Facharbeiter* (skilled worker) at between eighteen and nineteen years of age. The *Facharbeiterbrief* is a prerequisite for later progression to a two or three year part-time *Meister* course which itself is a prerequisite for promotion to foreman, or more accurately 'superintendant' in British terms.

This structure of training not only tends to minimize the distinction between 'maintenance' (skilled) and 'production' (semi-or unskilled) workers which characterizes British manufacturing industry, but also allies production engineering closely with management. This in turn results in a range and degree of skill, knowledge and experience that increases the functional autonomy and flexibility of production workers and their supervisors. It is this autonomy and associated flexibility between jobs that appears to reduce the staff component of managerial hierarchies in German industry. The hierarchical nature of training and qualifications works to produce technical qualifications in management with a major emphasis on practical skills. This can be contrasted with the academic emphasis amongst the minority of graduate managers in British industry whose courses, if they were at all technical, would have been derived from the assumed superiority (as opposed to mere difference) of 'science'.

The structure and operation of German firms

A number of factors concerning the structure of German enterprises may be considered important in terms of their performance in comparison with British counterparts. One of these is the influence of training as discussed in the previous section; others relate to the legal structure of enterprises and associated features of the employment relationship.

As Sorge and Warner (1980) point out, the role of culture has been relatively underplayed as a contingency factor in the debate about influences on organizational structure. If we consider the development of educational and training systems as cultural features, since they will be at least in part determined by the social, political and historical factors associated with industrialization, then it is possible to see culture at work influencing organizational forms.

We have already mentioned in this chapter how the German programme of vocational education and training may be interpreted as producing a relatively less formal, less 'staff'-oriented structure. The level and range of skills posessed by workers, and the technical qualifications of their superiors, produces a degree of autonomy and flexibility which in turn reduces staff functions and positively strengthens line functions. This produces a less top heavy and more flexible structure than in Britain, as suggested by Table 10.1.

The point about Table 10.1 is that it demonstrates the level of qualification possessed by German managers and supervisors in a chemical

Table 10.1 Vocational qualifications of managers and supervisory staff in chemicals factories in Germany and Britain

Germany (%)		Britain (%)	
Without formal qualifications	3	Without formal qualification	42
Craft	42	Craft	21
Meisterbrief/Techniker[1]	30	City & Guilds/ONC	4
Ing. Grad.[2]	17	HNC and equivalent	8
University degree	8	University degree	21[3]

1. Technician.
2. Engineering diploma, usually taken at a *Fachhochschule* (polytechnic equivalent).
3. Reflects emphasis on academic criteria. These will be 'science'-based or 'management'-related degrees. Also reflects concentration on staff as opposed to line functions/responsibilities.

Source: Maurice, Sorge and Warner (1980), pp. 59–86.

plant. Only 3 per cent of German managers and supervisors have **no** qualification at all, in comparison with 42% of their British counterparts. Whereas 33% of British managers and supervisors have qualifications ranging from craft to HNC level, this is the case for no less than 89% of German managers and supervisors.

The flexibility and autonomy resulting from training provides greater satisfaction for employees as well as reducing problems of coordination. This results in higher productivity since it facilitates more effective use of expensive human and technical resources. A 'job enrichment' programme is not necessary when as a matter of course workers are trained in, and paid for, a range of skills and are able to deal with many shopfloor problems without having to call in staff experts.

German supervisors do not apparently experience the feelings and problems of status and authority deprivation that have been the focus of British studies, for example Child and Partridge (1982). This is in part at least due to the fact that as a result of their level of qualification and training supervisors in German companies are able to make decisions which would be taken by their organizational superiors in Britain. German supervisors or superintendants will play a major part in the purchase and evaluation of new equipment for example, as well as in discussions with customers to establish how their needs can be met (Lawrence, 1984). It is worth emphasizing that whereas training courses for German supervisors concentrate on technical matters, those for their British counterparts have mainly been concerned with human relations matters.

Legal aspects

What we have said so far is of direct relevance to those aspects of structure which are determined by the legal framework. One of the ironies of the debate about lessons to be learnt from countries like Germany is that while British managers complain about the strait-jacket imposed by over-powerful unions who are 'outside the law', they have enjoyed a very much freer hand in labour relations than their German peers, certainly since the

Second World War. This applies also to issues such as maternity leave, for example, where entitlements in Europe generally are far greater than in Britain.

British workers have no right to be consulted about job changes and takeovers, for example. They have no right to strike or to refuse overtime, and only limited rights to information that would enable them to assess the company's financial and market position when negotiating. German workers have a constitutional right to withdraw their labour, and managers are obliged by law to take certain matters to the works council in a consensus-oriented process known as co-determination – *Mitbestimmung*. Case Study 10.2 explains the structure of a German company.

CASE STUDY 10.2

THE TWO-TIER STRUCTURE OF GERMAN COMPANIES

The legal structure of German companies involves a 'two-tier' board structure which is common in Europe. Unlike British companies with their single board of directors, even though comprising two major groups, excutive and non-executive directors, German companies have two separate boards: a supervisory board or *Aufsichtsrat*, and a decision-making executive board or *Vorstand*.

The supervisory board is made up of elected members who, while the great majority will be business people, are not full-time employees of the company. Neither will they be 'status loaders' such as retired senior officers from the armed services, politicians or aristocrats. The supervisory board appoints, and has the power to dismiss, the members of the executive board who are full time executives of the company.

Worker Representation

Worker representation was established in the Federal Republic in 1951 by the *Mitbestimmungsgesetz* or Co-determination Law which was passed (reluctantly it should be noted) by the Christian Democrat (CDU) government in the face of a threat by the unions to mount what in effect would have been a general strike. This particular legislation covered only the iron, steel and coal industries – the *Montanindustrie* – and provided for the equal representation of employer and employee representatives on the supervisory board, with the chair being elected by the shareholders' meeting. In addition, a labour director (*Arbeits-direktor*) was to be appointed to the *Vorstand* on the recommendation of the worker representatives on the supervisory board.

In 1952 the Industrial Constitution Law was passed which required all enterprises not included in the *Montanindustrie* to have at least one-third of the supervisory board made up of worker representatives. Also in 1952, legislation was passed which required all enterprises with more than five employees to establish a works council.

Works councils

Works councils and co-determination have a history which goes back before the Second World War. Poole (1986) suggests that the origins of

Continued over page

Continued from previous page

works council legislation can be traced back as far as the 1830s and 1840s. However, the first formal steps were taken in 1917 in an attempt to involve workers in cooperating to increase wartime production. This very modest beginning was subsequently influenced by the considerable social and industrial unrest following the defeat of Germany in which factories were occupied and joint worker and soldiers' soviets established.

In the early years of the Weimar Republic (1919–33) works councils as such were established which were entitled to negotiate local wage agreements. During the same period the Companies Act was modified to require that the supervisory board should contain two worker representatives – one for manual and one for non-manual groups.

These councils were abolished by the National Socialists at the same time as trade unions came under attack, and in some cases works councils formed the basis of resistance to the Nazis (Miller, 1978). After the Second World War, strong trade unions and works councils were regarded by the Occupying Powers as a means of preventing the dictatorial centralization which had occurred under the Nazi regime, and so they encouraged – required – the re-establishment of the councils. Paradoxically perhaps, one of the additional factors that made employers sympathetic to the idea of co-determination was, as Lawrence (1980) points out, the perceived commonality of interest between employers and workers in the face of the dismantling of factories and appropriation of equipment (e.g. locomotives and machine tools) for shipment under the Reparation Programme.

The rights of workers

The 1952 legislation on works councils established three sets of rights, the *Mitbestimmungsrecht*, the *Mitwirkungsrecht* and the *Informationsrecht*.

The *Mitbestimmungsrecht* requires that employers must obtain the consent of the works councils in matters concerning, for example, internal transfers of workers, dismissals, fixing start and finishing times and break periods, holiday periods, and prevention and investigation of accidents.

The *Mitwirkungsrecht*, or 'right to be consulted', covers decisions about plant closures or the opening of new plants, and the transfers of workers between sites.

The *Informationsrecht*, or right to information, is exercised through an Economic Committee (*Wirtschaftausschuss*) composed of members of the works council and management. This committee has the right to information covering the economic performance of the enterprise, including information relevant to investments and profits. There is an obligation of confidentiality placed upon members of the works council which means that worker representatives cannot divulge this information to their constituents though it can be used in collective bargaining.

Industrial relations

The question of industrial relations and the power of trade unions is a constant refrain in debates about the relatively poor performance of manufacturing industry in Britain. From the literature, and personal experiences of this author in discussions with German businessmen, such a concern is somewhat less overt, and possibly less developed, among German managers. Recently, in discussions with the chief executive of a major machine tool company in Germany, facing considerable competitive pressures from the value of the Deutschmark against the dollar, and from competitors in Japan, Switzerland and Italy, the only reference to trade union activity occurred when it was mentioned that the impact of the shorter working week was producing pressure from customers for even more highly automated products in order to maintain output targets!

This apparent absence of concern may well be the result of more 'responsible' union leaders or 'sensible' structures. It may also be the case that 'responsible' union behaviour and particular features of organizational structure are the result rather than the cause of success. A similar process may produce the apparent lack of concern with 'profit', as noted in the literature, in comparison with the constantly high profile of profitability where British managers are concerned. If you are successful in terms of market share, and are making a level of profit which enables product development to grow, pay to rise and the providers of debt (as opposed to equity) capital to be kept happy, then you do not have to spend too much time worrying about rates of profit. If on the other hand none of these things are happening, then attention is turned almost exclusively to profit. Such an overriding concern then has implications for the time-scale over which 'profit' and 'profitability' are considered, usually short-term and in the case of Britain focused on equity capital and the role of share prices.

It is also interesting to note that German managers tend not to use the equivalent of the term 'employees' when discussing numbers employed, or those in subordinate positions in the company generally. The term used on such occasions is *Mitarbeiter* – co-worker.

Despite a widely held belief that the Germans owe much of their current industrial relations system to an Allied commission responsible for re-establishing democratic institutions of industrial relations after 1945 (the British representative was Vic Feather, later to become General Secretary of the Trades Union Congress), the main features of the German system are much older. The development and acceptance of the post-war and post-Nazi system of industrial relations is intimately connected with the shared trauma of both employers and trade unions under National Socialism and the military defeat at the hands of the four major allies.

It is also important to note that the rights of German workers do not derive from the strength of trade unions (formidable as that is both organizationally and financially in comparison with those in Britain) but from the constitution and the law. In fact German trade unions are not allowed to operate within the enterprise as they do in this country. The system is formalized and institutionalized via the statutory requirements for worker representation and the role of the works council. It so happens that works councils often comprise significant numbers of trade union members, Lawrence (1980) suggests up to 80%, but they do not represent the union or only union members. Works council members represent those who are employed in the enterprise. According to Miller (1978) this absence of the union from the plant level stems from a conference decision of the metalworkers' union, IG Metall, in 1947 which actually took place in the British Zone of occupation. This structure was later incorporated into the 1952 legislation.

In 1976 a further piece of legislation was passed which required all enterprises employing more than 2000 people to have a supervisory board with membership divided equally between shareholders and employee representatives. The chair was to be taken by an elected representative of the shareholders who has a second – casting – vote. It was laid down that the worker representatives should include at least one white-collar worker, one senior manager (*leitende Angestellten*) and one blue-collar worker. An *Arbeitsdirektor* is appointed to the *Vorstand*, but she or he is elected by all the members of the *Aufsichstrat*, not just the worker representatives.

The rights of property

In 1977 29 employers' associations and nine independent industrial companies took the Federal Government to court on the grounds that the 1976 legislation was unconstitutional. It was argued that the requirements of the Act represented an infringement of the rights of property owners to dispose of their property as they saw fit. In 1979 the Federal Constitutional Court found against the employers on the grounds that the casting vote of the chair, a shareholders' representative, maintained the rights of property.

It should not be assumed that the existence of this legislation meets with the wholehearted approval and enthusiasm of employers. One consequence of the 1976 legislation was for large enterprises to restructure so as to fall below the 2000 employee limit. But as Lawrence (1980) writes: '. . . the effects of co-determination include advance regulation of particular issues, a measure of system induced co-operation between employers and employees, the diffusion of company performance information and a greater constraint on management to explain and justify its decisions.'

The implications of the German case for the United Kingdom

It should be apparent that any lessons which it might be possible to draw from the kind of material we have been considering are not particularly remarkable. They concern the significance of a skilled and motivated workforce who have confidence in their ability to exercise some control over their situation and confidence in their superiors. We will return to this latter point when looking at the experience of Japanese-managed firms in Britain in the next section of this chapter. The advantages of participation are very well-known to British managers through their own experience and research findings. Indeed a concern with the well-being of human resources forms a part of the common currency of managerial pronouncements and speeches.

It is possible that there is a component of the German character that renders their managers and workers particularly amenable to the dictates of capitalism, but it is not necessary to assume such qualities since the system under which they operate is quite consistent with the aspirations of British managers and workers.

However, there undoubtedly are factors which distinguish the German approach and which have given rise to it. These relate to historical factors which influence social and political relationships and which may also be considered under the rubric of 'culture'. Such factors can be grouped under two headings: those that are specific to the German experience, and those that relate to the experience of those societies that can be grouped under the heading of 'secondary industrializers', what Dore (1973) describes as 'a general late capitalist development syndrome'. Both Germany and Japan fit this syndrome.

To take those factors specific to the German case first, those used to explain German success after the Second World War are often taken to be the assumed advantages of losing the war. This of course fits with English sensibilities. But this argument does not stand up to close investigation. For example, while Germany did receive considerable funds from America, it is not widely realized that Britain actually received half as much again under the Marshall Aid Programme as Germany. Lawrence (1984) reports that although Germany received some $4.4 billion of mainly American aid under the Government and Relief in Occupied Areas Programme this was for **relief** in the form of food, fuel, seeds and fertilizers, not for industrial reconstruction. When the Marshall Plan was installed, 50% of the funds received was for food imports, 40% for raw materials and semi-finished goods, and only 3.5% was for machines and vehicles.

While these funds were of considerable significance in terms of reconstructing the infrastructure, housing suffered far more under Allied bombing than did manufacturing installations of which about 20% were destroyed, important social factors were also in operation to aid in the reconstruction of industry. These relate to the social and psychological consequences of defeat, the horrors of the Nazi regime, and the influx of refugees as a result of expulsions and border changes in the East as well as those fleeing Russion occupation. These population movements not only produced a reservoir of skilled labour, manual and non-manual, but also a population who had lost everything. The drive to reconstruct and redeem was powerful, very powerful. This drive was politically important at the national level as well as between managers and workers.

It is necessary to bear in mind other socio-historical factors that set the context for the reconstruction effort in both Germany and Japan. These relate to the fact that both countries were major industrial forces before the 1939–45 war. This is the context for considering the late development, or secondary industrializer, syndrome.

Late capitalist development

Secondary or late development industrializers are countries who industrialize in a world where there is already an established industrial power or powers. In the case of Germany (and other Continental countries and Japan) this meant Britain and then America. In such a situation it is likely that the strategies adopted will be different from those used by the primary industrializer. If a country industrializes when there are no other competitors, then certain strategies appear relevant which would not seem so if the situation was different.

In the case of Britain an emphasis on the role of the market (*laissez-faire*) as opposed to the state, and on 'free' trade, appeared reasonable. For a secondary industrializer such strategies have less appeal for obvious reasons. Free trade assists those who are already established, not those who are attempting to establish themselves. The lack of highly trained workers is less of a hindrance when the technology is relatively simple and competition minimal. For a secondary industrializer who is, by reason of the existence of established industries and products, forced to develop newer and more complex products the absence of suitable financial, educational and training system requires rapid and effective solutions.

For this reason at least, the state is likely to become involved. As Samuels *et al.* (1975) have shown, the development of financial systems is both a consequence and a cause of experience under industrialization. European financial systems developed a role in which banks became intimately involved in industrialization and this enabled them to acquire considerable expertise which could then be applied in aid of entrepreneurs. They became closely involved in manufacturing industry rather than developing as secondary sources of funds. German companies are much more concerned with banks since finance is largely debt not equity. Consequently, German banks are closely concerned with the long-term viability of their industrial customers since the security for the loans they have made (and for which shares in the company are largely the security) and interest payments, not to mention the prospect of further loans in the future, depend on long-term survival and growth. Secondary markets like the stock exchange are then relatively unimportant and insignificant. Only about 500 firms are quoted on the Frankfurt stock exchange, for example, compared with over 3000 in London.

This has implications for what are perceived to be the major indicators of performance, for example growth of market share based upon high quality, even if highly priced, products as opposed to a rise in share prices. The time-scale is also likely to be different with shareholders (secondary investors) in countries like Britain and America eager to sell one company or industry share in order to get into apparently better performing sectors or companies.

Some recent evidence relating to this aspect of the debate comes from a comparison of the allocation of venture capital investment in Britain and the USA, a country that also has a highly developed financial system, described in Case Study 10.3.

Education and training again

Pressure upon secondary industrializers is likely to make state involvement in education and training acceptable if not actually desired. As a result it is

Venture capital investment:	UK %	US %
Start up	16	18
Early stages	7	17
Expansion	27	44
Buy outs and acquisitions	44	17
Other	6	4

CASE STUDY 10.3

ALLOCATION OF VENTURE CAPITAL AND THE ROLE OF FINANCIAL INSTITUTIONS

Source: 'Venture Economics', *Financial Times*, 3 November 1987.

It is well recognized that major problems arise as companies expand, from small to medium or medium to large. Not only does this process put considerable strain on financial resources, it also puts considerable social and psychological strain on managers. The breakdown of figures shown is consistent with the observation that British companies tend to grow by acquisition rather than by internal growth as a result of increasing market share.

Relevant in this context – as examples of the different approaches in terms of the relationship between the banks and industrial companies – are the takeover bids for GEC from Metsun (a takeover company established by the one-time managing director of Westland Helicopters) and for BAT Industries involving Sir James Goldsmith, Jacob Rothschild and Kerry Packer.

The bid for GEC occurred at the time GEC was involved with Siemens in a bid for Plessey. Barclays Bank were involved with Metsun; at the same time they were GEC's bankers and the GEC chairman, Lord James Prior, was a director of Barclays. He resigned when he discovered Barclays involvement. The point is that Barclays were concerned to establish a reputation for putting together bid deals in order to take advantage of expected European growth in such activity as companies restructured after 1992. The object was to establish a presence in this particular market to cope with competition from other European institutions, but particularly the American and Japanese. They were concerned with the fee income that could be earned by such activity, and were not significantly concerned about the long-term viability of GEC should it be broken up.

Similar features can be seen in the £13bn leveraged offer for BAT Industries by Hoylake, a shell company jointly owned by Sir James Goldsmith, Mr Jacob Rothschild and Mr Kerry Packer. This bid was the largest ever for a British company and the second largest in corporate history. The deal was to be financed by debt and high interest 'junk' bonds and the return was to come from 'unbundling', i.e. selling off, the component businesses of BAT. It was reported in *The Financial Times* on the day the bid was announced, 12 July 1989, that institutional investors were somewhat concerned that a basically well managed company was to be broken up by 'corporate adventurers with no managerial or industrial skills'. However, it was acknowledged that a decision to accept the offer would depend on a purely commercial judgement. In other words, if the price was right, 'we'd sell'. It was also

Continued over page

Continued from previous page recognized that one consequence of such a bid, whether it was successful or not, would be pressure on other companies to increase their dividend payments in order to fend off similar bids. Merchant banks not involved in the bid were reported to be awed by its size, and envious of the fees that would be earned by those involved.

The point to be made here is that merchant banks, and the merchant banking arms of other financial institutions, earn their money from the fees derived from advising participants in bid situations (either those doing the bidding or those fighting it off), and from putting together the necessary loan funds. Success for a merchant bank, or other financial institutions, therefore is not closely related to the long-term market fortunes of a particular company.

more likely that national systems of provision and qualifications will be developed with industry being required to take part in both organizing and financing that provision.

Steadman (1988) shows how these factors appear to operate in the field of technical training in France, with a comparable population to that of the UK even if the proportion in manufacturing is smaller. After adjusting for the smaller workforce in France, Steadman concludes that per head of the workforce France produces three times as many craftsmen and two and a half times as many technicians in the area of mechanical and electrical engineering as Britain. The Report concludes that as a result of increasing the numbers gaining craft qualifications over the same period that the number in Britain declined, France is approaching the situation of Germany where the typical industrial worker is qualified to craftsman level. This means that French manufacturing industry will be able to move more rapidly than the British in introducing new technology and work practices, with supervisors trained to technician level and workers with craft skills. The report found that French vocational secondary schools taught to standards that are reached in Britain at colleges of further education.

A subsequent report from the NIESR dealing with training in retailing (Jarvis and Prais, 1988) comes to equally disturbing conclusions. The numbers qualifying in retailing over the last decade in France had doubled. Half of these qualified after a two to three year course at full-time vocational schools, while the other half are apprentices who have had day-release. The YTS type courses in retailing in Britain, which have expanded, are simply introductory and do not reach what would be considered acceptable levels in either France or Germany. It is important to note that such courses in France and Germany are not merely concerned with developing a narrow skills base but are also concerned to achieve high standards in general educational abilities. Some 40% of the curriculum of vocational courses in Germany is concerned with the continuation of general education, including foreign languages.

It is instructive to compare the approach in France and Germany, for example, with that illustrated in an article in the July 1989 issue of *Business*

Education Today describing a BTEC course on International Trade and Languages. The author says: 'Experience has shown that companies are not looking for knowledge specialists, but for students with skills such as communication (face-to-face/telephone/memos) and keyboarding (for keying-in details on, say, a bill of lading, or word processing a hand written letter). Naturally, students require an overview of the industry, particularly with regard to its jargon . . . .'

Even in the nineteenth century in the UK the problem of technical education and training was recognized to be less a problem about provision and much more to do with the apparent lack of demand for people with such a training.

It is worth noting that what might be considered **the** élite educational institution in France, the École Polytechnique, is an engineering school, and was established under Napoleon to produce a technically competent élite for a post-revolutionary, modern, France.

Japan and the United Kingdom

Here again, many assumptions taken for granted do not stand up to close investigation. Many of the same assertions are made about conditions that

Table 10.2 Copying or innovating

Proportion of Patents registered in the US by country:	1975	1984
UK patents	4.2%	3.5%
German patents	8.5%	9.5%
US patents	64.9%	57.3%
Japanese patents	8.9%	16.6%

Source: DTI (1987).

Table 10.3 Four nations compared

	West Germany	UK	USA	Japan
Labour cost in manufacturing (DM per hour 1986 incl. wages and social security)	31.4	17.6	29.0	25.3
Working hours (annual per capita 1985)	1640	1947	1913	2135
Private consumption (% of GDP 1985)	55.0	59.7	66.7	55.5
Investment (gross fixed capital formation % of GDP 1985)	19.9	18.4	21.2	30.0

Source: Institut der Deutschen Wirtschaft, quoted in *Financial Times,* November 4 1987.

Japanese managers and workers face as have been made about Germany. For example, Japanese workers are docile, almost passive, workaholics; they are low paid; Japanese manufacturers got where they are by copying Western products and so on. Some of the myths about Japan can be blown by starting with the assumption that Japan is in fact remarkably successful. Consider the figures in Tables 10.2 and 10.3 and Case Study 10.4.

While post Second World War Japan has made a significant impression upon the Western world, particularly the Anglo-Saxon component, it was already a major industrial power before the Second World War. At the time of the conflict with Russia before the First World War, Japanese warships were some of the largest in the world. The growth of Japan after the Second World War was based upon a period of development that began after the arrival of European and traders in the mid-nineteenth century. Dissatisfaction with the apparent failure of the feudal Tokugawa Shogunate to protect national interests against the arrival and future intentions of foreigners resulted in the aristocratic revolution of 1868,

---

CASE STUDY 10.4

HOW SUCCESSFUL IS JAPAN?

The following figures on trade comparisons (Gillan, 1986) are from different time periods, but do illustrate some important features of the Japanese case:

	Japan (1984)	UK (1983)
Exports per head	£1012	£1064
Manufactures as % of exports	97%	66%
Imports per head	£812	£1072
Manufactures as % of imports	27%	68%

The point is that while the UK actually exported more per head than Japan (but remember that Japan has a population nearly three times as large) only two-thirds of those exports were manufactured goods compared with 97% of Japanese exports. Similarly with imports: while the UK imports are 25% greater than the Japanese, over two-thirds of them are manufactured products in comparison with just over one-quarter of Japanese imports. Japanese exports will tend to be high value-added products such as electronics which are important in both consumer and industrial markets world-wide.

Consider also the following measures of success taken from Mirza (1984), Table 1 and based on Gatt, *International Trade 1981/2*:

	Exports ($bn)	Exports per capita ($)	Export/import ratio ($bn)
Japan	150	1,300	11
UK	110	2,000	2
USA	220	1,000	−45
West Germany	180	2,900	13
France	100	1,900	−19

known as the Meiji or Imperial Restoration. The intention of those involved was to restructure Japanese society so as to facilitate the creation of a state that would be able to negotiate with the Westerners from a position of wealth and strength.

This required both economic and military policies. The treaties that Japan had been forced to sign, with tariffs set by the Westerners, left domestic producers in agriculture and handcraft manufacturers at the mercy of dynamic and aggressive foreign (i.e. Western) economies. The result would have been the same as elsewhere in Asia with the decline and destruction of the domestic economy. To prevent this development, rapid and radical action was necessary.

Consequently the major role in industrialization was taken by the state with new factories, textile mills and shipyards established by the government. These were later to be sold to high-ranking families at virtually 'give-away' prices, so as to leave the government free to concentrate on strategy rather than their day-to-day operation. In order to implement strategic objectives and develop the necessary skills in management and production, the Western world was scoured in order to select the best methods and techniques from the point of view of Japan. In this way, using second-hand textile machinery from Lancashire, and a French expert in modern silk manufacture, the textile industry was rejuvenated. Similarly in shipbuilding (the Dutch and Scots), steel and government administration (Prussia), education (France again) – the best of what was available was eagerly adapted to the needs of the new Japan.

Competition for colonies was also perceived as a feature of modernization. Since the process of colonization implied up-to-date and technically efficient armed services, this in turn implied a well educated population from which to recruit. Basic education was established in 1890 and by 1900, 90% of male children were attending primary schooling.

The influence of Japanese feudalism

During the feudal period in Japan the Samurai had developed characteristics which became important in the context of modernization. Unlike European aristocratic warrior classes the Samurai did not own land, but exercised power as bureaucrats. This at least facilitated the development and implementation of government policies directed towards rapid industrialization, and was consistent with a strategy based upon the dictum of a 'rich country and strong army'. This has to be seen in the context of a perceived need to be able to stand up to the West economically and politically. Such an approach resulted in military (i.e. traditional feudal) values of loyalty to one's superior and one's group being incorporated into the new industrial system. A system of 'two governments', civil and military with the military as the 'secret' government, also facilitated adaptation of the Japanese bureaucracy to the rigours of the American Government of Occupation after 1945. In addition, the reconstruction of Japan after 1945 was considerably assisted by the policies of the Americans towards Japanese industry as a source of materials for the conduct of the Korean War.

Culture?

Undoubtedly there are features of Japanese culture which have been important in the process of industrialization, for example the fact that the starting point for discussions about the organization of work is the group rather than the individual. But much of what the Japanese put into practice over the last decades of the nineteenth century and after 1945 was learnt from the West. In the case of the post-1945 reconstruction it came from management manuals of the USAAF. The so called 'secrets' of Japanese management have been widely circulated over a period of time to Western managers in a mountain of indigenous management textbooks and business journals.

As Hafiz Mirza (1984) points out, while it is obviously the case that Japanese manufacturers pay particular attention to detail and quality in production processes, their ideas on quality control originated from the USA. The same can be said of many of the personnel policies commonly associated with modern Japanese management: life-long employment (which anyway only applies to about one-third of those employed in the larger companies) and cradle-grave security were not unique to Japanese employers. Neither was the operation of a seniority wage system. The English Quaker industrialists developed such policies in the nineteenth century, to be followed by others in Europe and America. The railways in Britain had highly developed systems of promotion based on seniority, and these were adopted to meet the demands of management as well as those of trade unions.

Education

Hirschmeier and Yui (1981) suggest comparisons between Germany and Japan in terms of the process of modernization, including the development of a national identity suited to the modern world. It is also possible to see such a comparison in the field of education, certainly in so far as the system in Germany and Japan differs from that in the United Kingdom.

Compulsory schooling from 6 to 15 years of age in Japan is followed by three years of upper secondary schooling which is undertaken by 94% of children. One-third of these students compared with one-tenth in Britain go on to university. There the first two years of the four-year course are given over to general education. At both upper secondary and university levels students follow courses in the social and natural sciences, humanities, foreign languages and health and physical education. In addition, both mathematics and science are taught to higher standards than in the United Kingdom and without the drop-out of girls. Even for quite ordinary production jobs the entry qualifications for Japanese workers are virtually equivalent to 'A' level in the UK. These entry qualifications are further developed by a systematic series of job-related qualifications associated with job rotation and mobility within the enterprise. This process creates and maintains a pool of ability and experience that can be called upon to facilitate functional flexibility and cooperation.

As with Germany, a major proportion of university students go on to study engineering, approximately 20%, with the result that Japanese industry has the highest proportion of qualified engineers and scientists in the world (Bergen and Miyajima, 1986). However, unlike the British situation, there is much less concern with 'industrial relevance' in the curriculum. Japanese engineering courses concentrate on teaching engineering principles in the knowledge that training will be given by employers (McCormack, 1988). The result is a highly flexible labour force which is further developed by the training undertaken by companies, especially the larger ones. Leading Japanese companies spend more than 3% of their income on training as compared with the figures reported in a *Financial Times* survey of February 1985 which showed that 65% of the organizations surveyed in Britain spent less than 0.5%. A subsequent study over a two-year period by the Training Commission (1988) found that employers spent some £809 on training for every person employed in the period 1986–7. However, £606 was the labour cost of trainees and trainers.

As was suggested in the German case, an important factor in the operation of Japanese production processes is not just the entry qualifications of workers and systematic further training, but the way in which such features facilitate what Nohara (1987) has termed a 'system of collective apprenticeship'. This term is used to describe how new work tasks required by new production technologies are delegated from engineers to maintenance workers to production workers as the new system becomes established. In this way the knowledge and skills required by the new processes are diffused throughout the groups involved. 'Japanese management makes greater use than the traditional management of Western countries of the knowledge and experience of people at the lower hierarchy levels, and of the knowledge and experience of production workers themselves' (Jurgens, 1989). Such a process is of course facilitated by the level of educational attainment attained by the average Japanese worker.

Finance

A further point of comparison with Germany (and in this case also with France) is to be found in the role played by the banks in Japan. Japanese industry has been able to obtain long-term low-interest loans without having to produce substantial short-term returns. In addition, banks have played an active part in the management of companies with favourable consequences for long-range planning. The ability to plan for the long term encourages strategies directed towards gaining and maintaining market share, as we saw when discussing the article by Wong *et al.* (1987) in Case Study 6.5. This approach to business philosphy is graphically illustrated by Case Study 10.5.

Research and development

Part of the Western folklore accounts for Japanese manufacturing success relates to the role of the Ministry of International Trade and Industry (MITI). It is undoubtedly the case that during the 1950s MITI played a crucial role in directing and assisting industrial development, much as government agencies had during the Meiji period. However, that period is now over, little government money now goes into R&D (Bergen and Miyajima, 1986). These authors quote a Japanese Science White Papter of 1982 which showed that while Japanese R&D consumed less of GNP

CASE STUDY 10.5	**NEC:** semiconductors and computers (1983):	
TWO PHILOSOPHIES OF BUSINESS	R&D expenditure	10.3% of sales
	Pre-tax declared profit liable to corporation tax at an effective rate of 54%	4.3% of sales
	Average pre-tax profit 1973–83	3.1% of sales

Result?   Success, the company grows at 14% per annum.

Thorn-EMI: defence and consumer electronics, leisure – adopts growth policies:

Pre-tax profit for 1984–5 *falls* to 5.7% of sales.

Result?   Chairman resigns!

Source: Gillan (1986).

than was the case for the UK (1.96% against 2.19%), Japan, with just over twice the population, had nearly three times as many R&D staff as Britain.

A crucial factor appears to be that an overwhelming proportion of UK expenditure on R&D is 'defence' related rather than being directed to product and process innovation in manufacturing industry. The problem, discussed in more detail by Weston and Gummett (1987), is the low spinoff from defence-related research to manufactured products. While the amount spent on industrial R&D has certainly increased in the UK no more is being spent in real terms now than was the case in 1964.

Related to the question of R&D is the myth that Japanese industry plagiarizes rather than innovates. Here again, while this may have once been the case it no longer applies, as was shown earlier by Table 10.2.

The problems of the US microchip industry are in large part due to the technological innovations and breakthroughs made by their Japanese competitors rather than being due simply to cut-price 'dumping'. There is also a view that the Strategic Defense Initiative, the so-called 'Star Wars' programme, is, or was, basically an attempt to channel government research funds into overtaking Japanese electronic innovations in a manner politically acceptable in a 'free market' economy.

One other myth that has currency is that the Japanese success has been achieved by paying low wages. Again, while this may have once been true – as it has been with all industrializing countries – it no longer applies and cannot be accepted as the basis for recent successes, as explained by Case Study 10.6.

Japanese managers in Britain

Finally, let us conclude this brief examination of the Japanese case with a consideration of the work of White and Tevor (1983). This is an

1960	35 manufacturers	130 400 units	20 000 workers
1969	8 manufacturers	66 137 units	6 000 workers
1979	1 (Meriden/Triumph)	19 500 units	

CASE STUDY 10.6

TWENTY YEARS IN THE HISTORY OF THE BRITISH MOTOR CYCLE INDUSTRY

Market performance 1968–74:

Markets	Market size (000 units)		Growth (% pa)	UK share (%)	
	1968	*1974*	*1968–74*	*1968*	*1974*
USA	458	1066	15	11	1
UK	38	91	16	34	3
Europe	100	290	19	2	<1

Was this caused by high wages?

Factory labour remuneration:

	1970	*1973*	*1975*
Honda	£125	£249	£296*
Norton Villiers Triumph	n/a	£143	£203

* = estimated.

These are monthly averages including all fringe benefits (bonuses and housing in the case of Honda).

| Net fixed Investment per head | Honda | approx. £5000 |
| | NVT | approx. £1300 |

Source: Boston Consulting Group (1975) *Strategy Alternatives for the British Motor Cycle Industry*, and Andrew Millward, Birmingham Polytechnic.

interesting study since it sets out to examine the experience of workers in Japanese-managed firms in Britain. White and Trevor commence by quoting the work of Takamiya (1979) who showed that whatever the significance of the assumptions about the role of personnel policies in Japan, such policies were not part of the style of Japanese management in their British subsidiaries. Takamiya found that Japanese companies in the UK were not offering life-time employment, exceptional welfare benefits or placing great emphasis upon 'human relations' techniques. Despite the absence of what many commentators saw as 'typical' Japanese policies, the British subsidiaries were achieving high levels of output and quality. Why? Takamiya argued that this was due to the way in which Japanese managers organized the actual process of production.

The significance of this finding is that it focuses attention upon less conspicuous features of Japanese management which are perhaps more easily transferable. Many of the more widely recognized or assumed characteristics which, if they are important at all, relate to the particular experience and problems of the Japanese process of industrialization are likely to be somewhat less transferable. What appear to be significant features about Japanese managers in the context of the production process are as follows:

- [ ] close attention to detail;
- [ ] emphasis on training;
- [ ] immediate rectification of defects;
- [ ] involvement of technicians and supervisors in the production task;
- [ ] small but continuous improvements both to products and to the production process.

As Limprecht and Hayes (1982) say of German manufacturers: '. . . . they prefer to pursue state-of-the-art products through a series of incremental improvements rather than through dramatic leaps to new technologies, which can quickly render obsolete the skills and reputations they have painstakingly built up over the years.'

One of the most striking aspects of the case studies carried out by White and Trevor relates to the responses of British workers to their Japanese managers. While Japanese companies are well known for the absence of status differentiating symbols, the Japanese as a people are not unconcerned about status and authority. As with many aspects of relations at work, what matters is not authority as such but how it is exercised. The view of the Japanese-managed workers interviewed by White and Trevor was that British managers displayed the 'arm's length' approach mentioned by Glover (1988).

British managers were not often to be seen on the shopfloor, and when they were, they were not often able to offer any constructive advice. The Japanese managers by contrast were well regarded by their British subordinates because of their technical knowledge and willingness to apply that knowledge in dealing with problems on the shopfloor. While, according to a number of authors referred to by McCormack (1988), British engineers seek to maximize the social distance between themselves and shopfloor workers, their Japanese peers make efforts to minimize such distance. A Japanese writer, Okuda (1983), argues that this is not the result of human relations type training, but due to economic and social conditions. These include membership of a common enterprise union, wages calculated on a common basis, and acceptance of a narrower wage differential.

Japanese managers were well regarded by their British subordinates because of their technical competence and their concern for high quality work which was seen as reflecting upon workers and the reputation of the company. The respect for their Japanese managers shown by British workers was in no way undermined by the strict enforcement of procedures. As White and Trevor observe in their discussion of managerial authority: 'It is not merely its strength, but its form, its purpose, and its method of legitimation which are at issue.' Being part of a competent and effective enterprise was what appeared to attract the British workers. So much so that workers actually regarded with apprehension the eventual replacement of expatriate managers by the home-grown variety!

Interestingly, the situation in the three City firms studied by Trevor and White, all banks, was not quite so satisfactory, although here again the ability of the Japanese to adapt to local conditions was noteworthy. The problem was explained in terms of the very different status of bankers and banking in the two countries. All the banks were considered 'first-class companies' (*ichiryu kaisha*) in Japan, and therefore recruited high-class (in terms of the university they had attended) graduates. Since graduate status is not necessary for a banking career in Britain, and since anyway many of the employees would not be expected to be graduates, differences in outlook and expectations were considerable.

To conclude this chapter on international comparisons, reflect again for a moment on Table 10.3 comparing Britain, West Germany Japan and the USA on a number of relevant dimensions.

Summary

The purpose of this chapter has been to turn attention to some of the ways in which countries differ in their approach to what may be regarded as common problems, and further to suggest that some of the differences may well be due to different experiences of the process of industrialization. The point of conducting such an exercise has been to highlight the fact that assumed national characteristics are probably neither necessary – and certainly are not sufficient – to explain differences in economic performance and behaviour in organizations.

It is possible to suggest, ironically, that what explains the relatively poor performance of British industry has rather less to do with the culture of, say, Germany and Japan, and rather more to do with that of the British or English. The point may not be to discover what others do that we do not, but why do we not do what others do . . . which is what appears to be associated with economic success! A possible answer can be found in different experiences of industrialization coupled with other political, social and historical features of the British experience. Particularly important here may well be the fact that, unlike other major industrial powers, the English social and political system has not been traumatized by either revolution or military defeat. Consequently there has not been the necessity to undertake a fundamental reappraisal of taken-for-granted assumptions. Anyone who does propose or undertake such a fundamental review is likely to be regarded as somewhat suspicious since they are calling into question what may be termed 'cherished illusions' about a system and its institutions that have not, as yet, demonstrably failed.

The core of Wiener's (1981) thesis is that the English experience of industrialization did not involve the replacement or defeat of a pre-industrial, largely feudal, aristocratic élite. The consequence was the survival of pre-industrial values and their acceptance, if not by the rising class of entrepreneurs, certainly by their sons. Wiener notes Habbakuk's observation that English landowners did not acquire their land in order to develop it but 'in order to enjoy it'. Wiener goes on to comment that: 'The adoption of a culture of enjoyment by new landowners and aspiring landowners meant the dissipation of a set of values that had projected their fathers as a class to the economic heights, and the nation to world predominance. In its place, they took up a new ideal – that of gentleman.' The philosopher Bertrand Russell is said to have observed: 'The concept of the gentleman was invented by the aristocracy to keep the middle classes in order.'

The continued hegenomy of a basically aristocratic élite resulted in the absorption by that élite of the rising middle classes of industrialism, the public school being one of the mechanisms through which this absorption operated by virtue of its dedication to the production of 'gentlemen'.

In the context of our discussions it is important to note that the problem is not one of the acceptability of 'wealth creation' *per se*, but of the acceptability of **forms** of wealth creation. This brings us back to the arguments made by Eatwell for the key role of manufacturing in economic growth. These arguments have to be borne in mind when examining the recent inprovement in the growth rate of the British economy and the economic problems of both Germany and Japan.

It may be that the British economy has recently been one of the fastest, growing in Europe, that the rate of growth in Germany is low, that the severity of their demographic decline in the numbers of young people will be more severe than ours, that Japan is going to experience demographic induced unemployment and is being hard pressed by even later industrializing economies of the 'Pacific rim'. However, it is necessary to remember that a factor in the German case is the slow-down in the world economy and the effect that will have on a country where about 50% of manufacturing output is exported. Competitive pressures on Japan are already forcing companies to look closely at such policies as life-long employment and seniority-based pay scales, all at a time when population pressures are likely to create demands for more, not fewer, jobs.

In this context it is necessary to note that even if the present levels of productivity improvements are maintained by British industry, it will take ten years to get to where the Germans are now in 1989. The problem may well not be, as is often alleged, a peculiarly British distaste for wealth creation and a propensity to consume wealth in the form of the public provision of transport, health care and education and so on, but the failure to recognize that the production process in manufacturing industry is the key to wealth creation. Without the development of respect for a concept like 'technik', and a more sophisticated approach to distinguishing forms of knowledge, where is the motivation to reward production engineers rather than accountants? Where will the motivation arise for rewarding investment in training and product development for the future, rather than simply seeking a rise in the share price as a result of relatively short-term factors? These are the issues to be faced if Britain is to 'catch up' with the economies of countries such as Germany and Japan, let alone currently industrializing economies.

Finally, it is important to recognize that in the effort to ensure consumate cooperation from a workforce, features of Japanese and German management and organization structure may play an important part and do not appear to be based upon some unique attribute of national character. The degree of technical competence and associated autonomy enjoyed by production workers in Germany, and a legal and organizational framework providing statutory support for the right to be informed and involved in decision-making, are important factors. They contribute to a sense of security that enables human beings to face an uncertain future with some confidence. Such confidence is necessary if innovations are to be developed and introduced quickly and effectively. This confidence is the basis of committed cooperation.

Study questions

1. What methodological problems are likely to arise when undertaking international comparative studies?
2. 'If culture is important in explaining the relative performance of the British and, say, German or Japanese economies, then that may well say more about British/English culture than about German or Japanese cultures.' Do you agree? Why?
3. In what ways may it be argued that British managers are less restricted in labour relations matters than their German counterparts?
4. How might a well-developed national technical training programme influence the structure and functioning of management?
5. To what extent do observed characteristics of Japanese management derive from essentially Japanese qualities rather than from the application of a generally applicable pragmatism?

Further reading

There is a considerable literature on international comparisons of management and organizations particularly as concerns Japan. Much of this material falls into the 'panacea promotion' category and is therefore to be treated with caution.

A now dated but classic work is Dore (1973). This was a comparative study based upon two factories of English Electric and two of Hitachi. While much of the descriptive material is no longer applicable in either Britain or Japan, Chapters 14 and 15 which examine the origins of the Japanese employment system and the 'late development' or 'secondary industrializing' thesis are still worth looking at in order to develop an understanding of the Japanese case in particular and of the significance of international comparisons in general.

A historical understanding of the development of modern Japan can be derived from, for example, Hirschmeier and Yui (1981). This, as does the two volume *Japanese Reader* (Livingstone, Moore, Oldfather, 1973) gives an account of the response of Japanese institutions, after two centuries of self-imposed isolation, to Commodore Perry's arrival in 1853. The significance of Perry's arrival, and its implications for Japan on the social, political and military levels, are all important in understanding the development of modern Japan and its approach to the future.

A similar background to an understanding of post Second World War Germany is to be found in Lawrence (1980). This gives a useful account of the aftermath of defeat in 1945 on German institutions and business. In all of these works, assertions taken for granted about the nature of 'culture' as an explanatory variable are assessed in terms of pragmatic responses to perceived strategic interests and objectives.

The English case is examined by Wiener (1981). This work considers the implications for the development of industrialization in Britain of the fact that the pre-industrial élite, the land-owning feudal aristocracy, were neither politically nor militarily defeated. The consequence was that they were able to absorb the new rising class of industrialists into what Wiener suggests was (and is) a fundamentally anti-industrial (because pre-industrial) value system.

References

Bergen, S.A. and Miyajima, R. (1986) Productivity and the R&D/production interface in Japan. *R&D Management*, **16**, (1), 15–24.

Child, J. and Partridge, B. (1982) *Lost Managers*. Cambridge University Press.

Department of Transport and Industry (1987) *Indentifying Areas of Strengths and Excellence in UK Technology*. DTI.

Dore, R. (1973) *British Factory – Japanese Factory*. Allen & Unwin.

Eatwell, J. (1982) *Whatever Happened to Britain*, Duckworth/BBC.

Fores, M. and Rey, L. (1977) Technik: the Relevance of a Missing Concept. *Nature*, **269**, 31–2.

Gillan, W.J. (1986) *The Japanese Secret: Are They Winning?* DTI Overseas Technical Information Unit.

Glover, I.A. (1988) *The Hobsbawm–Wiener Conundrum: Economics, History and Sociology in the Study of British Decline*. Mimeo, Dundee College of Technology.

Handy, C. (1987) *The Making of Managers*. Report on management education, training and development in the USA, West Germany, France, Japan and the UK. NEDO.

Hirschmeier, J. and Yui, T. (1981) *The Development of Japanese Business*, 2nd edn. Allen & Unwin.

Hutton, S. and Lawrence, P. (1981) *German Engineers: The Anatomy of a Profession*. Oxford University Press.

Jarvis, H. and Prais, S.J. (1988) *Two Nations of Shop Keepers: Training for Retailing in France and Britain*. NIESR Discussion Paper No. 140.

Jurgens, U. (1989) The transfer of Japanese management concepts in the international automobile industry. In Wood, S. (ed.) *The Transformation of Work?* Unwin-Hyman.

Lawrence, P. (1980) *Managers and Management in West Germany*. Croom-Helm.

Lawrence, P. (1984) *Management in Action*. Routledge and Kegan Paul.

Limprecht, J.A. and Hayes, R.H. (1982) Germany's world class manufacturers. *Harvard Business Review*, November/December, 137–45.

Livingstone, J., Moore, J. and Oldfather, F. (1973) *Japanese Reader*, 2 vols. Penguin.

McCormack, K. (1988) Engineering education in Britain and Japan: some reflections on the use of 'the best practice' models in interational comparison. *Sociology*, **22**, (4).

Maurice, M., Sorge, A. and Warner, M. (1980) Societal differences in organizing manufacturing units: a comparison of France, West Germany and Great Britain. *Organization Studies*, **1**, (1).

Miller, D. (1978) Federal Republic of Germany: an analysis of the post war Vertraunsleute policy of the German Metalworkers' Union (1952–77). *British Journal of Industrial Relations*, **16**, (3).

Mirza, H. (1984) Can – should – Japanese management practices be exported overseas? *The Business Graduate*, January.

Nohara, H. (1987) *Technical Innovation, Industrial Dynamics and the Transformation of Work: The Case of the Japanese Machine-Tool Industry*. Paper presented to a Conference on High Tech and Society in Japan and the FDR. Mimeo, West Berlin Wissenschaftszentrum, quoted in Jurgens, op. cit.

Nicholas, A.N. (1988) *Reform of Engineering Education in the Royal Navy to 1939*. Paper delivered at Manchester University, May.

Okuda, K. (1983) The role of Japanese engineers in industry and education. *Journal of Japanese Trade and Industry*, September/October, 18–22.

Poole, M. (1986) *Industrial Relations: Origins and Patterns of National Diversity*. Routledge and Kegan Paul.

Raimond, P., Hinard, M. and Weitkamp, J. (1988) 'Comparing European companies'. *European Management Journal*, **6**, (4).

Roderick, G. and Stephens, M. (1972) *Scientific and Technical Education in Nineteenth Century England*. David & Charles.

Samuels, J.M., Groves, R.E.V. and Goddard, C.S. (1975) *Company Finance in Europe*. Institute of Chartered Accountants in England and Wales.

Sorge, A. and Warner, M. (1980) Manpower training, manufacturing organisation and workplace relations in Great Britain and West Germany. *British Journal of Industrial Relations*, **18**, 318–33.

Steadman, H. (1988) *Vocational Training in France and Britain: Mechanical and Electrical Craftsmen*. NIESR Discussion Paper No. 130.

Takamiya, M. (1979) *Japanese Multinationals in Europe: International operations and their public policy implications*. Working Paper, International Institute of Management, Berlin.

The Training Commission (1988) *The Study of Funding of Vocational Education and Training*.

Weston, D. and Gummett, P. (1987) The economic impact of military R&D hypothesis, evidence and verification. *Defence Analysis*, (3).

White, M. and Trevor, M. (1983) *Under Japanese Management – The experience of British Workers*, PSI, Heineman.

Wiener, M.J. (1981) *English Culture and the Decline of the Industrial Spirit 1850–1980*. Cambridge University Press.

11 Conclusion

In this book we have examined factors which affect behaviour in business, following the structure of the Business in Context model which informs all the contributions to the series. We have carried out the examination in the context of the long-standing debate about aspects of the relatively poor performance of the British economy over a fairly lengthy period stretching at least as far back as the 1850s, and which has been almost continuous since the end of the Second World War. The factors considered have included:

□ the nature and experience of industrialization;
□ information and strategies;
□ organization size and structure;
□ ownership and goals.

We have also examined the influence on human behaviour of the role of the state, technology and culture, and the organizational context of work.

All of these aspects have been examined in terms of their influence upon the activities at the core of the model and which represent the key activities of business organizations in the manufacturing and service sectors – product development, production, marketing, purchasing, finance and accounting, and personnel.

The purpose of the examination has been twofold: first, to illustrate those factors which influence human behaviour in a business context in terms of the motivation of people and how they cooperate (or not) in order to achieve their goals. Work is the major organizing activity of human lives, and how that work is organized and controlled is a key feature of human experience which moulds, even where it does not precisely determine, human perceptions and activities.

Secondly, the purpose has been to illustrate how and why factors relating to the organization of work are important in explaining differential economic performance and adaptation to change. Important here has been the emphasis placed upon the differing experiences of industrialization as a formative feature of industrial societies in terms of the organization and control of work. The organization and control of work was argued to be the prime motivation for, and major characteristic of, industrialization in the first place (see Chapter 2).

The strategies and policies which are perceived as relevant for a particular society are determined to some degree by the environment in which that society industrializes. Thus 'secondary' industrializers developed rather different methods and solutions from those seen as being available and relevant to a primary industrializer.

Microelectronic and information technologies are creating, or at least make likely, a situation which is as different from traditional mass production as that was different from craft production methods. It is becoming clear that competitive advantage in both manufacturing and service industries requires companies increasingly to tailor their products to more precisely defined market niches. This in effect reverses the principle of mass production which originated in the nineteenth century and dominated most of the twentieth. The key to success in the last decades of the twentieth century – the basis of competitive ability – is increasingly perceived as depending upon the responsiveness of the producers of goods and services to developing and newly defined market segments: in a word, 'flexibility'.

An important component of the drive towards flexibility derives from the nature of new machines which, unlike the machine tools of mass production, are themselves immensely flexible. Unlike their predecessors, the new breed of machine tool does not require long runs of standardized parts to be profitable. Indeed, the whole point of the new machines is that they are capable of, and only effectively utilized when, production is organized around products tailored to relatively small and variable market segments or niches. Competition has changed from being based merely upon the ability to produce large quantities at some combination of cost and quality, to a situation where factors of cost and quality must be combined with the ability to respond rapidly to changes in the product market if success is to be achieved.

A similar process is at work in the service sector of the economy. Information technology and relatively cheap computing power enable service companies to tailor their services and the delivery of those services to more sophisticated and structured markets. In retail banking for example, the ability to automate the provision of low value-added services such as cash withdrawals and deposits enables banks to concentrate staff on high value-added services which require face-to-face contact with the customer. It is these kinds of service that form the basis of competition since the competitive advantage of large-scale cash handling has been minimized by developments in the industry to date.

The significance of such developments for the subject of this book is that the flexibility inherent in the new technology **must** be matched by flexibility in organizational and behavioural patterns. The advantages of technological advance can only be realized **if** human, especially managerial, behaviour changes also. An important factor here for the explanation and understanding of human behaviour is the way in which these advantages are to be realized in the context of management/labour relations, and how any benefits are to be distributed.

The consideration of human behaviour also involves a concept that has not been directly addressed in this volume, that of human nature. The problem with this concept is that it is very difficult to define. One only has to consider the considerable variations in the environments to which humans have adapted, and the forms that they have evolved in the process of adaptation, to realize that 'human nature' is in fact highly variable. As an explanatory variable, therefore, it is not very helpful. Conflict, like procreation, may well be endemic to the human species, but the form it takes and the manner of its regulation is extremely varied. This variation may well be supported by cultural distinctions but can also be supported and explained by pragmatic responses to particular conditions.

The point is that forms of behaviour that are taken for granted and their justifications – or 'culture' – are themselves the result of a particular social group adopting particular solutions to particular problems at a particular time. There is nothing 'inevitable' about them; the responses could have been different – and may develop differently in the future.

So, if human behaviour in the work situation has to change, what does this imply? This is the question to which this volume has been addressed in order to understand contemporary behaviour as well as to identify how behaviour will have to change in the future. The point is that the two are related. Factors influencing **contemporary** behaviour are relevant to understanding the demands of change, and hence **future** behaviour.

The adaptability of new technology can only be realized by utilizing the adaptability of human beings. This means skill flexibility on the part of people. This in turn implies flexible forms of organization and implies a restructuring of work organizations that has implications outside the work setting since the allocation of responsibility and knowledge will be changed within the work setting. This then is the sense in which the new technology is indeed 'revolutionary', or at least, of 'revolutionary' potential.

The point of the present volume has been to demonstrate that human behaviour is largely formulated by reference to what individuals and groups perceive as being in their interests in the kind of world they have come to inhabit. Suspicion of management is engendered by experience of the consequences of management actions in the past, a past known to individuals directly from their own lives and from what they have learnt from talking to or living among others who have directly felt the impact of management decisions. The same process operates among those who become managers of course. There is the possibility (probability?) of a self-fulfilling cycle: both groups have come to trust or mistrust the other. Each then behaves as though they were in reality scripted by the other group.

A company or country that aims to maintain or develop a growing economy and hence increase its share of domestic and/or international markets must then develop approaches to manufacturing and service provision, and the organization of work, that match human and technological flexibility. This implies some re-consideration of the way in which the benefits of economic growth or increasing market share are distributed.

This in turn implies rather different methods of organizing and controlling work from those characterizing the nineteenth and twentieth centuries. Flexible workers are highly trained and motivated people. Without training and motivation they are unable to carry out the tasks required of them let alone contribute to quality and innovation. Since flexibility also implies rapid responses, workers will require skill and motivation to exercise initiative when management do not, in many cases cannot, know the answers. Reflect upon the description of JIT in Chapter 7 – such a system requires that all involved be able to respond rapidly to events. Failure to respond in this way results in the whole process seizing up, and such a seizure will at least increase costs even if it does not result in lost market opportunities.

The comparative study of the manufacture of fitted kitchens carried out by Steadman and Wagner (1987) discussed in Chapter 8 illustrates very clearly the role of a highly qualified and motivated labour force in competitive success. What Willman calls 'consumate cooperation' requires and implies a workforce that is highly skilled and whose personal objectives are either consistent with, or at least not contrary to, those of the organization.

Establishing consumate cooperation requires that the organization of work and its control proceeds on a different set of assumptions from those that characterized mass production. The mission statement of Hewlett-Packard for example (Table 8.4), the observations of Lincoln on human motivation (Case Study 8.4), the work of Ouchi (also in Chapter 8) on the development of 'Theory Z' and the example of Mondragon discussed in Chapter 9, all suggest some, at least, of the organizational implications and prerequisites of flexibility and consumate cooperation.

Another example is provided by the legal framework within which, for example, German industrial and employment relations operate, as discussed in Chapter 10. This indicates further aspects of the change that is required in and by British management if they are to retain their grip on the future. Highly skilled and motivated people are likely to require rights to consultation, participation and information which are guaranteed by a legal framework rather than merely being available at the whim of management.

Similarly with training. Over a century and a half of industrialization has failed to establish a basic framework of training in Britain that approaches those operating in major competitor economies. Can British industry afford the luxury of being left to its own devices to overcome decades of, at best apparent, unconcern?

The two preceding paragraphs are not to be read as necessarily advocating any particular form of regulation. They are simply to be seen as indicating the kind of reappraisal that is necessary. In the areas of human relations and training, competitor economies require managers to operate under considerably more complex and intrusive legal frameworks than is the case for British managers. In the context of the 'demographic time-bomb' that is seen to confront employers as a result of the decline in the number of school-leavers available for employment, such differences in approach to regulation will become even more apparent. Will any changes in company policy provoked by demographic factors survive the period over which those factors are operative? Will British industry initiate, via the market mechanism, fundamental changes in their approach quickly enough to stay in contention in the post-1992 world?

Many larger British companies are responding to the demographic threat by enhancing the rights of part-time employees generally and women in particular – the Midland Bank has established a number of crèches for example. It is possible that population changes may very well bring about dramatic changes in employers' attitudes to training in general and to female employees in particular as a result of market forces. The point is, given the situation concerning employment and training rights currently in existence in competitor economies in Europe, both inside and outside the European Community, plus the more favourable provisions for female employment in those countries (e.g. maternity leave provision, rights to re-instatement and so on), can Britain afford to wait for the operation of market forces to bring about changes? Moreover, will any changes survive a future increase in the supply of (skilled) labour?

The regulatory frameworks which operate in Europe require that management give considerable thought to the development of strategies and their implementation. They also have the effect, intended or not, of ensuring that management take the time to set out their proposals for the consideration of the representatives of the workforce as well as those who have invested (debt) capital in the enterprise. The consequence is a situation well known to social psychology and noted in textbooks on organizational behaviour: those who have participated in decision-making are likely to be committed to the result. At the very least, people who have been informed and who have participated in a decision process will know what is going on and why, even if they would have preferred some other outcome. This kind of knowledge is important in the process of establishing consumate cooperation since it ensures that the workforce have sufficient knowledge to act appropriately in situations that demand rapid responses.

Not only do workers need to know why something has to be done, they also need to know how to do it. Training is therefore crucial if the competitive ability of an organization is to be developed. Here also the legal framework of competitor economies can be seen to be important.

French legislation for example has given workers the right, since 1970, to take unpaid leave to follow a training course of their own choosing whatever the size of the enterprise, and whether or not the proposed course relates to the business of the enterprise. Since 1971 any enterprise employing more than ten people has had to pay a percentage of the salary bill (1.2%) for training. This can be either spent internally or paid into statutory bodies which are administered jointly by equal numbers of managerial and union representatives, so-called 'parity organizations', for the provision of training.

Other provisions enable employees to take a period of sabbatical leave for retraining, or to develop new skills/knowledge areas. On completion of the sabbatical the individual is entitled to return to the same or similar job and remuneration that he or she enjoyed before the leave.

Originally, employers objected to these arrangements as interferences in their business. However, they now view these arrangements rather differently as they have come to realize the potentials for competitive advantage that follow from a formal system of training. Again, the point is not that a legal framework is necessarily the best or only way of establishing such a system, but that given the existence of such a framework management are required to give careful consideration to the issues covered by the legislation. The result is a more structured, formalized and consistent system of training that enables French employers and employees to benefit.

In the German case, vocational training after formal schooling is covered by the Vocational Training Act of 1969. This Act covers industrial and agricultural enterprises as well as civil servants and the professions. Even the qualifications required by training personnel are set out, in the Regulations on the Qualifications of Training Personnel, which are issued in accordance with the Vocational Training Act. Generally, instructors must have completed their own vocational training course/s, have several years of relevant work experience and be at least 24 years old. They are additionally required to have a specified level of theoretical knowledge relating to their work experience in general, and the methodology of vocational training in particular.

Examinations in the German system comprise practical, oral and written components and the examination boards are made up of equal numbers of employers and trade unionists and at least one teacher from a *Berufsfach-schule*, a full-time vocational school.

Consideration of the factors which mould the framework within which competitors operate suggests that it is not necessary to resort to vague assertions about cultural features which allegedly enhance competitive ability. The features of the framework important in determining competitive advantage can be seen to be the results of a pragmatic rather than distinctively cultural process.

This perhaps is the most important point for British managers. Whatever the characteristics of their German, French or Japanese competitors which appear so advantageous, the results in terms of human behaviour and performance are totally consistent with the results of research conducted in British and American firms for over seventy years. The system under which competitors operate appears to produce a result that is not peculiar to any one culture. For example, while there may well be features of Japanese society that facilitate the participation of individuals in groups, the consequences of participation in decision-making, i.e. commitment, is not a result peculiar to human beings of Japanese, or German, origin alone, and has been scientifically researched for fifty years.

Similarly, the apparent orderly nature of German industrial relations may well be associated with confidence in a system that gives workers and their representatives certain rights, rather than simply reflecting some cultural orientation towards rules.

The important question is, why are British managers so slow to implement systems that produce the beneficial results that are so widely desired? A second and more fundamental question is then: What is to be done?

Before attempting to answer this question consider the following. The characteristics of competitor economies that we have considered may well be the reason/s why those economies have got where they are. However, this does not mean that the strategies they have used to date are necessarily those that will enable them to maintain their pre-eminence in the future, nor does it mean that British managers slavishly following such 'lessons' will necessarily produce the desired results.

There is a sense in which Britain may be in the situation in which 'secondary' industrializers found themselves a hundred or more years ago. As then, the point will not be to try and emulate those currently in the lead, but to develop novel approaches to the problem: to leap-frog the competition. Leap-froging the competition, however, requires the rapid development of innovative methods of managing a highly skilled and motivated labour force.

As demonstrated several times in this book, flexibility does not just imply changes in attitudes towards training and motivation, it also implies changes in the organization of work flow and the structure of organizations. Highly trained and motivated people cannot be supervised as though they were untrained and lacking in motivation. To take advantage of both the flexibility of new technology and the flexibility inherent in trained and motivated people, organizational structures will also have to change. Ouchi's 'Theory Z' type organization is an attempt, and only one attempt, to specify some of the features which organizations in the future will have to display.

This is not to say that in the future organizations must display these features, but simply to point out some of the organizational implications of the material dealt with in this book. As Hirschorn has argued, work in the future will be different from that in the recent past since it (work) will largely focus on the controlling of control systems with all that implies for human behaviour and decision-making. Organizational structures will have to accommodate a degree of cross-referencing and communication that will undermine traditional structures and authority systems.

Social institutions are indeed monuments to old problems. Success in the immediate, and not so immediate, future will go to those who not only recognize the truth of this observation, but who can act upon its implied prescription.

Index

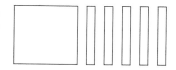